Pet Loss, Grief, and Therapeutic Interventions

This book recognizes and legitimizes the significance of pet and animal loss by exploring the various expressions of trauma and grief experienced by those who work with, live with, or own an animal or pet.

The chapters of *Pet Loss, Grief, and Therapeutic Interventions* weave together cutting-edge research with best practices and practical clinical advice for working with grieving clients. Beginning with an overview of the human–animal bond, the book guides readers through the many facets of pet loss, including topics such as animal hospice and euthanasia, offering a comprehensive account of one of the field's most rapidly emerging areas. Designed to help mental health professionals support clients coping with pet loss, the collection explores personal narratives, current theories, up-to-date research, and future directions.

This unique and comprehensive book will be of interest to students, clinicians, academicians, and researchers in the fields of counseling, psychology, and social work.

Lori Kogan is Professor of Clinical Sciences in the College of Veterinary Medicine and Biomedical Sciences at Colorado State University, US.

Phyllis Erdman is Professor of Counseling and Associate Dean for Academic Affairs in the College of Education, Washington State University, US.

Explorations in Mental Health

For more information about this series, please visit www.routledge.com/
Explorations-in-Mental-Health/book-series/EXMH

Pet Loss, Grief, and Therapeutic Interventions

Practitioners Navigating the Human–Animal Bond

Edited by
Lori Kogan and
Phyllis Erdman

Routledge
Taylor & Francis Group

LONDON AND NEW YORK

First published 2020 by Routledge

2 Park Square, Milton Park, Abingdon, Oxon, OX14 4RN
605 Third Avenue, New York, NY 10017

Routledge is an imprint of the Taylor & Francis Group, an informa business

First issued in paperback 2020

Library of Congress Cataloging-in-Publication Data
Names: Kogan, Lori, editor.
Title: Pet loss, grief, and therapeutic interventions : practitioners
navigating the human-animal bond / edited by Lori Kogan &
Phyllis Erdman.
Description: New York, NY : Routledge, 2020. | Includes bibliographical
references.
Identifiers: LCCN 2019020358| ISBN 9781138585577
(hbk : alk. paper) | ISBN 9780429505201 (ebk)
Subjects: LCSH: Pet loss–Psychological aspects. | Pet owners–
Psychology. | Human-animal relationships.
Classification: LCC SF411.47 .P483 2020 | DDC 636.088/7–dc23
LC record available at https://lccn.loc.gov/2019020358

ISBN: 978-1-138-58557-7 (hbk)
ISBN: 978-0-367-78477-5 (pbk)

Typeset in Baskerville
by Wearset Ltd, Boldon, Tyne and Wear

Contents

Illustrations

Contributors

Aubrey H. Fine has been a faculty member at California State Polytechnic University since 1981. He is now Professor Emeritus in the Department of Education.

Gail F. Melson is Professor Emerita at Purdue University in the Department of Human Development and Family Studies and in the Center for the Human–Animal Bond.

Clarissa M. Uttley is Professor of Education and the Program Coordinator of the MEd in Curriculum and Instruction at Plymouth State University.

Shelly Volsche is a Biocultural Anthropologist and Lecturer at Boise State University who studies the influence of social change on the practice of family and kinship.

Jessica Bibbo is a Research Scientist at the Center for Research and Education of the Benjamin Rose Institute on Aging in Cleveland, Ohio.

Maria Gore is a Counselor at Colorado State University's Veterinary Teaching Hospital working with the Argus Institute that offers counseling and support services related to pet loss and end of life decisions.

Erin Allen is a Counselor for the Argus Institute within the Colorado State University Veterinary Teaching Hospital.

Gail Bishop has been affiliated with Colorado State University's (CSU) Veterinary Teaching Hospital (VTH) since 2002. She is Director of CSU's Argus Institute.

Angela K. Fournier is a Licensed Psychologist in Minnesota and Professor in the Department of Psychology at Bemidji State University.

Brandon Mustful is the Executive Director of Great River Rescue, a companion animal shelter located in Bemidji, Minnesota.

Amy Johnson developed and directs Oakland University (Rochester, MI) online Animal Assisted Therapy Certificate Program and is the Director of its Center for Human–Animal Interventions.

Laura Bruneau is Professor of Counselor Education at Adams State University in Alamosa, Colorado.

Christine Kim is a Macro Social Worker at the intersection of animal welfare and human welfare.

Yvonne Smith is Assistant Professor in the School of Social Work at Syracuse University.

Amalia Golomb-Leavitt is a Master's student in the School of Social Service Administration at the University of Chicago.

Katy Schroeder is Assistant Professor of Companion Animal Science at Texas Tech University where she directs the Equine-Assisted Counseling and Wellness Research Lab and Community Clinic.

Mariko Yamamoto is Senior Lecturer in the Department of Animal Sciences at the Teikyo University of Science.

Lynette A. Hart is Professor of Human–Animal Interactions and Animal Behavior at the UC Davis, School of Veterinary Medicine.

Cara A. Miller is a Faculty Member in the Clinical Psychology doctoral program within the Department of Psychology at Gallaudet University in Washington, DC.

Emma K. Grigg is a Certified Applied Animal Behaviorist (CAAB; Animal Behavior Society, US), a lecturer and research associate at the University of California.

Tammy McCormick Donaldson has been a Certified Applied Animal Behaviorist since 2003.

Phyllis Erdman is Associate Dean for Academic Affairs at College of Education, Washington State University.

Kathleen Ruby was Director of Counseling and Wellness and on the faculty at the Washington State College of Veterinary Medicine for 19 years until retiring in 2017. She now serves as an Adjunct Professor at the college.

Katherine Goldberg is a dual Professional Veterinarian and Social Worker. She pursued her LMSW at Syracuse University after recognizing the significant human needs that arise in medical environments.

Cori Bussolari is Associate Professor at the University of San Francisco in the Counseling Psychology Department.

Wendy Packman is a Professor of Psychology, Palo Alto University.

Jeannine Moga is a Licensed Clinical Social Worker in private practice whose specialties include veterinary social work, grief and loss, and clinical ethics. She serves as an adjunct instructor for North Carolina State University's School of Social Work.

Acknowledgments

Perhaps one reason why there are so few books written that honestly and deeply explore the topics of pet grief and loss is because they are painful to write. We want to acknowledge this fact and express our gratitude to each contributor to this book. Each of you have had your own personal experience with the grief over a beloved pet. Some of you supported an animal through the transition, working through your own grief, sadness, and emptiness, while others of you supported the caretakers of these animals. We hope that the process of writing your chapter helped, at least in a small amount, to process some of this grief. Your wealth of memories and experiences are what has enabled you to help others understand the value of pets and the tremendous pain experienced upon their loss. For your willingness to feel your pain and thereby help others, we thank you. Many of us have experienced the disenfranchised grief that all too frequently accompanies the death of a pet. Your personal stories and contributions to this book indisputably demonstrate that the grief of a pet is equally, and often times, more painful than that of a human companion. Finally, we thank you for validating our own personal grief and, at the same time, recognizing the immeasurable joy our animals provide. These animals deserve to be honored, remembered, and valued during their lives and after their death. We hope our contributors and our readers alike have a lifetime of pet-related memories on which to reflect and many new memories yet to create.

The Editors

Introduction

It is likely that you are reading this book to learn more about how to help support those who have lost a companion animal. Yet, the chances are good that you, yourself, have shared your life – and your heart – with a companion animal and that the connection you shared with that animal was, or still is, a significant life relationship. As we all know, however, these relationships come with inevitable grief. As Dr. Leo Bustad, one of the early proponents of the human–animal bond, so aptly stated many years ago, "Grief is the price of loving." We created this book to help give you a better understanding of this particular type of grief; to define and normalize it, and assist you (and your clients) with the healing process. Each chapter in this book presents a unique aspect of the grief process as it relates to the human–animal bond and offers suggestions on how mental health care providers can guide and support their clients through this time in a supportive and validating way.

The book begins with an introductory chapter that reminds us of the importance of the human–animal bond and the profound impact of pet loss. Through the sharing of personal stories and relevant research of the mutual physiological and behavioral benefits of human–animal inter-actions, the chapter lays the foundation for the remainder of the book. Grief is experienced differently by each individual, yet looking at commonalities within groups can help us better support those who come to us for help. The first part explains how pet loss is experienced throughout the life span, from young children to older adults, and the unique needs associated with each of these periods. In Chapters 2 through 5, the authors provide valuable information to helping professionals on how to recognize and address the unique needs of grieving pet owners at each stage of life. For example, the knowledge that young children do not conceptualize grief in the same way as adults might dissuade parents from involving their children in the euthanasia of a family pet. Yet, as explained, involvement may actually help a child process his/her grief more effectively. On the other end of the life spectrum, the chapter on pets and aging reminds us that many older adults rely on their pets as their only source of companionship, and that their loss can have a grave impact on owners' mental and physical health.

The third part, "Special Populations," describes the impact of pet loss for those in unique contexts. For example, veterinarians and animal care agents often deal with animal death on a daily basis, yet we sometimes fail to comprehend the emotional toll this can present for them. Chapters 6 and 7 help us better understand the challenges these professionals face regarding animal loss. The next two chapters (Chapters 8 and 9) help open our eyes to how we can better support vulnerable populations by exploring the unique roles that companion animals can have with prison populations and those who experience homelessness. The last chapter in this part examines a critical, yet often overlooked, component of pet loss – the impact of different cultural perspectives.

Part IV of the book highlights the importance of understanding grief as it relates to special animal populations. Chapter 11 describes the relationship between horses and people, including the challenges of saying goodbye to our equine companions. Chapters 12 and 13 explore the complicated psychological burden that accompanies the loss of an assistance dog and how to support clients during this time. Lastly, Chapter 14 explains how helping professionals can assist clients with euthanasia decisions that stem from problem behaviors.

The last part explores the complexity of grief, including how mental health providers can help prepare their clients for an impending loss. Chapter 15 provides several models to better conceptualize grief, as well as exploring the concept of disenfranchised grief and the lack of validation that often accompanies pet loss. Chapters 16, 17, and 18 provide ways to help clients prepare for loss beforehand and work through their grief afterward, including the value of hospice care and the many ways that clients may choose to maintain a continued bond with their companion animal, even after death. The concluding chapter suggests how we, as professionals, can navigate interprofessional boundaries to better understand the many facets of pet loss from multiple professional perspectives to best serve those who are suffering a loss.

Working on this book has been both a joy and a challenge. It reminds us, as we read through these chapters, of the undeniable impact that animals have on our lives and the lives of our clients. Despite the long, rich history of these human–animal relationships, only recently has society begun to recognize and normalize the pain that comes from losing these companions. Yet, we still have a long way to go before this type of loss and grief is universally recognized. This book was written to help move us in that direction – by supporting mental health providers in their efforts to help their clients cope with loss and convey an understanding of its often profound impact. Through these teachings, it is the hope that we all can become better at validating the human–animal bond and the pain that accompanies its loss.

Phyllis Erdman and Lori Kogan

Part I
Foundation and Theory

1 The Eternal Bond

Understanding the Importance of the Human–Animal Bond and its Impact on Pet Loss

Aubrey H. Fine

Does it ever get easier? Will the pain and empty feelings ever subside, or at least appear more manageable? These are common questions frequently asked and considered when people experience the loss of their beloved companion animal. So, I rhetorically ask, why do most people consider getting another pet knowing that perhaps their heart will be broken once again? The answer for many is truly simple. The love that you receive from this relationship is so significant that you are willing to have your heart broken once again.

Over the past 40 years, my heart has been broken several times because of the losses that I have experienced. Goldie was our first Golden Retriever, and he changed my life. I fell in love with him the first time I saw his puppy eyes. Although I had other small animals as pets, I never had a dog. In fact, as a child, I grew up afraid of them. As an adult, I became more infatuated with golden retrievers, and they would become my breed of choice. From the first moment I met Goldie, our relationship was unbreakable. He became my running and riding buddy and was a big brother to my growing children. It was so much fun watching them romp in the fields near my house. Goldie went with us everywhere. Memories of those years will be etched in my mind for a lifetime.

However, we don't stay young forever, and as Goldie aged, he began to slow down. He didn't have many health impairments in his early years, but, when he was about 11 years of age, he developed brain cancer. It was at that time we realized that his life was coming to an end. I must confess, it was very difficult to let go, although, in my mind (not my heart), I knew it was in his best interest. I still vividly recall the afternoon we put Goldie down. We had scheduled a home visit with a veterinarian about four days earlier. When he arrived, I was devastated. I was not ready to let go of my beloved friend. In fact, the night before Goldie was to be put down, I remember barbecuing him steak and letting my wife know I was going to spend the night sleeping next to him (just like a little boy). At some point in the evening, I felt him gazing into my eyes, almost trying to tell me that it was OK to let him go. He even got up a few times to move away for a short time. When the veterinarian finally arrived the next day, he noted that he could give Goldie a short physical to be sure that our assessment was accurate. Quickly, the reality sunk in and it was clear that euthanasia was definitely appropriate. My eyes welled as we made the final decision. In my mind, I went through all of the stages of Kübler-Ross's grief. I would have bargained to the end of time not to let this occur, but reality did hit. The veterinarian was very comforting and explained everything that was going to happen. Goldie laid his head on my lap and after the injections were given, slowly closed his eyes and began to stop breathing. The veterinarian left me with Goldie for a while. I wept as I gently stroked his warm, soft fur. When the veterinarian returned, he told me that he would take Goldie to be cremated. As I watched Goldie being carried to his car, I remember standing there holding onto his collar and dog tags. His body was leaving, but his soul would be etched into my heart forever.

Although seemingly a cliché, the adage nonetheless is true and apropos: time heals all wounds but never erases the scars. So, as time went on, my heart lightened, and I eventually became ready for another pet to love. I must be clear that new pets are not replacements or substitutes! You never replace someone; instead, you find and embrace another soul with whom you can connect.

Years later, we adopted another Golden Retriever whom we named Magic. Magic became our family's "Forever Dog." There are many reasons why she deserved that accolade, but perhaps it was most related to the time in our lives that we got her. We got Magic two days before my wife Nya was diagnosed with breast cancer. Magic just jumped right into our family and the relationship she had my wife Nya was astonishing. They were always together. Magic lifted Nya's spirit, perhaps because she was so tiny and adorable and always seemed to be right next to her. There was a time during my wife's recovery when she looked at me and said, "I know now why we got Magic when we did. Magic is keeping me busy and brings me joy. She is helping me heal." And so right she was with that impression. What was so special to witness was that every evening they could be found holding hand and paw together. It was their special moment which they repeated daily for almost 12 years.

Losing Magic was devastating! Even though we had prepared ourselves for the couple months that she was ill, because of our connection, it was very difficult. Magic too was battling cancer and unfortunately it was winning the battle. We became her best advocate and put her welfare and quality of life as our top priority. It needed to be about her, not us! We elected not to have her endure any invasive procedures because a healthy prognosis was not there. However, our role was to monitor and evaluate her quality of daily life. When we believed that the quality of her life was unduly influenced by her illness, we would have to make *that* decision. It was only the last 24 hours of her life that she had a noticeable decline. We were told that it could happen quickly and her decline was evident. At dinnertime, she got up to eat and fell down. We knew quickly that her end was nearing, and it was time to say goodbye to our beloved friend. Nya actually realized that the end was coming earlier in the day before everything seemed to fall apart. Magic was always an early riser, and on that Monday she slept in. It was at that moment I realized how painful it was for Nya as I watched tears drop out of her eyes. She had beaten her battle with cancer, but she felt helpless that she could not help her buddy anymore. It was 6 o'clock that evening that Magic's body began to give out.

Early the next morning, we took our final drive with Magic. Although Nya accompanied us to the veterinarian, she didn't feel comfortable entering. I understood her feelings and respected them, although I have to admit that I called her twice while inside asking her if she had changed her mind. The outcome wasn't any different from the one I experienced 30 years earlier when Goldie passed on. It was hard for both of us because of the strong connection that we had with Magic. Both Magic and Goldie were integral parts of our family and it was hard to let go.

It's been close to a year and a half since Magic passed away, but there hasn't been a day that has gone by that I haven't thought about her, sometimes reflecting for a moment or shedding a tear. More often, as I think of times gone by too quickly, I smile and give thanks! Thanks for having her and all of my pets in my life. They have completed and made our days richer!

The goal of this chapter is to help conceptualize why the human–animal bond is so significant and unique. Attention will be given to these human–animal interactions, and provide information on the physical as well as psychosocial benefits of having animals in our lives. Finally, the chapter will provide a framework by which to better understand the various theories used to explain our bonds with other living beings. This foundation should be helpful in explaining why we have such a strong connection with our companion animals and develop these eternal bonds. In essence, our relationships with animals have evolved from having them live in the backyards of our homes or in our garages to now sleeping in our bedrooms and sharing our homes. Over the past 50 years, science has begun to catch up with what people have known intuitively for centuries – animals are good for our well-being, and they contribute tremendously to our quality of life.

Why We Love Animals

Over the years, pet ownership has grown in America. According to the 2017–2018 American Pet Products Association (APPA) National Pet Owner Survey, 68% of households own a pet, which equates to about 84.6 million homes. In fact, in 1988 when the first survey was conducted by APPA, only 56% of US households owned a pet, so we have seen a modest growth of about 12% in close to 30 years. Dogs are in approximately 60.2

million US households, while cats are in 47.1 million US households. Although cats are in fewer homes, there are more cats than dogs in the United States. There are 89.7 million dogs in our homes while there are 94.2 million cats.

Pets are now intimately connected with us, and we graciously and lovingly share our homes (bedrooms, kitchens, living areas) with them. No longer are they confined to the outskirts of homes (backyards, garages). They have become an integral part of our daily lives. People are now spending a great deal of their discretionary funds on pet keeping to ensure the quality of life for their animals. Demonstrating our commitment to our pets, our pets are now more pampered than ever before. Expenditures, including items like food, supplies, boarding, grooming, and veterinarian care, were estimated to be over $70 billion in 2017 (APPA, 2018). In essence, our relationships with our pets involves not only our heart, but also our pocketbooks. Many talk to their pets like fellow humans and attribute to them several human qualities such as reasoning, cognition, emotion, and perception. The science of canine cognition has been literally transformed in the past two decades and has unearthed new insights. Research into canine cognition has provided new insights into dog behavior and cognition. For example, Horowitz (2009) explained that dogs' strength in communicating with humans is related to their predisposed ability to look at our faces for critical information, for reassurance, and for guidance. These traits are a definite asset for their interaction with humans because they enable dogs to be keen observers of our reactions. Research suggests that dogs uniquely obtain information from facial cues and can use auditory as well as visual information to identify emotions in both canines and humans (Albuquerque et al., 2016). Furthermore, research has demonstrated the importance of mutual facial gazing in the bond between humans and dogs. For example, Nagasawa, Kikusui, Onaka, & Ohta (2015) argue that mutual gaze, a behavior signifying attachment between mother and child, is found in relationships between humans and their pet dogs. More current research now suggests that dogs are also capable of understanding human words. Andics et al. (2016) report that some dogs are able to recognize more than 1,000 human words. Their research found that regardless of how the words are pronounced, dogs process meaningful words in the left hemisphere of their brain.

Fine and Beck (2015) point out that it is apparent that dogs have been bred to co-exist with their human counterparts to fulfill many roles, including herding, guarding, hunting, fishing, and companionship. In fact, they suggest that the supportive nature of animals has played a tremendous role in human lives and believe that this could be one of the major reasons for their domestication in their use as pets. Fine (2014) points out that we established positive interactions with animals ever since we began domesticating them to co-exist with us – over 30,000 years ago. In most cases, humans befriended animals and welcomed them into their lives for a variety of reasons, including security and companionship. In a discussion with Temple Grandin (2013), she noted that she believed the animals that were the most intuitive, cooperative, helpful, and friendly to their human counterparts were those most welcomed into human circles. Those animals that lacked some of these traits were less likely to be accepted by humans. Furthermore, research also points out that pets can facilitate our social relationships with others. For example, we more easily connect with neighbors who have pets with whom we can interact. Animals are easier to talk to than people, or they act as a bridge into an introduction (Fine, 2014).

What is The Human–Animal Bond?

The American Veterinary Medical Association (AVMA) defines the human–animal bond:

> as a mutually beneficial and dynamic relationship between people and other animals that is influenced by behaviors that are essential to the health and well-being of both. This includes, but is not limited to, emotional, psychological and physical interactions with people, other animals, and the environment.
>
> (JAVMA, 1998, p. 1975)

In many ways, the metaphor *human–animal bond* (HAB) captures the spirit of the infant–parent bond (Fine, 2014). Beck (1999) noted that the term "bond" was borrowed from the terminology used to describe the relationship between parents and their children. In fact, Beck (1999) points out that the first "official" use of the term "human–animal bond" appeared in the *Proceedings of the Meeting of Group for the Study of Human-Companion Animal Bond* in Dundee, Scotland, March 23–25, 1979. An animal's dependence on humans appears to be a critical factor in establishing and sustaining this bond. Many individuals recognize their responsibility to their pets and how much their pets depend on them. Legally, animals are considered property, but most people view their pets as companions and family members (Fine, 2014). In essence, our healthy relationships with pets have a profound influence on both human and animal health and behavior.

The Physiological and Psychological Benefits of Human–Animal Interactions

Ever since the pioneering research by Erica Friedmann and her colleagues (1980, 1993) demonstrated that pet ownership was associated with better recovery in patients discharged from a coronary care unit, there has been great interest in studying the impact of the human–animal interactions on human health. Fine (2014) identified a plethora of studies that have high-lighted the value of these interactions on human health. Studies have revealed numerous outcomes, including the impact of stroking a pet on heart rate (McGreevy, Righetti, & Thomson, 2005; Shiloh, Sorek, & Terkel, 2003; Vormbrock & Grossberg, 1988), the presence of a pet dog or cat and its impact on heart rate and blood pressure in stressful situations (such as completing mental arithmetic) (Allen, Blascovich, & Mendes, 2002), pets' impact on reducing feelings of loneliness and isolation (Headey, 1998), and how walking with a dog impacts opportunities to initiate and sustain conversations with strangers (McNicholas & Collis, 2000). Furthermore, in research conducted by Purewal et al. (2017), they found evidence for childhood pet ownership and a wide range of psycho-logical health benefits. The study suggested that pet ownership provides support for increased social competence as well as enhancement of child-hood social networks.

Further research points out that during interactions with a perceived friendly dog, cortisol (stress hormone) levels decrease significantly, and both humans and dogs experienced an increase in oxytocin, an endor-phin that promotes a sense of happiness (Odendaal & Meintjes, 2003). It is evident that the presence of and the interaction with a companion animal makes people feel less stressed and anxious and increases feelings of security (Fine, 2014). Findings from research studies have helped explain how through the study of stress biomarkers such as cortisol and immunoglobulin A (Beetz, Julius, Turner, & Kotrschal, 2012; Krause-Parello, 2012, 2008;). In a study by Duvall Antonacopoulos (2017), they examined the effect of acquiring a dog and its impact on loneliness. The results from their study suggest that participants who acquire a dog experi-ence reduced levels of loneliness. Considerable evidence supports the position that pet ownership or interaction with animals decreases social isolation and loneliness, and facilitates social interaction (Wells, 2009). People may seek out animal companionship when they are lonely or feeling bad about their social situation. Even thinking about cats or dogs appears to provide relief from social rejection (Brown, Hengy, & McConnell, 2016).

Kingson (2018), in an article reported in the *New York Times*, cites com-ments by numerous scholars that support research related to the health benefits of animals. She underscores Dr. James Serpell's findings that having relationships and social experiences with animals is very helpful to people's health and has a positive impact on their immune system and car-diovascular functions. Serpell goes on in the interview to state that:

> The hormone oxytocin plays a key role in the way animals can soothe humans. The petting and the physical contact side of things is critical in terms of oxytocin release. Physical contact with something warm and fuzzy and soft is also a good trigger.

Research also highlights the role of pets in enhancing humans' quality of life. For example, a study by Hall, MacMichael, Turner, and Mills (2017), found that there were improvements in quality of life associated with owning a support dog for individuals with physical disabilities. Their research found that the improvements exceeded what was expected from the increased physical independence that was acquired because of having an assistance dog. Some of the lifestyle changes noted by the researchers included increased recreational and social engagement and more involvement in their communities. It appears that both service animals as well as pets contribute to the happiness of humans. Research and writings by Ryan and Deci (2001) highlight some current findings on emotional well-being. Their research point to two general perspectives of where they believe happiness stems. One of the roots can be attributed to a category classified as the hedonic approach, which defines happiness and well-being in terms of pleasure attainment and pain avoidance. On the other hand, they discuss the eudaimonic approach, which focuses on meaning and self-realization in life. Ryan and Deci (2001) define well-being "in terms of the degree to which a person is fully functioning." Some current research has documented the critical role that pets can play in eudaimonic aspects of well-being. The findings of these studies suggest that pets seem to have an impact on enhancing a sense of personal fulfillment (Kanat-Maymon, Antebi, and Zilcha-Mano, 2016) and understanding oneself more clearly (Hall et al., 2017).

Ample evidence supports the notion that the presence of an animal encourages social interaction. Perhaps one of the greatest benefits that animals provide is their role in acting as social capital. Lang and Hornburg (1998) define social capital as the glue that holds society together. Pets function as one source of social capital – they enhance communication and solidarity among people and act as lubricants for social interaction in the community (Wood, 2011; Wood, Giles-Corti, & Bulsara, 2005; Wood, Shardlow, & Willis, 2009). Additionally, pet owners perceive their communities as friendlier and more amiable than non-pet owners (Arkow, 2015). Wells (2009) prepared a tremendous review of the literature that synthesizes numerous studies that highlight the health benefits of animals. (Readers are encouraged to review this article as well as a chapter in Fine (2014), which highlight some of the same findings.)

Although there have been numerous studies supporting the value of pets in promoting psychological and physical well-being, there are some who argue the evidence is not conclusive. Herzog (2018) in a blog on the *Psychology Today* website entitled "Does having pets really make us healthier" argues that the idea that getting a pet will make you healthier and happier is not accurate. He points out a few studies that have found very little difference between the health of pet owners versus non-pet owners. For example, in a recent study by Mein and Grant (2018), the results showed very little difference between pet owners versus non-pet owners in regards to health issues. The study included 6,575 participants between the ages of 59 and 79, and about 2,000 of these individuals lived with a pet. Their findings seemed to suggest no differences between the groups in their general health and number of chronic illnesses. Very few of the variables under investigation were found to show any significant difference between pet owners and non-pet owners. One of the factors that did show a difference was in regard to the exercise of dog owners. It appears that dog owners engaged in considerably more mild to moderate exercise than the non-pet owners. These findings seem to be consistent with other research on the role animals can have on human exercise. Herzog (2018) concluded in his argument that the research on the so-called "pet effect" seems to have mixed results. In essence, Herzog (2018) argued that the findings are still inconclusive and that one still needs to use caution in regard to interpreting findings that pets are a definite source of well-being for their human counterparts. I agree with that position and encourage individuals not to view pet ownership and interactions as a panacea to both physical and mental health and to remain guarded and realistic with regard to human/pet interactions (Wright et al., 2016).

Theories Explaining the Human–Animal Bond

Many wonder why people appear to naturally gravitate towards meaningful relationships with non-human animals. Fine and Weaver (2018) and Fine and Mackintosh (2016) note that there are three theories that can shed light on explaining the human–animal bond phenomena. These three theoretical orientations include animals acting as a social support, the attachment theory, and the biophilia hypothesis. The first orientation suggests that animals serve as social support for their human counterparts. In essence, it is believed that animals can provide comfort and strength in difficult times and that many people have pets for this reason. People of all ages may turn to their pets as an outlet for their feelings during stressful circumstances as well as occasions where they just want companionship (Fine and Eisen, 2016; Melson, 2001; Strand, 2004). As research has previously documented, pets may be helpful in physically calming their owners by reducing blood pressure and heart rate, and decreasing the levels of stress hormones such as cortisol (Handlin et al., 2011). Furthermore, there has been some research that points out that interactions with animals impact several neurobiological hormonal agents including decreasing cortisol (de-stressing) as well as increasing serotonin, oxytocin and dopamine (Beetz, Uvnas-Moberg, Julius, & Kotrschal, 2012; Wohlfarth, Mutschler, Beetz, Kreuser, & Korsten-Reck, 2013). McConnell, Brown, Shoda, Stayton, and Martin (2011), in an interesting paper called "Friends with benefits," noted that pets seem to have the ability to stave off negativity caused by social rejection. The researchers summarize that pets can serve as an important source of social support. Furthermore, in a study by Stewart, Dispenza, Parker, Chang, and Cunnien (2014) regarding the therapeutic application of human–animal interactions, they noted that animal-assisted therapy outreach interventions seem to significantly decrease self-reported anxiety and loneliness of college students in need. They point out that today it is not uncommon to see animal visits used as a source of comfort for college students in difficult times.

Children, too, can benefit from the social connections formed with non-human animals. For example, how many times have you heard stories of children who turn to their pets during times of tremendous stress and anguish? Furthermore, for some children and adults who lack friendships and social contacts, turning to an animal can provide them with an otherwise missing sense of comfort and security. I recall a boy who was seven years old who was diagnosed as having Attention Deficit and Hyperactivity Disorder (ADHD). The child had limited relationships outside of school and was often considered lonely. His best friend was actually his dog, with whom many would frequently witness him playing with and walking. Ironically, it was his relationship with his dog that acted as a catalyst in gaining access to other children who wanted to interact with him and his dog. They approached him because of his strong connection with the dog, and peer relationships were created as a consequence.

In other situations, it's not uncommon to find people living in isolation who turn to their animals. They view the animal as being critical in providing them social support. Over the years in talking to elderly people, including those with chronic illnesses, it has not been uncommon for information to be shared about the perceived importance of their pets as strong contributors to their social support system. They recognized how their animals contributed to their quality of life and realized without them they would have even more profound challenges. Lisa is a 77-year-old widow who lost her husband 2 years ago and has battled feelings of isolation and loneliness. She attributes her decreased despair and internal strength to a new cat in her life. She loves taking care of him and his attention helps her in moments of supreme emptiness. She finds that when she feels stuck in a chasm of loneliness, she turns to her beloved cat for comfort and support.

The attachment theory provides an alternative perspective of why we are so connected to our pets. The theory suggests that our strong relationships with animals exist because of our innate attachment needs as caregivers. Attachment theory was developed by John Bowlby (1969), who described a major element in parent–child relationships that relates to humans' desire to protect their infants. This widely accepted theory has also been associated with why people want to have pets. The attachment theory explains the strong connection we have with our pets. Biologically, we can explain the attachment bond with the higher levels of oxytocin that are often found when this connection is elicited. Oxytocin, often considered the "love hormone," is a peptide hormone that is often released in

periods of hugging and other forms of interpersonal connection. It is
believed to be critical for the attachment that parents have with their children, and in our case the attachment between humans and their pets. In
essence, the literature has now provided tremendous support for our
understanding of the biology of attachment.

Zilcha-Mano, Mikuliner, and Shaver (2012) suggest that humans view
their companion animals in a similar fashion as those caring for an infant.
Taking care of an animal brings pleasure and joy and is the impetus of the
relationship. Furthermore, in a paper by Barba (1995), the author
described owners' relationships with their pets as parallel to the parent/
child relationship. In so many ways, our pets depend on us for their care
and protection (Fine, 2014). This caretaking role provides people of all
ages, including children, with opportunities to be caregivers rather than
receivers. In fact, it has been noted that in both boys and girls, taking care
of an animal and being a nurturer is a valued and accepted behavior
(Fine, 2014). Additionally, research by Carlisle (2014) indicated an
increase in social behavior among children with pets, suggesting that children too seem to show strong levels of attachment to their animals. Furthermore, there is also biological evidence that the neurotransmitter
oxytocin is prevalent not only in parent–child relationships (highlighting
familial love) but also between owners and their pets, which gives the
attachment theory a neurobiological basis (Odendaal & Meintjes, 2003).

Many examples come to mind that highlight the attachment theory. Pet
owners who feel a strong commitment to their pets and take care of them
as children could be used as examples of this position. I think of Diana,
who takes great pride in caring for her golden pups. She is their best advocate. When her eldest dog Savanna was very ill, she did what was humanly
possible to make sure she was comfortable. In many ways, just like Bowlby's
work suggested, she felt a strong kinship with her dog, and the instincts of
a parent taking care of an infant seem very comparable. These actions are
not uncommon and can be seen in homes of millions of families across
this country.

Finally, E. O. Wilson and Stephen R. Kellert developed a theory called
biophilia that suggests that humans evolved to bond with other forms of
life as a means of survival (Kellert, 1997; Wilson, 1984). According to
Edward O. Wilson (1984), biophilia is the inherent need of humans to
understand and relate to nature (Wilson, 1984). Furthermore, Stephen K.
Kellert asserts that humans are intimately reliant on the environment for
survival (Kellert, 1993). In essence, the theory suggests that biophilia
motivates humans to form relationships with other animals and to feel a
kinship in nature (Fine & Weaver, 2018). Fine and Weaver (2018) suggest
that biophilia is also the cause of an innate part of the human brain that
draws enrichment through connections to nature. The theory provides
another alternative to understanding human–animal interactions. In
essence, this orientation suggests that humans are very connected to their

natural environment, and there is a biological need for us to interact with nature as a whole – including animals. That is why we see people walking with their pets in nature, bird watching, or engaging in other forms of eco-tourism. We just seem to have a fantastic connection with nature as a whole. In summary, each of these orientations provide a different glimpse as to why we have unique relationships with pets. While each of these might not completely answer the question of why people relish being sur-rounded by animals, they do provide us with a solid foundation from which to start.

Conclusions

It is apparent that our relationships with animals have long been valued. Although science has not conclusively provided evidence that animals make a significant impact on our physical and emotional well-being, most people intuitively accept this belief. Many people would agree that pets provide humans with tremendous support that enrich their lives. Our relationships with animals help us endure and persevere in difficult moments and they help us find joy in everyday moments. In essence, animals are good for our well-being, and unfortunately their significance to us makes losing them even harder. Anatole France (n.d.) once stated: "that until one has loved an animal, a part of one's soul remains unawakened." How appropriate this quotation is in capturing the essence of our bond with animals. Their lives become so entangled with ours that we become richer as a consequence.

When Magic passed on, we tried to think of many ways to celebrate her life. We decided to engrave a portrait on her urn with a small etched passage written by Isla Paschal Richardson. The passage helped us put into perspective the significance of her life to our family. "*Grieve not, nor speak of me in tears, but laugh and talk to me as if I were beside you ... I loved you so – twas heaven here with you.*" When we develop such strong connections with our pets, it would be ridiculous to believe that their physical absence will not affect us. Most people adjust to their grief over time and hold onto a relationship that meant so much to them. This book will provide answers to many of your questions on how people cope and deal with loss, as well as covering some best practice approaches to supporting people who are bereaving the loss of their pets.

References

Albuguerque, N, Kun, G., Savalli, C., Otta, E., and Mills, D. (2016) Dogs recognize dog and human emotions, *Biology Letters*. doi: 10.1098/rsbl.2015.0883

Allen, K. M., Blascovich, J., & Mendes, W. B. (2002). Cardiovascular reactivity and the presence of pets, friends and spouses: the truth about cats and dogs. *Psychosomatic Medicine*, 64, 727–739.

American Pet Products Association. (2018). Industry statistics and trends. www. americanpetproducts.org/pressindustrytrends.asp.

Andics, A., Gábor, A., Gácsi, M., Faragó, T., Szabo, D., & Miklósi, A. (2016). Neural mechanisms for lexical processing in dogs. *Science*, 353, August, 1030–1032. doi: 10.1126/science.aaf3777.

Arkow, P. (2015). Animal therapy on the community level: The impact of pets on social capital. In A. Fine (Ed.), *Handbook on animal-assisted therapy: Theoretical foundations and guidelines for practice* (4th ed., pp. 43–52). San Diego, CA: Elsevier Inc.

Barba, B. E. (1995) A critical review of research on human/companion animal relationship: 1988 through 1993. *Anthrozoös*, 8(1) 9–20.

Beck, A. M. (1999). Companion animals and their companions: sharing a strategy for survival. *Bulletin Science, Technology & Society*, 19(4), 281–285.

Beetz, A., Julius, H., Turner, D., & Kotrschal, K. (2012). Effects of social support by a dog on stress modulation in male children with insecure attachment. *Frontiers in Psychology*, 3, 352. doi: 10.3389/fpsyg.2012.00352

Beetz, A., Uvnas-Moberg, K., Julius, H., & Kotrschal K. (2012). Psychosocial and psychophysiological effects of human–animal interactions: The possible role of oxytocin. *Frontiers in Psychology*, 2012(3), 1–15.

Bowlby, J. (1969). Disruption of affectional bonds and its effects on behavior. *Canada's Mental Health Supplement*, 69, 1–17.

Bowlby, J. (1980). *Attachment and loss*. New York, NY: Basic Books.

Brown, C. M., Hengy, S. M., & McConnell, A. R. (2016). Thinking about cats or dogs provides relief from social rejection. *Anthrozoös*, 29, 47–58.

Carlisle, G. K. (2014). The social skills and attachment to dogs of children with autism spectrum disorder. *Journal of Autism and Developmental Disorders*. Advance online publication. doi: 10.1007/s10803-014-2267-7

Duvall Antonacopoulos, N. M. (2017). A longitudinal study of the relation between acquiring a dog and loneliness. *Society & Animals: Journal of Human-Animal Studies*, 25(4), 319–340. doi: 10.1163/15685306-12341449

Fine, A. H. (2014). *Our faithful companions: Exploring the essence of our kinship with animals*. Crawford, CO: Alpine Publications.

Fine, A. H., & Eisen, C. (2016). *Afternoons with puppy: Inspirations from a therapist and his therapy animals* (2nd ed.). West Lafayette, IN: Purdue University Press.

Fine, A. H., & Weaver, S. (2018). The human–animal bond and animal assisted intervention. In M. van den Bosch & W. Bird (Eds.), *Oxford textbook of nature and public health* (pp. 132–138). Oxford, UK: Oxford University Press.

Fine, A. H., & Mackintosh T. K. (2016). Animal-assisted interventions: Entering a crossroads of explaining an instinctive bond under the scrutiny of scientific inquiry. In: H. S. Friedman (Ed.), *Encyclopedia of mental health* (2nd ed., Vol 1, pp. 68–73). Waltham, MA: Academic Press,.

Fine, A. H., & Beck, A. (2015). Understanding our kinship with animals: input for healthcare professionals interested in the human/animal bond. In A. H. Fine (Ed.), *Handbook on animal-assisted therapy: Theoretical foundations for guidelines and practice* (3rd ed., pp. 3–15). San Diego, CA: Elsevier Inc.

France, A. (n.d.). BrainyQuote.com. Retrieved November 8, 2018, from www.brainyquote.com/quotes/anatole_france_383929

Friedmann, E., Katcher, A. H., Lynch, J. J., & Thomas, S. A. (1980). Animal companions and one-year survival of patients after discharge from a coronary care unit. *Public Health Rep.*, 95, 307–312.

Friedmann, E., Locker, B. Z., & Lockwood, R. (1993). Perception of animals and cardiovascular responses during verbalization with an animal present. *Anthrozoös*, 6, 115–134.

Grandin, T. (2013). Personal communication, September 18, 2013.

Hall, S. S., MacMichael, J., Turner, A., & Mills, D. S. (2017). A survey of the impact of owning a service dog on quality of life for individuals with physical and hearing disability: a pilot study. *Health and Quality of life Outcomes*, 15(1), 59.

Handlin, L., Hydbring-Sandberg, E., Nilsson, A., Ejdebäck, M., Jansson, A., & Uvnäs-Moberg, K. (2011). Short-Term Interaction between dogs and their owners: Effects on oxytocin, cortisol, insulin and heart rate—an exploratory study. *Anthrozoös*, 24(3), 301–315. doi: 10.2752/175303711x13045914865385

Headey, B. (1998). Health benefits and health cost savings due to pets: preliminary estimates from an Australian national survey. *Social Indicators Research*, 47, 233–243.

Herzog, H. (2018). Does having pets really make us healthier? New studies find little support for a "Pet Effect" on physical or mental health. Retrieved September 8, 2018, from www.psychologytoday.com/ca/blog/animals-and-us/201808/does-having-pets-really-make-us-healthier

Horowitz, A. (2009). *Inside of a dog: What dogs see, smell, and know*. New York, NY: Scribner.

Journal of the American Veterinary Medical Association. (1998). Statement from the committee on the human–animal bond. *Journal of the American Veterinary Medical Association*, 212(11), 1675.

Kanat-Maymon, Y., Antebi, A., & Zilcha-Mano, S. (2016). Basic psychological need fulfillment in human–pet relationships and well-being. *Personality and Individual Differences*, 92, 69–73.

Kellert, S. R. (1997). *From kinship to mastery: Biophilia in human evolution and development*. Washington, DC: Island Press.

Kellert, S. R. (1993). The biological basis for human values of nature. In S. R. Kellert, & E. O. Wilson (Eds.), *The biophilia hypothesis*. Washington, DC: Clearwater Press.

Kingson, J. (2018). As animal-assisted therapy thrives, enter the cats. *The New York Times, September 6, 2018*. Retrieved September 12, 2018, from www.nytimes.com/2018/09/06/well/live/as-animal-assisted-therapy-thrives-enter-the-cats.html

Krause-Parello, C. A. (2008). The mediating effect of pet attachment support between loneliness and general health in older females living in the community. *Journal of Community Health Nursing*, 25, 1–14.

Krause-Parello, C. A. (2012). Pet ownership and older women: The relationships among loneliness, pet attachment support, human social support, and depressed mood. *Geriatric Nursing*, 33, 194–203.

Lang, R., & Hornburg, S. (1998). What is social capital and why is it important to public policy? *Housing Policy Debate*, 9(1), 1–16.

McConnell, A. R., Brown, C. M., Shoda, T. M., Stayton, L. E., & Martin, C. E. (2011). Friends with benefits: On the positive consequences of pet ownership. *Journal of Personality and Social Psychology*, 101(6), 1239–1252. doi: 10.1037/a0024506

McGreevy, P. D., Righetti, J., & Thomson, P. (2005). The reinforcing value of physical contact on the effect on canine heart rate of grooming in different anatomical areas. *Anthrozoös*, 2, 33–37.

McNicholas, J., & Collis, G. M. (2000). Dogs as catalysts for social interactions: robustness of the effect. *British Journal of Psychology*, 91, 61–70.

Mein, G., & Grant, R. (2018). A cross-sectional exploratory analysis between pet ownership, sleep, exercise, health and neighborhood perceptions: the Whitehall II cohort study. *BMC Geriatrics*, 18(1), 176.

Melson, G. F. (2001). Child development and the human-companion animal bond. *American Behavioral Scientist*, 47, 31–39

Nagasawa, M., Kikusui, T., Onaka, T., & Ohta, M. (2015). Dog's gaze at its owner increases owner's urinary oxytocin during social interaction. *Horm. Behav.*, 55, 434–441.

Odendaal, J., & Meintjes, R (2003). Neurophysiological correlates of affiliative behaviour between humans and dogs. *Vet. Journal*, 165(3) 296–301.

Purewal, R., Christley, R., Kordas, K., Joinson, C., Meints, K., Gee, N., & Westgarth, C. (2017). Companion Animals and Child/Adolescent Development: A Systematic Review of the Evidence. *International Journal of Environmental Research and Public Health*, 14(3), 27. doi: 10.3390/ijerph14030234

Ryan R., & Deci, R. (2001). On happiness and human potentials: A review of research on hedonic and eudaimonic well-being, *Annual Review of Psychology*, 52(1), 141–166.

Shiloh, S., Sorek, G., & Terkel, J. (2003). Reduction of state-anxiety by petting animals in a controlled laboratory experiment. *Anxiety, Stress, and Coping*, 16(4), 387–395.

Stewart, L. A., Dispenza, F., Parker, L., Chang, C. Y., & Cunnien, T. (2014). A pilot study assessing the effectiveness of an animal-assisted outreach program. *Journal of Creativity in Mental Health*, 9(3), 332–345. doi: 10.1080/15401383.2014.892862

Strand, E. B. (2004). Interparental conflict and youth maladjustments: the buffering effects of pets. *Stress, Trauma, and Crisis*, 7, 151–168.

Vormbrock, J., & Grossberg, J. (1988). Cardiovascular effects of human–pet dog interactions. *Journal Behav Med.*, 11(5), 509–517

Wells, D. L. (2009). The effects of animals on human health and well-being. *Journal of Social Issues*, 65(3), 523–543.

Wilson, E. O. (1984). *Biophilia*. Cambridge MA: Harvard University Press.

Wohlfarth, R., Mutschler, B., Beetz, A., Kreuser, F., & Korsten-Reck, U. (2013). Dogs motivate obese children for physical activity: key elements of a motivational theory of animal-assisted interventions. *Frontiers in Psychology*, 4, 796. doi: 10.3389/fpsyg.2013.00796

Wood, L., Giles-Corti, B., & Bulsara, M. (2005). The pet connection: Pets as a conduit for social capital? *Social Science & Medicine*, 61, 1159–1173.

Wood, L., Shardlow, T., & Willis S. (2009). Living well together: How companion animals can help strengthen social fabric. Petcare Information & Advisory 22 Service Pty Ltd and the Centre for the Built Environment and Health (School of Population Health), The University of Western Australia.

Wood, L. J. (2011). Community benefits of human–animal interactions … the ripple effect. In P. McCardle, S. McCune, J.A. Griffin, L. Esposito, and L.S. Freund (Eds,). *Animals in our lives: Human–animal interaction in family, community, and therapeutic settings* (pp. 23–52). Baltimore, MD: Paul H. Brookes Publishing Company.

Wright, H., Hall, S., Hames, A., Hardiman, J., Burgess, A., Mills, R., & Mills, D. (2016). Effects of pet dogs for children with autism spectrum disorders (ASD) and their families: Expectations versus reality. *Human-Animal Interaction Bulletin*, 4(2).

Zilcha-Mano, S., Mikuliner, M., & Shaver, P. R. (2012). Pets as safe havens and secure bases: The moderating of pet attachment orientation. *Journal or Research in Personality*, 46(5), 571–580.

Part II
Lifespan

2 Children's Experiences of Pet Loss and Separation

A Child Development Framework

Gail F. Melson

Introduction

Pets are everywhere in human society. Companion animals provide significant relationships in the lives of most children. A growing body of literature on Human–Animal Interaction (HAI) documents the multiple ways interactions with animals in general, and pets in particular, affect human development. (Note that although humans are clearly animals, I follow customary usage and refer to non-human animals as "animals" and human animals as "humans." In addition, the terms "pets" and "companion animals" are sometimes contested terms, implying exploitation or unacceptable power asymmetry to some people. While acknowledging these controversies, the terms "pets" and to a lesser extent, "companion animals" remain in wide usage. Hence, for clarity, I employ them.)

Within the HAI literature, there is now ample evidence that children develop close, affectionate bonds with pets and derive emotional and social support from these relationships, especially in times of stress. Physiological relaxation effects, as measured by heart rate, stress hormones such as cortisol, and galvanic skin response (GSR), may occur in the presence of a friendly pet, even one that is unfamiliar or belonging to another family. Ties with pets prompt children to consider moral questions concerning the human treatment of animals (Melson et al., 2009) and affect later attitudes toward animal welfare and environmental issues. There is also evidence that involvement with pets, including pet care, may help children to develop a more accurate understanding of biological processes. Thus, the child–pet relationship affects multiple dimensions of children's development – physiological, cognitive, emotional, social, and moral.

Another body of literature addresses children's developing understanding and experience with loss, separation, and death. Scholars have documented how the cognitive understanding of death unfolds, including a gradual understanding of key features of death, such as finality, universality, and causality. However, less research attention has been paid to understanding children's emotional responses to death, despite recognition that confronting the permanent loss of a loved one is, above all, an emotional experience. At the same time, practitioners have developed therapeutic interventions for adults and children facing human as well as animal losses. Many children's books dealing with death are available to parents. Thus, because of clients' needs, therapy, support, and interventions have outpaced research into evidence-based best practices.

Given the pervasiveness of pets in children's lives, for many children their first experience with death comes from the death of a pet. Yet, the two bodies of literature – that on children's ties with pets and that on children's experiences with death – have not been well integrated. This chapter addresses that gap. I advance a child development perspective, asking the following questions:

1. How do children's relationships with pets affect their experiences of pet loss, separation, and death?
2. In what ways are children's experiences of loss, separation, and death, involving human ties versus animal ties similar and different?
3. What individual, familial, and contextual factors affect children's experiences of pet loss, separation, and death?
4. What are the implications for therapeutic interventions with children and their families?

The Significance of the Child–Pet Relationship

Ever since the publication of Uri Bronfenbrenner's 1979 classic, *The Ecology of Human Development,* an ecological approach to child development has been central. This approach emphasizes that children grow up in widening circles of relationships and environments, from the most intimate – the family – to the most expansive – the wider culture and historical epoch. While children bring their own temperament, personality, and genetic heritage – the "nature" of the nature–nurture interaction – their development is shaped by these interrelated contexts.

Despite the complexity of Bronfenbrenner's descriptions of the multiple contexts and relationships in children's lives, he, along with most other psychologists, assumed that only relationships with other humans were consequential. This "anthropocentric" bias (Melson, 2001) has given way to a more "bio-centric" perspective, in which connections with other animals and nature are recognized as important contexts. The field of Human–Animal Interaction has now grown to host international conferences and produce scientific research journals dedicated to this subject.

Nonetheless, children's ties with the non-human world are still not fully integrated into our understanding of child development. Most child development textbooks, as they address social relationships fail to mention, let alone discuss in depth, ties with animals, especially pets. When scholars advance theories and conduct research on children's ties to pets and other animals, this academic work is often "siloed" in journals and books dedicated to the human–animal bond. Thus, we have little insight into how children's relationships with humans and non-humans are interwoven and interrelated. We need a perspective that integrates all relationships and environments, human and non-human.

We also need a developmental perspective to fully understand children's relationships with animals. This perspective recognizes both dynamic change and continuity in all living things from conception to death. Such a recognition mandates consideration of earlier experiences as shapers of the present. This is particularly true of early childhood experiences which often form a "template" or predisposition toward future experiences. In addition, children, indeed all humans, are influenced by their expectations of the future. A child development perspective further recognizes predictable maturational changes as children move from infancy through early childhood into middle childhood and then adolescence. Finally, a developmental perspective considers multiple domains or areas or development – physiological, cognitive, emotional, social, and moral. While conceptually distinct, each domain influences the others through mutual feedback loops. For example, a child's cognitive level in understanding death is likely to influence the child's emotions during a death experience and vice versa.

Pet Ownership

Even today, the US Census does not ask about non-human family members. Similarly, other countries rely on survey data and individual studies to project pet ownership rates. As a result, we only have estimates, not firm figures, of the extent of pet ownership in the US and worldwide. These estimates indicate that pet ownership is widespread, with recent surveys by the Humane Society of the US, the American Veterinary Medical Association and the American Pet Products Association estimating that about two-thirds of all US households had at least one pet. Ownership of multiple pets is common among pet owners. Rates are similarly high in other societies in Europe and Latin America, with rates in Asian countries rapidly increasing. For example, a 2018 online survey of 27,000 individuals across 22 countries found pet ownership rates highest in Latin America, with 80% of Mexican and 80% of Argentinian respondents indicating pets in the household. Seventy-three percent of Russian respondents identified as pet owners. By contrast, 31% of South Korean and 37% of Japanese respondents said they owned pets. However, the most rapid rate of increase in pet ownership is currently in Asian countries (see www.gfk.com/global-studies-pet-ownership). Moreover, households with children under 18 years of age are more likely than other household types to have pets. For example, a UK study found that 74% of families with a 10-year-old also had at least one pet (Westgarth et al., 2010).

Although pet ownership is widespread in families with children, there are contextual variations, not surprisingly, based on demographic characteristics such as race, social class, parental education, family living arrangements, culture, and geography, among others. Variables such as attitudes toward animals and parental history of pet keeping also may play a role. Unfortunately, precise data on pet ownership including such variables is often lacking. As research catches up to practice, therapists and others should keep in mind that every child–pet relationship is unique. The particular qualities of this relationship will impact how the child deals with pet loss and death.

Given the high incidence of pet ownership, it is surprising that recognition of children's relationships with animals continues to lag behind attention to human ties. Children have been growing up in close proximity to animals since the dawn of human evolution. In modern times, pets – a relationship centered on companionship and affection – have taken their place in a majority of households with children. Surveys indicate that most parents and children consider their pets "members of the family" and report getting pets "for the children," in the belief that pets enrich the child's development and bring the family members together (Melson, 2001).

The child–pet relationship emerges as even more important when considered against the background of demographic changes in family composition. Lower birth rates and smaller family size (long-term demographic trends) mean that children are less likely to have multiple siblings at home. Divorce often results in reduced contact with the non-custodial parent, usually the father. Multiple generations are less likely to be living under the same roof or in close proximity. Such trends, widespread in developed industrialized and post-industrial societies in North America, Europe, and Asia, may make the presence of pets even more salient, as the number of human family members dwelling together shrinks.

Pet Keeping History

In addition to demographic changes in the human composition of households, the presence of companion animals reveals additional complexities. Because of the shorter life span of companion animals compared to those of humans, children may grow up with a series of pets. Ecological systems theory (Bronfenbrenner, 1979) as well as child development perspectives (Kaplan & Garner, 2017) tell us that all family relationships mutually affect one another simultaneously. This is true for non-human family members as well. It is likely that any current relationship with a particular animal will be influenced by prior relationships with pets that are no longer physically present in the family.

The Child–Pet Bond

Pets are ubiquitous in children's lives, but are they important? The growing literature on the child–pet relationship indicates a firm "yes" (Monsen, 2001). Most children with pets at home identify their relationship to them as a close, affectionate bond. In interviews with children, they single out their pets as unique sources of support, more likely to last "no matter what" (Furman, 1989). In another study, 42% of 5-year-olds with pets at home said they turned to their pets when feeling sad, anxious, lonely or wanting to tell a secret. Deriving such emotional support from pets was associated with parental reports of lower anxiety and better adjustment as the children began kindergarten (Melson, 2001).

In addition, many children are involved in pet care. Unlike caring for human infants and young children, caring for animals does not seem to be gendered in the minds of children. Specifically, children over five years of age associate (human) infant care with feminine gender roles and as a result, boys are less likely to be interested in and involved in nurturing human young (Fogel & Melson, 1986). By contrast, boys and girls alike view pet care as "gender neutral," not associated with either femininity or masculinity. As a result, pet care may be one of the few culturally sanctioned opportunities for involving boys in nurturing and caregiving (Melson & Fogel, 1989).

For both boys and girls, pet care may be a more accessible way for children to be involved in caregiving, since parents, for safety and legal reasons, are likely reluctant to have older children take responsibility for the care of human infants, younger children, or frail elderly relatives. In addition, as noted earlier, humans in need of such care are increasingly absent in many children's households.

Like any close family relationship, the child–pet one is complex. While emotional support, bonding, nurturing, and other benefits have been emphasized in research, children also report worries and stress related to their pets, such as concern about pet safety when the child is away (Bryant, 1990). The economic costs of properly caring for companion animals can stress children and families. Zoonotic diseases, animal behavioral problems, and dog bites are risks of pet ownership. In families where domestic abuse occurs, animal abuse is a risk (Newberry, 2017). Attention to animal welfare and child socialization of proper pet "etiquette" can minimize some of these risks.

Evidence of worry, stress, and negative experiences with pets has implications for children's experiences with pet loss and death. When children express worry over pet safety, the children may already be aware, perhaps unconsciously, of the risks of pet loss or death. This anticipatory stress can prepare some children for later real losses. On the other hand, for some children, such worries may exacerbate their distress over later pet loss, or lead to hypervigilance while the pet is alive. Parents and other caregivers can play an important role in reassuring children about pet safety when the children are away at school or other activities.

The Significance of Pets for Child Development

A growing body of research has examined multiple domains of development, particularly physiological, cognitive, social, emotional, and moral development. While this chapter cannot fully document studies in each area (for further details, see Melson, in press), pets may play a role in all of these domains. However, research is far from conclusive. The "gold standard" of research – double-blind experiments with randomization – is not practical. Many studies conflate pet ownership (the mere presence of an animal in a human household) with pet attachment or bond (the emotional relationship of human and animal). In addition, too often research on the impact of pet ownership fails to control confounding variables or selection factors, making it difficult to attribute health or psychological outcomes to pet ownership alone (Saunders, Parast, Babey, & Miles, 2017). Finally, a cultural bias, the assumption that pets are good for humans and their effects are solely beneficial, may seep into scholarly studies, leading researchers to neglect findings of no effects or negative effects. Animal-assisted therapy (AAT) and animal-assisted activities (AAA) are now widespread, outpacing evidence-based studies on efficacy. As a result, some scholars may feel social pressure to report positive findings and minimize negative ones (Serpell, McCune, Gee, & Griffin, 2017).

With these caveats in mind, there is suggestive evidence of pets' physiological benefits: friendly companion animals (usually dogs have been studied) can produce relaxation effects, lowering blood pressure and stress hormones. With respect to cognitive influences, pet care can increase understanding of biology and of basic distinctions between living and non-living organisms (Inagaki & Hatano, 2006). In the social and emotional domains, there is evidence that children derive feelings of support, acceptance, and companionship, not only from the animals within their own households, but even friendly unfamiliar animals with whom they have brief involvement (Melson et al., 2009). Finally, interactions with animals prompt children to consider moral questions, such as the proper treatment of pets (Melson et al., 2009), and even issues of conservation and species protection. Animal care can promote empathy and better perspective-taking. At the same time, the moral domain regarding human relationships with animals is enormously complex, since animals are consumed as food, turned into clothing and hunted for sport as well as treasured as close companions. As Serpell (2009) notes, this "confronts us with fundamental questions about what it means to be human."

Implications for Understanding Pet Loss

Evidence for the pervasiveness of pet ownership and the myriad ways in which the presence of pets impacts children suggests important implications for how children experience pet loss, separation, and death. First, high rates of pet ownership combined with the average lifespan of many pets means that children are likely to experience death and permanent loss first with a companion animal. This first loss may form a template or "first understanding" of death and loss in general. Thus, pet loss may affect how the child responds to subsequent human or animal losses. Second, the well-documented emotional bonds that many children form with the animals in their household suggest that children are likely to experience pet loss as a significant break in an attachment or emotional bond. We need not compare this break to the death of a grandparent, other relative or even parent to recognize that pet loss will likely (though not inevitably) be significant. Third, how the child experiences pet loss or death may well affect the child's cognitive understanding of what death in general is. At the same time, the child's maturational level will shape both cognitive understanding and emotional experience of pet death or loss. Finally, in the moral domain, pet death raises many questions for child and family: How is it appropriate to memorialize or recognize the death? When, if ever, is it appropriate to bring another animal into the family? How does one understand the moral implications of naturally occurring death versus euthanasia? What circumstances justify pet relinquishment? Ethically, must one acquire pets only from rescue organizations or shelters? Given economic constraints in the family, how much expense is warranted in treating a sick animal, especially when those expenses may diminish care for other human family members? How does one ethically deal with animal suffering? When does one decide to withhold further medical treatment of an ailing animal, and on what ethical basis is that decision made? Living with companion animals "in sickness and in health" raises all these questions.

Children's Understanding of Death

An important aspect of cognitive development is the development of "naïve biology." This construct refers to children's (and adults') intuitive understandings of the biological world, including the distinction between living and non-living or never-living things, the characteristics of biological organisms versus non-biological things, and most pertinent to this chapter, what it means to be "alive" versus "dead" or "not alive." Well before formal instruction in biological sciences, children wrestle with these questions.

Studies of these understandings reveal, not surprisingly, a developmental progression with age. Before age 4, young children tend to view death as a different state of life, a prolonged sleep. Between ages 4 and 7, gradually a more accurate understanding of the characteristics of death emerge: death is universal for all living things, it is final, irreversible, and caused by the breakdown and permanent cessation of life processes, such as respiration. The finality of death tends to be understood first, with the causation of death understood last. This progression tends to hold across cultures. For example, in interviews with British Christian, British Muslim, and Pakistani Muslim children, all between the ages of 4 and 7 years, similar patterns of unfolding understanding of death emerged (Panagiotaki, Nobes, Ashraf, & Aubby, 2015).

Influences on Understanding Death

Nonetheless, there are contextual variations. For example, rural children and those in conflict zones are more exposed to both animal and human deaths. As a result, they show a more accurate understanding of death at an earlier age. Media exposure can affect children's understanding of death. Unfortunately, most media coverage contributes to distorted ideas about death; for example, believing that most people die from shootings. Religious beliefs also color understanding. Interestingly, research shows that mature biological understanding of death can co-exist with spiritual beliefs that are seemingly inconsistent. Both children and adults can understand the finality and irreversibility of death and, at the same time, hold religious beliefs in incarnation, resurrection, and immortality (Callahan, 2014). The way parents and other adults talk about death, or avoid the subject, affects children's understanding.

An important contextual factor is the particular being who has died, and the specifics of the death experience. For example, a death may be anticipated and accompanied by a gradual decline or may be sudden. Some deaths occur in violent contexts along with other traumatic events. Few studies specify these contextual factors but instead ask about death in general. Children may well understand death differently when applied to other humans, animals, or plants. Children may be affected by the nature of the relationship they had with the now dead being. On the other hand, there is evidence that the key characteristics of death, such as its finality and irreversibility, are universally applied in a mature understanding of the concept (Gutierrez, Miller, Rosengren, & Schein, 2014).

Children's Emotional Experiences of Death

An important limitation of studies that examine children's developing understanding of death is the neglect of emotion. As Callahan (2014) notes, death is always first and foremost an emotional experience. While children experience emotions confronting death, they may not have the vocabulary or self-understanding to label these emotions. In addition, as death is a cultural experience, children become aware of culturally sanctioned emotional expressions appropriate for the occasion. For example, in one study (Gutierrez et al., 2014), children were asked about their feelings in response to hypothetical scenarios of another child confronting the death of a human, a dog, or a plant. In response to all three scenarios, the children reported they would feel "sad." Interpreting these findings is difficult. Children may well react with the same sadness to the death of a plant versus a family member. On the other hand, the emotion label "sad" is readily available and culturally appropriate.

Other emotions, such as anger, feelings of abandonment and rejection, and guilt are common reactions to death or loss of a significant relationship. While children (as well as adults) may feel these emotions, they may not have words to identify them in themselves or others. Again, a child development perspective would take account of the child's developmental level in terms of labeling and understanding emotions. At any age, moreover, children may feel that such emotions are not appropriate and therefore, should not be expressed.

Emotional responses to death also are colored by the context of other losses. As Kaufman and Kaufman (2006) point out, multiple losses within a short period of time can compound grief. Bereavement in such a context can lead to depression, anxiety, social withdrawal, behavioral problems, and school difficulties. One loss, such as pet death, can trigger reactions to previous losses such as grandparent death or separation from a parent because of divorce. Similarly, pet death in the context of other human losses can result in more severe or, in the words of Kaufman and Kaufman (2006), "complicated grief."

Parents often feel their children should be shielded from the experience of death or feel awkward in discussing it. When caregivers are themselves in shock or distress over a death, immersed in the grieving process, they may lack the resources to address the child's emotions and understanding. Perhaps for such reasons, many children's books address death. In one analysis, 39% of 109 children's books dealing with death, published between 1938 and 2003, focused on the death of an animal. Of all the books, 63% included the emotion of sadness (Gutierrez et al., 2014). Children's media, such as Disney movies, also often depict the death of an animal or person and its effects on others. These portrayals are not always accurate. In a study of 23 death scenes taken from ten animated Disney films, the key features of death, such as its permanence and irreversibility, were not acknowledged. Importantly, the emotions surrounding death were sometimes omitted or distorted. For example, characters were shown celebrating and happy at the death of a villain (Cox, Garrett, & Graham, 2004). Books and videos can be useful supplements and catalysts for discussion when parents engage with their child in reading or viewing. However, literature or movies dealing with pet death used as substitutes for parental communication are likely to be at best, unhelpful to children or at worst, misleading.

Influences on the Emotional Experience of Death

As with the cognitive understanding of the concept of death, the emotions surrounding death are sensitive to contextual and individual effects. In addition to the particular relationship that the child has had with the deceased individual, the role of the family, particularly parents and care-givers, is particularly important. For many parents, as noted earlier, death (along with sex and money) is a subject often avoided in discussions with children. As Callahan (2014) notes, children may overhear adults talking to each other and recognize that something important is being hidden from them. In this way, the subject of death can take on the aura of a "for-bidden" topic, prompting children's curiosity and making them vulner-able to misinformation.

When a death of a loved one does occur, parents may be incapacitated by grief and unable to focus on how the child is reacting. Importantly, the death of a family member, such as a grandparent, may affect parents so deeply that the child feels psychologically abandoned during the period of intense grief.

Children's Experiences of Pet Loss and Separation

Much of the psychological literature on children's understanding of and emotional response to death can be applied to the experience of pet death. Although the evidence is sparse, it appears that the same developmental pro-gression in understanding the key features of death in general occur when applied to the death of a companion animal. Children report similar emo-tions (e.g., sadness) at the death of humans as well as animals. As with reac-tions to human deaths, children do not respond to animal deaths on a timetable. A child may express boredom or indifference in the immediate aftermath of the loss of a pet, only to process emotions many months later.

However, there are key features of children's relationships with pets that may make the experience of pet death different from other death experiences. First, the child–pet relationship is an asymmetrical one. Pets are physically dependent on human care and have limited, species-specific communication strategies to convey their needs and wants. Thus, humans are both dominant over, and responsible for, companion animals or other animals in their care. At the same time, humans must deal with the chal-lenges of discerning an animal's wishes and balancing those wishes against other factors. One implication is a possible sense of guilt over the death of a pet. The family may decide to forego complicated and expensive medical treatments for financial or other reasons. Pets may be permanently lost, as when a dog escapes a fenced yard. Family members may blame themselves for neglecting their responsibility to keep the pet safe. Healthy pets may be relinquished, and hence permanently lost to the family, because of such events as a family relocation.

A second feature of pet loss in some cases is its ambiguity. When a pet goes missing, as when an "outdoor" cat fails to return home, family members may search and for a time, hope that the errant animal will reappear. When that fails to happen, some family members may conclude that the pet is permanently gone, but others, including children, may continue to hope that the pet will return or believe that the pet is still alive somewhere. These feelings may result in unresolved loss.

A third feature of pet death is its cultural context. Unlike deaths of human family members, there are no culturally established rituals, such as a funeral, family visitation, (e.g., a wake or shiva), religiously sanctioned prayers, or established mourning periods. For many people, the loss of a pet is viewed as a loss of less importance than the loss of human family members. Some friends and relatives, seeking to be helpful, may urge the family to get a replacement pet. However, the child (as well as other family members) experiencing pet death may feel this loss intensely. Such a reaction is not uncommon. For example, a survey of 106 adults at a veterinary clinic indicated that 20% of clients suffered what the authors termed "significant grief," with symptoms of post-traumatic stress disorder (PTSD), after the loss (Luiz Adrian, Delirainuch, & Fruch, 2009). When pet loss and death are minimized by others, the child or adult pet owner is likely to feel a lack of support or sympathy for prolonged and intense expressions of grief. Grief and mourning that is not validated or even dismissed by one's social network has been termed "disenfranchised grief."

Implications for Practitioners

Perhaps the most important implication for practitioners working with children is simply enhanced awareness and appreciation of the depth of grief many pet owners feel at the loss or separation from their pets. Rituals such as a veterinary obituary or letter of condolence can help to validate a pet owner's feelings of loss. Transforming "disenfranchised grief" into "enfranchised" or culturally and socially validated grief is the first step. Children can be encouraged to explore their emotions through drawing, stories, plays, or arts projects, such as constructing a memorial. Adults should be aware that children may express feelings much later or at what might seem inappropriate times (for example, during a carpool ride). Emotions can be amplified when pet loss triggers memories of previous losses or occurs during stressful times, such as the start of a school year, during a family move or in the midst of parental conflict.

At the same time, parents also should give children space to *not* express emotions. Many mourners, regardless of the loss, are subject to social pressure concerning the expected expression of grief. The child who does not cry or look sad in the aftermath of a pet death, but can't wait to return to a videogame is not necessarily unfeeling. Avoidance is a typical way of dealing with overwhelming stress. Similarly, many parents are distressed when children express prolonged sadness or other negative emotions. The desire to "make everything better," to take away the hurt, can mean that children feel their emotions are not recognized and validated, but rather should be changed, and they should "cheer up." The urge to quickly replace the pet is a way for parents to "change the subject" and "move on" but is likely to short circuit the grieving process.

In a similar way, parents sometimes construct narratives that they feel will avoid the harsh reality of death. Adults may tell children that the pet has gone to live "on a farm" or "in a good home with other children" when in reality the pet has been euthanized or relinquished for economic or other reasons. As with other aspects of child-rearing, deception is never a winning strategy. Children are expert "lie detectors."

Finally, awareness of the developmental stage of the child is important. Young children are literal thinkers and may react to an explanation of pet death as "put to sleep" with fears that they too may never wake up when put to bed. As noted earlier, before age 7, most children have difficulty understanding the universality, irreversibility, and permanence of death. Parental explanations should be accurate but also take this into account. In fact, pet death is often an important "teachable moment" in advancing children's understanding of the concept of death.

Case Scenarios

Case Scenario #1

Roberta, a 37-year-old mother of two, has sought therapy because of concerns about her children's reactions to the death of their beloved beagle dog, Daisy, after 13 years. Roberta couldn't stop crying for days after Daisy died from complications of cancer. To help the family heal, Roberta organized a ceremony in the backyard. She dug a grave, buried Daisy's remains and asked her children to help construct a grave marker out of wood, writing on the plaque, "Here lies Daisy, beloved companion." Roberta's daughter Melanie, 12 years old, worked on the grave marker reluctantly, repeatedly saying it was "lame," while Ryan, her 4-year-old son, wanted to dig up the grave right away, "to check on how Daisy was doing." When Roberta gathered her children around the gravesite for a ceremony, they giggled and poked each other and finally ran away. Roberta is concerned her children are unfeeling, lacking in empathy, and behaving strangely. How should she cope with this situation? She is waiting to hear what her therapist recommends.

Discussion Questions:

1. How might the ages and genders of Roberta's children affect their responses?

2. What could Roberta say to each of her children about Daisy's death?
3. What other ways could Roberta address her own grief?

Case Scenario #2

The Gonzalez family recently settled in Portland, Oregon, after fleeing persecution and economic distress in Honduras. The three children – Luiz, Angelica, and Jose – ages 7 to 17, all witnessed violence, such as death threats, beatings, and people made to "disappear." Although the children are rapidly learning English and adjusting to their new home, each child is showing signs of stress. Luiz, age 7, has recurrent nightmares. Angelica, age 13, seems angry and sullen and often refuses to speak to her parents. Jose, at 17, has taken two part-time jobs to help the family and has little time for school. To help the children, the mother and father brought home several stray kittens they found in the neighborhood. After a few weeks, it became clear that one of the kittens was seriously ill. Money for veterinary care is lacking, and the parents are worried that the kitten will soon die, perhaps in front of the children. To avoid that, the parents are thinking about "putting the kitten out of its misery," or simply taking it away to a nearby field.

Discussion Questions:

1. How would you counsel this family, in a culturally sensitive manner?
2. How do the past experiences of this family affect how they might deal with the kitten's death or absence?
3. How might each child react differently to this situation, given each child's adjustment to their new environment?

References

Bronfenbrenner, U. (1979). *The ecology of human development.* Cambridge, MA: Harvard University Press.

Bryant, B. (1990). The richness of the child–pet relationship: A consideration of both benefits and costs of pets to children. *Anthrozoös, 3*, 253–261.

Callahan, M. (2014). Diversity in children's understanding of death. *Monographs of the Society for Research in Child Development, 79*, 142–180.

Cox, M., Garrett, E., & Graham, J. A. (2004). Death in Disney films: Implications for children's understanding of death. *Omega, 50*, 267–280.

Fogel, A., & Melson, G. F. (1986). *Origins of Nurturance: Developmental, biological and cultural perspectives on caregiving.* Hillsdale, NJ: Erlbaum.

Furman, W. (1989). The development of children's social networks. In D. Belle (Ed.), *Children's social networks and social supports* (pp. 131–172). New York, NY: Wiley.

Gutierrez, I. T., Miller, P. J., Rosengren, K. S., & Schein, S. S. (2014). Affective dimensions of death: Children's books, questions and understanding. *Monographs of the Society for Research in Child Development, 79*, 43–61.

Inagaki, K., & Hatano, G. (2006). Young children's conception of the biological world. *Current Directions in Psychological Science*, 15, 177–181.

Kaplan, A., & Garner, J. K. (2017). A complex dynamic systems perspective on identity and its development: The dynamic systems model of role identity. *Developmental Psychology*, 53, 2006–2051.

Kaufman, K. R., & Kaufman, N. D. (2006). And then the dog died. *Death Studies*, 30, 61–76.

Luiz Adrian, J. A., Delirainuch, A. N., & Fruch, C. (2009). Complicated grief and PTSD in humans responding to the death of pets/animals. *Bulletin of the Menninger Clinic*, 73, 176–187.

Melson, G. F. (2001). *Why the wild things are: Animals in the lives of children.* Cambridge, MA: Harvard University Press.

Melson, G. F. (in press). Rethinking children's connections with animals: A child-hoodnature perspective. In A. Cutter-MacKenzie, K. Malone, & E. B. Hacking (Eds.), *International Research Handbook on ChildhoodNature.* New Yrok, NY: Springer Publishing Co.

Melson, G. F., & Fogel, A. (1989). Children's ideas about animal young and their care: A reassessment of gender differences in the development of nurturance. *Anthrozoös*, 2, 265–273.

Melson, G. F., Kahn, P. H., Jr., Beck, A., Friedman, B., Roberts, T., Garrett, E., & Gill, B. T. (2009). Children's behavior toward and understanding of robotic and living dogs. *Journal of Applied Developmental Psychology*, 30, 92–102.

Monsen, R. (2001). Children and pets. *Journal of Pediatric Nursing*, 16, 197–198.

Newberry, M. (2017). Pets in danger: Exploring the link between domestic violence and animal abuse. *Aggression and Violent Behavior*, 34, 273–281.

Panagiotaki, G., Nobes, G., Ashraf, A., & Aubby, H. (2015). British and Pakistani children's understanding of death: Cultural and developmental influences. *British Journal of Developmental Psychology*, 33, 31–44.

Saunders, J., Parast, L, Babey, S. H., & Miles, J. V. (2017). Exploring the differences between pet and non-pet owners: Implications for human–animal interaction research and policy. *PLoS ONE*, 12, 1–15.

Serpell, J. A (2009). Having our dogs and eating them too: Why animals are a social issue. *Journal of Social Issues*, 65, 633–644.

Serpell, J. A., McCune, S., Gee, N., & Griffin, J. A. (2017). Current challenges to research on animal-assisted therapy. *Applied Developmental Science*, 21, 223–233.

Westgarth, C., Heron, J., Ness, A. R., Bundred, P., Gaskell, R. M., Coyne,K. P., German, A. J., McCune, S., & Dawson, S. (2010). Family pet ownership during childhood: Findings from a UK birth cohort and implications for public health research. *International Journal of Environmental Research and Public Health*, 7, 3704–3729.

3 Adolescence, Pet Loss, Grief, and Therapeutic Interventions

Clarissa M. Uttley

Developmentally, adolescence is the time when children are trying to find their place in the world. Although the properties of the developmental period of adolescence have changed over the course of generations, researchers have teased apart tasks, expectations, and relationships that accommodate global societal changes. The term adolescence as a social construct was first introduced by Hall (1904), and later defined by Crosnoe and Johnson (2011) as a period of human development that serves as a transition period between childhood and adulthood. Many researchers refrain from placing an age range on the term adolescent and instead focus on the developmental tasks (biological, emotional, social) of the life stage. Current developmental theorists often separate the traditional adolescence period into two distinct periods (early and later adolescence), each with specific tasks and goals (Newman & Newman, 2017). This chapter will use the terms early and later adolescence and discuss the impact of pets on children in each of these developmental periods.

As the understanding of adolescence has changed over generations, so too has the definition of pets and the importance of the relationships people have with their pets (Baker, 2015). During the highly agricultural periods of the early 1900s, pets were rarely a consideration. Most animals maintained on a property had a working purpose (cows for milk and meat; chickens for eggs; dogs and cats for protection). With the physical movement of humans from farming lands to cities, a desire to maintain connections to animals continued but the species and purpose of animals had to change (Francione, 1996). In 2018, the most popular house pets were fish, dogs, and cats. However, the types of animals considered pets encompass everything from reptiles and insectivores to livestock and exotics (American Pet Products Association, n.d.). This chapter will use a broad definition of the word "pet" to include any non-human animal that is cared for by a human. A growing awareness of how pets impact child development has resulted in millions of children living with pets and thereby dealing with challenges inherent in pet ownership (e.g., death, leaving the pet for college).

Developmental Stage of Early Adolescence

Early adolescence may be defined through several age-related factors such as cognitive, developmental, or chronological. The generally understood age range for the period of early adolescence is between 12–18 years of age (Newman & Newman, 2017). However, numerous aspects of human development influence the biological, cognitive, cultural, and societal attainment of adolescence.

Biological and physical changes begin to occur as puberty traditionally occurs during this developmental period (Erikson, 1968). Some of the physical changes include growth spurts, development of muscles and/or breasts, changes in voice, weight gain, etc. (Newman & Newman, 2017). These changes, while expected, can strain peer and familial relationships. For example, a child may appear advanced in physical maturity, yet be chronologically and cognitively at an age-appropriate developmental level. This divergence of developmental attainment across domains can pose challenges for parents, teachers, and the adolescent if his/her physical appearance provides people with unrealistic expectations of his/her abilities.

Romantic relationships, peer groups, and familial relationships change as new experiences and skills are assimilated into the adolescence life (Newman & Newman, 2017). New experiences in school and with extra-curricular activities support adolescents in the continued development of their cognitive skills. Areas such as memory and increased awareness of their actions' consequences result in changes to the adolescents' behavior. This growth may lead to an increased ability to take on more responsibilities at home or within peer relationships.

Gender issues become a focus as do peer relationships and the task of identify formation (Erikson, 1968; Newman & Newman, 2017). The social roles of male and females are influenced by many factors; however, researchers agree that traditional gender role expectations still exist and influence our relationships (Lindsey, 2011). For example, Little (2016) states that females experience greater expectations to be nurturing and to take care of others while males are more likely to be taught toughness and to be cautious with emotions.

Finally, the period of early adolescence is also a time for individuals to explore career opportunities (Newman & Newman, 2017). At this stage, adolescents begin realizing the importance of work in the lives of adults as well as the value of work to social capital, a sense of purpose and self-worth, and to society as a whole (Porfeli & Lee, 2012).

Developmental Stage of Later Adolescence

Later adolescence is often defined as occurring during the ages of 18–24 years and contains several significant milestones (Newman & Newman,

2017), including moving away from the family home. Historically, people in this age range have typically left home for the first time as they begin to become financially independent. However, there is an increasing number of later adolescents who are remaining at home for longer periods of time or returning to the family home after college due to several possible reasons including a challenging job market, increasing the cost of living expenses, or an increasing debt load (Fry, 2017).

Relationships with peers, family, and partners develop and change throughout our lives, yet the foundation of our relationship skills can be found in our early experiences. Adolescents observe the relationships of others, including their families, and take their cues from those around them. Attachment theory is a well-studied concept in human development used to better understand relationships people have with their parents, siblings, friends, and pets (Ainsworth & Bell, 1970; Bowlby, 1980; Hawkins & Williams, 2017). There are several attachment styles currently used to help understand the interpersonal relationships between adults:

Secure attachment: Securely attached people tend to have positive views of themselves and their attachments. They also tend to have positive views of their relationships.

Anxious-preoccupied attachment (Insecure): People with this style of attachment seek high levels of intimacy, approval, and responsiveness from their attachment figure. They sometimes value intimacy to such an extent that they become overly dependent on the attachment figure.

Dismissive-avoidant attachment (Insecure): People with this attachment style desire a high level of independence. The desire for independence often appears as an attempt to avoid attachment altogether.

Fearful-avoidant attachment (Insecure): People with losses or other trauma, such as sexual abuse in childhood or adolescence, may develop this type of attachment. They commonly view themselves as unworthy of responsiveness from their attachments, and they do not trust the intentions of their attachments.

Attachment issues have been linked to the quality of personal and professional relationships (Hong & Park, 2012). As adolescents are expanding their social networks and interacting with more people through school and work environments, maintaining positive relationships with others becomes increasingly more important. Knowledge of attachment styles is extremely useful when trying to understand our clients or ourselves.

Parenting styles also have a strong influence on how later adolescents develop relationships with others (Hoskins, 2014). Several parenting styles have been identified – ranging from neglectful to authoritarian (Maccoby, 1992; Darling & Steinberg, 1993; Baumrind, 1971). As adolescents expand their relationships from family unit friendships to self-selected friendships (including intimate relationships), the way they were parented holds some influence in the design of these new relationships (Lamborn, Mounts,

Steinberg, & Dornbusch, 1991). For example, some adolescents may enter a relationship with expectations of being "in-charge," deciding on aspects such as communication levels, activities, and even who the couple can be friends with (authoritarian parenting style). Other adolescents may take a more egalitarian approach to relationships and engage in conversations with their partner to come to agreements on issues of divergent views (authoritative parenting style).

As later adolescents begin to focus on exploring career opportunities and developing intimate relationships (Newman & Newman, 2017), success in these areas depend in part on their experiences earlier in life, including their experiences with their pets.

Importance of Pets in Early Adolescent Development

As children reach early adolescence (12 years of age), it is likely that they have already had experience with a pet. These experiences may come from a family pet, friends' pets, other family member's pets, or pets in their classrooms. Many couples decide to begin their families with a family pet and then expand their family with children (Reynolds, 2015). These reasons, and many more, contribute to the fact that millions of children are growing up with pet relationships central to their upbringing (Brenna, n.d.; Herzog, 2017; Stevens, 2018).

Children in the developmental stage of early adolescence deal with several emerging, evolving, and new challenges (Newman & Newman, 2017) and pets can help in navigating some of these trials. According to multiple sources, over 68% of US households indicated owning at least one pet in 2017 (APPA, n.d.). By far, freshwater fish are the most common household pet, followed by cats then dogs. Freshwater fish are also the most common pets found in classrooms (Uttley, 2013). This may be due to the ease of care and limited resources, since fish typically need less money, space, and attention than other species.

Another possible reason that fish are the most popular family pet could include the goal of increasing early adolescents' responsibilities. Early adolescents are beginning to take care of themselves through actions such as cooking, getting ready for school each morning, scheduling their extra-curricular activities, and, in general, starting to manage the majority of their life – albeit with family support. This support should ideally slowly decrease until the adolescent is ready to explore the tasks associated with later adolescence. Through the responsibility of taking care of themselves, adolescents may also feel the desire to care for others, including the family pet. A fish may provide a lower level of responsibility for the adolescent to prove to themselves and others that they can successfully care for another living being.

While fish may provide some level of exposure to responsibility and companionship for the adolescent, there is a different level of social interaction that an adolescent can have with pets such as dogs, cats, rabbits, or livestock (Hauge, Kvalem, Pedersen, & Braastad, 2013). These animals have increased mobility and, arguably, interactions with people. Memory, and other cognitive skills, are developing rapidly during the early adolescence period and having the responsibility of a pet can help to reinforce these skills (Schneider et al., 2014). Remembering to feed a pet on time and with the correct amount of food, training the pet to perform basic commands, and learning how to understand pet behavior, all support adolescent cognitive development.

Responsibilities such as walking, feeding, and grooming may also help adolescents develop self-confidence, self-worth, and self-esteem that can bridge relationships between their pet and their peers (McNicholas & Collis, 2001). These social skills can be transferred to relationships with the adolescents' peers and serve to establish and maintain relationships with people outside of the family home (Purewal et al., 2017). The ability to have positive social–emotional interactions with others is key to future developmental life stages and workplace environments. Additionally, having the capability to read and interpret the emotions of others is a life skill developed during adolescence that can be learned through inter-actions with animals (Rocha, Gaspar, & Esteves, 2016) and transferred to relationships with other humans.

Pets can also serve as a safe relationship for adolescents. Early adoles-cents are trying to find their place in their world, feeling a need to test their independence, while still being reliant on their parents. This struggle sometimes leaves the early adolescent feeling alone or having no one with whom to confide (Hall-Lande, Eisenberg, Christenson, & Neumark-Sztainer, 2007). The family pet is often considered a non-judgmental con-fidant and pillar of support for children. Pets are there to listen to the child after a great day at school or after a painful relationship dispute without providing any advice or attitude. Pets do not share secrets or hold grudges against a person's character. These important pet–child relation-ships help the early adolescent to navigate their own thoughts and make decisions about who and how to trust the people in their lives (Centers for Disease Control, 2018).

Importance of Pets in Later Adolescent Development

Adolescents, exploring their own independence, may feel a sense of loss and loneliness in their new lives. Many college students, away from home for the first time, acquire a "dorm pet" such as a fish, to help ease home-sickness and fill the void from leaving a family pet back home. Mentioned early, many couples make the conscious decision to "try their hands" at raising pets before they decide to have children. The role experimenta-tion of being a parent, albeit a "pet parent," is a vital step toward adult-hood, increased responsibility, and self-awareness.

Several important developmental milestones occur during the stage of later adolescence and serve to support positive human development. Some typical examples include moving away from the family home, attending college, establishing a profession, and beginning a family (Newman & Newman, 2017; Erikson, 1962). These activities encourage role experimentation and a growing sense of individual identity. These activities may foster a sense of capability and independence for some, but for others, can cause stress and anxiety.

Later adolescents may struggle with emotions related to leaving the family home and pet. Attachment issues from earlier developmental stages may be highlighted during this time and for some, manifest with behaviors exemplifying an avoidant attachment (Ainsworth & Bell, 1970). These can be extended to the family pet, whereby the adolescent, knowing they will be leaving, avoids the family pet. An anxious attachment style may result in different behaviors, in which the adolescent may feel unable to move away from home due to a high level of dependency on the pet. These relationship attachment styles and resultant behavior choices may carry over into romantic relationships and affect future relationships.

Parenting styles may also have a significant influence on the relationships that later adolescents have with their pets. If a child grows up in a family with unresponsive and undemanding parenting styles (Baumrind, 1971), they may treat their pets in a neglectful manner since that is what they experienced. Conversely, if an adolescent is raised in a responsive and demanding family, there is a strong likelihood that the adolescent will develop with a sense of maturity and responsibility. These experiences, too, are likely to carry over into relationships with other humans, including significant others and children.

Interactions with pets, taking responsibility for them, including them as part of the family, caring for and loving them, all have positive impacts on adolescents. They teach adolescents about relationships, aid with developmental tasks such as self-esteem, and serve as social supports. With all the positive benefits of having a relationship with a pet brings, there are also inevitably heartbreak and grief associated with the loss of a pet.

Grief/Bereavement in Early Adolescents

The average lifespan for family dogs and cats in the US is between 12–17 years. This means that numerous early adolescents face the loss of their companion, first friend, family member, and confident during a significant developmental period of life (Balk, 2009, 2011; Corr, Nabe, & Corr, 2009; Favazza & Munson, 2010). How early adolescents and their families address this loss can influence the rest of the child's life. Early adolescents may have built their identity around the pet and the responsibilities gained through their relationship with their pet. Once the pet is gone, or the adolescent has moved away from the family pet, there is a period of self-reflection and grief.

Grief can take many forms, especially during early adolescence, when children are developing more advanced cognitive and social strategies to help them understand their world (Adams, 2013; Balk, Zaengie, & Corr, 2011; Johnson, 2001; Krupnick, 1984). As developmentally expected, early adolescents observe those around them for social cues on how to deal with the loss of a pet. Some families hold pet funerals for their deceased family member and invite relatives and friends to celebrate the life of the pet. Some families try to ignore the death of the pet as much as possible, to the extent of quickly removing all components of the pets' presence in the house (beds, feeding bowls, leashes, etc.) and moving on with their daily activities. These experiences help teach the early adolescent how to cope with death and loss in the future (Servaty-Seib & Pistole, 2006).

Grief/Bereavement in Later Adolescents

In the previous developmental life stage, the grief over the loss of a pet focused on the premise that the pet dies. However, when examining grief over the loss of a pet during the life stage of later adolescence, it is important to note that this grief can come from pet death but can also include the adolescent leaving home.

Later adolescents are spreading their wings and learning to live away from the family unit and more independently (Newman & Newman, 2017). Moving away from home, either for college or independence, can be a stressful, traumatic experience for all involved. Depending on the reason and proximity of the move, later adolescents may be leaving their social network as well as their family members. Multiple changes occurring in a short amount of time can cause significant challenges to both mental and physical health. The Life Change Index Scale (Holmes & Rahe, 1967) measures the amount of change in a person's life over the period of 1 year. During later adolescence, it is likely that a person will experience several life events that cause stress. Examples of these events include marriage, pregnancy, outstanding personal achievement, change in residence, change in schools, change in social activities, and changes in sleeping or eating habits. The typical changes occurring in later adolescence can increase the likelihood of illness, according to the Life Change Index Scale.

These significant life changes may also include the loss of a pet who served as the adolescent's stress release, social support, and confident. Leaving the family home most often means leaving the family pet as well. For many adolescents, the family pet is a source of joy, entertainment, and comfort. Leaving home may mean leaving those experiences behind as well. This adds another layer of stress to an already challenging time.

In addition to physically losing the connection with the family pet, a later adolescent may also feel a psychological loss of the pet. This loss, based on the reduced access to and knowledge of the pet's well-being, can be considered an ambiguous loss (Cordaro, 2012). Ambiguous loss, or grief, occurs when the one being grieved is still alive. Moving away and leaving the family pet behind is a prime example of ambiguous loss. This type of loss also brings a sense of guilt and can cause the adolescent to question whether their move was the right thing to do or if they should have stayed at home to continue caring for their pet.

This guilt can become overwhelming and lead some adolescents into depression or anxiety, with some becoming withdrawn or developing compulsions (Cohen, Mannarino, & Deblinger, 2006; Manik, Smid, Kleber, & Boelen, 2017). Acknowledging these feelings of grief is important in helping later adolescents move forward with positive life experiences and relationships. Self-awareness, and acceptance of the impact of the grief allows the individual to seek and receive help, and learn from the experience.

If the grief is not acknowledged, the resultant stress can lead to negative behavioral, physiological, and social consequences. For example, a lack of sleep due to grief can cause irritability, leading to poor social interactions and negatively impacted relationships (Manik et al., 2017). Some defense strategies that adolescents might use to deal with the grief could push away friends, causing a greater sense of isolation and creating a negative sense of self-worth and value.

Grief and Bereavement Models

Several models of bereavement and grief can be applied to the period of adolescence. New models for coping with grief are emerging and those discussed here should be considered as a review of only a select few models.

Perhaps one of the most influential researchers in the field of grief was Kübler-Ross who, in 1969, detailed five stages of grief: denial, anger, bargaining, depression, and acceptance ("Grief, Loss, and Bereavement," 2018). Her framework of grief has been adapted to multiple situations and scenarios and serves as a guide to understanding emotions related to the loss of a loved one. When examining grief in adolescence, it may be helpful to employ these stages in an effort to increase self-awareness and develop a plan to move forward through the grief.

Denial is the first stage of grief and serves to question the importance of the relationship to the individual. Early adolescents will likely accept the loss of a pet more easily than a later adolescent or adult. This is due to the early adolescences ability to address problems (loss of a pet) with a logical, matter of fact, approach.

Anger is the second stage of the grief process and may manifest in numerous ways. As the early adolescent experiences anger over the loss of a pet, they may lash out at their parents and claim that the parent did not do enough to help save the family pet.

Bargaining is the third stage of the Kübler-Ross model of grief and involves a great deal of self-reflection. Early adolescents might review what they did wrong in their relationship with their pet. An early adolescent may also try to bargain with his or her family members to acquire another pet.

Depression is the fourth stage of grief and is considered an appropriate response to loss. The realization that the pet is not coming back and may not be replaceable physically or emotionally is difficult and may lead to a sense of melancholy and sadness.

The final stage of grief is acceptance. In this stage, the early adolescent will begin to understand that the loss of a pet is a reality and accept this as the only outcome. Accepting not only the loss of their pet but what that loss means to them as an early adolescent is important to successfully adapt to this new normal in their lives.

More recently, Worden (2008) presents a model of grief detailing Four Tasks of Mourning. In this model, there is flexibility in how individuals move through or process each task and flexibility in the order that the tasks are addressed (Perper, 2015). The four tasks include: accepting the reality of the loss, working through the pain of grief, adjusting to life without the deceased, and maintaining a connection to the deceased while moving on with life ("Grief, Loss, and Bereavement," 2018).

As adolescents are working through the grief of losing a pet, it may be easier for early adolescents to accept the reality of the loss due to their level of cognitive development. Later adolescents, who have developed a more abstract way of thinking, might experience greater degrees of difficulty in accepting the loss of a pet. Later adolescents can benefit from strategies to support their efforts in working through their grief. With advanced defense mechanisms being developed, later adolescents can put words to their emotions and share their experiences with others. The American Academy of Child and Adolescent Psychiatry (AACAP) (2016) recommends that families allow children to mourn pets in their own way and that may include drawing pictures or writing poems and stories about their pet. In addition to the actual writing or drawing, sharing the stories or drawings with friends or relatives may help the adolescent comprehend the scope of the loss of a pet.

The type and significance of the relationship between the adolescent and pet will play a critical role in how the adolescent adjusts to life without the pet. For example, an early adolescent who was responsible for the daily feeding and care of their pet may now have a large period of time available for other activities. This can be problematic if the adolescent is unable to fill the time with a positive activity.

Lastly, the ability to maintain a connection to the deceased pet could be enhanced by creating a memorial or photo album of the pet. Many early adolescents may suggest quickly replacing the pet and naming the new pet after the deceased pet. While this is developmentally appropriate, it may be difficult for others in the family to understand the rationale behind these actions. Helping the early adolescent grow during this period is important to their future development as well.

Another approach to grief can be found in the Dual Process Model (Stroebe, Schut, & Stroebe, 2005). This model encourages an understanding of both the positive and negative aspects of grief and how they both are critical in helping resolve feelings of grief. Providing adolescents with the skills and knowledge necessary to cope with and understand the feelings of grief will support them in the current period of bereavement and throughout future losses.

The Dual Process Model (Stroebe et al., 2005) proposes a loss oriented process that assists people in accepting their grief and mourning. In this process, adolescents are beginning to understand and cope with their grief. This is a critical time for the adolescent who may acknowledge the loss and begin to adapt to life without the pet or may become overwhelmed with the grief. The second process with the Dual Process Model is restoration oriented coping (Stroebe et al., 2005) and involves the adjustment to the loss. For some later adolescents, this adjustment may include finding new opportunities for friendships, activities to replace the time spent with the pet, or ways to feel that they are nurturing and caring for others.

Differences in Grief Experiences

Relationships with pets vary with each individual just as grief manifests differently in each individual. It is vitally important to understand how each individual person views the relationship and experiences the grief. Developmental life stage, gender, and culture are just some of the variables that will influence how an individual experiences their relationship with their pet and how grief is expressed upon the loss of the pet. As an example, if a child has spent most of their life as a caretaker and friend to a family pet, that relationship is likely to be very strong and the grief of losing the pet will be difficult to overcome. However, if a pet is not fully integrated as a member of the family, the emotional distance between the adolescent and the pet may cause the period of grief to be minimal.

Grief and Developmental Life Stage

Adolescents will rely on different defense strategies to mask their grief. Their strategies are most often called primitive defense mechanisms and are based on their level of emotional maturity (Newman & Newman, 2017). Two such defense mechanisms include passive-aggression and acting out. Passive-aggressive behavior is more likely seen with more mature adolescents. Examples of passive-aggressive behavior include procrastination, refusing requests to complete tasks such as homework or household chores, and ignoring people whom they associate with the grief

(Cherry, 2018). Acting out is more likely seen in early adolescents and occurs when the adolescent is unable to physically control his/her emotions and lashes out verbally or physically (Balk, 2011). This acting out could be directed toward others or directed inward. Acting out can be triggered by a variety of interactions or thoughts. For example, an adolescent may be watching television when a commercial with a pet that looks similar to their family pet is shown. This visual representation may create a level of emotion within the adolescent that he/she is unable to manage in an appropriate manner, leading to an outward expression of the emotion (acting out). How well those around the early adolescent understand, assist, and cope with these acting out behaviors can help or hinder the development of positive defense and coping mechanisms.

In later adolescence, primitive defense strategies begin to yield to more advanced defense strategies such as sharing stories and emotions, and seeking out ways to remember the subject of the grief (Balk et al., 2011). The increasing levels of cognitive development support adolescents in the verbalization of their grief and in the creation of positive coping mechanisms under periods of stress. Opportunities to share experiences with others, in a low-judgment setting, assists the later adolescent in feeling that their grief is normative and validated. In this way, family and friends can help support the adolescent's developing sense of identity and a growing understanding of their relationship needs.

Grief and Cultural Differences

Cultural influences impact our relationships with pets in a variety of ways – including how we are taught to value pets and how we should grieve the loss of a pet (Heath, Nickerson, Annandale, Kemple, & Dean, 2009). Cultural or social norms inform our actions and are constantly changing over time. In many cultures, pets are mainly considered family members and are treated as such (Kylkilahti, Syrjala, Autio, Kuismin, & Autio, 2016). Due to the close relationship people in the United States have with their pets, it is commonly understood that the loss of a pet is equally if not more devastating than the loss of a human family member (American Humane, 2016; Axelrod, 2016; Shelton, 2017). Some religions acknowledge the loss of a pet with specific rituals, prayers, and periods of mourning (Jerome, 2011). Still, some religions do not mourn death as an ending but as a beginning of a new life and formation. Understanding these differences, and being able to articulate how they are grieving, is necessary for adolescents as they work through their grief.

Grief and Gender Differences

Grief may also manifest differently across gender (Lindsey, 2011). For example, Lawrence, Jeflie, and Matthews (2006) found that while there were no differences in how college students experienced grief after the death of a parent, they were able to identify different utilization of coping strategies based on gender. Female college students, more frequently than males, reported using an avoidant coping strategy to help them deal with depression after the loss of a parent. Yet, employing this strategy isolates the individual, and reduces exposure to more healthy coping strategies such as talking with someone or spending time with friends and families.

Other researchers have presented the idea of masculine and feminine styles of grieving (Centre for Human Potential, 2018). Feminine grief may be indicated by an overwhelming desire to talk through the loss and to verbalize their feelings. Masculine grief has been explained by a need to fix the grief. When focusing on the grief surrounding the loss of a pet, the fixing may include immediately replacing the pet with another or quickly removing all signs of the pet (food bowls, leashes, bedding, etc.) in an effort to get over the grief in a rapid fashion.

Circumstances of the Pet's Loss

One of the many factors to consider when working with people who are experiencing grief over the loss of a pet is the manner in which the pet died. This may have a direct and meaningful impact on the grieving process (Dowshen, 2018). How the adolescent interprets the loss, and responsibility for the loss, will also depend on their developmental level. For example, an early adolescent may be more likely to blame the pet loss on others (parent or veterinarian) and claim that the loss is unfair. Later adolescents will typically try to rationalize and understand the specifics of the loss to learn from the experience.

When the loss occurs because of the pet's death, the finality of this loss can be difficult for an adolescent to understand (Harris, n.d.; Newman & Newman, 2017). For an early adolescent, this difficulty can be linked to their developing sense of identity and place in their social circle. It is likely that their pet served as a social mediator or a bridge for communication with peers (Axelrod, 2016). The loss of the pet may break, or challenge, the bonds between human friends. In cases when the pet served as the catalyst for friendship with others, the friendship may suffer once the pet is no longer present. The pet may have also have served as an entry point in establishing relationships with other adolescents. The entry point of being the kid with the cool pet may no longer be available, and the adolescent needs to find another interesting fact about them to use as a conversation starter. Having a pet may have provided the adolescent with the sense of being unique or having something in common with their peers, thereby increasing their confidence in establishing new friendships.

If the pet loss is due to a more unknown or ambiguous reason (i.e., pet ran away, or died when the adolescent was away from home), the grief may be more difficult to process. Adolescents, at both developmental stages, may struggle with feelings of ambiguous grief and be unsure how appropriate their reactions are to this loss (Adams, 2013; Balk, 2009). They may also experience difficulty in explaining their feelings to others. Later adolescents, especially females, may be more successful in dealing with this type of grief based on the development of their coping strategies, including talking through their grief with others (Havenwood Academy, n.d.).

Strategies to Assist Adolescents' Understand/Cope/Grow Through Their Grief

Grief is a normative experience and should be considered a typical and expected behavior (Balk, 2011). Understanding and recognizing the difference between healthy grieving processes and unhealthy grieving processes allows for timely interventions (Krupnick, 1984; Shapiro, 2008). It is common for adolescents to find comfort in a pattern, even if that pattern is unhealthy. In terms of grief, it is important to be able to identify when someone is experiencing chronic grief or when that grief is creating an inability to function.

It is critically important to understand the impact that developmental life stages have on how individuals react and cope with the loss of a pet. Taking the time to learn where your client is developmentally is necessary in order to create a plan to address their grief in a positive manner. This knowledge will help to establish a timely intervention and suggest appropriate intervention strategies (Ober, Granello, & Wheaton, 2011).

Several strategies and suggestions for helping clients work through their grief over a pet include: (modified from several sources: Grief Support Center n.d.; Hawn, 2015; Openshaw, 2011; Spuij, Dekovic, & Boelen, 2013; Vickio, 2008).

Normalize and validate the grief. Help the adolescent realize that it is normal to emotionally feel the loss of a pet. Do not diminish the emotions that the adolescent shares with you about their relationship with their pet. Use this information to help build trust with your client.

Take time to talk through the experience and emotions of losing a pet. While this might be difficult for both parties, it is likely that the adolescent has not verbalized their experience with anyone due to their inability to put words to their emotions or the lack of someone with whom to speak about this issue. Other family members may not be able to understand the differences in the developmental approach to the loss of a pet between adolescents and adults.

Be sure to know if you are the right person, at the right time, to discuss this topic with your client. It is important to understand your own emotions, how they may impact your work with a client, and when referring to another counselor will best serve the client.

Many times the adolescent needs the time to talk through the experience of losing a pet. Adolescents, especially early adolescents, are trying to negotiate their new identity without their pet as a support. This process of reorganizing a cognitive schema takes time and repetition.

Suggest, or create, peer support groups for adolescents who are experiencing grief due to the loss of a pet. In addition to being a safe place for an adolescent to share their experience, a support group environment may also serve as a way for the adolescent to rebuild their identity and help others.

Provide opportunities or suggestions for the adolescent for rechanneling their time, love, and emotions. Perhaps there is an animal shelter nearby where the early adolescent can volunteer to spend time socializing the animals available for adoption. A later adolescent may be in a position to foster an animal before deciding to permanent add a pet to their family again.

Assist the adolescent with preparing for events that may trigger emotions associated with the loss of a pet. As the anniversary of the loss approaches, help your client prepare by discussing how emotions may arise during this time. With an early adolescent, it may be a good time to create a scrapbook to remember the pet and to help develop the sense of permanence of the loss but also acknowledging the value the pet, and the relationship, had for the adolescent.

Case Scenarios

Case Scenario #1: Early Adolescence

Lucas grew up in a large family with four other siblings, some older, some younger. Being a middle child, Lucas tried to set himself apart from his other siblings but it was difficult to compete with high achieving siblings in academics and sports. He decided that he would ask his mom for a pet, someone who would be there to listen to him talk about his relationships with his siblings and peers but not provide a response. Someone who would be happy to see him when he came home from school every day. Someone he could know better than anyone else could.

His mom, after some debate, agreed that a pet might be a good option to help Lucas become more responsible and might help him come out of his shell. On his next birthday, Lucas turned 11 years old and his mom brought him to the local animal shelter to see the animals they had available. Lucas picked out a shorthaired lop-eared rabbit and spent the next nine months learning everything about this bunny he named Brady. Lucas and Brady would spend time together outside and inside the house and Brady lived in Lucas's bedroom. Lucas was responsible for cleaning and feeding Brady and he even made special treats and hideaways for Brady. Lucas would talk with his friends about Brady, had a picture of Brady taped in his school locker, and wrote class papers about his adventures with Brady.

During the summer vacation, Lucas and his family traveled away from home and left Brady in the care of a family friend. During this time, Brady suffered heat stroke and did not survive. Upon the family's return from vacation, Lucas was informed of Brady's death. Lucas emotionally withdrew from the family and began acting out at school. He started to befriend another group of friends at school, "the bad kids" and was shortly after suspended from school for the destruction of property.

Based on this suspension, Lucas was referred to the local restorative justice (RJ) program in hopes of avoiding legal and permanent ramifications. In consultation with the RJ coordinator and Lucas's parents, a plan was put in place to have Lucas work with animals as part of his RJ contract. After talking with Lucas about animals and his feelings of loss it was determined that a possible good fit would be to work with people who share their pets, and the love for their pets, with others. Lucas was connected with a pet therapy program in the area. This work included meeting people who work with animals and establishing a relationship with a dog therapy team. Together the dog therapy team and Lucas would visit nursing homes, hospitals, and schools to provide love and comfort to the residents. Working with a pet in these therapeutic settings helped Lucas to regain confidence and feel like a contributing member of his community once again.

Lucas was able to redirect his grief for the loss of Brady to his work with the pet therapy team. Through this experience, he heard other stories of grief and pet loss and realized that he was not alone with his feelings. He also witnessed positive role models, who also lost pets, but did not violently or illegal act out. This experience helped Lucas move from the primitive defense mechanism of acting out to a more mature defense mechanism such as sublimation.

Discussion Questions:

1. How might the experience of visiting the animal shelter to select the pet for Lucas influenced his development? What areas of early adolescent development may have been enhanced by that experience?
2. What types of supports or activities could have been used to support Lucas appropriately manage his emotions and reactions to the loss of Brady?
3. What would be the benefits and challenges of Lucas's family attempting to "replace" Brady, either immediately or shortly after his death?

Case Scenario #2: Later Adolescence

Catherine had just graduated from college and decided to adopt a cat to serve as a companion on this next stage of life. Pepper was a black and white shorthaired cat, approximately 6 years old, and instantly made herself at home on Catherine's lap. It was love at first sight for them both.

Over the course of a year, Catherine started a new job and moved to a new city. Pepper was very comfortable with the new home and seemed to thrive with the attention that Catherine paid to her. Pepper was allowed anywhere in the apartment and would cuddle with Catherine on the couch during binge-watching sessions or long video chats with friends and family back home. When Catherine was home, Pepper was by her side.

Catherine came home after work one day and Pepper did not meet her at the door. Instead, Pepper was curled up in her bed on the floor in the living room. Pepper was fairly unresponsive and Catherine immediately called a local veterinarian. The veterinarian visit, the following day, revealed that Pepper had diabetes and was in need of insulin injections to control her glucose levels. The veterinarian reviewed the treatment options and costs with Catherine. However, Catherine was unable to afford the financial costs to care for Pepper and made the heart retching decision to relinquish custody of Pepper to the veterinarian's office for care. One stipulation of this arrangement was that Catherine would not remain informed of Pepper's condition. Catherine believed she had no other choice and signed paperwork in the hopes of Pepper receiving life-saving treatment.

Since this experience, Catherine has been fairly standoffish in her relationships with others, avoiding video chats with friends and becoming more reclusive. Catherine moved all of Peppers toys, bedding, and photographs to one area of the living room and was not sure if she should be experiencing the levels of guilt, sadness, depression, and loss that she was feeling. Not knowing if Pepper was still alive was causing a deep sense of despair. Catherine decided to call the veterinarians office and schedule a time to talk about what had happened. While unable to confirm the outcome of Pepper, the veterinarian was able to talk Catherine through the grief process and helped her to understand that it is normal to feel this way. She also suggested that Catherine attend a pet grief support group so that Catherine did not feel alone in her feelings.

Discussion Questions:

1. In the case study above, Pepper served as a transition support for Catherine through changes in later adolescence. Discuss the other ways that Pepper helped Catherine through this developmental period.
2. How might the experience of choosing to relinquish Pepper impacted Catherine's self-esteem, self-worth, and confidence?
3. What other activities might assist Catherine is moving forward, in a healthy manner, after the loss of Pepper?

References

Adams, J. (2013). Understanding grieving teenagers. Child Bereavement UK. Retrieved July 22, 2018, from https://childbereavementuk.org/wp-content/uploads/2016/05/3.-Understanding-Grieving-Teenagers.pdf

American Academy of Child and Adolescent Psychiatry. (2016). Death of pets: Talking to children. Facts for families. Retrieved February 12, 2019, from www.aacap.org/aacap/families_and_youth/facts_for_families/fff-guide/When-A-Pet-Dies-078.aspx

American Humane. (2016). Pet loss & grief. Fact sheet. Retrieved July 20, 2018, from www.americanhumane.org/fact-sheet/pet-loss-grief/?gclid=Cj0KCQjw6MHdBRCtARIsAEigMxEhvcvtbIqSIvUcFFLRh2Bx1kHxCmARNzyZ5i5Yzez9K6N5Qn95VhgaAkqHEALw_wcB

American Pet Products Association. (n.d.). Household penetration rates for pet-ownership in the United States from 1988 to 2017/2018. Statista – The Statistics Portal. Retrieved August 13, 2018, from www.statista.com/statistics/198086/us-household-penetration-rates-for-pet-owning-since-2007/.

Ainsworth, M. D. S., & Bell, S. M. (1970). Attachment, exploration, and separation: Illustrated by the behavior of one-year-olds in a strange situation. *Child Development*, 41, 49–67.

Axelrod, J. (2016). Grieving the loss of a pet. Psych Central. Retrieved July 22, 2018, from https://psychcentral.com/lib/grieving-the-loss-of-a-pet/

Baker, L. W. (2015). *Animal Rights and Welfare: A Documentary and Reference Guide.* Santa Barbara, CA: ABC-CLIO.

Balk, D. E., Zaengie, D., & Corr, C. A. (2011). Strengthening grief support for adolescents coping with a Peer's death. *School Psychology International*, 32(2), 144–162.

Balk, D. E. (2009). Adolescent development: The backstory to adolescent encounters with death and bereavement. In D. E. Balk, & C. A. Corr (Eds.), *Adolescent encounters with death, bereavement, and coping* (pp. 3–20). New York, NY: Springer Publishing.

Balk, D. E. (2011). Adolescent development and bereavement: An introduction. *The Prevention Researcher*, 18(3), 3–9.

Baumrind, D. (1971). Current patterns of parental authority. *Developmental Psychology*, 4(1, Pt.2), 1–103.

Bowlby, J. (1980). Loss: Sadness & depression. Attachment and loss (Vol 3); (International psycho-analytical library no. 109). London: Hogarth Press.

Brenna, L. (n.d.). Children who grow up with pets make more sensitive and sympathetic adults. Retrieved November 20, 2018, from www.lifegate.com/people/lifestyle/pets-improve-child-development

Centers for Disease Control and Prevention. (2018). Young teens. Retrieved February 12, 2019, from www.cdc.gov/ncbddd/childdevelopment/positiveparenting/adolescence.html

Centre for Human Potential. (2018). How men and women grieve differently. Retrieved August 5, 2018, from www.cfhp.com.au/grieving-differences-men-women/

Cherry, K. (2018). How to understand and identify passive-aggressive behavior. Behavioral Psychology. Retrieved February 12, 2019, from www.verywellmind.com/what-is-passive-aggressive-behavior-2795481

Cohen, J. A., Mannarino, A. P., & Deblinger, E. (2006). *Treating trauma and traumatic grief in children and adolescents.* New York, NY: Guilford Press.

Cordaro, M. (2012). Pet loss and disenfranchised grief: Implications for mental health counseling practice. *Journal of Mental Health Counseling,* 34(4), 283–294.

Corr, C. A., Nabe, C. M., & Corr, D. M. (2009). *Death and dying, life and living* (6th ed.). Belmont, CA: Wadsworth.

Crosnoe, R., & Johnson, M. K. (2011). Research on adolescence in the twenty-first century. *Annual Review of Sociology,* 37, 439–460.

Darling, N., & Steinberg, L. (1993). Parenting style as context: An integrative model. *Psychological Bulletin,* 113(3), 487–496.

Dowshen, S. (2018). When a pet dies. KidsHealth. Retrieved July 30, 2018, from https://kidshealth.org/en/parents/pet-death.html

Erikson, E. H. (1968). *Identity: Youth and crisis.* New York, NY: Norton.

Favazza, P. C., & Munson, L. J. (2010). Loss and grief in young children. *Young Exceptional Children,* 13(2), 86–99.

Francione, G. L. (1996). Animals as property. Animal Legal and Historical Center. Michigan State University. Retrieved August 6, 2018, from www.animallaw.info/article/animals-property

Fry, R. (May 5, 2017). It's becoming more common for young adults to live at home – and for longer stretches. Pew Research Center. http://pewrsr.ch/2pdI0mq

Grief, Loss, and Bereavement. (2018). *GoodTherapy.* Retrieved from www.goodtherapy.org/learn-about-therapy/issues/grief

Grief Support Center. (n.d.). Helping a child cope with pet loss. Retrieved July 22, 2018, from www.rainbowsbridge.com/Grief_Support_Center/Grief_Support/Chrildren_and_petloss.htm

Hall, G. S. (1904). *Adolescence: Its psychology and its relations to physiology, anthropology, sex, crime, religion, and education.* New York, NY: Appleton.

Hall-Lande, J.A., Eisenberg, M. E., Christenson, S. L., & Neumark-Sztainer, D. (2007). Social isolation, psychological health, and protective factors in adolescence. *Adolescence,* 42, 265–286.

Harris, A. (n.d.). When a child loses a pet. Trauma and Grief Network. Retrieved July 30, 2018, from https://tgn.anu.edu.au/wp-content/uploads/2014/10/petloss.pdf

Hauge, H., Kvalem, I. L., Pedersen, I., & Braastad, B. O. (2013). Equine-assisted activities for adolescents: Ethogram-based behavioral analysis of persistence during horse-related tasks and communication patterns with the horse. *Human-Animal Interaction Bulletin,* 1(2).

Havenwood Academy (n.d.). Teen grief: Helping your daughter cope with the loss of a pet. Retrieved July 30, 2018, from www.havenwoodacademy.org/teen-grief-helping-your-daughter-cope-with-the-loss-of-a-pet/

Hawkins, R. D., & Williams, J. M. (2017). Childhood Attachment to pets: Associations between pet attachment, attitudes to animals, compassion, and human behavior. *International Journal of Environmental Research and Public Health,* 14(5), 490–505.

Hawn, R. (2015). 6 family friendly ways to help kids grieve after pet loss). Psychology Today. Retrieved July 30, 2018, from www.psychologytoday.com/us/blog/adoption-stories/201507/6-family-friendly-ways-help-kids-grieve-after-pet-loss

Heath, M. A., Nickerson, A. B., Annandale, N., Kemple, A., & Dean, B. (2009). Strengthening cultural sensitivity in children's disaster mental health services. *School Psychology International,* 30(4), 347–373.

Herzog, H. (July 12, 2017). Why kids with pets are better off. *Psychology Today.*

Holmes, T. H., & Rahe, T. H. (1967). The social readjustment rating scale. *Journal of Psychosomatic Research*, 11, 213.

Hong, Y. R., & Park, J. S. (2012). Impact of attachment, temperament, and parenting on human development. *Korean Journal of Pediatrics*, 55(12), 449–454.

Hoskins, D. H. (2014). Consequences of parenting on adolescent outcomes. *Societies*, 4, 506–531.

Jerome, A. (2011). Comforting children and families who grieve: Incorporating spiritual support. *School Psychology International*, 32(2), 194–209.

Johnson, P. (2001). Helping teens cope with grief. OptumHealth. Retrieved July 22, 2018, from http://cory.dpsk12.org/wp-content/uploads/2011/07/HelpingTeenswithGriefArticle.pdf

Krupnick, J. L. (1984). Bereavement during childhood and adolescence. In M. Osterweis, F. Solomon, & M. Green (Eds.), *Bereavement: Reactions, Consequences, and Care* (pp. 97–142). Washington, DC: Institute of Medicine (US) Committee for the Study of Health Consequences of the Stress of Bereavement.

Kylkilahti, E., Syrjala, H., Autio, J., Kuismin, A., & Autio, M. (2016). Understanding co-consumption between consumers and their pets. *International Journal of Consumer Studies*, 40, 125–131.

Lamborn, S. D., Mounts, N. S., Steinberg, L., & Dornbusch, S. M. (1991). Patterns of competence and adjustment among adolescents from authoritative, authoritarian, indulgent, and neglectful families. *Child Development*, 62(5), 1049–1065.

Lawrence, E., Jeflie, E. L., & Matthews, L. T. (2006). Gender differences in grief reactions following the death of a parent. *OMEGA – Journal of Death and Dying*, 52(4), 323–337.

Lindsey, L. L. (2011). *Gender roles: A sociological perspective* (5th ed.). Upper Saddle River, NJ: Prentice Hall.

Little, W. (2016). Introduction to sociology: 2nd Canadian edition. Retrieved from https://opentextbc.ca/introductiontosociology2ndedition

Maccoby, E. E. (1992). The role of parents in the socialization of children: An historical overview. *Developmental Psychology*, 28(6), 1006–1017.

Manik, M. J., Smid, G. E., Kleber, R. J., & Boelen, P. A. (2017). Early indicators of problematic grief trajectories following bereavement. *European Journal of Psychotraumatology*, 8(6).

McNicholas, J., & Collis, G. M. (2001). Children's representations of pets in their social networks. *Child: Care, Health, and Development*, 27(3), 279–294.

Newman, B. M., & Newman, P. R. (2017). *Development through life: A psychosocial approach.* (13th ed.). Boston, MA: Cengage Learning.

Ober, A. M., Granello, D. H., & Wheaton, J. E. (2011). Grief counseling: An investigation of counselors' training, experiences, and competencies. *Journal of Counseling & Development*, 90, 150–159.

Openshaw, L. L. (2011). School-based support groups for traumatized students. *School Psychology International*, 32(2), 163–178.

Perper, R. (2015). Worden's four tasks of grieving. Therapy Changes Blog. Retrieved November 20, 2018, from https://therapychanges.com/blog/2015/05/review-wordens-four-tasks-of-grieving/

Porfeli, E. J., & Lee, B. (2012). Career development during childhood and adolescence. *New Directions for Youth Development*, 134, 11–22.

Purewal, R., Christley, R., Kordas, K., Joinson, C., Meints, K., Gee. N., & Westgarth, C. (2017). Companion animals and child/adolescent development: A systematic review of the evidence. *International Journal of Environmental Research and Public Health*, 14(234).

Reynolds, J. (2015, March 24). Can adopting a pet help prepare you for parenthood? *Chicago Tribune*.

Rocha, S., Gaspar, A., & Esteves, F. (2016). Developing children's ability to recognize animal emotions – What does it take? A study at the zoo. *Human-Animal Interaction Bulletin*, 4(2).

Schneider, A. A., Rosenberg, J., Baker, M., Melia, N., Granger, B., & Biringen, Z. (2014). Becoming relationally effective: High-risk boys in animal-assisted therapy. *Human Animal Interaction Bulletin*, 2(1).

Servaty-Seib, H. L., & Pistole, M. C. (2006). Adolescent grief: Relationship category and emotional closeness. *OMEGA*, 52(2), 147–167.

Shapiro, E. R. (2008). Whose recovery, of what? Relationships and environments promoting grief and growth. *Death Studies*, 32, 40–58

Shelton, S. (October 2017). Understanding and coping with the loss of a pet. Retrieved July 22, 2018, from www.findapsychologist.org/understanding-and-coping-with-the-loss-of-a-pet-by-dr-sarah-shelton/?gclid=Cj0KCQjwx43ZBRCeARIsANzpzb-VKh1kQh16L9P27oDPL6k24B3DS75YKB_VwutYY6D6EeFmJBg_GDkaAtbuEALw_wcB

Spuij, M., Dekovic, M., & Boelen, P. A. (2013). An open trial of "grief-help": A Cognitive-behavioral treatment for prolonged grief in children and adolescents. *Clinical Psychology & Psychotherapy*, 22, 185–192.

Stevens, S. (April 6, 2018). Pets are good for your health, and we have the studies to prove it. *Mother Nature News*. Retrieved November 20, 2018, from www.mnn.com/family/pets/stories/11-studies-that-prove-pets-are-good-your-health

Stroebe, M., Schut, H., & Stroebe, W. (2005). Attachment in coping with bereavement: A theoretical integration. *Review of General Psychology*, 9, 48–66.

Uttley, C. M. (2013). Animal attraction: Including animals in early childhood classrooms to engage and inspire young learners. *Young Children Journal*, 68(4), 16–21.

Vickio, C. J. (2008). Designing and conducting grief workshops for college students. New directions for student services. In H. L. Servaty-Seib, & D. J. Taub (Eds.), *Assisting bereaved college students* (pp. 41–50). San Francisco, CA: Jossey-Bass.

Worden, J. W. (2008). *Grief counseling and grief therapy: A handbook for the mental health practitioner* (4th ed.). New York, NY: Springer Publishing Company.

4 Pet Parents and the Loss of Attachment

Shelly Volsche

Introduction

American pet owners spent over $69 billion on their pets in 2017 and are on track to spend an estimated $72 billion or more in 2018 ((APPA, 2018). While it is tempting to focus on the capitalism of this booming industry, it may be more valuable to consider where that money is being spent, and on whom. With over $29 billion spent on food and food treats, $17 billion on veterinary care and pet insurance, and $15 billion spent on supplies, including over the counter medicine and toys, clearly many American pet owners are increasingly invested in their pets' welfare and quality of life.

The APPA's survey and report includes all species of pet, but it is important to highlight the significant bias toward cats and dogs in these homes. More homes own dogs than any other species (60.2 million), with homes owning cats next on the list (47.1 million). Despite this, there are more total cats living in these households than dogs (94.2 and 89.7 million, respectively). This number suggests cat owners are more likely to obtain multiple pets, perhaps in the interest of providing conspecific companionship (see Tucker, 2016). In interviews, cat owners noted the reduced responsibility for direct care beyond daily necessities (feeding and grooming) as a benefit to having multiple cats. This is particularly relevant given the perception that cats are more independent. In contrast, this extended direct care is often perceived as a daily requirement for those who own dogs, provided in the form of walks, play, and training interactions (Volsche, 2018).

Using this analysis of the APPA's *National Pet Owners Survey*, and in consideration of comparative cognitive and emotional data (discussed below), one might surmise that the term "pet parents" references invested dog owners. Yet, prior research suggests that a deep, bonded attachment leading to a parent-like relationship with one's pet is not solely the domain of dog owners. For instance, Volsche (2018) spoke to one respondent who referred to herself as a "bunny mom." Likewise, individuals who live on a property with horses may also report a deep attachment to these animals.

So, while other species may certainly be "parented," this discussion will proceed under the assumption that most "pet parents" are raising dogs or cats. However, for the mental health practitioner, it is important to consider the perspective of the patient rather than the species of companion animal involved.

Regardless of the specific species, human–animal bonds can reach exceptional depths, involving emotional, financial, and temporal investments reportedly like those expressed toward human children (Volsche, 2018). These bonds result in routines that center around training classes, daycare drop-offs, veterinary visits, and pet-friendly travel. Rather than Saturdays at soccer practice or piano recitals, pet parents go to dog parks, pet festivals, and training classes. They may take long hikes or simply spend the day on the couch cuddling an aging pet. As a result, the loss of these relationships can be devastating. In addition to a loss that is often difficult to articulate within anthropocentric cultural norms, disruptions in routine, perceptions of pathology from family and friends, and the loss of a deep source of attachment make grieving a pet exceptionally difficult for many pet parents. This chapter seeks to define pet parents; understand how these individuals experience the loss of a pet; and provide guidance to the clinician with a foundation for supporting grieving pet parents in practice.

Defining Pet Parents

What makes someone a parent? Is it a biological relationship? Is it a cultural ascription? Or is it something more?

The *Merriam-Webster Dictionary* circumvents the necessity of biology by defining a parent as "a person who brings up and cares for another (*foster parent*)" (Parent, n.d.). A cursory search of the internet suggests parents are accountable for the physical, psychological, and financial support of their charges, including cognitive, emotional, and social development. For example, common themes in blogs and web magazines suggest good parents are loving and affectionate, good at communicating with their children, able to manage family stress, and respect the autonomy of their children while providing a safe environment within which to learn and grow (see Blau, 2017). Essentially, parents care for and raise the individuals for whom they are responsible while providing guidance on how to live successfully in the world around them. Within these definitions, is it possible to "parent" pets?

Far from images of trendy "pet parents" conjured by advertisements and marketing campaigns, invested pet parents are highly devoted individuals who emphasize welfare and quality of life for their pets. These individuals stay home from work or school when their pets are ill, take their pets on vacation, obtain pet insurance to assist in the expenses of veterinary care (Dmietrieva, 2014), and provide resources above and beyond basic care. In some cases, they may refuse compliance in their own medical care to instead provide more immediate necessities for their pets (Hodgson, Darling, & Kim, 2015). Ultimately, they are applying typical parenting strategies that involve deep investment, even at their own financial, physical, or emotional expense, to companion animals. This is distinct from the average pet owner and requires identifying pet parents as different than the broader scope of pet owners in general.

There are many types of associations people may have with animals. Blouin (2013) interviewed 34 dog owners, some in pairs, for a total of 28 in-depth interviews on their relationships with their own dogs and attitudes toward animals at large. Three primary owner orientations were represented in the data –dominionistic, protectionistic, and humanistic. Those who had a dominionistic orientation viewed dogs as lower species and replaceable, holding a primarily utilitarian value. Dogs were often kept outside, and problem behaviors most likely resulted in relinquishment. In a study of United Kingdom youth groups and gangs, Maher and Pierpoint (2011) found that dogs were often used as status symbols or weapons, control of whom used to display an individual's masculinity or social rank. The authors found that these dogs often suffered various forms of abuse as their owners demonstrated control of the dog, an extreme example of Blouin's dominionistic orientation.

A protectionistic orientation views dogs as equivalent or superior to humans, with the owner viewing themselves as charged with the protection of all similar animals (Blouin, 2013). These individuals regularly donate time and money to animal welfare organizations and view the relinquishment of animals as mistreatment. In the protectionistic orientation, animals are innocent, vulnerable beings whom humans are responsible for defending. Pierce (2016), in her discussion of the ethics of pet keeping, attempts to consider how an individual who keeps companion animals in the home seeks to reconcile the agency of the pet with the desire to protect and advocate.

Blouin's (2013) humanistic orientation most closely aligns with the ideology and practice of pet parenting. In this case, dogs are elevated to a status equal to humans, and often viewed as surrogate children. Whether in homes without children or as additional members of the family, these dogs sleep in their owners' bed or have a designated bed of their own somewhere within the house. They received regular, high-quality veterinary care, and owners reported they would never relinquish the dog. Though animal advocacy may be considered, these owners were most concerned with the care and quality of life of their own dog, much like parents of human children may emphasize the needs of their own children.

Veevers (1985) found that companion animals have the potential to approximate human companionship. These relationships may supplement the roles of friends, spouses, parents, and children. Likewise, individuals may gain social capital as an "animal person," symbolizing their nurturing tendencies. Veevers's (1980) earlier work noted the regularity with which pets serve as surrogate children in the homes of these voluntarily childless ("childfree") individuals. As such, persons identifying as "pet parents" are signaling to others that they perceive their relationship with their pet as existing beyond the traditional "owner/animal" context, perhaps to the extent of replacing children as an outlet for human nurturing behaviors. This phenomenon continues to be found frequently in the literature on the childfree (see Blackstone, 2014; Volsche, 2018).

By combining this research on the childfree with Blouin's humanistic orientation, a theoretical foundation for the pet parent identity emerges. These individuals value their relationships with their pets, often ascribing the status of "person" or "child," particularly to those animals in their own home. These pets receive high-quality care, sleep within the home, and often belong to persons without children. Much like the social capital gained in parenting children, pet parents embrace a means to convey something about their personality and self-image (i.e., invested pet owner, dedicated nurturer). Given the APPA pet ownership data, pet parents most likely raise dogs and cats and prioritize supporting the physical, emotional, and developmental needs of the animals in their care.

While there has been little research specifically seeking to establish the demographics of this population, both Pierce (2016) and Herzog (2010) argue that most parents choose to bring pets into the home with a utilitarian purpose. In short, many family pets play a role in helping teach children to understand the importance of care and responsibility toward others. Though it certainly occurs that pets, especially dogs, establish themselves as "one of the kids," research also suggests that this status is flexible and easily dismissed if superseded by the needs of another, human, family member (Shir-Vertesh, 2012).

To further understand the formation of a pet parenting identity, these individuals likely held close attachment bonds to pets early in life and developed a strong empathy toward animals. For example, Rothgerber and Mican (2014) found that high attachment to pets in childhood increased animal empathy in adulthood. As Veevers (1980) and Blackstone (2014) have found, most pet parents are also likely childless either by choice or circumstance. Though this suggests pets are fulfilling the role of surrogate children, this is not always the case, and rarely in a pathological way (Volsche, 2018). Rather, childfree pet parents often report understanding the pressures of society places upon parents and have chosen to nurture others in their lives, including pets. As for those who are childless by circumstance, pets provide a means to raise and nurture another when, for various reasons, having children was not a viable option.

Despite the lack of explicit research, some studies do suggest that invested pet parents are more likely not to have children. In 2016, Volsche and Gray surveyed over 650 women regarding their attachment to and training of pet dogs. Nearly 80% of the respondents reported not having children, with many specifying a lack of interest in having children in the future. Likewise, Blackstone (2014) reported that many of the childfree she had interviewed actively engaged in highly invested "parenting" of their pets. Finally, an ethnographic study of childfree pet owners found that terms such as "mom," "dad," and "the girls/boys" are frequently used to convey relationships between pets and owners in these homes (Volsche, 2018).

Understanding the Relationship

In 1984, Harris stated that "nonconventional human-animal bonds" put pet owners at risk for mental health concerns, particularly when euthanasia was imminent. Concerns regarding over-dependence upon the animal for security were common (see Keddie, 1977). Rynearson went so far as to state:

> The relationship becomes pathologic when the attachment interchange between human and pet assumes such significance for the human that it has greater priority than attachment interchange with other humans".
>
> (1984, p. 143)

This presents a conflict with Blouin's humanistic orientation and Veevers' findings that pets may supplement human relationships in positive ways. Are pet parents simply experiencing pathology?

The past few decades have seen extensive research into identity, personality, attachment, and cognitive and emotional capacities of both humans and companion animal species (see Bradshaw, 2017 for a discussion). As such, a new understanding of human–animal interactions provides insight into the pet parents' world view. While some individuals who identify as "pet parents" are post-reproductive adults whose children have left home, as previously noted, there is research to suggest that most "pet parents" are those without children either by circumstance or by choice. This abates the probability that people are neglecting children in the home in lieu of companion animals.

Given the cognitive and emotional abilities of dogs and cats, it is not a stretch to see how these animals may fill the need to nurture in homes without children. For example, research shows dogs are more likely to steal food when they are not being watched (Kaminski, Pitsch, & Tomasello, 2013), seek human assistance with unsolvable tasks (Marshall-Pescini, Rao, Virányi, & Range, 2017), copy human behaviors (Fugazza & Miklósi, 2015), and respond to human emotional and social cues (i.e., Custance & Mayer, 2012; Sanford, Burt, & Meyers-Manor, 2018). Researchers have also found that dogs are capable of deceptive-like behaviors (Heberlein, Manser, & Turner, 2017) and the ability to override their own preference to retrieve an item that appears to be preferred by their owner (Turcsán, Szánthó, Miklósi, & Kubinyi, 2015). As research into canine cognition continues, it becomes increasingly comprehensible why dogs are the most likely species to provoke a parent-like response from an owner seeking to fulfill the need to nurture.

Due to a lack of research, significantly less is known about cat cognition, emotionality, and sociality. However, in their review of feline cognition research, Shreve and Udell (2015) suggest that the emotional and cognitive capabilities of cats may be more like that of dogs than previously realized. While acknowledging that the area of study is still new, the authors suggest that what work has been completed supports the idea that cats may, in fact, be quite like dogs in their cognitive capacities and ability to bond and interact with humans. For example, human-socialized, domestic cats vocalize (meow) later into adulthood and significantly more frequently than their feral and wild counterparts (see Tucker, 2016 for further discussion).

This growing literature on the cognitive, behavioral, and emotional capacities of dogs and cats further explains the regularity with which pet owners display typical human parenting strategies toward their pets. To understand how attachment influences the use of aversion in dog training, Volsche and Gray (2016) surveyed over 650 women through online recruitment. The authors found that women who viewed themselves as their dogs' "parent" or "guardian" used training techniques that mirror middle-class, suburban mothers. Likewise, Steiner and colleagues (2013) found that when a new romantic partner joined a home with an existing pet, the level of investment in this new human–animal relationship mirrored those of step-parents taking on a partner's children.

Interestingly, the distribution of direct care and indirect care among pet parents is often different than homes with children. According to Hrdy (2009), direct care involves the feeding, grooming, and overall investment in the health and survival of the child (or pet). This may include pediatrician/veterinary visits, bathing, and providing daily security in times of stress. An extension of direct care involves social development, including play and teaching. Indirect care is the provisioning of resources, such as money for food, housing, and healthcare. In humans, direct care is often, nearly by biological imperative, the domain of the mother, given the mandates of breastfeeding and social expectations. In contrast, indirect care involves both the father and mother. However, as Blackstone (2014) found, most childfree pet parents are more egalitarian in this distribution. Since pet owners are already allomaternal (other than mother) caregivers, they have the ability to more evenly distribute the work of feeding, grooming, veterinary visits, training classes, shopping, working, etc. among adults in the home. This is much more like a two-income, middle-class family with school aged or older children than a home with an infant. Arguably, one of the draws of parenting pets over parenting children for these individuals is the flexibility of "skipping" the time-intensive care of an infant.

These similarities continue in the daily practice of pet parenting. For example, a growing number of people now report sleeping with their pets (Smith et al., 2017). Additionally, similar to parents of children, an increasing number of pet owners are conscious of the impact of their romantic relationship on their companion animals. This results in a mediating effect of pets on relationships as pet parents respond to the sensitivities of pets during disagreements (i.e., Cloutier & Peetz, 2016). Likewise, the preferences and autonomy of pets are often considered. For example, more pet parents are beginning to enjoy what Horowitz (2016) calls "smell walks" and emphasizing the walk as designated parent-pet time (Fletcher & Platt, 2016). Others purchase monthly subscriptions of toys and treats (see BarkBox® for an example) in order to share the delight of trying new things with their pets.

Anecdotes from social media participant observations with pet owners further support the child-like displays of dogs and cats in the home (Volsche, unpublished data). Conversations in social media groups with names like "Childfree Pet Parents" involve daily conversations of the jovial behavior, mischief, and empathy displayed by pets. Individuals use words that express deep attachment, and often, conversations turn to "parenting advice" and support seeking from others who can appreciate one's attachment to their pets. In this vein, a cursory scan of social media rapidly returns an outpouring of support for individuals who have lost pets. Photo and story sharing often takes place in solidarity with the grieving pet parent. Pets are such integral members of many childfree homes, that one Facebook group had to designate the 12th of each month as "pet whoring day" in order to alleviate the constant sharing of animal pictures in an otherwise "not pet-related" group (Volsche, forthcoming).

Returning then to the Rynearson's (1984) argument that human–pet bonds which supersede human–human relationships are "pathological," more recent research challenges this perception. While pathology in the human–animal bond likely exists, pet parents report knowing the difference between parenting children and parenting companion animals (Volsche, 2018). Rather, they may choose to parent pets to express a desire to nurture while being able to better balance this responsibility with other areas in their life. For example, pets may be left home alone for stretches of time unlike young children, allowing parents to work and go out without societal pressure and guilt. However, they argue, the relationship is still one of parenting, such that their pets' needs and desires are considered in perspective to the daily routine of the home. As stated by a respondent in Volsche's interview of pet parents:

I know they are dogs, not children. That is by choice. This doesn't change the fact that I will sit up with them at night if they are sick, move a meeting if they need to go to the vet, and prioritize their comfort when we travel [driving instead of flying]. If that isn't parenting, what is it?

Pet Parents and Loss

Pets exist in a liminal space – not quite human, yet no longer "just an animal" (Fletcher & Platt, 2016). This in-betweenness is accentuated for pet parents, given the exceptionally deep attachment that forms over the course of the relationship. The shared history of waking to care for sick animals during the night or experiencing the first embarrassing training class error bonds these individuals. Yet, pet parents are intimately aware of the social norms of "othering" companion animals as not human. As such, they may struggle to reconcile social expectations with the lived experience of sharing their lives with an emotive, autonomous being to whom they become deeply attached but are expected to see as replaceable.

An example of this comes from the discourse that occurs online between parents and pet parents. Blogs and media articles, written primarily by parents, dismiss raising pets as "nothing like parenting a child" (see Cross, 2011). They may diminish the attachment and subsequent grief felt as dramatic or "pretending" to understand what a parent feels. These posts express a cultural norm that may deepen the misunderstanding and lack of sympathy toward pet parents during grief. Echoing those early psychological writings (see Keddie, 1977), others in the pet parents' lives may view this grief as pathological or excessive.

These responses may come from a multitude of places. Depending upon the pet parents' social circle, they may expect conflict from employers and co-workers, family, and friends. As discussed above, most pet parents are also childfree by choice. These individuals may also be deeply invested in their extended families (as aunts and uncles) or in their communities through various outreach and caretaking careers (Volsche, forthcoming). While others may find it endearing and even ascribe social capital to pet parents while the pet is alive, expressing too much grief over the loss of this non-human "other" may cause ostracism for pet parents. In response, pet parents may hide their sense of grief or be embarrassed to admit to others the depth of the loss felt.

With deep attachment comes deep suffering at the loss of that attachment. Eckerd, Barnett, and Jett-Dias (2016) found that, whether recalling the death of a pet or person, the closeness felt by the individual surveyed was the strongest predictor of the sense of grief. It therefore stands to reason that a person who identifies as a pet parent will experience similar if not the same sense of loss as any parent grieving a human child. While the loss may be equally felt, one mitigating factor is the expressed understanding of differences in life expectancy. As Volsche (2018) found, many pet parents are aware of the species-specific differences in needs and motivations, and hence, are likely more prepared to lose their pet children within their own lifetime.

McAndrew (2017), writing in an essay for *The Conversation*, summarizes the depth of loss and conflicting obligation to social norms:

> Research has confirmed that for most people, the loss of a dog is, in almost every way, comparable to the loss of a human loved one. Unfortunately, there's little in our cultural playbook – no grief rituals, no obituary in the local paper, no religious service – to help us get through the loss of a pet, which can make us feel more than a bit embarrassed to show too much public grief over our dead dogs.
>
> (para. 4)

This sentiment can be even stronger for pet parents, whose perspective is such that they have lost more than a pet. A grieving childfree pet parent stated in an interview, "I was told that if I 'just get another dog' it would help me heal. Who says that to a grieving parent? If someone loses a child, no one says, 'If you just have another baby, you'll feel better'" (Volsche, forthcoming).

In response to the lack of norms in our "cultural playbook," pet parents often seek to mirror the same practices they observe during the loss of a close, human family member. Pet specific crematoriums now provide services for private cremation, allowing pet parents to obtain their individual pet's ashes after euthanasia. Relatedly, a growing number of pet product companies market a range of headstones, urns, and memorial art pieces with which to pay tribute to pets. Additionally, some pet parents find it helpful to create shrines or places of tribute within the home with which they can honor the life they lived with their pet (Bekoff, 2018).

These practices allow pet parents to maintain what Habarth et al. (2017) refer to as "continuing bonds." Continuing bonds are expressed in a range of ways, from sharing fond memories to holding on to possessions of the pet (i.e., collars, toys, favorite blankets). By creating a shrine or place of tribute in the home, pet parents are creating a centralized location for their continued bonds that allows them to have a focal point with which to interact with their lost pet. In many ways, this practice reflects the ritual of visiting a loved human's grave or memorial to seek connection. Habarth et al. (2017) noted the existence of social constraints on the ability to maintain continuing bonds, whether because of sensitivity to social pressures outside the home or as a result of conflict within the home, resulting in negative mental health outcomes and reduced daily functioning. Ultimately, continuing bonds help pet parents grieve and can be vital in processing and accepting the loss, providing they can find emotionally safe ways to engage these resources.

These continued bonds may also help partnered pet parents maintain their relationship. Schwab (1998) found that, despite commonly held assumptions regarding the impact of child bereavement on a marriage, there are more factors than simply the loss of the child. For example, the quality of the pair bond, cause of death, and circumstances surrounding the death all influence relationship outcomes. In many ways, the same is true for pet parents, with one additional factor – did both partners ascribe the same family role to the pet?

In many cases, the answer is yes – particularly for deeply invested pet parents who have spent years developing the attachment. Cloutier and Peetz (2016) found links between pet empathy and relationship outcomes. The more closely romantic partners align in their view of pets in the home, the more harmonious the relationship is reported to be. This appears to be the result of perceived empathy and social capital as a caring "pet person" and mutual concerns regarding the influence of conflict on the pet's behavior and mental health. Much like parents are often advised not to argue in front of children due to the potential consequences on the child's mental health and behavior (see Lee Ng, Cheung, & Yung, 2010, for a review and case study), pet parents inherently apply this same advice to their relationship when parenting pets.

The challenge, then, is to assist coupled pet parents to continue appreciating each other during the bereavement process. Much like marriages that may struggle depending upon the circumstances and cause of death of a child, so too may pet parents need guidance remaining bonded in their grief rather than seeking to blame. Whether through a shared space for grief such as a shrine or other visible focal point in the home or through efforts to remind each other of positive memories, allowing for shared continuing bonds may provide space for the pet parents to see each other as empathetic to each other's loss. Through this bond, the couple can continue practicing their agreement "not to fight in front of the pet" by supporting each other in grief instead.

The presence of pets has been found to have mitigating influences on the loss felt during the bereavement of a child in the home (Adkins & Rajecki, 1999). Likewise, Gibbons (1992) suggested the importance of a family-centered approach in assisting children through the bereavement of siblings. Given the similarities in cognition and emotional capacity of companion animals (particularly dogs and cats) to young children, it is likely her recommendations would also benefit the family who is grieving the loss of a pet "child" while needing to support other, surviving pets. These families need to be cautious not to detach from or neglect living pets. In this way, reemphasizing the needs of the remaining pet may benefit the bereaving pet parents immensely.

What about the surviving pets and their experience of loss? Sadly, little to no research has been done on the grief process of companion animals. King (2013) argues for the need to understand the intensity of emotion displayed by pets who may be grieving the loss of a conspecific friend. Sharing research and anecdotes, King attests to the deep emotion and attachment animals are capable of feeling. As such, her work suggests the need to further understand how pet parents may support the surviving "siblings" in the home.

It is well understood that non-human animals are capable of extreme cases of mental health and illness (see Braitman, 2014 for a full discussion). Anecdotes litter social media and online forums regarding displays of loss and grief from the remaining pet. This includes laying in or smelling the deceased pet's favorite bed or resting place, refusing to eat alone, and periodically searching the house for the missing family member. In some cases, signs of separation anxiety such as laying near the exit of the home or pawing at door frames can result. An online anecdote mentioned a dog who lay by the garage door of the home for nearly four days waiting to "go get Oliver."

Relatedly, many of the companion animals are from highly social species who bond deeply to conspecifics, known humans, and other deeply social species with whom they share their home (it is a myth that dogs and cats cannot get along). As such, it makes logical sense that they do in fact grieve. Depression, anxiety, and separation related stress may all be concerns for pet parents who have surviving pets for whom they continue to care. For example, Becker (2015) suggests the importance of watching for signs of depression (lack of interest in food, lethargy) in the remaining pets. Making pet parents aware of these concerns may help them focus on the needs of the remaining pets and provide a source of "normal" while working through the grieving process.

Working with veterinarians and trainers, support can be provided for pet parents based upon species characteristics. Likewise, continuing to maintain a routine that includes consistent feeding times, increased exercise, and training can benefit the surviving pets as well as the grieving pet parent. This return to the "new normal," with an increase in walking or training, can provide much-needed distractions for all while time provides space to grieve, process, and move forward. It may also be beneficial for the mental health clinician to maintain an easy to distribute reference of online and local pet loss and bereavement support groups, as well as local trainers or veterinarians who may specialize in separation anxiety, loss, and pet behavior.

Conclusion

While research supports the idea that the strength of the attachment may influence the amount of grief felt by pet owners (i.e., Field, Orsini, Gavish, & Packman, 2009), more research is needed to consider if and how the identity of pet parent interacts with the loss. For example, do self-identified pet parents grieve more deeply than traditional pet owners, establishing yet another similarity to parents of children? Or, when faced with the separation of this long-held, secure attachment, do they take a utilitarian approach and distance themselves from the animal "other," akin to Shir-Vertesh's (2012) "flexible personhood"?

Participant observations of social media groups, online essays, and interviews with pet parents suggest this loss may be more impactful for those who held their pets so close. However, to-date, most research emphasizes the practice and lived, daily experience of pet parenting (Owens & Grauerholz, 2018; Volsche, 2018). Perhaps it is because of an unspoken understanding of the depth of pain felt by these individuals' losses that research into this area has yet to occur.

Case Scenarios

Case Scenario #1:

A single, working woman in her mid-30s presents with extreme lethargy and depressed mood. At the beginning of the visit, she confesses to having lost her 12-year-old cat to cancer. She has shared her home with the cat from kittenhood, first bringing the kitten home as a college graduation present for herself. She has struggled to maintain her work and expresses a sense of "absurdity" for being so upset over a cat and worries about being a "crazy cat lady." However, after further discussion, she admits this cat was her "closest companion … almost a child."

Discussion Questions:

1. What are some ways you can begin to help this client deal with her grief?
2. What can you say to her to ease her denial of the importance of this companion animal in her life?

Case Scenario #2:

A middle-class, childless married couple in their late-20s has been seeing you for a few weeks to work through their inability to conceive. They had been making progress, accepting the biological struggle. During this visit, the wife begins to cry uncontrollably, and states that she "feels she has lost everything." Finally, the husband admits they euthanized their senior, rescue dog after a sudden, acute illness. The husband states that it is difficult to lose their pet, but he does not understand why his wife has taken this so hard. "We both loved Scout, but he was still just a dog." In contrast, the wife explains that she had begun to love Scout as the "child they would never have."

Discussion Questions:

1. How can you help these clients see each other's perspective on the loss of the dog?
2. What are local services you may be able to recommend or provide as support for the couple, who is now grieving two losses?

Case Scenario #3:

A married couple in their early-40s comes to see you for grief counseling. They both work full-time in professional careers, one in a standard office setting and one from home. The couple states that they are childfree by choice but are struggling to accept the loss of their 16-year-old dog to cancer. Since the husband works from home, he has the flexibility to deal with his grief, and has begun to ask for a puppy to "fill the silence." The wife states that she feels she has not been able to find time to let go and is not ready. They also express concern over the impact their grief is having on their surviving dog. "She is also our child, but we feel oddly disconnected. It's like we can't 'feel' her right now."

Discussion Questions:

1. How can you help the wife deal with her grief?
2. What practices or therapies can you offer to help the couple bond together through this time rather than fighting over how to deal with the loss?
3. What recommendations can you provide that may help the couple support each other and their remaining dog?

References

Adkins, S., & Rajecki, D. (1999). Pets' roles in parents' bereavement. *Anthrozoös*, 12(1), 33–42.

APPA. (2018). Pet industry market size & ownership statistics. Retrieved from www.americanpetproducts.org/press_industrytrends.asp.

Becker, K. (2015). 10 tips for helping your surviving pet deal with a loss. Healthy Pets with Dr. Karen Becker, Retrieved from https://healthypets.mercola.com/sites/healthypets/archive/2015/09/19/helping-surviving-pet-deal-with-loss.aspx

Bekoff, M. (2018). Saying goodbye to a canine friend with respect and love. PsychologyToday.com, Retrieved from www.psychologytoday.com/us/blog/animal-emotions/201810/saying-goodbye-canine-friend-respect-and-love

Blackstone, A. (2014). Doing family without having kids. *Sociology Compass*, 8, 52–62.

Blau, L. (2017). What are the essential characteristics of a good parent? Livestrong.com, Retrieved from www.livestrong.com/article/560215-what-are-the-essential-characteristics-of-a-good-parent/.

Blouin, D. (2013). Are dogs children, companions, or just animals? Understanding variations in people's orientations toward animals. *Anthrozoös*, 26, 279–294.

Bradshaw, J. (2017). *The animals among us: How pets make us human*. New York, NY: Hachette Book Group, Basic Books.

Braitman, L. (2014). *Animal madness: How anxious dogs, compulsive parrots, and elephants in recovery help us understand ourselves*. New York, NY: Simon & Schuster, Inc.

Cloutier, A., & Peetz, J. (2016). Relationships' best friend: Links between pet ownership, empathy, and romantic relationship outcomes. *Anthrozoös*, 29, 395–408.

Cross, L. (2011). Sorry, having a dog is nothing like parenting a child. Retrieved November 12, 2018, from www.mommyish.com/sorry-having-a-dog-is-nothing-like-parenting-a-child-482

Custance, D., & Mayer, J. (2012). Empathic-like responding by domestic dogs (Canis familiaris) to distress in humans: an exploratory study. *Animal Cognition*, 15(5), 851–859. doi: 10.1007/s10071-012-0510-1

Dmietrieva, K. (2014). Dogs loved like children fuel pet insurance sales. Bloomberg, November 12, 2014. Retrieved April 20, 2017, from www.bloomberg.com/news/articles/2014-11-13/dogs-loved-like-children-fuel-pet-insurance-sales

Eckerd, L., Barnett, J., & Jett-Dias, L. (2016). Grief following pet and human loss: Closeness is key. *Death Studies*, 40(5), 275–282. doi: 10.1080/07481187.2016.1139014

Field, N., Orsini, L., Gavish, R., & Packman, W. (2009). Role of attachment in response to pet loss. *Death Studies*, 33(4), 334–355. doi:10.1080/07481180802705783

Fletcher, T., & Platt, L. (2016). (Just) a walk with the dog? Animal geographies and negotiating walking spaces. *Social & Cultural Geography*, 2, 211–229.

Fugazza, C., & Miklósi, Á. (2015). Social learning in dog training: The effectiveness of the Do as I do method compared to shaping/clicker training. *Applied Animal Behaviour Science*, 171, 146–151. doi: 10.1016/l.applanim.2015.08.033

Gibbons, M. (1992). A child dies, a child survives: The impact of sibling loss. *Journal of Pediatric Health Care*, 6(2), 65–72. doi:10.1016/0891-5246(92)90123-L

Habarth, J., Bussolari, C., Gomez, R., Carmack, B., Ronen, R., Field, N., & Packman, W. (2017). Continuing bonds and psychosocial functioning in a recently bereaved pet loss sample. *Anthrozoös*, 30(4), 651–670.

Harris, J. (1984). Nonconventional human/companion animal bonds. In W. Kay, H. Nieburg, A. Kutscher, R. Grey, & C. Fudin (Eds.), *Pet loss and human bereavement* (pp. 31–36). Ames, IA: The Iowa State University Press.

Heberlein, M., Manser, M., & Turner, D. (2017). Deceptive-like behaviour in dogs (Canis familiaris). *Animal Cognition*, 20, 511–520.

Herzog, H. (2010). *Some we love, some we hate, some we eat: Why it's so hard to think straight about animals.* New York, NY: Harper Perennial.

Hodgson, K., Darling, M., & Kim, F. (2015). Pets' impact on your patients' health: Leveraging benefits and mitigating risk. *The Journal of the American Board of Family Medicine*, 28, 526–534.

Horowitz, A. (2016). *Being a dog: Following the dog into a world of smell.* New York, NY: Scribner.

Hrdy, S. (2009). *Mothers and others: The evolutionary origins of mutual understanding.* Cambridge, MA: Harvard University Press.

Kaminski, J., Pitsch, A., & Tomasello, M. (2013). Dogs steal in the dark. *Animal Cognition*, 16(3), 385–394. doi: 10.1007/s10071-012-0579-6

Keddie, K. (1977). Pathological mourning after the death of a domestic pet. *The British Journal of Psychiatry*, 131(1), 21–25.

King, B. (2013). *How animals grieve.* Chicago, IL: The University of Chicago Press.

Lee, W., Ng, M., Cheung, B., & Yung, J. (2010). Capturing children's response to parental conflict and making use of it. *Family Process*, 49(1), 43–58.

Maher, J., & Pierpoint, H. (2011). Friends, status symbols and weapons: The use of dogs by youth groups and youth gangs. *Criminal Law & Social Change*, 55, 405–420. doi: 10.1007/s10611-011-9294-5

Marshall-Pescini, S., Rao, A., Virányi, Z., & Range, F. (2017). The role of domestication and experience in "looking back" towards humans in an unsolvable task. *Scientific Reports*, 7, 46636. doi: 10.1038/srep46636

McAndrew, F. (2017). Why losing a dog can be harder than losing a relative or friend. The Conversation. Retrieved from https://theconversation.com/why-losing-a-dog-can-be-harder-than-losing-a-relative-or-friend-68207

Owens, N., & Grauerholz, L. (2018). Interspecies parenting: How pet parents construct their roles. *Humanity & Society*, 0160597617748166. doi: 10.1177/0160597617748166

Parent. (n.d.) In *Merriam-Webster Dictionary*, Retrieved from www.merriam-webster.com/dictionary/parent

Pierce, J. (2016). *Run, spot, run: The ethics of pet keeping*. Chicago, IL: The University of Chicago Press.

Rothgerber, H., & Mican, F. (2014). Childhood pet ownership, attachment to pets, and subsequent meat avoidance. The mediating role of empathy toward animals. *Appetite*, 79, 11–17. doi: 10.1016/j.appet.2014.03.032

Rynearson, E. (1984). Owner/pet pathologic attachment: The veterinarian's nightmare. In W. Kay, H. Nieburg, A. Kutscher, R. Gre, & C. Fudin, (Eds.), *Pet loss and human bereavement* (pp. 143–148). Ames, IA: The Iowa State University Press.

Sanford, E., Burt, E., & Meyers-Manor, J. (2018). Timmy's in the well: Empathy and prosocial helping in dogs. *Learning & Behavior*, 1–13. doi: 10.3758/s13420-018-0332-3

Schwab, R. (1998). A child's death and divorce: dispelling the myth. *Death Studies*, 22(5), 445–468.

Shir-Vertesh, D. (2012). "Flexible Personhood": Loving animals as family members in Israel. *American Anthropologist*, 114, 420–432.

Shreve, K., & Udell, M. (2015). What's inside your cat's head? A review of cat Felis silvestris catus cognition research past, present and future. *Animal Cognition*, 18(6), 1195–1206. doi: 10.1007/s10071-015-0897-6

Smith, B., Hazelton, P., Thompson, K., Trigg, J., Etherton, H., & Blunden, S. (2017). A multispecies approach to co-sleeping. *Human Nature*, 28(3), 255–273. doi: 10.1007/s12110-017-9290-2

Steiner, E., Silver, N., Hall, P., Downing, C., Hurton, D., & Gray, P. (2013). Raising canine: Cross-species parallels in parental investment. *Human-Animal Interactions Bulletin*, 1, 38–54.

Tucker, A. (2016). The lion in the living room: How house cats tamed us and took over the world. New York, NY: Simon & Schuster.

Turcsán, B., Szánthó, F., Miklósi, Á., & Kubinyi, E. (2015). Fetching what the owner prefers? Dogs recognize disgust and happiness in human behaviour. *Animal Cognition*, 18(1), 83–94. doi:10.1007/s10071-014-0779-3

Veevers, J. (1980). Childless by choice. Toronto: Butterworth & Co. (Canada) Ltd.

Veevers, J. (1985). The social meanings of pets: Alternative roles for companion animals. *Marriage & Family Review*, 8(3–4), 11–30.

Volsche, S. (2018). Negotiated bonds: The practice of childfree pet parenting. *Anthrozoös*, 31(3), 367–377.

Volsche, S., & Gray, P. (2016). "Dog Moms" use authoritative parenting styles. *Human-Animal Interaction Bulletin*, 4(2), 1–16.

5 Pet Loss in Older Adulthood

Jessica Bibbo

The human–animal bond is the central focus of the owner–pet relationship, regardless of a person's age or stage in life. In older adulthood, specific features of this relationship often become more salient. The companionship and emotional support from a pet can be particularly important for older adults with smaller social or support networks (Garrity, Stallones, Marx, & Johnson, 1989; Pruchno, Heid, & Wilson-Genderson, 2018), as can the opportunity to provide nurturance (i.e., the opportunity to care for someone else) (Enders-Slegers, 2000). Pets have also been found to be a motivator for older adults' commitment to health-promoting behaviors (Curl, Bibbo, & Johnson, 2017; Johansson, Ahlström, & Jönsson, 2014). These three aspects of the owner–pet relationship are likely to be particularly important when an older adult is grieving for a beloved pet. Practitioners working with older adults who are bereaving a pet should be aware of each of these relationship facets, as well as acknowledge the older adult's strengths and resources.

The Death of a Pet in Older Adulthood

The ability to employ effective emotion regulation strategies (i.e., positive reappraisal, positive refocusing, and putting situations into perspective) has been associated with experiencing less grief, anger, trauma, and guilt following the death of a pet (Green, Kangas, & Fairholm, 2018). Empirical evidence strongly suggests that older adults are better able to effectively employ coping strategies compared to people in earlier adulthood. In a study of 177 Canadian adults whose pets died within the previous two weeks, older age was associated with fewer socioemotional/physical consequences (e.g., sleeplessness, crying) and intrusive thought processes (e.g., guilt, rationalization, preoccupation with death; Adams, Bonnett, & Meek, 2000). A study of 82 Japanese adults whose pets had died within three weeks of the survey found that older age was negatively associated with somatic or social dysfunction, anxiety, insomnia, and depression (Kimura, Kawabata, & Maezawa, 2014). Findings from a sample of 409 adults in the United States whose pets had died within the past year found that being older was correlated with fewer feelings of guilt surrounding the pets' death (Barnard-Nguyen, Breit, Anderson, & Nielsen, 2016). Older adults have almost certainly experienced the deaths of human and non-human loved ones prior to the loss of this pet. These prior experiences are likely to underlie their abilities to cope effectively and to put this death into perspective.

These abilities do not invalidate or annul the grieving process. The circumstances surrounding the pet's death are likely to have more of a direct impact on the grieving process than an individual's chronological age (Barnard-Nguyen et al., 2016). The aspects of the human–animal bond, which can become more salient with age (e.g., social support, the opportunity to provide nurturance, and motivation) are likely to shape and be shaped by this process. Unfortunately, this area remains largely unexplored by research. The evidence that does exist suggests that older adults often choose not to bring a new pet into the home following a pet's death (Chur-Hansen, Winefield, & Beckwith, 2008). New pet owners anticipate that they will outlive their pet, and concerns about dying before a pet is one reason older adults choose not to take on a new animal companion.

The End of Pet Ownership

Older adults may not only be mourning the individual pet who has died, but also their identity as a pet owner. Individuals make the decision to no longer live with an animal companion for various and often multiple reasons. This decision-making process is generally based on assessing whether one has the abilities (e.g., physical and/or cognitive) and resources (e.g., financial, housing) to adequately provide for the physical health and socioemotional well-being of the future pet (Chur-Hansen et al., 2008; Wells & Rodi, 2000). Older adults appear to impartially assess their current status, while estimating changes which could occur within the next decade. Consequently, the difficult decision to no longer live with an animal companion may be made well before any functional limitation exists.

Falling due to a pet is a concern for many older adults as well as the individuals who care for and about them. Pets are statistically less of a fall risk for older adults than people of younger ages; however, older adults are more likely to experience a fracture due to the fall (Stevens & Haileyesus, 2009). The consequences of a fall can extend well beyond the acute physical injuries. For older adults, falls can result in loss of functional abilities, the loss of independence, institutionalization, and even death (Ambrose, Paul, & Hausdorff, 2013; Bergen, 2016). Experts suggest that the fall hazard presented by older adults' pet ownership be weighed against the potential psychological benefits (Stevens & Haileyesus, 2009). This may be an important issue when bereaved older adults are deciding whether to take on a new pet.

Mourning a pet may also conjure up thoughts of previous pets. Thinking about pets, one has shared one's life with is likely to evoke memories of other interpersonal relationships with family and friends, along with experiences and specific times in one's life associated with those pets. This may be particularly difficult when one is concurrently mourning a part of one's identity. Encouraging individuals to talk about and reminisce about their pets, the roles they have played, and the memories of people, places, and times that they are connected to, may help older individuals process their grief.

When the decision to no longer be a pet owner is based in any measure to being survived by the future pet, an individual is acknowledging their own inevitable death. Few making this choice may actually be in their end-of-life stage (i.e., a period in which it is known a person will die within a period of months or less, Hui et al., 2014), yet the impact of this issue can still be powerful and distressing. Acknowledging death, regardless of one's physical health is likely to be difficult, not only for the older adult but also for their family and friends (Hallberg, 2004; Missler et al., 2012).

Case Anecdote: Queen Elizabeth II and Willow

Queen Elizabeth II of the United Kingdom has lived with Corgis since 1933 when her father, King George VI, introduced Dookie to the family (Gold, 2018). She was given her own Corgi as an 18th birthday present in 1944. She has spent her life with dogs, and dogs have been entwined throughout her public and private life.

On Sunday, April 15, 2018, Queen Elizabeth made the decision to euthanize Willow. Willow was a 14 (almost 15)-year-old Pembroke Welsh Corgi. The decision was made when the dog's health had taken a very sudden change for the worse following a cancer-related diagnosis. Though the final decision to euthanize was necessarily immediate, years earlier the Queen had made the decision to not take on any more pet dogs. Queen Elizabeth understandably chose to keep her grief process private. Consequently, understanding her reasoning behind the decision to no longer take on new pets cannot be directly cited; however, her documented public life provides insights.

In 2015, the press reported that the Queen was no longer breeding Pembroke Welsh Corgis. A "senior courtier" stated the Queen was concerned that a young dog could lead to a fall and possible serious injury, which would in turn keep her from performing "… her duties for many weeks if not months, and that would upset her greatly" (Tominey, 2015). Monty Roberts, the famous "Horse Whisperer" who worked with Queen Elizabeth for decades said, "She didn't want to leave any young dog behind" (Ward, 2015). Naturally, the life of a monarch is a unique human experience, but this story raises issues which many older adults are likely to encounter.

The Queen's reported reasoning for not taking on a new dog exemplifies what is found in the scientific literature. Older adults make this decision based on issues surrounding their own well-being along with the well-being and welfare of the future animal companion. While the duties of a queen are unlike those most of us have, not being able to care for oneself and perform one's everyday tasks is a common and significant stressor. The Queen's desire to not "leave any young dog behind" is a profound example of older adults' concerns regarding being survived by a pet (Chur-Hansen et al., 2008). Queen Elizabeth's worries could not have been based on the basic needs of her dogs being met. Certainly, the dog would continue to receive the finest food, housing, and veterinary care available following the death of the monarch. However, she felt that taking on a dog who would almost surely live longer than her would not be fair to the dog nor the subsequent guardian(s). Her decision illustrates the centrality of the bond to the human–pet relationship. The individual may worry for the psychological and emotional needs of the pet and experience anticipatory guilt over not fulfilling the responsibility of caring for the pet throughout its life.

Euthanasia and Relinquishment

Issues surrounding euthanasia are discussed in more detail elsewhere in this book, and they also apply to older adults. The decision to relinquish the care of a pet to a shelter or other organization is similarly a difficult decision for the majority of pet owners (DiGiacomo, Arluke, & Patronek, 1998). Much like the decision to not take on another animal, the needs, functional abilities, quality of life, and welfare of both the animal and the individual are taken into account when encountering the matters of euthanasia and relinquishment. Issues such as complicated and anticipatory grief are likely to be exacerbated when a person is simultaneously mourning their life-long role as a pet owner. Factors which may be unique to older adults include the issues of health, housing, and human agency (older adults' health is considered in other sections of this chapter, physical functioning is discussed in more detail above, cognitive impairment and dementias are examined later in this chapter).

Housing issues are a frequently cited reason for relinquishing pets to an animal shelter (Salman et al., 1998; Shore, Petersen, & Douglas, 2003). Older adults' physical and cognitive functioning, along with their socioeconomic status, significantly impact their housing options. A lack of available pet-friendly affordable housing may further constrain older adults' options and lead to considerations of relinquishment and even euthanasia (Toohey, Hewson, Adams, & Rock, 2017; Toohey & Rock, 2019).

The transition from living in the community to a long-term care facility (e.g., assisted living, nursing home) may be another reason for facing these decisions. Pets (i.e., residents' pets, not visiting human–animal teams involved in animal-assisted interventions) have traditionally been prohibited from these facilities. Older adults living in a nursing home who had previously lived with a pet reported they would like to have a pet and it bothered them not to live with an animal companion (Banks & Banks, 2002). Evidence suggests that more facilities are allowing residents to move in with pets; however, the percentage remains low and there is great variation in policies (Stull, Hoffman, & Landers, 2018). Regardless of these changes, many older adults may still be forced to decide what to do with a pet whom they cannot take with them upon moving into a long-term care facility.

The decision-making process surrounding the transition from the community into long-term care is multifaceted and can be a source of conflict with family and caregivers (Roy, Dubé, Després, Freitas, & Légaré, 2018). People working with older adults must be aware that including the older individual in decision-making and facilitating a sense of agency, regardless of a dementia diagnosis, is imperative for the success of this transition (e.g., the older adults' acceptance of it, the ability to adjust and following the transition) (Johnson & Bibbo, 2014; Miller, Whitlatch, & Lyons, 2016; Sullivan & Williams, 2017). Involving older pet owners in pet care decisions while providing a non-judgmental environment to talk about these complex issues may not only assist owners in working through these challenges, but also promote agency.

Case Anecdote: Nora's Letter

In November of 2017, a cat named Holly was relinquished to an animal shelter in west-central Indiana. Holly's online description said her owner had been an older woman who felt she could no longer properly care for the cat. The woman had written a thank-you letter to Holly's future adopter which was attached to Holly's cage and available for the public to read.

The body of the letter was in clean, black, slanted cursive. It began, "Hi, I just want to let you know how much I appreciate you adopting Holly." The letter went on to describe that she had been a rescue cat, had lived with the author for 10 years, and provided a brief medical history. It went on to describe her good behavior ("She does not jump on countertops or furniture except for my bed.") along with her personality ("She is very shy at first."). Underneath, in larger blue handwriting was, "Thank You So Much – Nora."

Nora had likely dictated the letter; possibly indicating Nora's recognition of her reliance upon others and the limitations of their own functional abilities. The existence of the letter implies that Nora had an active role in the decision-making process regarding what would happen to her cat. Writing the letter may have provided a Nora a feeling of involvement in her cat's future, even if she could not participate in it directly. Holly was not relinquished because Nora no longer cared for her; Holly was relinquished because Nora knew she was unable to care for her.

Support Groups

Participating in a pet loss support group may be beneficial to people of any age. For older adults who have made the decision to no longer live with a pet, this may be a way to reengage in the role of a pet owner. People who are grieving a euthanized or relinquished pet may find other people who have had to make the same difficult decision. Pet loss support groups can be located through the web, a local veterinarian, or veterinary schools. Support is also available for people who cannot leave their home through online groups, chatrooms, and social media pages, as well as telephone hotlines, many of which are toll-free.

Connecting with others who are also grieving for a pet may also be beneficial for those with extensive social or support networks. Support groups are non-judgmental spaces in which to actively deal with the grieving process. They can also be an opportunity to engage and find comradery based on shared experiences and emotions.

Important Issues

Social Isolation and Loneliness

Social isolation (i.e., lacking interpersonal contact) and loneliness (i.e., the emotional state of feeling isolated) are viewed as public health concerns for the older adult population due to their associations with an increase in mortality and a decline in cognitive functioning (Holt-Lunstad, 2017; Poey, Burr, & Roberts, 2017). Socially isolated older adults report that the bond they have with their pet is central to their well-being (Garrity et al., 1989). The death of a pet may be particularly detrimental for these individuals.

People who work with older adults should assess their clients' social support network. Incorporating existing social connections into the immediate and long-term bereavement processes may provide essential emotional and instrumental support. Older people with smaller support networks may experience profound grief. Older pet owners, regardless of their degree of interpersonal social contact, may have included their pet in their support network (Miller & Lago, 1990), and thus be experiencing deep loss. Socially isolated or lonely individuals whose pet was a motivator (e.g., for daily activities, health behaviors, etc.) are likely to need particular assistance in their grief and may benefit from support groups or hotlines (discussed above).

Cognitive Impairment and Dementia

Pets continue to be an important relationship for older adults with declining cognitive functioning. Individuals with cognitive impairment or dementia consistently report that their pets provide a sense of purpose, companionship, and a way to feel connected to others (Duane, Brasher, & Koch, 2013; Phinney, Chaudhury, & O'Connor, 2007; Shell, 2015; Wiles, Wild, Kerse, & Allen, 2012).

Living with dementia can be a stressful experience (Sharp, 2017) and may intensify the grieving process. No scientific literature addressing the topic of pet bereavement for those living with cognitive impairment or dementia could be located. The existing literature does suggest that the ability to employ problem-solving coping strategies decreases as cognitive impairment increases (de Souza–Talarico, Chaves, Nitrini, & Caramelli, 2009). Regardless of the presence or level of impairment, a pet owner should always be included in the decision-making process. The family caregiver literature strongly supports the inclusion of individuals living with Alzheimer's disease and other forms of dementia in their own care planning (Miller et al., 2016). Once again, the inclusion of members of the individuals' support network, including family caregivers, may be effective in the bereavement counseling process.

Beyond Pet Ownership

Not living with a pet does not mean that an individual must cease all contact with companion animals. Community-dwelling older adults may encounter other people's pets in public or have contact with pets belonging to their neighbors, friends, or family members. People living in long-term care may have contact with visiting human–animal teams. Visitation programs have been shown to be enjoyable, engaging, and beneficial for older adults, particularly those living with dementia (Borgi, Collacchi, Giuliani, & Cirulli, 2018; Olsen, Pedersen, Bergland, Enders-Slegers, & Ihlebæk, 2016; Yakimicki, Edwards, Richards, & Beck, 2018). However, interacting with visiting teams may not promote a sense of agency or purpose. The bi-directional relationship and emotional bond that pet owners experience is not likely to be established in a single, or even multiple visits, with a visiting animal. A visit can provide companionship, but is unlikely to provide the socioemotional support or nurturance that are meaningful for older adults. Fortunately, pet ownership is not the only way to establish a bond or provide for a non-human animal.

Volunteering

Volunteering with an animal organization (e.g., a shelter or rescue group) may be an effective way to foster agency and purpose. Formal volunteering, such as for an animal organization, may improve the bereavement process, particularly for those no longer living with a pet. Formal volunteering was found to lessen the negative impact of losing a major role (e.g., spouse, employee, parent) in a group of older adults (Greenfield & Marks, 2004). Older men and women who began volunteering two or more hours a week following the death of their spouse experienced less loneliness over a 4-year period than those who did not begin volunteering (Carr, Kail, Matz-Costa, & Shavit, 2018). Formal volunteering may not only attenuate the loss of the beloved pet and role of pet owner, but can also increase older adults' social contact and improve general well-being (Morrow-Howell, Hinterlong, Rozario, & Tang, 2003).

Fostering a cat or dog from a local shelter or rescue group is an ideal way to have a pet in the home without making a long-term commitment or taking on financial responsibility. A foster parent takes on the day-to-day care of an animal. Often the animal needs a quiet place away from the shelter and time to socialize, while at other times, a shelter may not have room for the animal. Fostering programs should make sure to match the animal to the preferences and abilities of the foster volunteer. Many shelters have a "Seniors for Seniors" program in which they match an older cat or dog with an older adult. Some of these programs have been created specifically for people living in assisted living facilities.

Fostering is only appropriate for individuals who can physically care for a pet, and it may be beneficial to include individuals from an older adults' support network in this decision. Fostering is not an appropriate option when there are cognitive impairments which could negatively impact the welfare of the adult or the animal.

Robotic Pets

The use of robotic pets (i.e., interactive robots developed to mimic the behaviors of animals) has become more prevalent with older adults (e.g., in long-term care facilities and adult day programs). The most well-known of these robotic pets is PARO, a small harp seal who engages with people by reacting to voice and touch through its own movements and vocalizations. Empirical studies have found PARO and other robotic pets can have benefits for older adults living with dementia such as increased engagement, social interaction, and emotional well-being (Banks, Willoughby, & Banks, 2008; Moyle et al., 2013; Pu, Moyle, Jones, & Todorovic, 2018; Šabanović, Bennett, Chang, & Huber, 2013). Older adults who are not living with any cognitive impairment or dementia also find PARO engaging (McGlynn, Kemple, Mitzner, King, & Rogers, 2017). PARO was designed and is sold as a medical device, and therefore is not a financially feasible suggestion for most older adults or their families.

Other robotic pets are becoming more accessible. Joy for All is a line of robotic dogs and cats Hasbro developed specifically for older adults (Ageless Innovation, 2018). Like PARO, these robotic pets are designed to be engaging and respond to vocalizations and movement; but unlike PARO, they are developed to mimic familiar species. Robotic pets can be a suitable option when either physical or cognitive functioning limitations prevent someone from having a living animal in the home. This technology can allow for engaging bi-directional non-human interaction without raising potential safety or animal welfare issues.

Conclusion

Mourning the loss of a pet is difficult at any age. The fact that many older adults have developed abilities to effectively cope with this stressor does not remove the emotional consequences of the loss. Providing older adults a non-judgmental environment to discuss the loss and pet ownership decisions can help them to more successfully navigate their decisions and transitions. Though the relationship with their pet can never be replaced, incorporating existing and new support networks throughout the bereavement process can provide older adults the support and agency necessary to manage their grief.

Case Scenarios

Case Scenario #1: Dennis, Mae, and Bear

Dennis (age 75) and Mae (age 71) are married and have consistently had a pet in their home since their children (now ages 44 and 47) were little. Three weeks ago they made the decision to euthanize Bear. Bear was 11 and had been sick for about a year. Dennis is starting to think about getting a new dog, but Mae does not want to bring another dog into the house.

Their respective doctors told them they were in good physical health at their last check-ups. Dennis is a cancer survivor and Mae takes a statin for her cholesterol. They are physically active and socially engaged with friends and family. Dennis works part-time and Mae continues to work full-time.

Mae is reluctant to take on a commitment of 10 or more years. She is worried that her health status may suddenly change. Her father died of a stroke at 75 and her mother developed dementia in her early eighties. Dennis counters that a dog will encourage them to remain physically active and does not want to live without a dog or cat in the house.

Discussion Questions:

1. What pet ownership issues are most important to Dennis and which are most important to Mae?

2. How could Dennis and Mae's family or friends be productively involved in this situation?
3. What are possible solutions that would address the pet ownership issues for both spouses?

Case Scenario #2: Maria, Timothy, and Abby

Maria is 82 years old. She has lived in the same home for 58 years and she has been living alone in the house for the past nine. Six months ago, Maria lost her balance while getting dressed and broke her hip. She called her son Timothy for help and he continues to assist her throughout her rehabilitation and help her continue to live in her home.

Two months ago, Timothy began to insist that his mother relinquish her 13-year-old dachshund, Abby. He wanted to do everything he could to minimize the chances of another fall. Maria adamantly refused to do so when the topic first came up. Timothy researched breed-specific rescue groups and continued to discuss his concerns for her health and independence.

A rescue group placed Abby in a carefully screened foster home three weeks ago. Maria continues to grieve. She is lonely without Abby; she had known Abby since she was a three-month-old puppy. However, Maria is not angry with her son. She knows he wants to do the best he can for her. Timothy knows that his mother loves Abby. He wants his mom to be happy as well as healthy.

Discussion Questions:

1. How could you help Timothy better understand the emotions his mother is experiencing?
2. How could you help Maria with her grief?
3. What are possible ways for Timothy to enable Maria to have contact with a pet?
4. What individuals (e.g., family, friends, or neighbors) or institutions/ organizations could be involved in improving this situation?

References

Adams, C. L., Bonnett, B. N., & Meek, A. H. (2000). Predictors of owner response to companion animal death in 177 clients from 14 practices in Ontario. *Journal of the American Veterinary Medical Association*, 217, 1303–1309. doi: 10.2460/javma.2000.217.1303

Ageless Innovation (2018, May 15). Ageless Innovation press release: Hasbro's Joy for All Brand acquired by management-led group to focus on increasing impact in the older adult market [press release]. Retrieved from https://joyforall.zendesk.com/hc/en-us/articles/360003588153-Ageless-Innovation-Press-Release-5-15-18

Ambrose, A. F., Paul, G., & Hausdorff, J. M. (2013). Risk factors for falls among older adults: A review of the literature. *Maturitas*, 75, 51–61. doi: 0.1016/j. maturitas.2013.02.009

Banks, M. R., & Banks, W. A. (2002). The effects of animal-assisted therapy on loneliness in an elderly population in long-term care facilities. *The Journals of Gerontology: Series A*, 57, M428–M432. doi: 10.1093/gerona/57.7.M428

Banks, M. R., Willoughby, L. M., & Banks, W. A. (2008). Animal-assisted therapy and loneliness in nursing homes: Use of robotic versus living dogs. *Journal of the American Medical Directors Association*, 9, 173–177. doi: 10.1016/j.jamda.2007.11.007

Barnard-Nguyen, S., Breit, M., Anderson, K. A., & Nielsen, J. (2016). Pet loss and grief: Identifying at-risk pet owners during the euthanasia process. *Anthrozoös*, 29, 421–430. doi: 10.1080/08927936.2016.1181362

Bergen, G. (2016). Falls and fall injuries among adults aged ≥65 years – United States, 2014. *MMWR. Morbidity and Mortality Weekly Report*, 65. doi: 10.15585/mmwr.mm6537a2

Borgi, M., Collacchi, B., Giuliani, A., & Cirulli, F. (2018). Dog visiting programs for maintaining depressive symptoms in older adults: A meta-analysis. *The Gerontologist*. Advance online access. doi: 10.1093/geront/gny149

Carr, D. C., Kail, B. L., Matz-Costa, C., & Shavit, Y. Z. (2018). Does becoming a volunteer attenuate loneliness among recently widowed older adults? *The Journals of Gerontology: Series B*, 73, 501–510. doi: 10.1093/geronb/gbx092

Chur-Hansen, A., Winefield, H., & Beckwith, M. (2008). Reasons given by elderly men and women for not owning a pet, and the implications for clinical practice and research. *Journal of Health Psychology*, 13, 988–995. doi: 10.1177/1359105308097961

Curl, A. L., Bibbo, J., & Johnson, R. A. (2017). Dog walking, the human–animal bond and older adults' physical health. *The Gerontologist*, 57, 930–939. doi: 10.1093/geront/gnw051

de Souza-Talarico, J. N., Chaves, E. C., Nitrini, R., & Caramelli, P. (2009). Stress and coping in older people with Alzheimer's disease. *Journal of Clinical Nursing*, 18, 457–465. doi: 10.1111/j.1365-2702.2008.02508.x

DiGiacomo, N., Arluke, A., & Patronek, G. (1998). Surrendering pets to shelters: The relinquisher's perspective. *Anthrozoös*, 11, 41–51. doi: 10.1080/08927936.1998.11425086

Duane, F., Brasher, K., & Koch, S. (2013). Living alone with dementia. *Dementia*, 12, 123–136. doi: 10.1177/1471301211420331

Enders-Slegers, M-J. (2000). The meaning of companion animals: Qualitative analysis of the life histories of elderly cat and dog owners. In A. L. Podberscek, E. S. Paul, & J. A. Serpell (Eds.), *Companion animals & us: Exploring the relationships between people and pets* (pp. 237–256). Cambridge: Cambridge University Press.

Garrity, T. F., Stallones, L., Marx., M. B., & Johnson, T. P. (1989). Pet ownership and attachment as supportive factors in the health of the elderly. *Anthrozoös*, 3, 35–43. doi: 10.2752/089279390787057829

Gold, M. (2018, August 7). 8 decades of British royal corgis reportedly at an end. *The New York Times*. Retrieved from www.nytimes.com/2018/04/18/world/europe/corgi-dogs-queen-elizabeth.html

Green, C., Kangas, M., & Fairholm, I. (2018). Investigating the emotion regulation strategies implemented by adults grieving the death of a pet in Australia and the UK. *Journal of Loss and Trauma*. Advanced online publication. doi: 10.1080/15325024.2018.1478934

Greenfield, E. A., & Marks, N. F. (2004). Formal volunteering as a protective factor for older adults' psychological well-being. *The Journals of Gerontology: Series B*, 59, S258–S264. doi: 10.1093/geronb/59.5.S258

Hallberg, I. R. (2004). Death and dying from old people's point of view. A literature review. *Aging Clinical and Experimental Research*, 16, 87–103. doi: 10.1007/BF03324537

Holt-Lunstad, J. (2017). The potential public health relevance of social isolation and loneliness: Prevalence, epidemiology, and risk factors. *Public Policy & Aging Report*, 27, 127–130. doi: 10.1093/ppar/prx030

Hui, D., Nooruddin, Z., Didwaniya, N., Dev, R., De La Cruz, M., Kim, S. H., Hutchins, R., Liem, C., & Bruera, E. (2014). Concepts and definitions for "actively dying," "end of life," "terminally ill," "terminal care," and "transition of care": A systematic review. *Journal of Pain and Symptom Management*, 47, 77–89. doi: 10.1016/j.jpainsymman.2013.02.021

Johansson, M., Ahlström, G., & Jönsson, A.-C. (2014). Living with companion animals after stroke: Experiences of older people in community and primary care nursing. *British Journal of Community Nursing*, 19, 578–584. doi: 10.12968/bjcn.2014.19.12.578

Johnson, R. A., & Bibbo, J. (2014). Relocation decisions and constructing the meaning of home: A phenomenological study of the transition into a nursing home. *Journal of Aging Studies*, 30, 56–63. doi: 10.1016/j.jaging.2014.03.005

Kimura, Y., Kawabata, H., & Maezawa, M. (2014). Frequency of neurotic symptoms shortly after the death of a pet. *Journal of Veterinary Medicine*, 76, 499–502. doi: 10.1292/jvms.13-0231

McGlynn, S. A., Kemple, S., Mitzner, T. L., King, C.-H. A., & Rogers, W. A. (2017). Understanding the potential of PARO for healthy older adults. *International Journal of Human-Computer Studies*, 100, 33–47. doi: 10.1016/j.ijhcs.2016.12.004

Miller, L. M., Whitlatch, C. J., & Lyons, K. S. (2016). Shared decision-making in dementia: A review of patient and family carer involvement. *Dementia*, 15, 1141–1157. doi: 10.1177/1471301214555542

Miller, M., & Lago, D. (1990). The well-being of older women: The importance of pet and human relations. *Anthrozoös*, 3, 245–252. doi: 10.2752/089279390787057504

Missler, M., Stroebe, M., Geurtsen, L., Mastenbroek, M., Chmoun, S., & Van Der Houwen, K. (2012). Exploring death anxiety among elderly people: A literature review and empirical investigation. *OMEGA – Journal of Death and Dying*, 64, 357–379. doi: 10.2190/OM.64.4.e

Morrow-Howell, N., Hinterlong, J., Rozario, P. A., & Tang, F. (2003). Effects of volunteering on the well-being of older adults. *The Journals of Gerontology: Series B*, 58, S137–S145. doi: 10.1093/geronb/58.3.S137

Moyle, W., Cooke, M., Beattie, E., Jones, C., Klein, B., Cook, G., & Gray, C. (2013). Exploring the effect of companion robots on emotional expression in older adults with dementia: A pilot randomized controlled trial. *Journal of Gerontological Nursing*, 39, 46–53. doi: 10.3928/00989134-20130313-03

Olsen, C., Pedersen, I., Bergland, A., Enders-Slegers, M.-J., & Ihlebæk, C. (2016). Engagement in elderly persons with dementia attending animal-assisted group activity. *Dementia*. doi: 10.1177/1471301216667320

Phinney, A., Chaudhury, H., & O'Connor, D. L. (2007). Doing as much as I can do: The meaning of activity for people with dementia. *Aging & Mental Health*, 11, 384–393. doi: 10.1080/13607860601086470

Poey, J. L., Burr, J. A., & Roberts, J. S. (2017). Social connectedness, perceived isolation, and dementia: Does the social environment moderate the relationship between genetic risk and cognitive well-being? *The Gerontologist*, 57(6), 1031–1040. doi: 10.1093/geront/gnw154

Pruchno, R., Heid, A. R., & Wilson-Genderson, M. (2018). Successful Aging, Social Support, and Ownership of a Companion Animal. *Anthrozoös*, 31, 23–39. doi: 10.1080/08927936.2018.1406199

Pu, L., Moyle, W., Jones, C., & Todorovic, M. (2018). The effectiveness of social robots for older adults: a systematic review and meta-analysis of randomized controlled studies. *The Gerontologist*. Advanced online publication. doi: 10.1093/geront/gny046

Roy, N., Dubé, R., Després, C., Freitas, A., & Légaré, F. (2018). Choosing between staying at home or moving: A systematic review of factors influencing housing decisions among frail older adults. *PLOS ONE*, 13, e0189266. doi: 10.1371/journal.pone.0189266

Šabanović, S., Bennett, C. C., Chang, W., & Huber, L. (2013). PARO robot affects diverse interaction modalities in group sensory therapy for older adults with dementia. IEEE 13th International Conference on Rehabilitation Robotics. doi: 10.1109/ICORR.2013.6650427

Salman, M. D., John G. New, J., Scarlett, J. M., Kass, P. H., Ruch-Gallie, R., & Hetts, S. (1998). Human and animal factors related to relinquishment of dogs and cats in 12 selected animal shelters in the United States. *Journal of Applied Animal Welfare Science*, 1, 207–226. doi: 10.1207/s15327604jaws0103_2

Sharp, B. K. (2017). Stress as experienced by people with dementia: An interpretative phenomenological analysis. Dementia. Advanced online publication. doi: 10.1177/1471301217713877

Shell, L. (2015). The picture of happiness in Alzheimer's disease: Living a life congruent with personal values. *Geriatric Nursing*, 36, S26–S32. doi: 10.1016/j.gerinurse.2015.02.021

Shore, E. R., Petersen, C. L., & Douglas, D. K. (2003). Moving as a reason for pet relinquishment: A closer look. *Journal of Applied Animal Welfare Science*, 6, 39–52. doi: 10.1207/S15327604JAWS0601_04

Stevens, J. A., & Haileyesus, T. (2009). Nonfatal fall-related injuries associated with dogs and cats – United States, 2001–2006. *MMWR: Morbidity and Mortality Weekly Report*, 58, 277–281. Retrieved from www.cdc.gov/mmwr/preview/mmwrhtml/mm5811a1.htm

Stull, J. W., Hoffman, C. C., & Landers, T. (2018). Health benefits and risks of pets in nursing homes: A survey of facilities in Ohio. *Journal of Gerontological Nursing*, 44, 39–45. doi: 10.3928/00989134-20180322-02

Sullivan, G. J., & Williams, C. (2017). Older adult transitions into long-term care: A meta-synthesis. *Journal of Gerontological Nursing*, 43, 41–49. doi: 10.3928/00989134-20161109-07

Tominey, C. (2015, February 1). The end of the line draws near for The Queen's corgis. Retrieved from www.express.co.uk/news/royal/555464/The-end-of-the-line-draws-near-for-the-Queen-s-corgis

Toohey, A. M., Hewson, J. A., Adams, C. L., & Rock, M. J. (2017). When places include pets: Broadening the scope of relational approaches to promoting aging-in-place. *Journal of Sociology & Social Welfare*, 44, 119–146.

Toohey, A. M., & Rock, M. J. (2019). Disruptive solidarity or solidarity disrupted? A dialogical narrative analysis of economically vulnerable older adults' efforts to age in place with pets. *Public Health Ethics*, 12, 15–29. doi: 10.1093/phe/phy009

Ward, V. (2015, July 14). Queen stops breeding corgis as "she doesn't want to leave any behind." Retrieved from www.telegraph.co.uk/news/uknews/theroyalfamily/11738382/Queen-stops-breeding-corgis-as-she-doesnt-want-to-leave-any-behind.html

Wells, Y., & Rodi, H. (2000). Effects of pet ownership on the health and well-being of older people. *Australasian Journal on Ageing*, 19, 143–148. doi: 10.1111/j.1741-6612.2000.tb00167.x

Wiles, J. L., Wild, K., Kerse, N., & Allen, R. E. S. (2012). Resilience from the point of view of older people: "There's still life beyond a funny knee." *Social Science & Medicine*, 74, 416–424. doi: 10.1016/j.socscimed.2011.11.005

Yakimicki, M. L., Edwards, N. E., Richards, E., & Beck, A. M. (2018). Animal-assisted intervention and dementia: A systematic review. *Clinical Nursing Research*. 28, 9–29. doi: 10.1177/1054773818756987

Part III
Special Populations

6 Helping Veterinary Professionals with Grief and Loss

Maria Gore, Erin Allen, and Gail Bishop

Many children dream of one day of working professionally with animals. The path into the veterinary medical profession, as a doctor, technician, or assistant, is paved with hard work and dedication, and seeded in a deep love for animals. In addition, veterinary professionals face a multitude of stressful and emotionally challenging situations, including often having to bear the weight of protecting the human–animal bond. Empathic caregivers are found at every career level in the veterinary field, whether it be a front desk receptionist, veterinary technician, or the doctor. They are the ones taking care of animal patients or talking with crying pet owners on the phone. These caregivers spend their working hours taking care of others and often, when they are faced with the loss of their own pets, the accumulative risk factors and demands of the veterinary profession can prompt them to seek support from mental health professionals. Empirical evidence shows that these individuals are at a higher risk than other professions for work-related stress, compassion fatigue, burnout, mental health issues, and suicide (Allison et al., 2016). A recent study cited that suicide deaths are higher among veterinary professionals than that of the general US population (Tomasi et al., 2019). Mental health professionals can benefit from understanding pet loss from the perspective of people who work in the veterinary field to better support these clients.

Grief and Pet Loss for the Veterinary Professional

Grief is an individual journey, unique to a person's life experiences, personal coping skills, as well as situational to a specific loss. There are many manifestations of grief that can impact an individual emotionally, physically, and spiritually. Pet loss for the veterinary professional can be even more significant as these individuals are surrounded at work by pets on an almost daily basis. They may find themselves being continually triggered by situations at work that can magnify their existing grief. Although grief is a natural, unavoidable reaction to loss that requires acknowledgment and expression, sometimes veterinary professionals have to suppress those emotions in order to perform the work they do with pets and pet owners.

Supporting a veterinary professional through the natural process of grieving can present extra challenges. Having a general understanding of the common mental health risk factors faced by those working in the veterinary field can enable the mental health professional to tailor treatment and therapeutic approaches to be more effective.

Risk Factors for Veterinary Professionals' Mental Health

One of the most frequently discussed risk factors in the research on the mental health of veterinary professionals is compassion fatigue, described by Figley (1995) as a secondary traumatic stress reaction resulting from helping or desiring to help a person suffering from traumatic events. Its symptomology is nearly identical to that of post-traumatic stress disorder (PTSD), except compassion fatigue applies to caregivers who were affected by the trauma of others. Caregivers experiencing compassion fatigue may develop signs of persistent arousal and anxiety as a result of this secondary trauma. This arousal state can include difficulties sleeping, irritability, anger, or exaggerated startle responses. Most importantly, these caregivers ultimately experience a reduced capacity for, or interest in being empathic toward the suffering of others (Boyle, 2011). It develops over time, building slowly, resulting in an accumulation that goes beyond normal fatigue. Compassion fatigue affects a person's physical body as well as their emotional well-being, therefore influencing a person's ability to handle their own traumas and/or losses. Though there is currently a lack of research in the specific area of a veterinarian's own grief, it could be assumed that the emotional toll of an individual's personal loss could potentially make him/her more susceptible to compassion fatigue. A veterinary professional who loses their beloved personal pet and returns to a job where there is a high need to be mentally present to serve both patient and client could potentially begin comparing their losses to those of their clients. This could place them at a higher risk of experiencing a loss of empathy for other's suffering or increase the impact of secondary trauma if events trigger something about their own loss. The reality of the veterinary profession is that most individuals in this field will be continually reminded of the powerful human–animal bond and can find themselves in the midst of an end-of-life conversation with a pet owner when they themselves have just recently faced their own similar decision. Unlike other professionals that experience pet loss, these individuals will face continual reminders of the trauma, illness, and the life and death of pets that are loved just as much as they loved their own pets. This unique aspect of the profession can make the grief related to a pet a very long and complicated experience.

Whereas compassion fatigue can develop from witnessing another's events, burnout evolves from dissatisfaction with working conditions. Scholars assert that, in general, compassion fatigue has a more sudden and acute onset than burnout, which gradually wears down caregivers who are overwhelmed and unable to effect positive change within the system which they work (Boyle, 2011). Burnout is defined as being driven by issues within the workplace organization, such as policies and procedures that inhibit feelings of job satisfaction (Crump & Thamm, 2011). It can be associated with the "hassles and stress" involved in one's profession. It has been noted burnout cumulates over time and is predictable in helping professions where work environments are demanding and staff maintain perceptions of feeling underappreciated (Lachman, 2016). Burnout can result in individuals feeling inadequate, contributing to lower self-esteem and lower job satisfaction. It can result in poor job performance and have negative consequences on a person's physical and emotional well-being.

When compassion fatigue, burnout, or a combination of the two occur, an individual's emotional and physical resilience dissipates. For someone experiencing grief, adding compassion fatigue or burnout can create a complicated grief process. For example, if an individual is already

Table 6.1 Manifestations of Compassion Fatigue

Emotional	Intellectual	Physical
Anger	Boredom	Increased somatic
Apathy	Concentration	complaints
Breakdown	impairment	Lack of energy
Cynicism	Disorderliness	Loss of endurance
Desensitization	Weakened attention to	Loss of strength
Discouragement	detail	Proneness to accidents
Dreams/flashbacks		Weariness, sense of fatigue,
Feelings of being		exhaustion
overwhelmed		
Attitude of hopelessness		
Irritability		
Lessened enthusiasm		
sarcasm		

Social	Spiritual	Work
Callousness	Decrease in discernment	Absenteeism
Feelings of alienation,	Disinterest in	Avoidance of intense
estrangement, isolation	introspection	patient situations
Inability to share in or	Lack of spiritual	Desire to quit
alleviate suffering	awareness	Diminished performance
Indifference	Poor judgment regarding	ability (i.e. medical
Loss of interest in	existential issues	errors, decreased
activities once enjoyed		documentation accuracy,
Unresponsiveness		record keeping)
Withdrawal from family		Stereotypical/impersonal
or friends		communications
		Tardiness

Source: Boyle, 2011.

Table 6.2 Characteristics differentiating Burnout from Compassion Fatigue

Variable	Burnout	Compassion Fatigue
Etiology	Reactional: response to work or environmental stressors	Relational: consequences of caring for those who are suffering
Chronology	Gradual. Over time	Sudden, acute onset
Outcomes	Decreased empathic responses, withdrawal, may leave position or transfer	Continued endurance or 'giving' results in an imbalance of empathy and objectivity; may ultimately leave position

Source: Boyle, 2011.

experiencing feelings of isolation, being overwhelmed, and a loss of interest in normal activities, these factors can have a negative impact on their capacity to handle grief. It is in this period that veterinary professionals may find themselves in crisis and seek mental health support. As a mental health professional working with this population, being able to identify compassion fatigue and burnout compounded with the manifestations of grief can be of huge importance in the success of any therapeutic intervention as each factor will need to be addressed.

Suicide Risk

A recent study that surveyed over 10,000 practicing veterinarians found that one in ten have experienced serious psychological distress and one in six reported having considered suicide (Larkin, 2015). The rate of suicide within the veterinary profession has been identified as more than twice that of the medical profession (Halliwell & Hoskin, 2005) and four times the rate of the general population (Bartram & Baldwin, 2010; Tomasi et al., 2019). Given the risk factors that veterinary professionals encounter, appropriate mental health interventions are critical.

Exposure to Euthanasia

Veterinary professionals are regularly involved in the ending of an animal's life. It is estimated that veterinarians and their staff experience death approximately five times as frequently as their counterparts in human medicine (Mitchener & Ogilvie, 2002). Although humane euthanasia reflects the value of ending suffering, the repeated exposure to death and loss can take its toll. Given that the veterinary profession is filled with individuals who have a deep affinity with animals, it is easy to acknowledge that there can be risks of caring too much. Veterinary professionals are faced with attending to their clients' emotions related to the loss of a pet in addition to handling their own emotions over the loss (White, 2018). This demand for high levels of compassion and empathy contributes to both compassion fatigue and burnout.

Active participation in the ending of animal life, often referred to as "good death," may alter personal perspectives on death and the sanctity of human life, and in the face of life's challenges, enable self-justification and reduce inhibitions towards suicide, making suicide seem a rational solution (Stoewen, 2015). One study (Witte, Correia, & Angarano, 2013) found that veterinary students' habitual exposure to euthanasia is associated with a fearlessness about death. Additionally, veterinary professionals have knowledge of and often access to prescription medications, including drugs for anesthesia and euthanasia. Accessibility increases the potential for these drugs being used as (maladaptive) means of coping and potentially as a means to suicide, theoretically being a key factor in the high rate of suicide in the profession (Hawton, 2007) A mental health professional supporting any client through a loss will continually assess for suicidal ideation. Understanding the unique perception many veterinary professionals have on what it means to have a good death and the potential accessibility to euthanasia drugs should prompt an open discussion on a client's thoughts on suicide. This kind of open discussion will create a safe space for a client to disclose any suicidal ideations.

Individual Risk Factors

The personality of an individual in the veterinary profession tends to be a combination of perfectionist or high-achiever, with those of caregiver and doer – resulting in a driven person with high self-expectations, whose self-perception is enmeshed within their work. Often, they place high standards for themselves within their medical role; increasing their vulnerability to distress if those standards are not met. A link between the high academic requirements for acceptance into veterinary school and perfectionistic, highly achieving veterinary students suggests those individuals may be at higher risk for mental health concerns and suicide. It has been suggested that the demanding curriculum may impede the development of emotional intelligence and social skills, limiting the development of coping skills and resilience (Stoewen, 2015). Understanding this potential deficiency should prompt a mental health professional to inquire and evaluate a client's past coping skills (both negative and positive) in order to aid the client in their grief process.

Perfectionism is the tendency to employ overly critical self-evaluation and high standards (Frost, Marten, Lahart, & Rosenblate, 1990). While some manifestations of perfectionism can be adaptive and beneficial, the majority of effects of perfectionism are maladaptive and create challenges for the individual. Perfectionism has been associated with mental health issues including depression, obsessive-compulsive disorders, eating disorders, social phobia, and suicidal thoughts (Allister, 2014; O'Connor,

2007). People who are perfectionistic are at increased risk of depression (Hewitt & Flett, 1991), and tend to judge their work critically and experience negative affects before, during and after evaluative tasks (Frost et al., 1990). Failure may be a very difficult experience for someone with a high level of perfectionism (Hamilton & Schweitzer, 2000). Within veterinary medicine, failure is an inevitable part of clinical work and those with perfectionistic traits may have difficulty adapting in a clinical environment.

These personality traits, prevalent among veterinary professionals, can predispose some individuals to be less resilient to workplace stressors (Bartram & Baldwin, 2010). This vulnerability can be linked to increased risk for suicide hence the importance of early intervention by mental health providers.

High standards and a propensity for critical self-evaluation can play a major part in an individual's grief related to the loss of their own pet. Mental health professionals working with veterinarians may often hear expressions of guilt with statements such as "I am a doctor and I couldn't save him" or "I help people make these kind of end-of-life decisions every day and I could not make one myself." Working with a client, a veterinarian is allowed a level of compassionate detachment and professional separation from their client's emotional process. However, when making medical decisions for their own beloved pet, it can be challenging to filter facts and science through their emotional bond to that animal. As a mental health professional, it may be important to remind clients that when it comes to their own pets, being a veterinary professional does not negate the intense emotions experienced when making decisions for their pets; they are pet owners first and foremost.

Professional Challenges

Professional challenges faced by those in the veterinary field add additional risk factors and place them at an increased risk for mental health issues. These challenges include long hours, high student loan debt, difficult client interactions, academic pressure, and perceived competition, and medical mistakes. One may question what impact student loan debt could have on veterinarians' grief process. For Doctor of Veterinary Medicine, the average student loan debt is staggering. A 2018 report indicates that 44% of veterinary graduates have borrowed $100,000 or more (Larkin, 2018). As pet owners, even veterinarians must consider finances in their pet care decision-making process. When a veterinary professional has the knowledge of potential treatments but cannot afford it for their own pet, thus influencing an end-of-life decision, feelings of guilt can accompany their grief of the pet.

Another challenge is the demanding work schedule of a veterinary professional that often includes long workdays, late nights, and/or overnight shifts. This can make it difficult to maintain a work–life balance, negatively impacting one's social support network. Social support is reported to be a protective factor for mental health as it relates to workplace stressors (Larkin, 2015). Decreasing one's social activities or time spent with family and significant others in response to long work hours can burden personal relationships and exacerbate existing family issues. If these issues are present at the time of a significant loss, it can have negative consequences on an individual's resilience and ability to cope with the loss. Mental health professionals can aid their clients by inquiring about their social support, how their job impacts their relationships and help clients develop effective strategies for achieving a work-life balance that will allow time for the self-care needed during grief.

Professionals in the veterinary field, often perfectionistic in nature, may self-judge their work harshly after evaluative tasks in the clinical environment (Allister, 2014). Additionally, veterinary students report an extremely competitive environment in veterinary school (Stoewen, 2015). Even after graduating and moving into private practice, veterinarians report feelings of elevated competition among peers and with competing for private practices (Allister, 2014). This competitive mind frame may negatively influence the perspective of appropriate self-care practice. An individual may perceive self-care efforts, such as taking time off after the loss of a pet, expressing emotions, or asking for a lighter caseload at their job, as a sign of weakness. This might make them reluctant to implement these types of supportive measures. Mental health professionals can help normalize grief and encourage clients to ask for what they need.

Work-Related Risk Factors

The veterinary work environment creates its own demands that can have a negative impact on an individual's mental health. When one dreams of working with animals in the veterinarian profession, the vision of helping animals often excludes the human counterparts accompanying the animals. Veterinarian professionals are faced with highly charged emotional situations on a daily basis. The human connections sometimes cause the most stress within these situations. Seeking to find a balance between ensuring the welfare of a patient while accommodating a client's expectations or demands, often with financial limitations, presents many ethical dilemmas that test the resilience of the veterinary professional (Rollin, 2006). Having to serve both patient and client interests within the boundaries the client presents can cause great moral conflict within the veterinary professional and their team (de Graff, 2005; Tannenbaum, 1993) Veterinary professionals may find themselves facing ethical dilemmas as often as three to five times per week (Kahler, 2015; Larkin, 2015). This can include veterinarians performing a euthanasia they would rather refuse to do, nurses treating animals that they perceive to have a poor quality of life, and professionals feeling conflicted at owner decisions related to their pet's treatment versus their own personal values. The stress from these dilemmas is not easily eliminated by typical interventions of stress management. Research in moral stress management among human nurses suggest there may be some positive benefits for empowering nurses to be active in ethics training, serving on hospital ethical committees and having a safe place to debrief ethical dilemmas among peers (Boyle, 2011). The emotional weight of these ethical dilemmas can be taxing even without a recent personal loss. However, the loss and grief experience can sometimes alter one's perception of a situation and make it difficult to clearly explain information to a client without filtering it through one's own experience. For instance, if a veterinarian feels guilty about a decision they made for their own pet, it may prove difficult for them to not allow that personal experience to influence how they assist their client's decision-making process. Validation of these tough situations will be helpful in therapy. This process starts by identifying and acknowledging the situation (e.g., a technician who gets triggered by working with a dog that has the same disease that their dog battled) and take appropriate actions to address it – the technician can request to be assigned to a different case. Additionally, as the study of human nurses suggests, there can be positive benefits in creating safe spaces where staff can debrief these situations. As a mental health professional, this safe space can be created during a session or in resources such as peer support groups for the client.

High expectations from clients, client complaints, online reviews, and the potential for litigation can all induce anxiety and thereby contribute to compassion fatigue and burnout (Stoewen, 2015). One study reported that veterinarians deem professional mistakes as one of their top three work-related stressors (Nett et al., 2015). Medical mistakes significantly impact a person's overall resiliency to combat the more common stressors of this profession. There is an indication that the traumatizing event of a medical mistake with negative outcomes for the patient can lead to a mental health crisis and potentially to suicidal thoughts (Stoewen, 2015; White, 2018). For some individuals, the long-term effects of clinical failures or mistakes can lead to difficulty in continuing to work in the profession and some individuals report moving on to other areas of the profession that do not involve direct patient care (Kogan, Hellyer, Rishniw, Schoenfeld-Tacher, 2018; Scott et al., 2009). In the human medical care profession, the term "second victim" is utilized when describing care providers involved in an adverse event (Seys et al., 2012). Studies report that these victims suffer emotional and physical distress that can lead to feelings of self-doubt, inadequacy, guilt, and symptoms of depression (White, 2018). Many veterinary professionals do not have the luxury of taking time off work following the loss of a pet, so they may find themselves struggling with grief at work, leaving them emotionally and physically depleted. Lack of sleep, inability to focus, and a decreased attention to detail can be manifestations of grief that put an individual at high risk for making a medical mistake. Gentle reminders of this potential situation from a mental health professional may aid the client in recognizing the importance of self-care during a time of loss and grief.

Supporting Veterinary Professionals

Pet loss, in addition to all of the other inherent risk factors within veterinary medicine, both individual and work-related, combined with compassion fatigue and burn out, paint a distressing picture for veterinary professionals. Given the high rate of reported contemplated suicide, early and effective intervention at the time of loss is important and just like many mental health issues, there are things that can help.

With the weight of caring compassionately, meeting the needs of clients and patients, and balancing professional obligations with personal desires on a veterinary professional's shoulders, how is one to have the time and energy needed for healthy grieving? First, it is important to acknowledge that the very nature of the profession itself puts people "at risk." There are many strategies that will help veterinary professionals manage the "cost of caring" within the profession. Taking a pre-emptive approach in recognizing the risk factors each individual faces and the signs of fatigue is important. Acknowledging personal losses and grief can help separate personal emotions from professional expectations.

Though not specific to veterinary professionals, the following widely utilized instruments are beneficial in assessing an individual's level of compassion fatigue:

- The Compassion Fatigue Scale (Adams et al., 2006)
- The Professional Quality of Life Scale (Stamm, 2009)

Veterinarians and veterinary professionals can learn from positive coping strategies developed for individuals working in a generalized healthcare setting as well as those specifically designed for workers in animal care fields. Grief support for the veterinary professional may often include a plan to achieve a balance between personal and professional life by establishing and maintaining appropriate boundaries. Boundaries may include not going to the office on "off" days, not sharing personal contact information with clients, and not allowing family/personal time to be interrupted by work. Work–life balance allows for the individual to create opportunities to nurture themselves as they prepare to nurture their clients and patients. These boundaries will aid in dealing with future losses and the grief that accompanies those losses. This requires ongoing introspection and action to achieve a satisfying professional longevity through experiences of personal pet loss. Mental health professionals that make an effort to understand the unique nature of working in the veterinary field, the reported risk factors and the effects these can have on their client will be in a better position to fully support their clients.

Case Scenarios

Case Scenario #1:

Tim has been a veterinarian technician for 15 years in a busy small animal clinic and has typically loved his work. Recently he had to euthanize his 7-year-old female Labrador retriever named "Joy." This was an unexpected loss as "Joy" was hit by a car. He brought "Joy" into the clinic he works for but they couldn't save her and he had to have her euthanized. "Joy" was his best friend and he thought he would have her for many more years.

At the animal clinic, Tim is often the team member helping veterinarians who are euthanizing client's pets, and it just feels too raw and overwhelming for him. This too is unexpected, and he is surprised by how deeply he feels conflicted when working these types of cases. He has come to you because he is questioning how to cope at work; he needs his job, and loves it normally, but with the loss of "Joy" and needing to be a viable team member, he is suppressing his feelings of loss. He states that work has always been his "go to" when life gets tough, but now … that is not the case. Tim wants to "turn back the clock" and get back to a place where he can enjoy and look forward to work again. He expresses that he feels like he is going to explode.

Discussion Questions:

1. How can you help Tim with his suppressed feelings of grief?
2. How can you guide Tim towards identifying alternative coping mechanisms?
3. What strategies might you employ with Tim to work through and re-write the narrative around "Joy's" death so that he can engage at work without being triggered?

Case Scenario #2:

Dr. Julie Buttons is a relatively new client of yours. She is coming to you because she is extremely upset about a medical error she believes squarely falls on her shoulders. During a routine urinary cystocentesis (where a needle is placed into the urinary bladder through the abdominal wall of an animal and a sample of urine is removed), her patient, a 10-year-old male Maltese named "Peanut" flinched and the needle lacerated a large vein and he bled to death. This has devastated "Peanut's" family and they have voiced that they blame her for his death. They want nothing to do with her and have forbidden her to call them. They have also refused to pay for the procedure.

The error happened a month ago and she has lost sleep and focus ever since. She states that she can't stop crying and feels worthless in both her professional life and also her personal life.

Discussion Questions:

1. What strategies might you employ to help Dr. Buttons?
2. Do you think that her assertions of her worthlessness bears exploring and if so, how do you do so?
3. How do you help Julie with her feelings of guilt and blame, especially in light of the fact that she cannot reach out to "Peanut's" family?

References

Adams, R.E., Boscarino, J. A., & Figley, C. R. (2006). Compassion fatigue and psychological distress among social workers: A validation study. American *Journal of Orthopsychiatry*, 76(1), 103–108. doi: 10.1037/0002-9432.76.1.103

Allison, S. O., Eggleston-Ahearn, A. M., Courtney, C. J., Hardy, C. D., Malbrue, R. A., Quammen, J. K., Sander WE, Swartz AA, Wexler SR, & Zedek, A. S. (2016). Implementing wellness in the veterinary workplace. *Journal of the American Veterinary Medical Association*, 249(8), 879–881. doi: /10.2460/javma.249.8.879

Allister R. J. (2014). Veterinary perfection why good enough should be good enough *Practice Life*, September/October, 24–26.

Bartram, D. J., & Baldwin, D. S. (2010). Veterinary surgeons and suicide: a structured review of possible influences on increased risk. *Veterinary Record: Journal of the British Veterinary Association*, 166(13), 388–397. doi: 10.1136/vr.b4794

Boyle, D. A. (2011). Countering Compassion Fatigue: A Requisite Nursing Agenda. *Online Journal of Issues in Nursing*, 16(1), 1. doi: 10.3912/OJIN.Vol. 16No01Man02

Crump, K., & Thamm, D. (2011). *Cancer chemotherapy for the veterinary health team.* Chichester, UK, Ames, IA: John Wiley & Sons.

de Graaf, G. (2010) Veterinarians' discourses on animals and clients. *Journal of Agriculture and Environmental Ethics*, 18, 557–578.

Figley, C. R. (Ed.). (1995). *Compassion fatigue: Coping with secondary traumatic stress disorder in those who treat the traumatized.* Philadelphia, PA: Brunner/Mazel, Brunner/Mazel psychological stress series, No. 23.

Frost, R. O., Marten, P., Lahart, C., & Rosenblate, R. (1990). The dimensions of perfectionism. *Cognitive Therapy and Research*, 14(5), 449–468. doi: 10.1007/BF01172967

Halliwell, R. E. W., & Hoskin, B. D. (2005). Reducing the suicide rate among veterinary surgeons: how the profession can help. *Veterinary Record: Journal of the British Veterinary Association*, 157(14), 397–398. doi: 10.1136/vr.157.14.397

Hamilton, T. K., & Schweitzer, R. D. (2000). The cost of being perfect: perfectionism and suicide ideation in university students. *Australian & New Zealand Journal of Psychiatry*, 34(5), 829–835. doi: 10.1080/j.1440-1614.2000.00801.x

Hawton, K. (2007). Restricting access to methods of suicide: Rationale and evaluation of this approach to suicide prevention. *Crisis: The Journal of Crisis Intervention and Suicide Prevention*, 28(Suppl 1), 4–9. doi: 10.1027/0227-5910.28.S1.4

Hewitt, P. L., & Flett, G. L. (1991). Perfectionism in the Self and Social Contexts: Conceptualization, Assessment, and Association With Psychopathology. *Journal of Personality and Social Psychology*, 60(3), 456–470.

Kahler, S. C. (2015). Moral stress the top trigger in veterinarians' compassion fatigue. *Journal of the American Veterinary Medical Association*, 246(1), 16–18. Retrieved from https://ezproxy2.library.colostate.edu/login?url=http://search.ebscohost.com/login.aspx?direct=true&AuthType=cookie,ip,url,cpid&custid=s4640792&db=aph&AN=100203433&site=ehost-live

Kogan, L. R., Hellyer, P. W., Rishniw, M., & Schoenfeld-Tacher, R. M. (2018). Veterinarians' experiences with near misses and adverse events. *Journal of the American Veterinary Medical Association*, 252(5), 586–595. doi: 10.2460/javma.252.5.586

Lachman, V. D. (2016). Ethics, law, and policy. Moral resilience: Managing and preventing moral distress and moral residue. *MEDSURG Nursing*, 25(2), 121–124. Retrieved from https://ezproxy2.library.colostate.edu/login?url=http://search.ebscohost.com/login.aspx?direct=true&AuthType=cookie,ip,url,cpid&custid=s4640792&db=aph&AN=114665017&site=ehost-live

Larkin, M. (2015). Study: 1 in 6 veterinarians have considered suicide. *Journal of the American Veterinary Medical Association*. Retrieved from www.avma.org/News/JAVMANews/Pages/150401d.aspx

Larkin, M. (2018). Salaries, debt for new graduates continue to increase. Journal of the *American Veterinary Medical Association News*. Retrieved from www.avma.org/News/JAVMANews/Pages/181215f.aspx

Mitchener, K., & Ogilvie, G. (2002). Understanding compassion fatigue: Keys for the caring veterinary healthcare team. *Journal of The American Animal Hospital Association*, 38(4), 307–310.

Nett, R., Witte, T., Holzbauer, S., Elchos, B., Campagnolo, E., Musgrave, K., Carter K. K., Kurkjian, K. M., Vanicek, C. F., O'Leary, D. R., Pride, K. R., & Funk, R. (2015). Risk factors for suicide, attitudes toward mental illness, and practice-related stressors among US veterinarians. *Javma-Journal of The American Veterinary Medical Association*, 247(8), 945–955.

O'Connor, R. C. (2007). The Relations between perfectionism and suicidality: A systematic review. *Suicide and Life-Threatening Behavior*, 37(6), 698–714.

Rollin, B. (2006). *An introduction to veterinary medical ethics: theory and cases*. Hoboken, NJ: John Wiley & Sons, Incorporated.

Stoewen, D. (2015). Suicide in veterinary medicine: Let's talk about it. *The Canadian Veterinary Journal = La Revue Veterinaire Canadienne*, 56(1), 89–92.

Scott, S., Hirschinger, L., Cox, K., Mccoig, M., Brandt, J., & Hall, L. (2009). The natural history of recovery for the healthcare provider "second victim" after adverse patient events. *Quality and Safety in Health Care*, 18(5), 325–330.

Seys, D., Scott, S., Wu, A., Van Gerven, E., Vleugels, A., Euwema, M., Panella, M., Conway, J., Sermeus, W., Vanhaecht, K. (2012). Supporting involved health care professionals (second victims) following an adverse health event: A literature review. *International Journal of Nursing Studies*, 50(5), 678–687.

Stamm, B. H. (2009). The concise ProQOL manual. The concise manual for the professional quality of life scale. Retrieved from www.proqol.org/uploads/ProQOL_Concise_2ndEd_12-2010.pdf

Tannenbaum, J. (1993). Veterinary medical ethics: A focus of conflicting interests. *Journal of Social Issues*, 49(1), 143–156.

Tomasi, S., Fechter-Leggett, E., Edwards, N., Reddish, A., Crosby, A., & Nett, R. (2019). Suicide among veterinarians in the United States from 1979 through 2015. *Journal of the American Veterinary Medical Association*, 254(1), 104–112.

White, S. (2018). Veterinarians' emotional reactions and coping strategies for adverse events in spay-neuter surgical practice. *Anthrozoös*, 31(1), 117–131.

Witte, T., Correia, C., & Angarano, D. (2013). Experience with euthanasia is associated with fearlessness about death in veterinary students. *Suicide and Life-Threatening Behavior*, 43(2), 125–138.

7 Loss and Grief in Animal-Care Agents

Angela K. Fournier and Brandon Mustful

This chapter provides information for mental health professionals serving clients who work in the direct care of sheltered animals. This includes volunteers, employees, and administrators working in animal shelters, animal rescues, and municipal facilities (i.e., "the pound"). We collectively refer to this group as animal-care agents (ACAs). The reviewed literature suggests that ACAs experience significant loss as part of the job, and that subsequent grief may be complicated by the nature of their work. Grief can be complicated and even disenfranchised when the loss is a non-human animal (Doka, 2003), and when it is part of the job (e.g., Kaplan, 2000). ACAs have twice the risk of disenfranchised grief since their losses are non-human animals *and* part of their job. Animal-care work poses significant challenges and is associated with substantial strain and distress (Figley & Roop, 2006; Fournier & Mustful, 2018). Unfortunately, resources for counseling this population are limited. Loss and grief are likely to be an issue for many in this field, and despite growing resources for pet owners experiencing the loss of a companion animal (e.g., Dolan-Del Vecchio & Saxton-Lopez, 2013; Sife, 1998), there are no writings on ACA loss and grief and no resources for mental health professionals counseling this population. This chapter addresses that need, describing the nature of ACA loss and issues that may complicate the grief process. Because there is no literature on ACA loss and grief, we integrate the literature on the complication of grief in other areas, for which there are similarities to ACA work (e.g., nursing, hospice work, foster parenting). We conclude with treatment and prevention suggestions for mental health practitioners.

Loss in Animal-Care Work

According to the American Society for the Prevention of Cruelty to Animals (ASPCA), approximately 6.5 million companion animals enter animal shelters in the US each year (ASPCA, 2017). These are facilities where stray, lost, abandoned, or surrendered animals are kept to rehabilitate, adopt out, or euthanize (Arluke & Sanders, 1996). Animal shelter is a broad term and can include (1) municipal facilities (i.e., "the pound") with limited housing and no medical treatment, (2) public or private facilities with ample space and resources for animals to receive medical and rehabilitation services (e.g., behavioral training), and (3) animal control facilities, which are governmentally-operated facilities for housing stray or lost animals with staff enforcing ordinances related to animal control and cruelty (Association of Shelter Veterinarians, 2017).

Animal rescues, on the other hand, are generally privately-funded groups, often made up of volunteers, who rescue and rehome animals. A rescue organization may be run from a personal home with volunteers paying for animal expenses out of their own pocket (Harbolt, 2003). Referring to them as animal-care agents (ACAs), we discuss those who work in shelters and rescues together because people in both types of organization are directly responsible for the day-to-day care of animals and can experience similar losses and complicating factors.

It is estimated there are over 3,500 animal shelters and rescues in the US (Rowan & Kartal, 2018). The organizations can vary in many ways, including space, mission, resources, and policies. They could also vary in the kinds of losses that are experienced (e.g., some must euthanize more than others), the way losses are perceived, and the support available for the ACAs who work there.

Examples of direct-care tasks that can impact ACA well-being include caring for an abused animal or euthanizing a healthy one. Research indicates that the death of a pet can result in feelings similar to that of a human death (Sharkin & Knox, 2003). Feelings can move from disbelief or denial to anger, sadness, and depression. The person may be preoccupied with thoughts and memories of the pet and have poor concentration for other things (Sharkin & Knox, 2003). The main losses experienced by ACAs are (1) death of an animal by euthanasia, (2) death of an animal by illness or injury, and (3) adoption. Each of these is explored in the context of potential ACA grief and loss.

Euthanasia

Approximately 2.4 million companion animals are euthanized each year in the US, with the largest proportion of those being otherwise healthy cats and dogs euthanized in animal shelters (HSUS, 2018). Studies suggest up to 57% of cats and 40% of dogs in some individual shelters are euthanized, with rates being higher for governmental shelters and lower for privately-owned shelters (Bartlett, Bartlett, Walshaw, & Halstead, 2005). Arluke's ethnographic study in an animal shelter (as described in Arluke & Sanders, 1996) revealed that ACAs often enter the field unaware that euthanizing animals is part of the job.

Arluke (1994) described the *caring-killing paradox* as a contributing factor in euthanasia-related strain for animal shelter workers. Unfortunately, people who choose to work in the animal care field because they care for and want to help animals can become the individuals responsible for euthanizing them. In other words, those who care must kill. This contradiction results in great stress and strain.

ACAs can also experience stress from an internal conflict between a logical understanding and acceptance of euthanasia policy and strong negative emotions around killing animals. In addition to internal conflict, there may be interpersonal disagreements about the euthanasia of an animal between shelter staff, between staff and administration, or among volunteers. Research indicates that disagreement around euthanasia can result in anger and resentment between those responsible for the animal (Barton Ross & Baron-Sorensen, 2007).

The consequences of carrying out animal euthanasia are significant. Reeve, Rogelberg, Spitzmüller, and DiGiacomo (2005) studied euthanasia-related strain among ACAs in animal shelters. The respondents reported substantial strain from performing euthanasia. The strain negatively impacted job satisfaction and overall well-being. Specific experiences included trouble concentrating, losing sleep, feeling depressed, having nightmares, and questioning their self-worth.

In another study of animal shelter workers (Taylor, 2010), participants reported that negative emotions around euthanasia were accepted and expected. Staff reported engaging in emotion management daily. This consisted of transferring negative emotions into a missionary zeal for the cause, empathy for the animals, and anger and hostility toward the public. Baran et al. (2009) surveyed euthanasia technicians at 62 different animal shelters, investigating strategies they use to cope with the euthanasia-related strain. The authors concluded that euthanizing animals is a major stressor and shelter workers cope in a variety of ways, including working to separate themselves from the animals, seeking professional help, and leaving the job.

It is important to note that although regular euthanasia is a reality for many ACAs, it is not experienced by all. A growing number of shelters are categorized as "no-kill" or limited admission, meaning they do not euthanize otherwise healthy animals due to lack of space or resources (HSUS, 2012). However, even ACAs who work at no-kill organizations can expect to experience animal death from other causes.

Illness or Injury

Animal shelters and rescues take in many animals, including those who are injured or ill. In some cases, an animal is surrendered because the owner cannot or will not care for an ill pet (New et al., 2000). In other cases, an animal is not identified as ill until it is already under ACA care. Some of the animals who enter shelters have been abused and/or neglected and suffer physical injuries that cannot be treated. Seeing an abused or neglected animal is distressing in and of itself, and can also result in the animal dying. Finally, animals can die from ailments acquired at the shelter or rescue facility. Studies consistently show that infections such as gastrointestinal parasites are higher in shelter animals than pets living in homes (e.g., Palmer, Robertson, Traub, Rees, & Thompson, 2010; Villeneuve et al., 2015). Some of these infections can cause serious illness and death, particularly in young animals (Raza, Rand, Qamar, Jabbar, & Kopp, 2018). For all these reasons – surrendered animals are ill, abused animals are severely injured, and the shelter environment fosters infectious diseases – ACAs will experience animals dying while in their care. The death of any individual animal may be perceived by the ACA as an emotional loss, eliciting a grief response. Beyond the more obvious grief around animal *death*, ACAs might also experience grief around animal *adoption*.

Adoption

There is great variability in animals' length of stay at animal shelters or rescues, ranging anywhere from one day to 2 years or longer (Brown & Morgan, 2015). The more time spent with an animal, the greater the opportunity to bond with the animal, making separation difficult. And although adoption is the desired outcome for the animal, ACAs may still feel an emotional loss when an animal they have been caring for leaves for its new home. Although there is no research to date on the psychological impact of animal adoption on ACAs, the literature on (human) foster parenting provides insight, as there are similarities between ACAs and foster parents.

Both involve providing care for others on a temporary basis, and both groups experience non-death losses relatively frequently. While those fostering children or animals can experience someone transitioning out of their care for positive reasons (the child or animal is adopted), they may also experience it as a loss and need to grieve. There are considerable resources to help foster parents cope with children transitioning out of the home (e.g., Baldino, 2009). For foster parents, it is suggested they take time before another child is placed in their care, talk to foster agency staff, and attend foster parent support groups and trainings (Baldino, 2009). Situations that may complicate the grieving process include (1) the child leaving has been a behavior challenge so caregivers are conflicted with relief and sorrow, (2) caregivers are too busy caring for others to grieve the departing child, and (3) caregivers worry about being perceived as emotionally weak or ill-equipped for the work. The latter two may be most relevant for ACAs, who may be too busy caring for other animals to process the adoption of an individual animal, and either not perceive it as a loss to process or feel too ashamed to discuss the loss with anyone. The loss experienced when a person or animal is adopted is more ambiguous than the clear-cut loss of a death. As we will see in a later section, ambiguous losses can hinder the grief process, resulting in negative outcomes. This is just one of several factors unique to ACA work that can complicate the grief process.

Unique Aspects/Complicating Factors

There are several aspects of the work ACAs do that are unique and may complicate the experience of animal loss and the grief process. These factors are important to understand when working with ACAs in a mental health capacity. Treating professionals should have a basic understanding of the complicated losses ACAs experience, and may impart this information onto the ACA to validate their experience.

Isolation and Ostracism

Despite the need for social support during times of loss and grief, ACAs may feel isolated from family, friends, and co-workers. Baran et al. (2012) found that shelter workers who performed euthanasia, compared to workers not involved in euthanasia, were more likely to avoid discussing their work with others. In addition to their own avoidance, animal-care work can be perceived as negative by others, resulting in poor social support. ACAs are sometimes associated with the "dirty work" (Hughs, 1962) of cleaning up after animals and performing euthanasia, being villainized by family, friends, and society in general (Arluke & Sanders, 1996). Even within the shelter community, there is tension that can result in greater stress, criticism, and poor social support. For example, there is a controversy between "kill" and "no-kill" animal shelters with those from both types of shelters perceiving the other as causing harm to companion animals (Arluke, 2003). Whether ACAs are avoiding or being avoided, these findings suggest ACAs may have limited social support, which can negatively affect an already disenfranchised grief.

Disenfranchised Grief

Doka (1989) coined the term disenfranchised grief, defined as grief that is not acknowledged by society. While in many cultures, grief is socially acknowledged, sanctioned, and supported, loss and grief that fall outside of what is socially accepted and expected is disenfranchised. This may occur because (1) the relationship between the griever and the one being grieved is not recognized, (2) the loss is not acknowledged, (3) the griever is excluded from the grieving process, (4) the circumstances of the death or loss deem it ungrievable, or (5) one's grieving style is inconsistent with socially-accepted practices (Doka, 1989, 2003). For ACAs, the first two may be especially important.

Disenfranchised Grief of an Animal

Doka suggests that because society undervalues animals and the relationships they can share with people, our attitudes and beliefs about animals block recognition, respect, and enfranchisement of the human–animal bond and thus the loss of an animal relationship (2003). Packman, Bussolari, Katz, and Carmack (2016) discuss the grieving process for pet owners, highlighting the potential intensity of the loss, positive association between attachment and grief, and the potential for invalidated grief.

Disenfranchised Grief of a Patient or Client

For ACAs, caring for a shelter animal is part of the job. Because it occurs within a work context, the relationship and subsequent loss may not be validated. Spidell et al. (2011) studied disenfranchised grief in healthcare chaplains. Over 500 chaplains completed a survey in which they reported substantial grief associated with their work. Symptoms included low energy, moodiness, apathy, and self-isolation. A significant proportion of the sample felt their grief was not affirmed or supported at work.

Foster parents may experience disenfranchised grief after a foster child leaves to reunite with their parent(s) or is adopted by another family. It is assumed that, because the foster parent–child relationship was to be temporary, there is no real loss (Anderson, Gurdin, & Thomas, 1989; Doka, 1989). This is true of shelter animals as well; because the shelter is a temporary home for the animals, the animals' adoption may not be perceived as a loss. Yet, ACAs could experience an emotional loss. Without the loss being acknowledged by them or others, there is no opportunity for grief. Over time, this type of ambiguous loss and subsequent frozen grief (Boss, 1999) can impact the individual emotionally and physically.

Ambiguous Loss

Boss (1999) discusses ambiguous loss, in which it is unclear if there has been a loss or if a traumatic experience can be labeled a loss. Though she focuses on the loss of those who are physically present but psychologically absent (e.g., a family member with dementia) and the loss of someone who is psychologically present but physically absent (e.g., veteran missing in action), insights from the ambiguous loss literature may elucidate the ACA experience. Loss of a shelter animal, whether through death or adoption, could be ambiguous for the ACA. The relationship with the animal who is gone may not be recognized (i.e., this was not a pet, there was no relationship) and the loss may not be perceived as grievable (e.g., this is just part of the job). For these reasons, it may not be clear to the ACA that they have experienced a loss. Managing feelings of grief or sorrow without a clear loss to attribute them is challenging. Boss suggests "the greater the ambiguity around one's loss, the more difficult it is to master it and the greater one's depression, anxiety, and family conflict" (Boss, 1999, p. 7). She discusses grief from ambiguous loss as frozen; survivors can't move through the grieving process. Boss finds that labeling something as a loss, and specifically an ambiguous loss, can be helpful for clients. It helps to de-pathologize their experience, understanding they are distressed because of this difficult *situation*, rather than a problem within *themselves.*

Cumulation of Multiple Losses

The effects of a loss are influenced by several factors, including whether the individual has experienced any other recent losses. It has been shown that experiencing multiple losses close together in time can result in a compounded loss effect (Barton Ross, 2013). Mercer and Evans (2006) studied the impact of multiple losses on the grieving process. They found that multiple losses had wide-ranging effects (e.g., health, relationships, finances) and the grief lasted longest when the losses occurred close in time. For ACAs, this can happen with disease outbreaks at the shelter. Marino (1998) defines cumulative grief as the emotional reaction when there is no time or opportunity to completely or adequately grieve for each person who has died. This concept is typically discussed in the context of the healthcare field; research indicates cumulative losses can lead to compassion fatigue and burnout for hospice nurses (Wright, 2017).

It is likely that ACAs will experience frequent losses through adoption, euthanasia, and illness or injury, and that any of the losses can have an emotional impact on the ACA. Since the loss is an animal and not a human, and a shelter/rescue animal rather than a pet, there are likely differences in the manifestation of cumulative grief. Research is necessary to study this issue, regarding prevalence, treatment, and prevention and whether the psychological literature on cumulative grief can be translated to understanding the grief of ACAs. For the clinician seeing ACAs now, it is important to investigate the potential experience of multiple losses and identify signs of cumulative grief. Symptoms can include depression, anxiety, substance abuse, apathy, and suicidal thoughts (Brosche, 2003; Conte, 2012; Feldstein & Gemma, 1995) and can cause caring professionals to detach emotionally or overinvest in those they are caring for, both which increase the risk of compassion fatigue (Boyle, 2011).

Anticipatory Grief

When a death is expected, the survivors are allowed time to search for understanding of the death, resolve conflicts with the dying person, say goodbye, and do things for the dying person to make their last days easier (Nolen-Hoeksema & Larson, 1999). This is termed anticipatory grieving – finding meaning in the loss and adjusting to the loss before the loved one dies. Anticipatory grief is thought to allow for easier adjustment than when the death is unexpected (Rando, 1986). It is possible the same is true for the expected death of a shelter or rescue animal. When an animal is scheduled to be euthanized, ACAs could take actions that help in understanding and accepting the loss, and focus on making the animals' remaining time as pleasant as possible. Despite these positive aspects of anticipatory grief, it may also bring challenges. According to Becvar (2003), an expected death can elicit mixed emotions in survivors, feeling sad about the loss but also relief, which can turn to guilt (Becvar, 2003).

Furthermore, the literature on the effects of anticipatory grief are mixed, with some data indicating it can complicate and hinder the grieving process (Reynolds & Botha, 2006). Literature suggests anticipatory grief can cause physical symptoms (e.g., sleep and appetite changes, fatigue), negative emotions (e.g., anxiety, helplessness, guilt, anger, sadness), and cognitive difficulties (e.g., confusion, forgetfulness, disorganization) (Simon, 2008). It is important to note that literature on anticipatory grief is currently limited to the experience of humans dying from an extended illness and those caring for them. While the psychological processes may be similar for animals who die naturally or are euthanized following an extended illness, research is needed to address the issue. Furthermore, the literature does not provide insight into the potential anticipatory grief of ACAs working in an environment where euthanasia of healthy animals due to lack of resources is common practice, and that the one anticipating the euthanasia is also the one carrying it out. Mental health professionals working with ACAs should discuss these issues, assessing for the potential of anticipatory grief and negative or positive consequences.

Presenting for Mental Health Treatment

Given the challenges of ACA work and the frequent losses, ACAs may experience levels of distress that call for professional help. Although grief may be the issue, it could manifest in various ways. For example, clients could present with symptoms of psychological disorders (e.g., depression, anxiety), problem coping behaviors (e.g., substance abuse, aggression), or relationship problems (e.g., strain interrupts their role as a partner or parent). It is important to note that any of these presenting problems could exist for the ACA independent of their work. Still, the grief they experience at work could exacerbate symptoms, impact presentation, or complicate treatment progress.

Whether a primary or secondary factor, grief is an important layer to address in treatment. The goals of bereavement counseling in general apply to ACAs: (1) providing information, (2) normalizing and validating the individual's experience, (3) maximizing social support and reducing isolation, (4) promoting adaptive coping strategies, and (5) providing a safe environment to express the emotions of mourning (Nolen-Hoeksema & Larson, 1999). In addition to these goals, we make the following recommendations specific to ACAs, based on the literature.

Use a Stress and Coping Framework

Psychological models on grief and loss were originally derived from psychoanalytic (Freud, 1917) and attachment theories (e.g., Bowlby, 1982), emphasizing the importance of close relationships to the self-concept. In these models, symptoms of distress were attributed to an individual's adjustment, or lack of adjustment, to the loss of a relationship. While these theories remain influential, there is a lack of empirical evidence for some of the theories' assumptions (Nolen-Hoeksema & Larson, 1999). Furthermore, these models may not fit in explaining ACA grief, as they rely on a significant attachment figure or close relationship. While these models may help address grief around pet loss, the stress and coping models of bereavement may be more useful in understanding the losses experienced by those working in animal shelters or rescues.

Stress and coping models view bereavement in the greater context of stressful life events, focusing on ways of thinking about and coping with the loss to address symptoms of bereavement (Nolen-Hoeksema & Larson, 1999). Bereavement caused by death can be considered a psychosocial transition, in which a change occurs that is lasting, takes place over a relatively short period of time, and requires revision of personal assumptions about the world (Parkes, 1988). Losses experienced by ACAs could meet each of these criteria, particularly with regard to the latter. An animal being abused or killed could cause one to question the belief many of us hold – that the world is just and meaningful, and that things happen for a good reason (Lerner, 1980) – particularly someone who identifies as an "animal person." Beyond that, the cumulative effect of hundreds of animals coming and going through shelters could agitate one's understanding of what is good and bad, as well as cloud the meaning and purpose of their work.

If we think about ACAs' loss and grief from a stress and coping perspective, coping models can give suggestions for helping those presenting with work-related grief. Coping is often discussed in two broad categories – problem-focused and emotion-focused. Problem-focused coping is aimed at solving the problem causing the stress, while emotion-focused coping is aimed at controlling the emotional response to the stressor (Lazarus & Folkman, 1984). For the everyday loss and grief experienced by ACAs, emotion-focused coping strategies would be most relevant, aimed at helping the individual to cope with the emotions around animal harm and loss. Table 7.1 lists some emotion-focused strategies for bereavement described by Nolen-Hoeksema and Larson (1999). For each strategy, an example is given in the context of animal shelter work. In working with

Table 7.1 Emotion-Focused Coping for Animal-Care Agents

Strategy	Definition	Example
Healthy Strategies		
Support Seeking	Reaching out to others for help	AWA colleagues, supervisor, support groups, professionals, family/friends
Emotional Expression	Expressing emotions openly (e.g., talking, yelling, crying)	Create time and space for expression at work, home, etc.
Reappraisal	Trying to find understanding and something positive about the stressor	Remembering positive times with an animal that is gone, remembering positive aspects of the job, success stories
Distraction	Engage in positive activities to keep oneself occupied	Focus on tasks of the job you enjoy, develop hobbies
Unhealthy Strategies		
Avoidance	Avoiding the loss or engaging in unhealthy activities (e.g., drugs, alcohol)	Drinking after work to relieve the stress and forget the trauma of the loss
Rumination	Passively focusing on the negative thoughts and emotions around the loss	Thinking about how unfair it is, and how awful I feel

Source: Nolen-Hoeksema, Larson, & Larson, 1999.

ACA clients, it may be helpful to discuss their loss and grief in the context of stress, identify their ways of coping with the stress, and work to address any unhealthy coping or help develop new healthy coping strategies.

In studying euthanasia-related strain, Baran et al. (2009) asked 242 animal shelter euthanasia technicians about their own coping strategies. Their responses were summarized into 26 distinct coping recommendations in eight categories. The coping recommendations were of two basic types – methods of dealing with euthanasia-related stress on and off the job. Table 7.2 provides these coping strategies.

Explore Meaning of the Animal/Loss/Work

Chur-Hansen (2010) suggests a thorough history and exploration of the animal's meaning for the client is important when addressing grief and bereavement around the loss of an animal. Doing so will help determine the placement of grief within the individual's mental health context and allow for validation and processing of emotions. To understand the meaning of an animal's death, it is important to gather information on previous losses, both human and animal, and the responses to those losses;

Table 7.2 Coping Strategies Recommended by Euthanasia Technicians

Type of Strategy	Example
Coping at Work	
Develop Competence or Skills	Seek education and training; have confidence in your ability
Euthanasia-Behavior Strategies	Have someone else euthanize special "pets"; Don't euthanize large amounts at one time
Self-Talk	Know that euthanasia is sometimes the best option; understand it is part of the job; don't blame yourself
Emotion Regulation	Acknowledge and vent feelings; alter emotional attachment level
Coping Outside of Work	
Separation	Keep separate from personal life; seek a diversion; mediate, pray, or reflect
Get Help	Discuss concerns with management; Seek external help (e.g., counseling)
Seek Long-Term Solutions	Promote responsible pet ownership
Withdrawal	Know the job is not for everyone; get a different job if necessary

Source: Baran et al., 2009

the death of someone today can bring up powerful emotions from previous deaths (Freeman, 2005). This is true whether the deceased is human (Freeman, 2005) or animal (Sharkin & Knox, 2003).

It is also important to understand the meaning of pets, animals, shelter animals, and shelter work for the ACA. Research suggests ACAs give the animals they care for personal meaning, perceive them as future family members or pets in waiting, not just animals. They use the term *adoption*, rather than *purchase*, despite the exchange of money between the shelter and the new owner (Taylor, 2010). Giving an animal the meaning of being a future family member may result in a different response to the animal's death or adoption than seeing them as just animals. Assessing for meaning, and any maladaptive placement of meaning, is but one important area of assessment when treating ACAs.

Assessment

Assessment is an important component of any mental health treatment. Beyond measuring symptoms or psychosocial functioning, it may be important to measure grief and bereavement, stress level and coping style, and meaning of their work. Table 7.3 provides a sample list of instruments in each of these areas.

Grief

Measuring grief is key to determining whether grief is the whole or part of the presenting problem. For ACAs who are experiencing grief, measuring it will be important in developing a treatment plan and detecting treatment progress. Although instruments specific to grieving an animal are limited, other grief instruments may be just as useful. The Pet Bereavement Questionnaire is a 16-item self-report instrument designed to measure the psychological impact experienced after the loss of a pet (Hunt & Padilla, 2006). The instrument measures grief, anger, and guilt and has demonstrated good reliability. There are also several useful non-pet-related measurement tools. The Texas Revised Inventory of Grief (Faschingbauer, 1981) is designed to measure "normal" or "typical" grief. It has good psychometric properties and has been used to measure non-pathological grief in other caregiver populations (Chentsova-Dutton et al., 2002). The Inventory of Complicated Grief (Prigerson & Jacobs, 2001) measures pathological grief, or grief accompanied by symptoms that disrupt functioning such as anger, disbelief, and hallucinations.

Stress and Coping

Taking a stress and coping perspective to understanding ACAs' loss and grief necessitates the use of instruments to measure stress levels and

Table 7.3 Measurement Instruments for Assessment of Animal-Care Agents

Instrument	Source	Description
Grief & Bereavement		
Pet Bereavement Questionnaire	Hunt & Padilla, 2006	16-item self-report instrument designed to measure the psychological impact experienced after the loss of a pet
Texas Revised Inventory of Grief	Faschingbauer, 1981	13-item self-report designed to assess non-pathological grief
Inventory of Complicated Grief	Prigerson & Jacobs, 2001	19-item measure to assess for pathological grief
Stress & Coping		
Perceived Stress Scale	Cohen, Kamarck, & Mermelstein, 1983	10-item scale to measure perceived stress in the past month
COPE Inventory	Carver, Scheier, & Weintraub, 1989	14 four-item scales that measure a variety of coping strategies
Meaningful Work		
Work as Meaning Inventory	Steger, Dik, & Duffy, 2012	10-item self-report designed to measure how meaningful one's work is
Meaningful Work Scale	Lips-Wiersma & Wright, 2012	28-item instrument designed to measure multiple dimensions of meaningful work

coping styles. The Perceived Stress Scale is widely used; it's designed to measure the degree to which one perceives situations in their life as stressful (Cohen, Kamarck, & Mermelstein, 1983). The instrument measures stress by assessing how unpredictable, uncontrollable, and overloaded they see their life. Regarding coping style, The COPE Inventory can be used to assess an individual's coping style (Carver, Scheier, & Weintraub, 1989). The instrument measures both problem-focused and emotion-focused coping strategies and could be used to confirm the use of effective strategies and identify the use of maladaptive strategies which could be addressed in treatment.

Meaningfulness

It may be important to assess whether the ACA perceives their work as meaningful, as is discussed below. This could be helpful in initial assessment and identification of treatment goals, while reframing negative aspects of work to focus on positive aspects, and deciding whether to stay in the field. There are several self-report instruments designed to measure whether work is meaningful, including the Work as Meaning Inventory (Steger, Dik, & Duffy, 2012) and the Meaningful Work Scale (Lips-Wiersma & Wright, 2012). Both instruments are appropriate for use with any type of work.

Validate the Ambiguous Loss(es)

While many clients need a certain degree of validation of their feelings and experience, those with disenfranchised grief may be in particular need of validation. Losses that are deemed ungrievable leave the person grieving without a means to express their feelings (Doka, 1989). As discussed earlier, loss of an animal may be met with less-than-sympathetic responses from family and friends (Packman et al., 2016), and caregivers for the dying who experience loss on the job report invalidated feelings of grief (Spidell et al., 2011). In addition, ACAs may be ostracized by family and friends for their work. This leaves ACAs at risk for limited validation of their feelings by others.

Because losses involve *animals* at *work*, the loss is somewhat ambiguous. Therefore, the ACAs themselves may not perceive their feelings as valid. Again, Boss (1999) suggests that labeling the loss as ambiguous helps to validate the experience of an ambiguous loss. It is important for the mental health practitioner treating ACA clients to be aware of their personal beliefs about animals and animal loss. A clinician with strong feelings that an animal death or adoption is not a significant loss may find it difficult to provide genuine validation and thus would need to refer the client elsewhere.

Reframe and Refocus

Just as foster parents gain personal and professional satisfaction in knowing they have played an important role in helping a foster child move toward a happier life (Baldino, 2009), ACAs can take satisfaction in knowing they have helped an animal find its forever home. Although euthanasia may be more difficult to reframe, there can be some satisfaction in knowing the animal is not suffering from illness, homelessness, or abuse.

The growing literature on post-traumatic growth may also be helpful in guiding ACA clients through a reframing of their work. Post-traumatic growth consists of positive emotional and behavioral changes following traumatic experiences. These changes can include an increased appreciation for life, changed priorities, and more meaningful interpersonal relationships (Tedeschi & Calhoun, 2004). Related to death and bereavement, studies show post-traumatic growth does occur, particularly with regard to transformations in self-concept and reappraisal of life and priorities (Michael & Cooper, 2013). More relevant to this chapter, research suggests post-traumatic growth is also possible following the loss of a pet.

Packman, Bussolari, Katz, Carmack, and Field (2017) surveyed pet owners who had lost a pet through death. The participants discussed positive changes in relating to others, appreciating life, personal strength, spiritual change, and new possibilities. Of these, the greatest number of responses focused on relating to others. Specifically, respondents indicated a greater sense of closeness with others and more compassion for others. Regarding personal strength, a significant proportion said the loss helped them discover that they are stronger than they thought, particularly in cases where the animal was euthanized. Rates and types of post-traumatic growth may vary by culture (Bussolari et al., 2017). It is unknown if post-traumatic growth occurs for ACAs and if so, how. Nevertheless, clinicians could discuss the concept of post-traumatic growth with ACA clients and explore for positive outcomes that have been experienced but not identified. This focus on growth from the loss experience may be part of the client refocusing on more positive aspects of the job.

There are rewarding aspects of ACA work, which might be forgotten among the challenges. But doing meaningful work has many benefits, including greater job satisfaction (Kamdron, 2005) and personal well-being (Arnold, Turner, Barling, Kelloway, & McKee, 2007). Clinicians can help their ACA clients shift their focus from the negative to the positive. The rewards of animal care and welfare work include providing good care for the animal while it is at the shelter or rescue, facilitating a successful adoption for the animal and new pet owner, and doing one's part in the larger, societal problem of pet overpopulation.

Develop and Maintain Healthy Boundaries

There is significant evidence in the literature that the intensity of grief is related to the intensity of the relationship, such that relationships with stronger attachment or more intense time spent with the deceased result in more grief. For example, the intensity of hospice-worker grief, in response to a patient death, is related to the intensity and duration of contact with the patient (Doka, 2003). To cope, hospice workers are encouraged to practice strategies to separate themselves from the work, such as doing enjoyable non-work activities and engaging in self-reflection before returning home (Bradley & Cartwright, 2002). Research suggests that the more attached one is to their pet, the greater their grief when they die (Field, Orsini, Gavish, & Packman, 2009). This relationship between attachment and grief is likely to also exist for ACAs, such that becoming attached to an animal increases the sense of loss and subsequent grief when the animal leaves the shelter. ACAs may prevent some grief by maintaining healthy boundaries with the animals. This can include thinking about and treating the animals as recipients of shelter and care rather than pets. One of the most common coping recommendations suggested by ACAs performing euthanasia is to alter one's emotional attachment to the animal; euthanasia technicians manage job strain, in part, by finding a healthy balance between emotional attachment to and detachment from the animals in their care (Baran et al., 2009).

It is important to note that those working in animal rescues could be especially challenged in developing and maintaining healthy boundaries. Since rescue workers can often shelter animals in their own home (Harbolt, 2003), the line between rescue animal and pet can be blurred. Having an animal in one's home around the clock, interacting with other people and pets in the family, can make the animal's transition – even to a happy, healthy home – an emotional one. Even with healthy boundaries, the ACA may experience an adoption or euthanization as a loss. Therefore, it is helpful for the individual ACA, and their employing organization, to have practices in place that allow for healthy management of those emotions.

Create Loss-Based Practices

Ceremonies and Rituals

Performing rituals and holding ceremonies are powerful actions that help to maintain order within a culture by transmitting group beliefs and expectations (Becvar, 2003). A funeral is a type of ceremony in which we say goodbye to the deceased in the context of a set of spiritual or religious beliefs; it also functions to allow for open expression of grief (Imber-Black, 1991). Death without ceremony can make it difficult to find closure and put grief to rest (Kohner & Henley, 1997). As an organization, shelters or rescues could hold a ceremony when an animal dies. On the other hand, ACAs may be more comfortable creating their own private ceremonies for animals who die. Whether large or small, formal or informal, public or private, holding a ceremony may be helpful in ACA work-related grief.

Beyond ceremonies, ACAs could perform rituals or use symbols to commemorate animal loss. For example, a balloon could be released when an animal dies, serving as a symbol of the deceased transitioning or a means of expressing one's feelings around the loss of the deceased. It is possible for ACAs to practice such grief rituals at an individual or organizational level. Some shelters have regular practices to acknowledge and memorialize animals that have transitioned in and out of the facility. These may be events held to remember all animals that have died, a permanent fixture at the shelter facility to represent animals who die there, or smaller-scale rituals carried out for individual animals (e.g., lighting a candle, giving a brief eulogy, saying a prayer). In practice, mental health professionals could help their ACA clients find or develop a ceremony or ritual for animals that leave the shelter.

Bereavement Debriefing Sessions

Keene, Hutton, Hall, and Rushton (2010) studied bereavement debriefing sessions as an intervention for healthcare professionals (e.g., nurses, physicians, social workers) grieving a patient's death. The sessions were offered, but not mandatory, within a week of the death. Sessions included a case review, discussion of group members' role in caring for the deceased patient, emotional processing of the loss, discussion of coping strategies, and discussion of lessons learned from caring for that particular patient. Those attending the sessions reported it was helpful, informative, and meaningful. Attendees reported the sessions helped them see the importance of self-care. Finally, the healthcare professionals reported that seeing how others were affected would impact how they interact with their colleagues in the future. Although these bereavement debriefing sessions were offered at one particular medical facility, similar practices could be adopted at animal shelters or rescues. Sessions could be provided after an animal death, or at regular intervals, depending on need. Mental health professionals can introduce this idea to clients experiencing shelter-related grief.

Hess-Holden, Monaghan, and Justice (2017) give suggestions for mental health professionals developing pet bereavement support groups. They recommend, based on best practices in psychiatric and veterinary medicine, that pet bereavement support groups (1) are led by a licensed mental health professional, (2) are held in a private location biweekly, (3) provide psychoeducation on grief, loss, and coping, (4) facilitate acknowledgment of the importance of pet loss and validation of members' grief process, and

(5) include evaluation of group efficacy by administering pre-post assessments (e.g., Pet Bereavement Questionnaire).

Practice Self-Care

Self-care is an important aspect of good physical and mental health, particularly for those in the helping professions (Bamonti et al., 2014). Figley and Roop (2006), in discussing the needs of those working in animal care and welfare, recommend the self-care guidelines provided by the Green Cross Academy of Traumatology (Green Cross Academy of Traumatology, n.d.). Self-care can be comprised of many activities, such as engaging in professional development, engaging in spiritual practices, refocusing on the rewards of the job and the meaning of the work, and practicing healthy escapes (e.g., breaks, recreation) (Norcross & Guy, 2007). Mental health professionals working with ACAs should discuss the concept of self-care with their clients, help them develop a self-care plan if they don't have one, and help them monitor the effectiveness of the plan and adjust if necessary.

Summary

Working to care for animals in a shelter or rescue is difficult work. One of the major challenges of the work is the experience of loss and grief. ACAs will undoubtedly encounter a significant amount of animal death, whether from euthanasia, abuse, illness, or injury. In addition, ACAs may experience non-death loss when animals are adopted. These losses can result in grief for the ACA. Grief in animal-care work is complicated because the loss is that of an animal and the loss occurs in the context of work. This can result in ambiguous loss and disenfranchised grief. In addition, ACAs experience multiple losses, which can have a cumulative effect. For these reasons, ACAs may be experiencing a great deal of loss and have limited means for healthy grief and mourning. Mental health professionals working with ACAs would do well to become aware of the loss and grief issues facing ACA clients. There are several assessment instruments that may be useful in determining the client's level of grief and stress, their coping style, and the meaning they see in their work. Suggestions for treatment and prevention of grief complications include, but are not limited to, shifting cognitions from the challenges of the job to the rewards, engaging in bereavement debriefing sessions, creating loss-based practices, and practicing self-care.

Case Scenarios

The following cases describe fictional characters, but the details are based on actual situations that occur in animal shelters and rescues. Read the case information and answer the questions that follow.

Case Scenario #1: Aggressive Animal Euthanasia

Kevin is a 24-year-old man who has been referred for anger management for some trouble he had at work. He had been working as a kennel attendant at his local animal shelter for six months when he met Rusty, a male chocolate lab. Rusty was transferred to the shelter from another animal welfare organization where he had been for several months. Kevin's shelter manager decided to take in Rusty despite the fact that he had two incidents of aggressive behavior reported. Both incidents were minor and did not involve a bite.

Kevin fell in love with Rusty immediately. Rusty exhibited some nervous behavior around strangers but behaved friendly after a proper introduction. Kevin bonded especially well with animals like Rusty, since he had struggled with his own anxiety and had been in jail for aggressive behavior in the past. Kevin spent as much time with Rusty as he could and enjoyed showing him off to potential adopters.

A few months went by and, although some people had shown interest in adopting Rusty, no one had applied to adopt him. As the days went by, shelter workers noted more and more nervous behavior from Rusty. Kevin noticed this as well, and responded by spending even more time with Rusty, working on behavior modification. The extra time had brought the two quite close, so that Rusty responded better to Kevin than any other shelter worker and Kevin began referring to Rusty as "my boy." One day, Rusty was spending time with a family with preteen children. In the middle of the visit, one of the children attempted to pick up a toy in front of Rusty and he quickly snapped at the child and bit him on the hand. It left a severe puncture wound.

The shelter manager and other administrators met to discuss Rusty's situation. Due to his apparent deteriorating behavior, the difficulty of adopting a dog that has bitten someone, and other safety considerations, the decision was made to euthanize Rusty. The euthanasia took place three days after the bite incident, and, just as quickly as Rusty had entered Kevin's life, he was gone.

Much of the shelter staff was saddened by the situation with Rusty, but none more than Kevin. He had spent many hours with Rusty and despite the reports from others, thought that Rusty was making improvements in his behavior. Kevin was not part of the decision to euthanize Rusty. Although he usually agrees with shelter policies and understands the need to euthanize, Kevin disagreed with this decision. He was hurt and angry and began having difficulties with his co-workers because of it. He was easily irritated and started drinking more after work, to "calm his nerves." He became so upset when arguing with a co-worker last week that he punched him. Kevin was suspended from work and his boss suggested he seek professional help for anger management.

Discussion Questions:

1. Is the presenting problem anger management, grief, or both? Explain.
2. Discuss anticipatory grief as a potential factor in this case.
3. Develop a potential treatment plan for Kevin, incorporating suggestions from the chapter.

Case Scenario #2: Kitten Disease Outbreak

Brooke is a 40-year-old single mother of two who has been working at her local animal shelter for a few years. She had a variety of job responsibilities, which included providing care for cats and kittens and spending time socializing them. Brooke really enjoyed her job and especially liked seeing the cats go to homes with excited adopters. Some days were better than others, but for the most part things were going well at the shelter.

Every summer, the shelter gets hit with more requests to take cats than they can handle, but this summer had been particularly challenging. The shelter had taken in a number of pregnant cats resulting in several litters of kittens. This put a lot of pressure on the shelter's capacity to provide adequate care. In the middle of it all, when the shelter was completely overloaded with cats, Brooke started noticing signs of illness in the kittens. Several kittens had diarrhea, runny noses and eyes, and just seemed listless. The shelter's animal health manager ordered the kittens to be quarantined and treated them with medication, but most of them didn't seem to be getting better. Not only that, but more and more kittens were getting sick. Brooke and other shelter staff were fighting to save these kittens and get them healthy and strong again, but nothing was changing.

A few of the kittens that had been treated for their illness did recover, and Brooke was feeling optimistic. But one morning she came to the shelter and found two kittens that had been housed together dead in their kennel. Brooke was devastated. They looked okay yesterday, but suddenly they had no life left. The shelter stopped taking in cats and implemented other standard practices to stop the spread of disease. However, over the next two weeks, seven more kittens died much like the first two had. Brooke and the other staff were sad, but also frustrated. Truthfully, they didn't have time to be sad. They still had to try to save the other kittens no matter how futile it seemed.

By the end of the summer, the outbreak of disease had been stopped from spreading. But the shelter lost a total of 17 cats in two months. The animal health manager told Brooke that they had all done everything they could. This type of outbreak happens in shelter environments and sometimes there isn't much that can be done. Brooke believed the health manager, but still felt responsible for what happened. She felt like every kitten that died was a happy home that would never happen. She presents for counseling at the suggestion of a co-worker, who is concerned about her.

Although everyone at the shelter was upset about the kitten outbreak, Brooke can't seem to get over it and move on. It's been several months, and she still talks about it constantly, whether at work or at home with her family. At work she's been preoccupied and forgetful, she's always tired, and she's been seen crying in the break room on several occasions. The final straw was two days ago, when a cat showed signs of a minor respiratory infection. Brooke immediately flashed back to the kitten outbreak. She started to panic and had to leave early that day. Now she's questioning if she can even continue working at the shelter. Maybe she's not strong enough to do this work. Brooke takes her co-worker's advice and seeks professional help.

Discussion Questions:

1. Which assessments, discussed in the chapter or elsewhere, might be useful in working with this client?
2. Discuss how the death of multiple kittens may be different from the death of one animal, and how that impacts mental health treatment.
3. If Brooke decides to continue working at the shelter, what can she do to prevent this level of distress in the future?

References

American Society for the Prevention of Cruelty to Animals. (2017). Pet statistics: Shelter intake and surrender. Retrieved July 15, 2017, from www.aspca.org/animal-homelessness/shelter-intake-and-surrender/pet-statistics

Anderson, G. R., Gurdin., P., & Thomas, A. (1989). Dual disenfranchisement: Foster parenting children with AIDS. In K. Doka (Ed.), *Disenfranchised grief: Recognizing hidden sorrow* (pp. 43–53). New York, NY: Lexington Books.

Arluke, A. (1994). Managing emotions in an animal shelter. In A. Manning, & J. Serpell (Eds.), *Animals and human society* (pp. 145–165). New York, NY: Routledge.

Arluke, A. (2003). The no-kill controversy: Manifest and latent sources of tension. In A. N. Rowan, & D. J. Salem (Eds.), *The State of the Animals II*, (pp. 67–83). Washington, DC: Humane Society Press.

Arluke, A., & Sanders, C. R. (1996). Regarding animals. Philadelphia, PA: Temple University Press.

Arnold, K. A., Turner, N., Barling, J., Kelloway, E. K., & McKee, M. C. (2007). Transformational leadership and psychological well-being: The mediating role of meaningful work. *Journal of Occupational Health Psychology*, 12, 193–203. doi:10.1037/1076-8998.12.3.193

Association of Shelter Veterinarians. (2017). Shelter terminology. Retrieved from www.sheltervet.org/assets/PDFs/shelter%20terminology.pdf

Baldino, R. G. (2009). Success as a foster parent: Everything you need to know about foster care. New York, NY: Penguin.

Bamonti, P. M., Keelan, C. M., Larson, N., Mentrikoski, J. M., Randall, C. L., Sly, S. K., Travers, R. M., & McNeil, D. W. (2014). Promoting ethical behavior by cultivating a culture of self-care during graduate training: A call to action. *Training and Education in Professional Psychology*, 8(4), 253–260.

Baran, B. E., Allen, J. A., Rogelberg, S. G., Spitzmüller, C., DiGiacomo, N. A. (2009). Euthanasia-related strain and coping strategies in animal shelter employees. *Journal of the American Veterinary Medical Association*, 235(1), 83–88.

Baran, B. E., Rogelberg, S. G., Carello Lopina, E., Allen, J. A., Spitzmüller, C., & Bergman, M. (2012). Shouldering a silent burden: The toll of dirty tasks. *Human Relations*, 65(5), 597–626.

Bartlett, P. C., Bartlett, A., Walshaw, S., & Halstead, S. (2005). Rates of euthanasia and adoption for dogs and cats in Michigan animal shelters. *Journal of Applied Animal Welfare Science*, 8(2), 97–104.

Barton Ross, C. (2013). *Pet loss and human emotion: A guide to recovery*. New York, NY: Routledge.

Barton Ross, C., & Baron-Sorensen, J. (2007). *Pet loss and human emotion: A guide to recovery* (2nd ed.).New York, NY: Routledge.

Becvar, D. S. (2003). *In the presence of grief: Helping family members resolve death, dying, and bereavement issues*. New York, NY: Guilford Press.

Boss, P. (1999). *Ambiguous loss: Learning to live with unresolved grief*. Cambridge, MA: Harvard University Press.

Bowlby, J. (1982). Attachment and loss: Retrospect and prospect. *American Journal of Orthopsychiatry*, 52(4), 664.

Boyle, D. A. (2011). Countering compassion fatigue: A requisite nursing agenda. *Online Journal of Issues in Nursing*, 16 (1), 2.

Bradley, J. R., & Cartwright, S. (2002). Social support, job stress, health, and job satisfaction among nurses in the United Kingdom. *International Journal of Stress Management*, 9(3), 163–182.

Brosche, T. A. (2003). Death, dying and the ICU nurse. *Dimensions of Critical Care Nursing*, 22, 173–179.

Brown, W. P., & Morgan, K. T. (2015). Age, breed designation, coat color, and coat pattern influenced the length of stay of cats at a no-kill shelter. *Journal of Applied Animal Welfare Science*, 18(2), 169–180.

Bussolari, C., Habarth, J., Kimpara, S., Katz, R., Carlos, F., Chow, A., Osada,H., Osada, Y., Carmack, B. J., Field, N. P., & Packman, W. (2017). Posttraumatic growth following the loss of a pet: A cross-cultural comparison. *OMEGA-Journal of Death and Dying*, 0 (0), 1–21. doi: 0030222817690403.

Carver, C. S., Scheier, M. F., & Weintraub, J. K. (1989). Assessing coping strategies: A theoretically based approach. *Journal of Personality and Social Psychology*, 56(2), 267.

Chentsova-Dutton, Y., Shucter, S., Hutchin, S., Strause, L., Burns, K., Dunn, L., Miller, M., & Zisook, S. (2002). Depression and grief reactions in hospice caregivers: from pre-death to 1 year afterwards. *Journal of Affective Disorders*, 69(1–3), 53–60.

Chur-Hansen, A. (2010). Grief and bereavement issues and the loss of a companion animal: People living with a companion animal, owners of livestock, and animal support workers. *Clinical Psychologist*, 14(1), 14–21.

Cohen, S., Kamarck, T., & Mermelstein, R. (1983). A global measure of perceived stress. *Journal of Health and Social Behavior*, 24 (4), 385–396.

Conte, T. (2012). Pediatric oncology nurse and grief education: A telephone survey. *Journal of Pediatric Oncology Nursing*, 28, 93–99. doi: 10.1177/1043454210377900

Doka, K. J. (1989). *Disenfranchised grief: Recognizing hidden sorrow*. Lexington, MA: Lexington.

Doka, K. J. (2003). Disenfranchised grief: New directions, challenges, and strategies for practice. Champaign, IL: Research Press.

Dolan-Del Vecchio, K., & Saxton-Lopez, N. (2013). The pet loss companion: Healing advice from family therapists who lead pet loss groups. North Charlestone, SC: CreateSpace Independent Publishing.

Faschingbauer, T. (1981). *The Texas Inventory of Grief – Revised.* Houston, TX: Honeycomb Publishing.

Feldstein, M. A., & Gemma, P. B. (1995). Oncology nurses and chronic compounded grief. *Cancer Nursing,* 18, 228–236.

Field, N. P., Orsini, L., Gavish, R., & Packman, W. (2009). Role of attachment in response to pet loss. *Death Studies,* 33(4), 334–355.

Figley, C. R., & Roop, R. G. (2006). Compassion fatigue in the animal-care community. Washington, DC: Humane Society Press.

Fournier, A. K., & Mustful, B. (2018). Compassion fatigue: Presenting issues and practical applications for animal caring professionals. In, L. Kogan, & C. Blazina (Eds.), *Clinician's Guide to Treating Animal Companion Issues.* New York, NY: Elsevier.

Freeman, S. J. (2005). *Grief & loss: Understanding the journey.* Belmont, CA: Brooks/Cole.

Freud, A. (1917). Mourning and melancholia. *The standard edition of the complete psychological works of Sigmund Freud,* 14, 1914–1916.

Green Cross Academy of Traumatology. (n.d.). Standards of self-care guidelines. Retrieved from http://home.cogeco.ca/~cmc/Standards_of_Self_Care.pdf

Harbolt, T. L. (2003). Bridging the bond: the cultural construction of the shelter pet. Ashland, OH: Purdue University Press.

Hess-Holden, C. L., Monaghan, C. L., & Justice, C. A. (2017). Pet bereavement support groups: A Guide for mental health professionals. *Journal of Creativity in Mental Health,* 12(4), 440–450.

Hughes, E. C. (1962). Good people and dirty work. *Social problems,* 10 (1), 3–11.

Humane Society of the United States. (2012). The HSUS shelter advocate toolkit. Retrieved from www.humanesociety.org/assets/pdfs/pets/shelter-advocate-toolkit/all_shelters_are_not_alike_.pdf

Humane Society of the United States. (2018). Pets by the numbers. Retrieved from www.animalsheltering.org/page/pets-by-the-numbers

Hunt, M., & Padilla, Y. (2006). Development of the pet bereavement questionnaire. *Anthrozoös,* 19 (4), 308–324.

Imber-Black, E. (1991). Rituals and the healing process. *Living Beyond Loss: Death in the Family,* 207–223.

Kamdron, T. (2005). Work motivation and job satisfaction of Estonian higher officials. *International Journal of Public Administration,* 28, 1211–1240.

Kaplan, L. J. (2000). Toward a model of caregiver grief: Nurses' experiences of treating dying children. *OMEGA-Journal of Death and Dying,* 41(3), 187–206.

Keene, E. A., Hutton, N., Hall, B., & Rushton, C. (2010). Bereavement debriefing sessions: An intervention to support health care professionals in managing their grief after the death of a patient. *Continuing Nursing Education,* 36 (4), 185–190.

Kohner, N., & Henley, A. (1997). *When a baby dies: The experience of late miscarriage, stillbirth and neonatal death.* London: Harper Collins.

Lazarus, R. S., & Folkman, S. (1984). Coping and adaptation. In D. Gendery (Ed.), *The handbook of behavioral medicine* (pp. 282–325). New York, NY: Guilford Press.

Lerner, M. J. (1980). *The Belief in a just world* (pp. 9–30). Boston, MA: Springer.

Lips-Wiersma, M., & Wright, S. (2012). Measuring the meaning of meaningful work: Development and validation of the comprehensive meaningful work scale (CMWS). *Group & Organization Management,* 37(5), 655–685.

Marino, P. A. (1998). The effects of cumulative grief in the nurse. *Journal of Intravenous Nursing*, 21(2), 101–104.

Mercer, D. L., & Evans, J. M. (2006). The impact of multiple losses on the grieving process: An exploratory study. *Journal of Loss and Trauma*, 11(3), 219–227.

Michael, C., & Cooper, M. (2013). Post-traumatic growth following bereavement: A systematic review of the literature. *Counselling Psychology Review*, 28(4), 18–33.

New Jr, J. C., Salman, M. D., King, M., Scarlett, J. M., Kass, P. H., & Hutchison, J. M. (2000). Characteristics of shelter-relinquished animals and their owners compared with animals and their owners in US pet-owning households. *Journal of Applied Animal Welfare Science*, 3(3), 179–201.

Nolen-Hoeksema, S., Larson, J. (1999). *Coping With loss*. Mahwah, NJ: London: Routledge.

Norcross, J. C., & Guy, J. D. (2007). *Leaving it at the office: A guide to psychotherapist self-care*. New York, NY: Guilford Press.

Packman, W., Bussolari, C., Katz, R., & Carmack, B. J. (2016). Continuing bonds research with animal companions: Implications for men grieving the loss of a dog. In C. Blazina, & L. R. Kogan (Eds.), *Men and their dogs* (pp. 303–320). Switzerland: Springer.

Packman, W., Bussolari, C., Katz, R., Carmack, B. J., & Field, N. P. (2017). Posttraumatic growth following the loss of a pet. *OMEGA-Journal of Death and Dying*, 75(4), 337–359.

Palmer, C. S., Robertson, I. D., Traub, R. J., Rees, R., & Thompson, R. A. (2010). Intestinal parasites of dogs and cats in Australia: The veterinarian's perspective and pet owner awareness. *The Veterinary Journal*, 183(3), 358–361.

Parkes, C. M. (1988). Bereavement as a psychosocial transition: Processes of adaptation to change. *Journal of Social Issues*, 44(3), 53–65.

Prigerson, H. G., Jacobs, S. C. (2001) Traumatic grief as a distinct disorder: A rationale, consensus criteria, and a preliminary empirical test. In: M. S. Stroebe, R. O. Hansson, W. Stroebe, & H. Schut (Eds.), *Handbook of bereavement research: Consequences, coping and care* (pp. 613–647). Washington, DC: US Psychological Association,

Rando, T. A. (1986). A comprehensive analysis of anticipatory grief: Perspectives, process, promises, and problems. *Loss and Anticipatory Grief*, 3–37.

Raza, A., Rand, J., Qamar, A. G., Jabbar, A., & Kopp, S. (2018). Gastrointestinal parasites in shelter dogs: Occurrence, pathology, treatment and risk to shelter workers. *Animals*, 8(7).

Reeve, C. L., Rogelberg, S. G., Spitzmüller, C., & DiGiacomo, N. (2005). The caring-killing paradox: Euthanasia-related strain among animal-shelter workers. *Journal of Applied Social Psychology*, 35(1), 119–143.

Reynolds, L., & Botha, D. (2006). Anticipatory grief: Its nature, impact, and reasons for contradictory findings. *Counselling, Psychotherapy, and Health*, 2(2), 15–26.

Rowan, A. N., & Kartal, T. (2018). Dog population & dog sheltering trends in the United States of America. *Animals*, 8, 68.

Sharkin, B. S., & Knox, D. (2003). Pet loss: Issues and implications for the psychologist. *Professional Psychology: Research and Practice*, 34(4), 414.

Sife, W. (1998). *The loss of a pet: A guide to coping with the grieving process when a pet dies*. Nashville, TN: Howell Book House.

Simon, J. L. (2008). Anticipatory grief: recognition and coping. *Journal of Palliative Medicine*, 11 (9), 1280–1281.

Spidell, S., Wallace, A., Carmack, C. L., Nogueras-González, G. M., Parker, C. L., & Cantor, S. B. (2011). Grief in healthcare chaplains: An investigation of the presence of disenfranchised grief. *Journal of Health Care Chaplaincy*, 17 (1–2), 75–86.

Steger, M. F., Dik, B. J., & Duffy, R. D. (2012). Measuring meaningful work: The work and meaning inventory (WAMI). *Journal of Career Assessment*, 20(3), 322–337.

Taylor, N. (2010). Animal shelter emotion management: a case of in situ hegemonic resistance? *Sociology*, 44(1), 85–101.

Tedeschi, R. G., & Calhoun, L. G. (2004). Posttraumatic growth: Conceptual foundations and empirical evidence. *Psychological Inquiry*, 15(1), 1–18.

Villeneuve, A., Polley, L., Jenkins, E., Schurer, J., Gilleard, J., Kutz, S., Conboy, G., Benoit, D., Seewald, W., & Gagné, F. (2015). Parasite prevalence in fecal samples from shelter dogs and cats across the Canadian provinces. *Parasites & Vectors*, 8(1), 281.

Wright, P. M. (2017). *Fast facts for the hospice nurse: A concise guide to end-of-life care.* New York, NY: Springer.

8   Prison Populations and Pet Loss

Amy Johnson and Laura Bruneau

Prisoners do not receive a lot of compassion from the general public. However, without providing opportunities for connection and inter-action, inmates may lack the skills to succeed as members of their community (Furst, 2011; Kolstad, 1996). Further, by offering rehabilitative options of varying therapeutic and experiential opportunities, inmates may develop increased levels of patience, impulse control, prosocial skills, and empathy (Allison & Ramaswamy, 2016) Britton & Button, 2005; Furst, 2011). Indeed, a person who can feel the emotions of others may be less likely to steal from or physically harm them. Therapeutic rehabilitation methods that include caring for companion animals have demonstrated increased levels of responsibility, self-esteem, patience, and compassion among the adjudicated (Seivert, Cano, Casey, Johnson, & May, 2016). Prison-based Animal Programs (PAPs) (Furst, 2011) appear to be a cost-effective way to rehabilitate prisoners, reinforce relationship building, and reduce feelings of isolation. The number of PAPs are growing, but more research is needed to support the existing anec-dotal evidence (Mulcahy & McLaughlin, 2013; van Wormer, Kigerl, & Hamilton, 2017).

This chapter guides professionals in better understanding the unique ways in which prisoners experience pet loss. Indeed, the loss of an animal can be minimized by those in the general population and often even more so within the prison setting. Psychotherapists who work with prisoners are in an optimal position to help inmates work through disenfranchised grief. However, psychotherapists do not always understand how to address animal loss, especially within the context of this unique population. There-fore, this chapter examines these issues, with a special focus on PAPs, and concludes with recommendations for counseling practice.

Prison Population

For the 1.5 million inmates in the US (Bureau of Justice Statistics, 2018), life behind bars is extremely stressful. Aside from the obvious stressors of life in prison (e.g., violence, racism, isolation), there is also the potential

Table 8.1 Characteristics of Prison Animal Programs (PAPs)

PAPs should …	Ideal PAPs include …	PAPs should not …
Have participants working to rehabilitate non-human animals in an effort to improve the life circumstances of the animals.	A vocational component, e.g., the opportunity to train for certification as a veterinarian technician or animal groomer.	Produce non-human beings that benefit others by being consumed or otherwise exploited; the care for the welfare of the animals should not be so as to result in increased agricultural profits or value.
Involve humanitarian and compassionate work with animals where life is nurtured regardless of its form.	An educational component whereby participants gain a deeper understanding of the animals with which they work.	Have animals that are present for entertainment purposes, such as a rodeo.
Have a positive social value that allows the participants to engage in a form of restitution to society.	Teaching participants how to administer medicine and other healing techniques to the animals.	Have inmates perform jobs connected to animals that non-incarcerated people can and frequently do choose not to accept, e.g., slaughterhouse and agricultural programs.
Have potential for psychosocial therapeutic benefits for participants.		

Note
Adapted from Furst (2011, pp. 51–53) and used with permission.

loss of self. For example, an inmate wrote in an online blog about his gradual loss of identity:

> I'm reminded every day that my identity is under constant threat. Those in control want me to believe that it is an identity which no longer belongs to me. I can never allow this to be true; my identity is mine alone, it's unique, ever-growing, and it can never be bottled up or contained.
>
> (Ballard, 2015, para. 3)

Despite his crime, this inmate sees himself as a man with value. Incarceration can rob a prisoner of dignity and self-worth, which society often believes is quid pro quo. Punishment is often the goal in prisons, not rehabilitation.

Fifty years ago, the generally accepted belief was that "nothing works" in regard to treatment in prison and recidivism rates (Kolstad, 1996). This perception, unfortunately, persists today. Indeed, the public and judicial systems do not believe in rewarding prisoners with educational and therapeutic programming (Furst, 2011; Strimple, 2003). However, rehabilitation provides the necessary social skills to restore or change self-image as an offender or criminal, thus keeping inmates from returning to prison (Kolstad, 1996).

Furthermore, promoting humanity through various programs can help offenders become better citizens as opposed to better criminals (Furst, 2011). All humans need to feel connected and experience mutual, meaningful relationships (Baumeister & Leary, 1995), as much as they require oxygen, food, and shelter. Because society attempts to dehumanize inmates, prisoners often feel isolated – physically and psychologically. Having animals to love unconditionally provides a critical sense of companionship and belonging, and can enhance the existential need for purpose and meaning (Pachana, Massavelli, & Robleda-Gomez, 2011). It is important to note, however, that in PAPs the animals are not solely present for the therapeutic benefit of the prisoner, as the inmate intentionally interacts with the animal for a specific goal, i.e., wildlife rehabilitation programs, livestock care programs, etc. (Furst, 2007). In fact, in some training programs, puppies are socialized and trained by the inmates to become guide dogs for the visually impaired, or trained for search and detection, while other dogs are given obedience training to increase their chances of being adopted. For more information, Table 8.1 provides a summary of how to design and implement PAPs (Furst, 2011).

Prison-Based Animal Programs

In many PAPs, homeless dogs from animal shelters or assistance dog organizations are brought into the facilities for obedience training with the end goal of adoption in the community, or prisoners may train animals for more specialized work (e.g., service dogs, search and rescue dogs) (Furst, 2011; Mulcahy & McLaughlin, 2013). PAPs can also include various programming, including vocational training, inmate visitation, wildlife rehabilitation, or livestock care (Furst, 2011). In 2006, Furst noted there were around 70 PAPS across the US, and that number is rapidly growing due to the popularity of non-profit programs such as *Cell Dogs, Death Row Dogs, and New Leash on Life* (Millman, 2014). Ten years later, the number of PAPs more than tripled, with Cooke and Farrington (2016) identifying 290 US correctional facilities with dog-training programs. Many of these programs help rescue animals, providing a much-needed service to the community, in addition to meeting animal welfare needs.

Overall, PAPs allow inmates to feel that they are making a contribution to society, rather than taking from or harming society (Furst, 2011). Other benefits to inmates can include an increase in (1) self-esteem, (2) self-worth, (3) self-efficacy, (4) patience, (5) self-control, (6) social skills, (7) well-being, and (8) responsibility, along with decreases in stress and disciplinary actions (Allison & Ramaswamy, 2016; Cooke & Farrington, 2016; Pachana et al., 2011; Turner, 2007). While these programs benefit the inmates, they also benefit the animals. For example, if not provided the opportunity to participate in the program, these animals may be euthanized. In sum, these programs are beneficial to the inmates, institutions, and community (van Wormer et al., 2017), and if the needs of the animals are appropriately addressed, the programs can be positive for the animals too (Huss, 2013).

Research on Prison-Based Animal Programs

A famous example of PAPs is the "Birdman of Alcatraz," which was the basis of a book and movie. Robert Stroud was a violent man who served life in prison for multiple murders. During his imprisonment, Stroud cared for approximately 300 canaries and wrote two books about his findings from raising the birds (Pollock, 2001), earning him the nickname "Bird Seed" (Strimple, 2003). Because of his violent nature, Stroud spent much of his time in solitary confinement. During this time, he found a nest of injured birds and nursed them back to health. Over time, Stroud was provided two extra cells to house and care for his birds (Pollock, 2001). Having the birds provided Stroud with a sense of purpose, and he was able to make several contributions to the study of birds.

The first formal evaluation of a PAP occurred at the Lima State Hospital for the Criminally Insane (Lee, 1983). Established in 1975, this PAP was implemented at a maximum security population (Mulcahy & McLaughlin, 2013; Strimple, 2003). After finding a wounded bird, several of the male inmates provided care by catching insects and feeding the bird. Staff noticed how well the inmates were spontaneously working together to care for the bird, and also noticed an improvement in interactions with staff. As a result, the facility conducted a 1-year study, comparing the unit to a control group of inmates who did not work with animals. Results indicated the inmates in the PAP unit required less medication and had fewer incidents of violence. In particular, the PAP unit had no suicide attempts, whereas the control group has eight suicide attempt the same year (Mulcahy & McLaughlin, 2013; Strimple, 2003).

In a qualitative study, Furst (2007) interviewed 15 female inmates who socialized dogs for later specialized training. Overall, the participants described positive effects. In particular, the inmates developed a variety of prosocial behaviors and enjoyed engaging in the program as a way of giving back to society, or altruism. The inmates also enjoyed the companionship of the animals, which helped to alleviate their emotional needs. In particular, for the female inmates, the dogs often served as surrogate children, which can make the dogs leaving the program much more difficult and emotional for the inmates (Furst, 2007). The concept of female inmates seeing the dogs as children was also a finding in Britton and Button's (2005) qualitative study on dog-adoption programs in prisons.

Although there are some thorough evaluations on PAPs in the scholarly literature (e.g., Furst, 2011), there are very few well-designed empirical studies, and much better research is needed (Bachi, 2013; Mulcahy & McLaughlin, 2013). For dog-training programs, a significant mean effect size was identified for both externalizing outcomes such as recidivism, behavioral consequences, and impulse control and internalizing outcomes that included self-esteem, depression, and self-efficacy (Cooke & Farrington, 2016). Further, a recent study indicated that a service dog training and dog-adoption program could lead to a reduction in infractions, grievances, and sanctions, in addition to higher levels of responsibility among male inmates (van Wormer et al., 2017). Another study in Japan examined a multi-modal PAP as a means to improve stress management of male inmates, resulting in mood improvement as measured by subjective evaluations and decreased salivary cortisol values (Koda et al., 2016).

Further, positive effects have been found in male and female adjudicated youth, including programs such as Teacher's Pet: Dogs and Kids Learning Together in Michigan, which pairs shelter dogs with youths in detention facilities for the dog's eventual adoption in the community. Recently, a study examined 138 juveniles who completed the program and discovered that developing increased patience was listed as a key benefit for the youths (Seivert et al., 2016). Other themes found included increased perseverance and hope, and a desire to give back to the community. This concept of "mutual rehabilitation" was also seen in a study with 70 Scottish male young offenders (Leonardi, Buchanan-Smith, McIvor, & Vick, 2017).

Overall, the aim of any prison program is reduced recidivism. In focusing on these efforts, the promotion of evidence-based programming is critical (Cooke & Farrington, 2016). Moreover, in addition to focusing on recidivism, other critical outcomes such as improving the psychological well-being of inmates (Mulcahy & McLaughlin, 2013), and providing benefit to the community (van Wormer et al., 2017) must be addressed. As previously discussed, many believe that prisons should only exist to provide public safety, rather than to rehabilitate inmates (Furst, 2011). However, as prisons are rapidly becoming "the new mental health institutions" (Jasperson, 2010), PAPs are becoming a viable and logical option.

Why PAPs Work

The numbers of PAPs have been steadily increasing over the past two decades, most likely due to the proliferation of the human–animal bond research which has demonstrated a positive relationship between companion animals and human health and well-being (Mulcahy & McLaughlin, 2013). Prisoners, who are especially vulnerable to social isolation, can interact with loving, sentient beings who do not judge them on their past actions (Furst, 2011). In particular, because of their ability to empathize with rescued animals, many inmates have an easier time connecting with animals than with people (Bekoff, 2008).

Social bonding is necessary for mental and psychological well-being. The similarities between the inmates and animals increase the bonding process. When animals have been homeless, unwanted, abused/neglected, the parallels between these animals and inmates make these animals well-suited for connecting with the inmates (Furst, 2011; Johnson & Bruneau, 2016). Indeed, animals and inmates share a history of not being recognized as having value (Furst, 2007). By working with animals who are viewed as less-fortunate and vulnerable, the inmates may see themselves in a different, more positive light – the animals can impact how inmates label themselves (Furst, 2011). Similarly, inmates in PAPs notice that corrections officers (COs) and staff may treat them a little better due to their interactions with their animals. As one inmate noted, "The COs treat us differently because we're doing something special and worthwhile" (Furst, 2011, p. 128). Practicing prosocial skills with the animals can provide a bridge to these same experiences with humans.

Attachment theory also plays a critical role in explaining human–animal interactions. Current studies posit that attachment exists between humans and companion animals as these bonds meet the four prerequisites of attachment: (1) proximity seeking, (2) safe haven, (3) secure base and, (4) separation distress (Zilcha-Mano, Mikulincer, & Shaver, 2011). Moreover, oxytocin, the "attachment hormone," plays a vital role in attachment and bonding between mothers and their offspring in all mammals (Handlin, Nilsson, Ejdeback, Hydbring-Sandberg, & Moberg, 2012). Oxytocin, a hormone released during human skin-to-skin contact, is also released during interactions between owners and their dogs, possibly leading to a reduction in blood pressure and cortisol levels in both species

(Handlin et al., 2012). Therefore, human–animal interactions may mutually benefit both the human and companion animal.

Certainly, the companionship and unconditional positive regard offered from a non-human animal are of special significance to humans (Cohen, 2015). But what happens when inmates open themselves up to animals, expose their vulnerabilities, and experience unconditional love, only to have the animals leave the facility, become adopted, retire, or die? Invariably, separation will occur between the inmate and the animal.

Grief/Loss with Companion Animals

Pet owners often view companion animals as safe havens, providing stability, unconditional love, loyalty, and authenticity (Zilcha-Mano et al., 2011). When an animal who provides this need for humans is no longer present, the pain can be significant. Humans may form emotional attachments to companion animals that are different from those they share with other humans. Whereas people may not have or feel connections to human beings in their lives, animals can provide an alternative source of love, safety, support, stability, comfort, and unconditional love (Wrobel & Dye, 2003). When that source of connectedness and acceptance is gone, the grief can be overwhelming.

However, grief is not only experienced by those who have pets. Even *knowing of* an animal can result in a person becoming attached in some manner (Cohen, 2015). For example, consider the public outcry in response to the loss of Harambe, the gorilla who was shot by zookeepers due to a tragic incident (Willingham, 2016). Various groups of people, including the media, primatologists, celebrities, and laypersons spoke out angrily in defense of what they deemed a senseless death of a beautiful, powerful, and endangered animal (Kim, 2017).

Moreover, grief for a beloved animal can be severe and can mimic that of the loss of a human (Brown & Symons, 2016; Cohen, 2015; Packman, Field, Carmack, & Ronen, 2011). Signs of grief can be similar in intensity (Podrazik, Shackford, Becker, & Heckert, 2000) in both these situations, and include: (1) feeling angry, (2) having difficulty eating and/or sleeping, (3) avoiding painful reminders, and (4) trouble concentrating (Packman et al., 2011). Other possible symptoms include preoccupation with memories and thoughts of the deceased animal, having flashbacks, and experiencing regret (Packman et al., 2011). Indeed, complicated grief can often mimic symptoms of post-traumatic stress disorder, including intrusion and avoidance (Wagner, Knaevelsrud & Maercker, 2006). Complicated grief is also referred to as prolonged grief disorder and may follow the loss of a close relationship, particularly when the loss is sudden or violent (Shear, 2015). During the initial mourning period, disbelief and numbness are common, as the person might be blaming him or herself, or others for the loss (Cordaro, 2012).

For people who feel isolated from others and have few human attachments, the unconditional support and love from an animal may be even more significant (Sharkin & Knox, 2003). Indeed, people who have strong attachments to the animal, limited social support, and accrued stresses may be at a greater risk for intense grief, and possible social isolation (Toray, 2004; Wrobel & Dye, 2003). In addition, adults with an anxious attachment style (e.g., excessive worrying, dependency) are more likely to develop complicated grief in response to pet loss (Field, Orsini, Gavish & Packman, 2009). Overall, the sense of closeness a person feels to the deceased companion animal is the most relevant factor in determining how severe the grief (Cordaro, 2012; Eckerd, Barnett, & Jett-Dias, 2016).

Cohen (2015) outlined three explanations for the intense, emotional responses to pet loss: (1) the role of pet, (2) the manner in which the pet died, and (3) the person's unique life experiences. When considering the prison population in each of these three areas, the animal may take on several roles (Cohen, 2015), including that of a *bridge* to other social interactions, a *companion* for the inmate to spend time with, and a *significant other* for the inmate – serving as the most important emotional relationship. Regarding the manner in which the animal died, inmates may lose animals due to a variety of reasons, including death, or because the animal left the program. Finally, the context in which the death or loss occurs is unique for incarcerated persons.

Grief and Prisoners

When examining the prison population, many factors impact the inmates' ability to grieve. More than 90% of prisoners have witnessed or been the victim of physical or sexual abuse, regardless of gender (Maschi, Gibson, Zgoba, & Morgen, 2011) which increases the likelihood of mental illness. Living in prison compounds the already fragile mental health of inmates, as prison can be another source of trauma and stress (Maschi et al., 2011). These stresses can include a multiple of losses, in addition to unresolved grief. Indeed, inmates experience many losses, in addition to death, including loss of freedom and control, possessions and jobs, relationships and spirituality, and hopes and dreams (Olson & McEwen, 2004).

In general, however, little is known about grief among inmates (Harner, Hentz, & Evangelista, 2011; Olson & McEwen, 2004). A qualitative study by Harner and colleagues (2011) indicated that for female inmates, there are limited counseling options for addressing complicated grief. The female inmates in this study expressed themes such as feeling frozen in time, having no space for grieving, needing to bury feelings, and feeling lonely. For many of the participants, the interviews were the first time they felt they could even talk about their grief with another (Harner et al., 2011). Certainly, for some inmates, the consequences of exhibiting normal grief behaviors may include being medicated, being placed in an alternative cell, or being put on suicide watch (Schetky, 1998).

Besides, trusting other inmates and exposing vulnerabilities can be harmful within this environment. Inmates can torment each other as a way to remain a *top dog*, making it difficult for inmates to show emotion, further perpetuating the cycle of shame (Schetky, 1998). Because of the need to maintain a strong image, mourning the loss of an animal might be seen as showing vulnerability. For example, the first author has often heard adolescents in a PAP express that being "soft" (e.g., showing emotion, being empathic) was dangerous to their well-being. In addition to society, and the prison system, inmates themselves may also dismiss the *right* to grieve, denying their dignity (Attig, 2004a),

Without the proper acknowledgment, the griever does not have access to appropriate support, which results in disenfranchised grief (Doka, 2008). Disenfranchised grief comes from three factors (Humphrey, 2009): (1) the relationship is not recognized by society, (2) the griever is not socially recognized as capable of grieving, or should get over the loss quickly, and (3) death is not recognized as a legitimate loss. Although awareness of the human–animal bond has increased in recent years, many people refuse to acknowledge that pets can be a legitimate attachment figure, and consider the loss insignificant because pets can be easily replaced (Wrobel & Dye, 2003). Often, because it is "just an animal," the sadness over the loss is minimized or dismissed by others.

Most cultures allow for specific rituals to mourn the loss of a human (e.g., funeral) but the loss of non-human animals might often be ignored (Cohen, 2015). This minimization may be a lack of awareness or understanding of the level of attachment a person had with the animal (Packman et al., 2011). As inmates are removed from their natural support system (Olson & McEwen, 2004), they are especially prone to disenfranchised grief. When people are not allowed to grieve, or when the loss is not recognized as valid, certain emotions can result, including anger and powerlessness (Olson & McEwen, 2004).

Psychotherapists must consider a variety of ways to conceptualize the impact of the loss of an animal (Cohen, 2015; Toray, 2004; Worden, 2008). Table 8.2 provides an overview of questions to consider when assessing grief and loss and extends these to the prison population. By having an understanding of these various factors, the psychotherapist can be better prepared to assist inmates in the healing process. Further, asking questions about a beloved companion animal can be a venue to discuss attachments and related behaviors with the inmates.

Table 8.2 Conceptualizing Grief and Loss for Prisoners

Question	Potential Impact
How much time did the animal and inmate spend together?	The more time spent together, the stronger the inmate may feel the loss of the animal.
Does the relationship with the animal represent another relationship in his life?	Taking care of the animal may be a substitute for other important relationships.
What role does the animal play in the life of the inmate?	If the animal was seen as a friend or confidant, this loss might be a critical void for the inmate.
How did the animal die, or leave the program?	If the animal died suddenly or traumatically, the inmate may not feel prepared or and may feel angry and out of control. Conversely, if the animal was adopted, the inmate may accept the transition and/ or feel proud.
What else was going on at that time for the inmate?	Other stresses and difficult life events can compound the loss for an inmate. Inmates have few options for getting help in prison.
Does the inmate have attachment issues?	Having a considerable amount of previous loss can complicate the grieving process. The inmate may feel intense emotions and have little coping skills.
How does the inmate identify with the animal?	Inmates may feel as if the animal understands them, strengthening the connection and bond.

Note
Adapted from (Cohen, 2015; Toray, 2004; Worden, 2008).

Implications for Practice

Addressing grief is not a "one-size-fits-all" approach (Hall, 2014). There is no single theory available to explain the grief process (Toray, 2004); however, there are suggestions to aid in the healing process. First, it's essential to understand that if the grief is not addressed properly, the inmate can lose the benefits gained from PAPs. For example, an inmate may see him or herself differently, such as being a healer (Cohen, 2015). The animal may have also served an important social role for the inmate, and that void needs to be examined and understood in order not to hinder progress made.

Next, it's critical to address maladaptive symptoms, such as suicidal thoughts and depression. The prison population, and in particular young offenders, are especially vulnerable to suicide (Finlay & Jones, 2000; Stroebe, Schut, & Stroebe, 2007). Young adult inmates are also more likely to have lost a first-degree relative, often due to violence or suicide (Finlay & Jones, 2000), leading to potentially complicated grief reactions. Staff will also want to be sure to assess for increased risk of physical health problems (Stroebe et al., 2007).

At the core, it is also necessary to acknowledge the loss to demonstrate non-judgmental acceptance and to validate the person's experience (Sharkin & Knox, 2003). Acknowledging the possibility of, and educating about, disenfranchised grief with the inmate can help to normalize stigmatized emotions, as well as affirm the grief (Cordero, 2012). For psychotherapists, this means *re-enfranchising* the grief through validation of pain (Cordaro, 2012; Doka, 2008). Helping people work through feelings of guilt and regret will help move them along the continuum of grief and loss (Kessler & Kübler-Ross, 2005).

Uncovering the meaning of the relationship with the animal will shape treatment techniques (Cordaro, 2012; Hall et al., 2004). Knowing the depth of the bond between inmate and animal, and the role the animal played allow psychotherapists to be most responsive to the unique grief process (Cordaro, 2012). Essentially, psychotherapists will want to ensure there is open communication with the inmate, taking the time to process the loss in full, therefore demonstrating an interest in the inmate's relationship with the animal (Worden, 2008).

Further, being able to express intense emotions, including anger, is a necessary part of the healing process for grief (Stroebe et al., 2007). A support group is a useful modality for grief work (Cohen, 2015) as it provides an opportunity for social support within the context of the unique prison culture (Olson & McEwen, 2004). Specific interventions that could be helpful in an individual or group modality, include: (1) implementing rituals (e.g., funeral), (2) supporting spirituality, (3) using writing assignments, (4) incorporating creative techniques (e.g., memory book or album), (5) initiating fundraising campaigns for other animals in need,

(6) integrating bibliotherapy or self-help approaches, and (7) developing psychoeducational materials regarding grief and loss (Cordaro, 2012; Cohen, 2015; Hall, 2014; Packman et al., 2011; Podrazik et al., 2000; Wagner et al., 2006; Worden, 2008).

With PAPs, in particular, it will be necessary for the inmate to process the loss of an animal before they can take care of another animal in the program. In these circumstances, there can be predetermined expectations for the new animal, or guilty feelings in caring for a new animal (Cordaro, 2012). The grief process can also happen before ending the relationship with the animal. For example, if an animal is adopted or retires, it will be important for the psychotherapist to recognize the signs of anticipatory grief, and normalize this type of reaction (Cordaro, 2012). The first author has experienced this phenomenon on several occasions. As the PAP nears completion, the residents may state they no longer like their dogs, or that they dislike the program as a defense mechanism. These instances, however, provide an opportunity to discuss the pain of saying goodbye to the animal. For examples, the residents are encouraged to share common feelings with other residents, or complete writing exercises (e.g., journaling, writing letters to the adopters).

However, grief and loss are not always negative experiences. New research is exploring post-traumatic growth associated with loss, considering how loss can be transformational and result in close relationships and a different perspective on life (Packman et al., 2011). The essence of grieving is finding meaning in suffering (Attig, 2004b). Indeed, death may be a meaning-seeking adventure. Hall (2014) concurred with this idea and proposed that grief work is about making sense of loss, as well as finding benefits associated with the loss. The benefits of loss are not always clear at first, and may only come with time.

Conclusion

Although the field of bereavement has transformed in recent years (Hall, 2014), there is still little known about how prisoners experience grief, and how this might impact their participation in a PAP. Indeed, this is a new area of inquiry. What we do know is that psychotherapists must recognize that inmates also experience grief, and this loss can extend to the animals within the PAPS. Validating the loss of the animal and processing the meaning behind the loss is enormously helpful in furthering the potential benefits gained from the PAP.

Finally, there is a high risk of burnout for psychotherapists who work in the prison setting due to increased incidents of suicide and sexual assault, in addition to mental illness (Carrola, Olivarez, & Karcher, 2016). This burnout, which may include emotional exhaustion and depersonalization, may hinder self-awareness and ability to connect with inmates' loss. Overall, self-care for practitioners in this setting should be encouraged.

Case Scenarios

Case Scenario #1:

In a juvenile justice center, Marcus, aged 15, participated in a PAP. Marcus had been in the facility a total of two times, with the first sentence for assault on his mother's boyfriend. The second sentence was for probation violation. After the initial assault, Marcus claimed he was physically and sexually harmed by the boyfriend, but the mother did not believe him and pressed charges against him for the attack. His mother subsequently moved out of state with his siblings, and Marcus had no other immediate family in the area. A grandmother whom Marcus was especially close to had recently passed away due to illness.

At the facility, the staff assessed Marcus as a good candidate for the PAP. In this program, homeless dogs were brought into the facility, five-weeks at a time for training. The goal of the program was for the dogs to be adopted by a community member. The first dog that Marcus worked with was a 3-year-old, mixed breed (Labrador/Pitbull) named "Abbie." Marcus worked with Abbie approximately ten hours a week. During her training, Marcus worked hard to keep her from jumping on people and from being overly active. Yet, with patience and persistence, Marcus excelled at teaching her basic commands, and Abbie was adopted within a month.

Marcus was excited about Abbie and her new family but was sad to lose his friend who loved him unconditionally. However, Marcus never told anyone he was upset, but when his next dog entered the program, he refused to work with him. Marcus stated he was proud of his work with Abbie, and no other dog was going to compare to her. While the other residents worked with their dogs, Marcus sat off to the side, sometimes making negative comments about the program or the other trainers. Other residents and the program facilitator introduced Marcus to new dogs, but he would turn his head away and mutter, "No thanks."

Discussion Questions:

1. How could the psychotherapist approach the idea of grief and loss with Marcus?
2. Why might Marcus not want to continue in the program? How might the psychotherapist help him make a different decision?
3. Describe two activities a psychotherapist could implement that would help Marcus work through his grief and loss.

Case Scenario #2:

Gina, a 32-year-old woman, spent the last 22 months in prison. Gina had a history of substance abuse and was a victim of intimate partner violence.

After consuming too much alcohol and smoking marijuana at a friend's house one night, Gina left with her 2-year-old daughter. While driving, Gina fell asleep and went through a red light where she hit an oncoming car. Neither her daughter, Sienna, nor the couple in the other car survived the crash. Subsequently, Gina was charged with vehicular manslaughter and was serving the first part of her 15-year sentence.

After initially having a difficult time adjusting to life in prison, Gina decided to participate in a PAP in which she raised a puppy for up to 1-year. In this program, the puppies were undergoing training for a service dog organization. At first, Gina was hesitant to become a puppy raiser, but she wanted to make a change in her life and asked if she could participate. The staff saw this as a good sign and put her into the program. Gina handled responsibility for the puppy's care without complaint and gave him plenty of affection and attention. She would often joke with other inmates or corrections officers that "Joey," the Labrador retriever puppy, was her son. Gina was often seen carrying Joey around like a baby. Overall, while in the PAP, her behavior has been positive and she followed the rules without consequence.

However, after several months of raising the puppy, he developed an illness and died due to complications. Gina was inconsolable, refusing to leave her cell and to eat. When she would leave her cell, she would stare off into the distance, and not engage with the other inmates of staff. When someone tried to talk with her, Gina would brush them off, stating she was "fine."

Discussion Questions:

1. How could the psychotherapist approach the loss of the puppy with Gina?
2. Why might Gina be having such difficulty with the loss of the puppy? How might the psychotherapist help her identify her unresolved grief?
3. Name two activities a psychotherapist could implement that would help Gina work through her grief and loss.

References

Allison, M., & Ramaswamy, M. (2016). Adapting animal-assisted therapy trials to prison-based animal programs. *Public Health Nursing*, 33(5), 472–480. doi: 10.1111/phn.12276

Attig, T. (2004a). Disenfranchised grief revisited: Discounting hope and love. *Omega*, 49, 197–215.

Attig, T. (2004b). Meanings of death seen through the lens of grieving. *Death Studies*, 28, 341–360.

Bachi, K. (2013). Equine-facilitated prison-based animal programs within the context of prison-based animal programs: State of the science review. *Journal of Offender Rehabilitation*, 52, 46–74. doi: 10.1080/10509674.2012.734371

Ballard. (2015, April). Stress in prison. *The Beat Within*. Retrieved from https:// thecrimereport.org/2015/04/17/2015-04-stress-in-prison/#

Baumeister, R. F., & Leary, M. R. (1995). The need to belong: Desire for interpersonal attachments as a fundamental human motivation. *Psychological Bulletin*, 117(3), 497–529.

Bekoff, M. (2008). Why "Good Welfare" isn't "Good Enough": Minding animals and increasing our compassionate footprint. ARBS Annual Review of Biomedical Sciences. Theme Topic on "Unraveling Animal Welfare." Retrieved from https://animalstudiesrepository.org/cgi/viewcontent.cgi?article=1060&context =acwp_awap

Britton, D. M., & Button, A. (2005). Prison pups: Assessing the effects of dog training programs in correctional facilities. *Journal of Family Social Work*, 9(4), 79–95. doi: 10.1300/J039v09n04_06

Brown, O. K., & Symons, D. K. (2016). "My pet has passed": Relations of adult attachment styles and current feelings of grief and trauma after the event. *Death Studies*, 40(4), 247–255.

Bureau of Justice Statistics (2018). Key Statistics – Prisoners. Retrieved from www. bjs.gov/index.cfm?ty=kfdetail&iid=488

Carrola, P. A., Olivarez, A., & Karcher, M. J. (2016). Correctional counselor burnout: Examining burnout rates using the counselor burnout inventory. *Journal of Offender Rehabilitation*, http://dx.doi.org/10.1080/10509674.2016.1149134

Cohen, S. P. (2015). Loss of a therapy animal: Assessment and healing. In A. H. Fine (Ed.). *Handbook on Animal-Assisted Therapy* (pp. 341–355). San Diego, CA: Elsevier.

Cooke, B. J., & Farrington, D. P. (2016). The effectiveness of dog-training programs in prison: A systematic review and meta-analysis of the literature. *The Prison Journal*, 96(6), 854–876. doi: 10.1177/0032885516671919

Cordaro, M. (2012). Pet loss and disenfranchised grief: Implications for mental health counseling practice. *Journal of Mental Health Counseling*, 34(4), 283–294.

Doka, K. J. (2008). Disenfranchised grief in historical and cultural perspective. In M. S. Stroebe, R.O. Hansson, H. Schut, & W. Storebe (Eds.), *Handbook of bereavement research and practice: Advances in theory and intervention* (pp. 223–240). Washington, DC: American Psychological Association.

Eckerd, L., Barnett, J., & Jett-Dias, L. (2016). Grief following pet and human loss: Closeness is key. *Death Studies*, 40(5), 275–282. doi: 10.1080/07481187. 2016.1139014

Field, N. P., Orsini, L., Gavish, R., & Packman, W. (2009). Role of attachment in response to pet loss. *Death Studies*, 33(4), 334–355.

Finlay, I. G., & Jones, N. K. (2000). Unresolved grief in young offenders in prison. *British Journal of General Practice*, 50, 569–570.

Furst, G. (2011). *Animal programs in prison: A comprehensive assessment*. Boulder, CO: First Forum Press.

Furst, G. A. (2007). Without words to get in the way: Symbolic interactions in prison-based animal programs. *Qualitative Sociology Review*, 3(1), 96–109.

Hall, C. (2014). Bereavement theory: Recent developments in our understanding of grief and bereavement. *Bereavement Care*, 33(1), 7–12.

Hall, M. J., Ng, A., Ursano, R., Holloway, H., Fullerton, C., & Casper, J. (2004). Psychological impact of the animal-human bond in disaster preparedness and response. *Journal of Psychiatric Practice*, 10, 368–374.

Handlin, L., Nilsson, A., Ejdeback, M., Hydbring-Sandberg, E., & Uvnas-Moberg, K. (2012). Associations between the psychological characteristics of the human–dog relationship and oxytocin and cortisol levels. *Anthrozoös*, 25(2), 215–228.

Harner, H., Hentz, P., & Evangelista, M. (2011). Grief interrupted: The experience of loss among incarcerated women. *Qual Health Res*, 21(4), 454–464. doi: 10.1177/1049732310373257.

Humphrey, K. (2009). *Counseling strategies for loss and grief.* Alexandria, VA: American Counseling Association.

Huss, R. (2013). Canines (and cats) in correctional institutions: Legal and ethical issues relating to companion animal programs. *Nev. LJ.*, 14, 25–62.

Jasperson, R. A. (2010). Animal-assisted therapy with female inmates with mental illness: A case example from a pilot program. *Journal of Offender Rehabilitation*, 49, 417–433. doi: 10.1080/10509674.2010.499056

Johnson, A., & Bruneau, L. (2016). Healing bonds: Animal-assisted interventions with adjudicated male youth. In C. Blazina & L. Kogan (Eds.). *Men and their dogs: A new psychological understanding of "man's best friend"* (pp. 113–132). New York, NY: Springer.

Kessler, D., & Kübler-Ross, E. (2005). *On grief and grieving: Finding the meaning of grief through the five stages of loss.* New York, NY: Simon & Schuster.

Kim, C. (2017). Murder and mattering in Harambe's house. *Politics and Animals*, 1–15.

Koda, N., Watanabe, G., Miyaji, Y., Kuniyoshi, M., Mijayi, C., & Hirata, T. (2016). Effects of a dog-assisted intervention assessed by salivary cortisol concentrations in inmates of a Japanese prison. *Asian Criminology*, 11, 309–319.

Kolstad, A. (1996). Imprisonment as rehabilitation: Offenders' assessment of why it does not work. *Journal of Criminal Justice*, 24(4), 323–335.

Lee, D. R. (1983). Pet therapy – helping patients through troubled times. *California Veterinarian*, 5, 24–25.

Leonardi, R., Buchanan-Smith, H., McIvor, G., & Vick, S. J. (2017). "You think you're helping them, but they're helping you too": Experiences of Scottish male young offenders participating in a dog training program. *International journal of environmental research and public health*, 14(8), 945.

Maschi, T., Gibson, S., Zgoba, K., & Morgen, K. (2011). Trauma and life event stressors among young and older adult prisoners. *Journal of Correctional Health Care*, 17(2), 160–172. doi: 10.1177/1078345810396682

Millman, J. (2014, March 18). Prisons give unruly rescue dogs a second chance. *Wall Street Online.*

Mulcahy, C., & McLaughlin, D. (2013). Is the tail wagging the dog? A review of the evidence for prison animal programs. *Australian Psychologist*, 48, 369–378. doi:10.1111.ap. 12021

Olson, M. J., & McEwen, M.A. (2004). Grief counseling groups in a medium-security prison. *Journal for Specialists in Group Work*, 29(2), 225–236.

Pachana, N., Massavelli, B., & Robleda-Gomez, S. (2011). A developmental psychological perspective on the human–animal bond. In C. Blazina, G. Boyraz, & Shen-Miller, D.N. (Eds.). *The Psychology of the human-animal bond* (pp. 151–165). New York, NY: Springer.

Packman, W., Field, N. P., Carmack, B. J., & Ronen, R. (2011). Continuing bonds and psychosocial adjustment in pet loss. *Journal of Loss and Trauma*, 16(4), 341–357.

Podrazik, D., Shackford, S., Becker, L., & Heckert, T. (2000). The death of a pet: Implications for loss and bereavement across the lifespan. *Journal of Personal & Interpersonal Loss*, 5(4), 361–395.

Pollock, C. (2001). The Birdman of Alcatraz. *Journal of Avian Medicine and Surgery*, 15(2), 131–132.

Schetky, D. (1998). Mourning in prison: Mission impossible? *Journal of the American Academy of Psychiatry Law*, 26(3), 383–391.

Seivert, N. P., Cano, A., Casey, R. J., Johnson, A., & May, D. K. (2016). Animal assisted therapy for incarcerated youth: A randomized controlled trial. *Applied Developmental Science*, 22(2), 139–153.

Sharkin, B. S., & Knox, D. (2003). Pet loss: Issues and implications for the psychologist. *Professional Psychology: Research and Practice*, 34(4), 414–421.

Shear, M. (2015). Complicated grief. *The New England Journal of Medicine*, 372(2), 153–160.

Strimple, E. O. (2003). A history of prison inmate–animal interaction programs. *American Behavioral Scientist*, 47(1), 70–78.

Stroebe, M., Schut, H., & Stroebe, W. (2007). Health outcomes of bereavement. *The Lancet*, 370, 1960–1973.

Toray, T. (2004). The human–animal bond and loss: Providing support for grieving clients. *Journal of Mental Health Counseling*, 26(3), 244–259.

Turner, W. (2007). The experiences of offenders in a prison canine program. *Federal Probation*, 71(1), 38–43.

van Wormer, J., Kigerl, A., & Hamilton, Z. (2017). Digging deeper: Exploring the value of prison-based handler programs. *The Prison Journal*, 97(4), 520–538.

Wagner, B., Knaevelsrud, C., & Maercker, A. (2006). Internet-based cognitive behavioral therapy for complicated grief: A randomized control trial. *Death Studies*, 30, 429–453. doi: 10.1080/07481180600614385

Willingham, A. J. (2016). Harambe, Cecil: Why we mourn animal deaths so intensely. *CNN*. Retrieved from www.cnn.com/2016/06/02/health/harambe-gorilla-cincinnati-zoo-why-we-mourn-trnd/index.html

Worden, J. (2008). Grief counseling and grief therapy: A handbook for the mental health practitioner (4th ed.). New York, NY: Springer.

Wrobel, T., & Dye, A. (2003). Grieving pet death: Normative, gender and attachment issues. *Omega*, 47(4), 385–393.

Zilcha-Mano, S., Mikulincer, M., & Shaver, P. (2011). An attachment perspective on human–pet relationships: Conceptualization and assessment of pet attachment orientations. *Journal of Research in Personality*, 45, 345–357.

9 Grieving Without a Home

Homelessness and the Loss of an Animal

Christine Kim

Introduction

Home is a deceptively simple concept – one that is innately understood yet difficult to articulate, and one that encapsulates both the "where" and the "who" of our most intimate selves. It is a product of our nesting behavior, linked to instincts that far predate modern society. Belonging to a home is a primitive human experience, which is perhaps why we are so confounded when confronted by its material absence. Today, over half a million people in the United States are homeless (US Department of Housing and Urban Development, Henry et al., 2018), and although there are proven methods to end and prevent homelessness, the conversation about bringing people home on a national scale seems ever more wrought with disagreement. While home is something we fundamentally grasp (Mallett, 2004), there is nothing simple about the real application of securing this most basic need for all people and all families (Minnery & Greenhalgh, 2007).

Intimately linked to the concept of home is the similarly simple and complex concept of family. While today's progressive discussions on family move beyond husband, wife, and 2.5 children, those with compositions outside the conventional mold will still have difficulty navigating the already onerous homeless services system. Recent movements to reduce the number of street homeless individuals on the West Coast of the United States have given rise to a clever catchphrase developed to demarcate new and old ways of thinking about shelter access, as well as chosen family units – ones that accept or do not accept the "three p's": pets, partners, and possessions (Beekman, 2017; Orrock, 2016).

Major metropolitan areas like San Francisco, Los Angeles, Sacramento, and Seattle, as well as other smaller municipalities dotted along the West Coast, have embraced the low-barrier shelter model, which lowers the threshold for accessing a shelter bed (National Alliance to End Homelessness, 2018a). In this model, substance use, pets, possessions, and unmarried partners are not criteria to shut people out of the shelter, making such facilities havens for people who are often the most difficult for the system to engage.

The importance of such spaces should not be underestimated. While a low-barrier shelter bed may be far from a permanent home, it is often the first step to housing assistance and access to a wide variety of services that can help address other life stressors. Pets, while largely ignored by homeless services until recently, can play an integral role in the lives of the people who love them, and a space which welcomes furry family members can open up a whole new realm of possibilities for their human caregivers. But this also presents new challenges for homeless service workers and mental health practitioners who may be witnessing the human–animal bond in such circumstances for the first time.

Among the many human–animal bond specific clinical issues which may arise in the context of homelessness, pet loss and grief is one for which mental health practitioners should prepare. Given the violence, trauma, and precariousness that characterize the experience of homelessness, the loss of a consistent source of companionship and security can take an even greater toll on the lives of people who have little else besides their faithful animal.

Little is known about simultaneously enduring homelessness and pet loss grief, except that it is a significant theme during the experience of homelessness itself (Slatter, Lloyd, & King, 2012). Despite the lack of research that has been dedicated to this topic so far, clinicians should be aware of this subpopulation and the unique challenges individuals face during pet loss bereavement. With the increasing integration of mental health treatment into homeless services, more clinicians may find themselves exposed to pet loss grief with this population in their practice. This chapter is a brief primer about homelessness and animal companionship for clinicians. The chapter will also give opportunities to apply themes of pet loss and grief to this population through two in-depth case studies.

Who is Homeless?

Homelessness is a growing problem in the United States, with a steady 3-year uptick after years of a declining population count. Data compiled from the 2018 point-in-time count, a national homeless census, revealed that there were approximately 552,830 people experiencing homelessness on a given night in the United States (US Department of Housing and Urban Development, Henry et al., 2018). The same report revealed the following themes in American homelessness:

- 65% of people experiencing homelessness stayed in sheltered locations, such as an emergency shelter, transitional housing program, or a safe haven, while 35% stayed in unsheltered locations not designated for regular sleeping accommodations, such as the streets, vehicles, or parks.
- 70% of unsheltered people were men or boys.

- 60% of people experiencing homelessness overall (both sheltered and unsheltered) were men or boys, 39% were women or girls, and less than 1% were either transgender or gender non-conforming.
- Two out of every three people experiencing homelessness were adults in households without children, and the remaining 33% of the population experienced family homelessness.
- African Americans are disproportionately represented among the homeless population compared to the overall US population. African Americans account for 13% of the US population, 40% of all people experiencing homelessness, and 51% of people experiencing homelessness with children.

It is also important to note that many people experiencing homelessness get up, get dressed, and contribute to commercial society every day but still struggle to reconcile their stagnant, low wages and the rising cost of living (National Alliance to End Homelessness, 2013, 2017). New data reinforces the particular importance of the cost of housing, poverty rates, and their impact on community homelessness rates – communities where people spend more than 32% of their income on rent can expect a more rapid increase in homelessness (Glynn, Byrne, & Culhane, 2018). Unfortunately, the National Alliance to End Homelessness (2017) reported that there were nearly 7 million people who faced a severe housing cost burden who contributed greater than 50% of their income toward rent in 2016. In such financial circumstances, there are multitudes who are just one emergency away from becoming homeless.

But homelessness and its causes are more complex than a rent to income ratio. Although there are groups of people who are more vulnerable to homelessness due to social location and social determinants of life outcomes, homelessness is still ubiquitous and can affect people from diverse backgrounds and income brackets (National Alliance to End Homelessness, 2018b; Shelton, Taylor, Bonner, & van Den Bree, 2009). Mental health practitioners, even those who are not specifically employed by homeless service organizations, may encounter clients experiencing homelessness due to the growing affordable housing crisis and the expansion of health care coverage.

It is important to remember that while the point-in-time census and other quantitative data provide an understanding of the breadth of homelessness, the experience of homelessness should not simply be reduced to numbers. People who experience homelessness are individuals, parts of family units, and have complex stories often colored by trauma narratives.

Homelessness, Mental Health, and Trauma

The US Department of Housing and Urban Development, the federal agency responsible for overseeing and administering funds to the country's homeless service organizations, reported that of the 552,830 people experiencing homelessness on a given night in January, 20% had a severe mental illness, and another 16% engaged in chronic substance abuse (2018). While severe behavioral health conditions may present themselves among individuals experiencing homelessness, it should be noted that these disorders are not evenly distributed across all homeless subpopulations (Lippert & Lee, 2015). The homeless population as a whole is made up of diverse subgroups, within each a plethora of nuanced individual and group experiences (North, Smith, Pollio, & Spitznagel, 1996). Clinicians seeking a deeper understanding of the prevalence of certain mental health conditions among people experiencing homelessness should better understand the key subgroup differences.

However, one mental health experience which traverses all categorical boundaries is trauma, which is endemic to homelessness. Not only is the experience of homelessness itself traumatic, but traumatic events are both an antecedent and consequence of homelessness (Browne, 1993; Goodman, Saxe, & Harvey, 1991; Rayburn et al., 2005). It is well documented that people who experience homelessness, especially those who have been chronically or repeatedly homeless, have higher rates of early childhood traumatic experiences (Bassuk, Perloff, & Dawson, 2001; Christensen et al., 2005; Deck & Platt, 2015; Kim, Ford, Howard, & Bradford, 2010). Mental health practitioners in the service of a client experiencing homelessness should expect to treat compounded trauma over the life course (Kim & Ford, 2006; Lippert & Lee, 2015). Also, rates of violent and traumatic incidents such as physical and sexual assault, particularly for women, skyrocket once they have entered into homelessness (Kushel, Evans, Perry, Robertson, & Moss, 2003; Lewinson, Thomas, & White, 2014; Rayburn et al., 2005).

Treating trauma is now understood to be critical to the mental health care of the homeless population, to address distress and affect the individual's ability to cope with the obstacles of exiting homelessness (Bassuk et al., 2001). Yet programs which do not make explicit efforts to create a trauma-informed care framework may miss translating that general awareness into practice. Unfortunately, the adoption of trauma-informed care within homeless services is still in its early stages (Hopper, Bassuk, & Olivet, 2010). Thus, it is not uncommon for homeless service workers and entire programs to engage trauma survivors without a direct awareness of how trauma may present or how to specifically treat trauma.

Implementing trauma-informed care requires a heavy organizational lift, committing staff on every level to understand and develop tools for responding to trauma. As a first step, mental health practitioners should be informed of trauma-specific services for their own clinical work with this population, including any work that is done around the traumatic loss and grief over a pet. But clinicians who understand the importance of this work must also educate and advocate for changes on an organizational scale, helping to ensure that staff along all points of the continuum of services are equipped to "do no harm" to clients with complex needs (Deck & Platt, 2015; Foster, LeFauve, Kresky-Wolff, & Rickards, 2010; Hopper et al., 2010; Lewinson et al., 2014).

Introduction to Homelessness and Animal Companionship

There are federal resources dedicated to understanding the various sub-groups of people experiencing homelessness, but animal guardians have yet to be seen as a legitimate subpopulation. As a result, little is known about people who experience homelessness with an accompanying animal, including their ubiquity. There are no federal statistics and few other formal data sets that quantify animal guardianship among people experiencing homelessness, revealing homeless services' lack of attention to the human–animal bond (Kim, 2019a). And until recently, there has been infrequent academic exploration of the special clinical, programmatic, and policy related interventions that can be implemented to address the specific needs of this subpopulation.

What is understood, however, are some of the benefits and liabilities of animal companionship for people experiencing homelessness. Homelessness is often characterized by feelings of isolation, stigma, greater rates of incarceration, poor physical health, and high rates of physical and sexual assault, as well as other types of traumatic experiences (Goodman, 1991; Greenberg & Rosenheck, 2008; Kushel et al., 2003; National Health Care for the Homeless Council, 2011; Phelan, Link, Moore, & Stueve, 1997). But animal guardianship in the homeless population has been identified as a buffer against many of these negative outcomes, and it has been shown to assist both adults and youth coping with depression and other mental health conditions (Bender, Thompson, McManus, Lantry & Flynn, 2007; Rew, 2000; Singer, Hart, & Zasloff, 1995). Qualitative interviewees have described animal caregiving as providing them with a sense of responsibility and contributing to the construction of a positive moral identity. Moreover, animals can provide constant companionship and unconditional love, protection, and as act as deterrents to engaging in risky behaviors which may lead to incarceration or other circumstances that will separate them from their animal (Bender et al., 2007; Irvine, 2013; Irvine, Kahl, & Smith, 2012; Lem, Coe, Haley, Stone, & O'Grady, 2013; Rhoades, Winetrobe, & Rice, 2015).

Due to the important role companion animals play in the lives of people experiencing homelessness, the loss of an animal might result in severe grief. As one study shows, the strongest indicator of grief severity is not species (loss of a human as opposed to loss of an animal), but closeness (Eckerd, Barnett, & Jett-Dias, 2016). Gosse and Barnes (1994) also found that high levels of attachment, limited social support, and accumulated stressful events were predictive of high levels of grief over the death of a pet – all of which permeate the experience of homelessness. Although neither study focused specifically on homelessness, findings may translate to the homeless population given that people experiencing homelessness have even greater empathy and attachment scores than the average scores collected from the domiciled, as measured by the Lexington Attachment to Pets Scale and adapted version of the Animal Empathy and Companion Animal Bonding Scales (Johnson, Garrity, & Stallones, 1991; Kim, 2019a; Singer et al., 1995; Taylor, Williams, & Gray, 2004).

Existing literature also shows that certain types of death may lead to excessive or traumatic grief reactions, particularly violent death (e.g., vehicle collisions, homicide, etc.) (Kaltman & Bonanno, 2003; Lehman, Wortman, & Williams, 1987; Murphy et al., 1999; Thompson, Norris, & Ruback, 1998). Given the violent nature of homelessness, pet death by violence, as opposed to natural means, may very well occur.

In addition to potential severe reactions to pet loss, there are other drawbacks of animal guardianship for people experiencing homelessness. For example, veterinary care has been noted as very difficult to obtain (Kidd & Kidd, 1994; Rhoades et al., 2015). It is also well documented that accompanying animals can become a barrier to accessing social services for people experiencing homelessness. Due to the no-pets-allowed culture in most service organizations, animal guardians experiencing homelessness often find themselves barred from shelter, housing, medical, and food services (Garrett et al., 2008; Pedersen, Tucker, & Kovalchik, 2016; Rhoades et al., 2015; Slatter, Lloyd, & King, 2012; Thompson, McManus, Lantry, Windsor, & Flynn, 2006). Accordingly, Taylor, Williams, and Gray found highly significant differences for medical care use between people experiencing homelessness with dogs and those without dogs. People with dogs were less likely to use medical care facilities and had lower health scores (2004).

Among these many crucial services, diminished access to shelter and housing is perhaps the most critical in the context of treating pet loss grief. Conventional shelter and housing models normally follow a Treatment First philosophy (Padgett, Gulcur, & Tsemberis, 2006; Padgett, Stanhope, Henwood, & Stefancic, 2011). Such programs have sobriety requirements and other challenging benchmarks for people to achieve in order to access services, as opposed to harm reduction and Housing First philosophies. Harm reduction and Housing First strategies operate on the principle that once people have their basic shelter or housing needs met, they may be able to more easily work on other life objectives such as sobriety, employment, physical health, and mental health goals.

Harm reduction and Housing First models have not only shown promise for ending homelessness, but they are seen much like a prebiotic for treating the conditions that can accompany homelessness (Padgett et al., 2006). Maslow's Hierarchy of Needs provides a theoretical basis for the Housing First rationale in which physiological needs, including shelter, form the base of the pyramid. The theory purports that fulfilling the needs at the base is the first step in the climb towards fulfillment in the other categories of safety, love and belonging, esteem, and self-actualization (Greenwood, Stefancic, & Tsemberis, 2013; Maslow, 1943). If healthy processing of the loss of a pet is contained in one of the higher steps on the pyramid, securing housing or shelter seems to be an intuitive first step into the therapeutic intervention for companion animal bereavement with clients experiencing homelessness.

Despite the logic of focusing on securing shelter first, lack of housing should not preclude people experiencing homelessness from working through pet loss grief. Recent research shows that while fulfilling basic needs makes abstract goals more attainable, the journey to self-actualization for people experiencing homelessness is more complex than this ladder-like approach. Findings from this research show the importance of person-centered care planning for people experiencing homelessness, which might include goals that go beyond basic needs. Aspirational goals which skip steps in the Hierarchy of Needs can help sustain motivation and commitment to change, and thus should be included in care planning regardless of housing or shelter status (Henwood, Derejko, Couture, & Padgett, 2015).

Unfortunately, the vast majority of homeless service programs have "no-pets-allowed" rules. No-pets-allowed spaces not only contribute to withholding resources from this subpopulation, but it may also impede trust building between clients and staff. In one study, research participants experiencing homelessness reported that unwelcoming encounters with health care professionals negatively influenced their desire to seek out future health care (Wen, Hudak, & Hwang, 2007). A lack of trust is a significant hurdle to effective therapeutic engagement, particularly for homeless clients who have co-occurring mental health and substance use disorders. This population is perhaps hardest to reach, engage, and retain in therapeutic services, and successful engagement may be impossible without significant trust building (Brunette, Mueser, & Drake, 2004; Calsyn, Klinkenberg, Morse, Miller, & Cruthis, 2004; Rowe, Fisk, Frey, & Davidson, 2002). For people with animals, the key to trust building may be in the provider's acceptance of one's pet. One study which examined service usage patterns of homeless youths, another population difficult to engage in services, found that youths with dogs were more likely to use and trust providers that allowed their dogs to also access the facility (Thompson, et al. 2006). The relationship between trust and pet-friendly policies in homeless services should be further examined. Such study findings may have important implications on social service usage and access.

There is still much to discover about delivering effective treatment to people experiencing homelessness who are simultaneously experiencing pet loss grief. However, clinicians can combine and apply what is known about homelessness and pet loss grief to support clients through this difficult period. Major challenges clinicians and clients experiencing homelessness may face include:

- More severe pet loss grief due to compounded stressors;
- High attachment to their animals;
- Limited social support systems;
- A distrust of mental health professionals;
- Limited access to mental health services due to a "no-pets-allowed" rule and inequitable distribution of health care resources;
- Resurfacing of prior trauma due to the loss of the pet, which acted as a protective factor against other stressors;
- The lack of a "home base," which may complicate the grieving process.

Despite multiple challenges, the resiliency of people experiencing homelessness should not be overlooked. As shown by the following case studies, people find ways to cope with difficult emotional circumstances, even with limited access or use of professional services. Nina and Sarah showcase the strength of individuals and remind us that people have a propensity for survival, are resourceful in the way they navigate their grief, and find ways to exercise their autonomy over their own mental health recovery.

Case Scenarios

To help give a real sense of the individuals who comprise this population, two in-depth case studies have been included. They are written from the perspective of the following women.

Sarah is a single, white woman in her mid-40s. During her latest episode of homelessness, Sarah and her two dogs have been sleeping in her car, camping, and staying with friends in a large city in Colorado for approximately 1 year. She has never been a user of the homeless shelter system, although she has experienced other periods of precarious housing and homelessness prior to her current episode. Sarah was interviewed at a pop-up street clinic providing free veterinary care for animals accompanying people experiencing homelessness.

Nina is a single, white woman in her mid-50s. She was recently housed through her participation in a Section 8 voucher program, which requires participants to contribute 30% of their income towards rent while the government entity which issued the voucher pays the remainder of the rental fee. Prior to being housed, Nina was considered chronically homeless, meaning that she has a disabling condition and was either homeless for at least 1 year continuously, or she experienced at least four episodes of homelessness in the past 3 years. Nina was recruited for an interview by a nonprofit group which provides free veterinary care for animals accompanied by people experiencing homelessness in a large city in Colorado.

Elements of these stories have been changed to protect the identities of the interview participants.

Case Scenario #1: Sarah

I got Zelda when I couldn't have kids. I did get pregnant a couple of times but Mother Nature just spontaneously aborted. That was the biggest thing that led to my divorce. So I wanted a dog and we got Zelda. I rescued her, and so she was my first fur baby.

My ex-husband and I lived in Switzerland. Zelda came back with me to the US after the divorce. My divorce in Europe was quite intense. It's supposed to take 2 years, but it ended up taking 4 years. All of my finances were frozen in the meantime. The government said if you're not married to a European citizen anymore, you need to go. So they sent me back to Houston, even though I didn't want to go back. And then I was diagnosed with cancer.

Zelda and I had been living with my family on and off, and my family kept telling me, "You've got to make money to take care of your dogs." So I got a job and I worked in town for a year but then that fell apart. A lot of other things kept falling apart too. I just wanted to do something different. I felt abandoned and hopeless, and my parents just carried on. They were actually embarrassed that I was there. They wouldn't even tell my relatives that I was staying with them.

I felt like I was 12 again. I had no control over my life. And I just hated all the pressure because they'd say, "Well what's wrong with you now? You're divorced. You don't have kids." I just felt really stuck and like I let everybody down.

I left home and came to Colorado to look for work. That first time, I didn't have a home, so I was going between house sitting for people, staying with friends, camping, and trying to make ends meet. Then Zelda was diagnosed with lupus, and she wasn't doing well. Even though I didn't have much money, I gave her all her medication. But she was still deteriorating and she got to the point where she wouldn't even go outside to relieve herself. It affected my entire work situation. At that time, I was living with a friend in a low-income hotel, and I was working this really remedial job. I couldn't keep calling out of work to take care of Zelda, so I got fired. They paid me so little that I didn't have any savings, so I didn't have anything to pay the next day's bill. Everything just fell apart in one day. I didn't have anywhere else to go, so I ended up driving back to Houston to stay with my parents. My parents had retired, and when I got back I actually slept for about a month. I was so stressed out and I was so upset.

After about a month or two of being there, I had to put Zelda down. I took her to the vet. I even fed her mac and cheese and barbeque that day. Zelda knew what was happening. And my other dog, Jessica, was with me.

She knew too. Everyone knew what was happening but me. I used to sing the Sunshine Song, so I was just singing to her the whole time when they were giving her the shots. And then she was gone. I don't even know how to explain it.

Afterwards, I didn't get out of bed for months. My parents weren't very supportive. My mother's like, "This is just crazy. You had a life in Colorado, and you just need to go." So I left. I took Zelda's ashes and I went to a place called Sunshine Canyon, which was a place we spent a lot of time camping when we were homeless in Colorado. I told Zelda, "This is your canyon. When it happens, I promise I'll bring you back here and I'll release you." So I drove there and had this huge ceremony out on that cliff for Zelda. I was crying as I was releasing her ashes. And I wanted it to be released. I didn't want it to stay in the box. So I just kept throwing it and then all of a sudden, I swear to God, Zelda was there. All these ashes just ended up on me. I was throwing them and throwing them and all of a sudden there was like this huge wind and I said, "Zelda, I know you're here. I know you're here." And so I released her there because I promised her I would.

I wish I had some real therapy after Zelda died, but I didn't have any health insurance. I really secluded myself and was really depressed when Zelda was gone. But I did go to Al-Anon for my dad's drinking. Even though it wasn't exactly about pet death, just talking to people helped because now that I didn't have Zelda, I had all these other issues that Zelda was probably buffering me from.

But I do feel like I have some closure now. We're camping back at Sunshine Canyon. I was out on the ledge where I let her go, and I was taking a video of these crows that came by. When I looked at the video, there was an orb flying through it and I know it's Zelda. I know she's with me, so I don't have to be scared. I think the biggest thing I've learned is that I've never really had unconditional love unless I've had my dogs. Even with my ex-husband, even with my parents, or even people I've gone out with. It's just not the same.

Discussion Questions:

1. Describe the compounded trauma and life stressors that may be affecting Sarah's grief experience.
2. What are Sarah's case management needs and therapy needs? How are they related?
3. Describe how Sarah's bereavement might be different if she had a stable place to live.

Case Scenario #2: Nina

Me and Killer met when I was at my old apartment a long time ago. One of the neighbors came over with a pack of 3-year-old dogs and she told me

I could have one. So I ended up taking Killer. I became homeless shortly after I got him. I had him for 23 years. About 2 years into being homeless, I met Dr. K. She opened up a free veterinary clinic for pets of the homeless. Dr. K gave Killer great care and has seen him through some tough times. Killer and I got into an apartment at the end of June last year, and by June or July of this year he just started getting really sick and going down. I asked Dr. K for advice, and she said he was too far along in his sickness, so I put him to sleep. That was a hard job. I'm just glad I wasn't on the streets when it happened. If I was on the streets when it happened, I'd probably be in jail.

I would have so much anger built up because I basically wanted him to pass at home. I didn't want it on the streets. So I figured if it was on the streets I would have lost it a lot more. Because it was already hard for myself and for the rest of my friends. But I just could not imagine being on the street knowing 100 people were going to come up to me daily and ask where he's at. And then I'd end up turning to depression and then I'd start getting angry at people for asking me because everybody knows everybody on the street. It's like a bush. But my one grateful thing was that he did pass at home, and ever since I found Dr. K I continue going to her. There's been times that Killer's been attacked by dogs. Dr. K went out of her way to come and check him out. She also tells me if anything else comes up, give her a call.

Killer was very intelligent. Killer was my service dog, and he had him a good personality. He was very smart. A lot of people loved him, but the men hated him. But then again, he hated the men because that's what he was abused by.

But having Killer while I was homeless was really tough. The summers, the fall, and the spring wasn't so bad. It was that winter. Wintertime was the worst. I never let him walk on the sidewalk unless it was sunny and the sidewalks were clear of snow. Nine times out of ten he was in a bag that I could sling over my shoulder. He was in there wrapped up in blankets and those hand warmers to keep him warm. I felt bad and I thought about putting him in a foster home, and I was like, you know what? I can't. I can't. Because one, he is my service dog.

I get really bad anxiety. If I'm in the middle of a grocery store and I'm in the aisle all by myself and you come one way and there's someone else coming the other way, I feel like y'all are going to block me in. Then I go through panic attacks real bad. So having him, I can see both of you two coming down the aisle and I just pet my dog and mind my own business.

When I had Killer and I was on the streets, the first time I went to a homeless shelter I snuck him in. He was in the bag. Nobody knew he was there. Nobody knew I had him. He'd lay in that bag all night long covered up and wouldn't make a sound. He was great. I took him in that shelter for a month and a half before I ended up getting busted. And I said to them, "I knew you guys weren't going to let me in with my dog. I had to hide him in order to be in a safe spot." They gave me a lot of grief about it.

Last winter Killer got sick. Killer's death threw me in depression for a while. But then I had to come to terms and realize that what I did to him – putting him to sleep – was the right thing to do. He was suffering. He didn't move. He stayed in one spot. But I gotta tell myself he lived a long and happy life. Putting him down was hard but it also put me at ease because I knew he wasn't suffering. I went through a depression for a little bit. And then I had to talk myself out of it and say, he did live a long life, 23 years. He didn't die on the streets. We were in a home when he passed away.

When Killer passed on, it was basically all my decision. When I did it, I didn't let anybody know. My friends told me, "When it's time, we'll go down there and we'll be with you." But it was such a spur of the moment decision. I went to talk to Dr. K and she told me to bring him in right away. It was real quick and when I called everybody and told them about it, they asked, "Why didn't you tell us? We would've been there for you. We would have been down there. We would have helped you through it." But it's something I had to do on my own.

If I was homeless, I'd probably be in the psych ward waiting to go to jail. But seeing as how I was in a house, I did what I had to go do. I locked myself in my house and I did my own depression and my own grieving on my own. I didn't want nobody around me. Not nobody. I didn't want a friend, I didn't want a fly on the wall. I didn't want nothing. So I basically locked myself up until I finally convinced myself I did the right thing. I only talked to Dr. K about his death. Dr. K and her whole crew at the vet clinic, they were awesome. I do say that. When I was in the room with Killer, they came in and checked on me, made sure that everything was ok with me. They were like, "It's normal to cry. Cry all you want." And they were like, "Well you did what you had to do. And just remember he had a long good life. He's not suffering no more." And they ended up getting Killer cremated for me. They got me his ashes, a plaque with his paw, a certificate for his cremation. To tell you the truth I just thought I was just gonna get the ashes. I started a memorial for Killer at home with all these things.

But I would do it the same way. Because I had to do it. I didn't want all the rest of the family to see it. It was hard enough for me. I didn't answer my phone. I'd call and get my meds. I'd go and get food. But there was no friends over, no phones, no nothing. I locked the world out, and that's the best way for me to handle with my grieving, because I don't want to start grieving and they start talking about it and I blow up.

I did tell my psychiatrist about Killer, but I didn't find it helpful. I wasn't expecting it to be. Therapists need to know that a loss of a pet is almost the same thing as losing a child. I have no biological kids. None. Killer was my son. More therapists need to understand that our four-legged creatures are our children.

Discussion Questions:

1. How has housing affected Nina's bereavement process?
2. Nina describes her interaction with several formal social services. Review what those interactions were like and how a trauma-informed approach might have changed those experiences.

References

Bassuk, E., Perloff, J., & Dawson, R. (2001). Multiply homeless families: The insidious impact of violence. *Housing Policy Debate*, 12(2), 299–320.

Beekman, D. (2017, October 12). Seattle may try San Francisco's "radical hospitality" for homeless. *The Seattle Times*. Retrieved from www.seattletimes.com/seattle-news/homeless/seattle-may-try-san-franciscos-radical-hospitality-for-homeless/

Bender, K., Thompson, S. J., McManus, H., Lantry, J., & Flynn, P. M. (2007). Capacity for survival: Exploring strengths of homeless street youth. *Child and Youth Care Forum*, 36(1), 25–42.

Browne, A. (1993). Family violence and homelessness: The relevance of trauma histories in the lives of homeless women. *American Journal of Orthopsychiatry*, 63(3), 370–384.

Brunette, M. F., Mueser, K. T., & Drake, R. E. (2004). A review of research on residential programs for people with severe mental illness and co-occurring substance use disorders. *Drug and Alcohol Review*, 23(4), 471–481.

Calsyn, R. J., Klinkenberg, W. D., Morse, G. A., Miller, J. & Cruthis, R. (2004). Recruitment, engagement, and retention of people living with HIV and co-occurring mental health and substance use disorders. *AIDS Care*, 16, S56–S70.

Christensen, R., Hodgkins, C., Garces, L., Estlund, K., Miller, M., & Touchton, R. (2005). Homeless, mentally ill and addicted: The need for abuse and trauma services. *Journal of Health Care for the Poor and Underserved*, 16(4), 615–622.

Deck, S., & Platt, P. (2015). Homelessness is traumatic: Abuse, victimization, and trauma histories of homeless men. *Journal of Aggression, Maltreatment & Trauma*, 24, 1022–1043.

Eckerd, L., Barnett, J., & Jett-Dias, L. (2016). Grief following pet and human loss: Closeness is key. *Death Studies*, 40(5), 275–282.

Foster, S., LeFauve, C., Kresky-Wolff, M., & Rickards, L. (2010). Services and supports for individuals with co-occurring disorders and long-term homelessness. *The Journal of Behavioral Health Services & Research*, 37(2), 239–251.

Garrett, S., Higa, D., Phares, M., Peterson, P., Wells, E., & Baer, J. (2008). Homeless youths' perceptions of services and transitions to stable housing. *Evaluation and Program Planning*, 31(4), 436–444.

Glynn, C., Byrne, T. H., & Culhane, D. P. (2018). Inflection points in community-level homeless rates. Retrieved from http://files.zillowstatic.com/research/public/StaticFiles/Homelessness/Inflection_Points.pdf

Goodman, L. (1991). The relationship between social support and family homelessness: A comparison study of homeless and housed mothers. *Journal of Community Psychology*, 19(4), 321–332.

Goodman, L., Saxe, L., & Harvey, M. (1991). Homelessness as psychological trauma: Broadening perspectives. *American Psychologist*, 46(11), 1219–1225.

Gosse, G., & Barnes, M. (1994). Human grief resulting from the death of a pet. *Anthrozoös*, 7(2), 103–112.

Greenberg, G., & Rosenheck, R. (2008). Jail incarceration, homelessness, and mental health: A national study. *Psychiatric Services*, 59(2), 170–177.

Greenwood, R., Stefancic, A., & Tsemberis, S. (2013). Pathways housing first for homeless persons with psychiatric disabilities: Program innovation, research, and advocacy. *Journal of Social Issues*, 69(4),645–663.

Henry, M., Mahathey, A., Morrill, T., Robinson, A., Shivji, A., & Watt R. (2018). The 2018 annual homelessness assessment report (AHAR) to Congress: Part 1: Point-in-Time estimates of homelessness, US Department of Housing and Urban Development. Retrieved from www.hudexchange.info/resources/documents/2018-AHAR-Part-1.pdf

Henwood, B., Derejko, K., Couture, J., & Padgett, D. (2015). Maslow and mental health recovery: A comparative study of homeless programs for adults with serious mental illness. *Administration and Policy in Mental Health and Mental Health*, 42(2), 220–228.

Hopper, E., Bassuk, E., & Olivet, J. (2010). Shelter from the storm: Trauma-informed care in homeless service settings. *The Open Health Services and Policy Journal*, 3, 80–100.

Irvine, L. (2013). Animals as lifechangers and lifesavers: Pets in the redemption narratives of homeless people. *Journal of Contemporary Ethnography*, 42(1), 3–30.

Irvine, L., Kahl, K., & Smith, J. (2012). Confrontations and donations: Encounters between homeless pet owners and the public. *The Sociological Quarterly*, 53(1), 25–43.

Johnson, T. P., Garrity, T. F., & Stallones, L. (1991). Psychometric evaluation of the Lexington Attachment to Pets Scale (LAPS). *Anthrozoös*, 5, 160–175.

Kaltman, S., & Bonanno, G. (2003). Trauma and bereavement: Examining the impact of sudden and violent deaths. *Anxiety Disorders*, 17(2), 131–147.

Kidd, A., & Kidd, R. (1994). Benefits and liabilities of pets for the homeless. *Psychological Reports*, 74(3), 715–722.

Kim, C. (2019a). Homelessness and animal companionship in Bloomington. A report on homeless animal guardians' needs and resources in the Bloomington community. *Human-Animal Interaction Bulletin*, 7(1), 58–76.

Kim, C. (2019b). Homelessness and animal companionship. In L. Kogan, & C. Blazina (Eds.), *Clinician's guide to treating companion animal issues: Addressing human–animal interaction* (pp. 365–378). San Diego, CA: Elsevier.

Kim, M., Ford. J., Howard, D., & Bradford, D. (2010). Assessing trauma, substance abuse, and mental health in a sample of homeless men. *Health & Social Work*, 35(1), 39–48.

Kim, M., & Ford, J. (2006). Trauma and post-traumatic stress among homeless men. *Journal of Aggression, Maltreatment & Trauma*, 13(2), 1–22.

Kushel, M., Evans, J., Perry, S., Robertons, M., & Moss, A. (2003). No door to lock: Victimization among homeless and marginally housed persons. *Archives of Internal Medicine*, 163(20), 2492–2499.

Lehman, D., Wortman, C., & Williams, A. (1987). Long-term effects of losing a spouse or child in a motor vehicle crash. *Journal of Personality and Social Psychology*, 52(1), 218–231.

Lem, M., Coe, J., Haley, D., Stone, E., and O'Grady, W. (2013). Effects of companion animal ownership among Canadian street-involved youth: A qualitative analysis. *The Journal of Sociology & Social Welfare*, 40(4), 285–304.

Lewinson, T., Thomas, M., & White, S. (2014). Traumatic transitions: Homeless women's narratives of abuse, loss, and fear. *Journal of Women and Social Work,* 29(2), 192–205.

Lippert, A., & Lee, B. (2015). Stress, coping, and mental health differences among homeless people. *Sociological Inquiry,* 85(3), 343–374.

Mallett, S. (2004). Understanding home: A critical review of the literature. *Sociological Review,* 52 (1), 62–89.

Maslow, A. H. (1943). A theory of human motivation. *Psychological Review,* 50(4), 370–396.

Minnery, J. & Greenhalgh, E. (2007). Approaches to homelessness policy in Europe, the United States, and Australia. *Journal of Social Issues,* 63(3), 641–655.

Murphy, S., Braun, T., Tillery, L., Cain, K., Johnson, L., & Beaton, R. (1999). PTSD among bereaved parents following the violent deaths of their 12- to 23-year-old children: A longitudinal prospective analysis. *Journal of Traumatic Stress,* 12(2), 273–291.

National Alliance to End Homelessness. (2013). Overcoming employment barriers. Retrieved from https://endhomelessness.org/resource/overcoming-employment-barriers/

National Alliance to End Homelessness. (2017). The state of homelessness in America. Retrieved from https://endhomelessness.org/homelessness-in-america/homelessness-statistics/state-of-homelessness-report/

National Alliance to End Homelessness. (2018a, April 3). Advice on lowering shelter barriers – From those who have done it. In The Basics: Introduction to Low-Barrier Emergency Shelter webinar series. Retrieved from https://endhomelessness.org/resource/emergency-shelter/

National Alliance to End Homelessness. (2018b). Racial inequalities in homelessness, by the numbers. Retrieved from https://endhomelessness.org/resource/racial-inequalities-homelessness-numbers/

National Health Care for the Homeless Council. (2011). Homelessness & health: What's the connection? Retrieved from www.nhchc.org/wp-content/uploads/2011/09/Hln_health_factsheet_Jan10.pdf

North, C., Smith, E., Pollio, D., & Spitznagel, E. (1996). Are the mentally ill homeless a distinct homeless subgroup? *Annals of Clinical Psychiatry,* 8(3), 117–128.

Orrock, T. (2016). Hope for the homeless. Retrieved from www.dhcs.ca.gov/services/mh/documents/2015_hopeforthehomeless.pdf.

Padgett, D., Gulcur, D., & Tsemberis, S. (2006). Housing first services for people who are homeless with co-occurring serious mental illness and substance abuse. *Research on Social Work Practice,* 16(1), 74–83.

Padgett, D., Stanhope, V., Henwood, B., & Stefancic, A. (2011). Substance use outcomes among homeless clients with serious mental illness: Comparing housing first with treatment first programs. *Community Mental Health Journal,* 47(2), 227–232.

Pedersen, E., Tucker, J., & Kovalchik, S. (2016). Facilitators and barriers of drop-in center use among homeless youth. *Journal of Adolescent Health,* 59(2), 144–153.

Phelan, J., Link, B., Moore, R., & Stueve, A. (1997). The stigma of homelessness: The impact of the label "homeless" on attitudes toward poor persons. *Social Psychology Quarterly,* 60(4), 323–337.

Rayburn, N., Wenzel, S., Elliot, M., Hambarsoomiams, K., Marshall, G., & Tucker, J. (2005). Trauma, depression, coping, and mental health service seeking among impoverished women. *Journal of Consulting and Clinical Psychology,* 73(4), 667–677.

Rew, L. (2000). Friends and pets as companions. Strategies for coping with loneliness among homeless youth. *Journal of Child and Adolescent Psychiatric Nursing,* 13(3), 125–132.

Rhoades, H., Winetrobe, H., & Rice, E. (2015). Pet ownership among homeless youth: Associations with mental health, service utilization and housing status. *Child Psychiatry & Human Development,* 46(2), 237–244.

Rowe, M., Fisk, D., Frey, J., & Davidson, L. (2002). Engaging persons with substance use disorders: Lessons from homeless outreach. *Administration and Policy in Mental Health,* 29(3), 263–272.

Shelton, K., Taylor, P., Bonner, A., & van Den Bree, M. (2009). Risk factors for homelessness: Evidence from a population-based study. *Psychiatric Services,* 60(4), 465–472.

Singer, R., Hart, L., & Zasloff, R. (1995). Dilemmas associated with rehousing homeless people who have companion animals. *Psychological Reports,* 77(3), 851–857.

Slatter, J., Lloyd, C., & King, R. (2012). Homelessness and companion animals: More than just a pet? *British Journal of Occupational Therapy,* 75(8), 377–383.

Taylor, H., Williams, P., & Gray, D. (2004). Homelessness and dog ownership: An investigation into animal empathy, attachment, crime, drug use, health, and public opinion. *Anthrozoös,* 7(4), 353–368.

Thompson, M., Norris, F., & Ruback, R. (1998). Comparative distress levels in inner-city family members of homicide victims. *Journal of Traumatic Stress,* 11(2), 223–241.

Thompson, S., McManus, H., Lantry, J., Windsor, L., & Flynn, P. (2006). Insights from the street: Perceptions of services and providers by homeless young adults. *Evaluation and Program Planning,* 29(1), 34–43.

US Department of Housing and Urban Development. (2018). HUD 2018 Continuum of Care Homeless Assistance Programs Homeless Populations and Subpopulations. Retrieved from www.hudexchange.info/resource/report management/published/CoC_PopSub_NatlTerrDC_2018.pdf.

Wen, C., Hudak, P., & Hwang, S. (2007). Homeless people's perceptions of welcomeness and unwelcomeness in healthcare encounters. *Journal of General Internal Medicine,* 22(7), 1011–1017.

10 The Loss of a Pet

Cultural Perspectives on Cross-Species Grief and Healing

Yvonne Smith and Amalia Golomb-Leavitt

Introduction

It can be a source of great opportunity and deep sadness that we tend to outlive our animal companions. Except for some long-lived birds and reptiles, pets enter and leave our lives in short cycles – reminders of our continuity and a microcosm of our own finitude. That people tend to outlive their pets, however, may be one of the few universal claims that can be made about the experience of losing a pet through death or separation. In fact, these experiences, like *all* human experiences make sense to us only through the various lenses of our cultures. In this chapter, we consider the relatively under-investigated topic of pet loss as a cultural phenomenon. We explore some of the research about pet loss across cultures with attention to how such knowledge can help us work effectively with a diversity of clients. We argue that clinical professionals must take our duty seriously to provide culturally competent *and* culturally humble practice in regard to pet loss, particularly since so little is currently known about the myriad of ways pet loss is experienced. We also argue that in order to practice culturally competent and humble mental health care, we must contextualize contemporary, middle-class US beliefs and practices surrounding pet-related grief and mourning as culturally-based rather than universally normative. We suggest that, by viewing such practices as culturally and historically specific, we can help avoid ethnocentric assumptions about how "best" to grieve the loss of an animal companion, and help legitimize and support cultural practices (e.g., death and remembrance rituals) that may prove a source of support to some clients.

In recent decades, scholars in all of the mental health professions have alerted us to the importance of understanding the diversity of human experience and the challenge of working knowledgeably, ethically, and effectively with clients whose cultures and worldviews are different from those of the clinician (Sue, Zane, Nagayama Hall, & Berger, 2009). If we wish to provide just and respectful treatment, informed attention to cultural differences in how clients experience the world and how forms of oppression and privilege differentially affect them is crucial. Many practitioners have had significant – if not always helpful – education and training in "cultural sensitivity" and "human diversity." But in practice, providing just and respectful care requires our continuous engagement in a process of working toward both cultural competence (Cross, Bazron, Dennis, & Isaacs, 1989; Sue, Arredondo, & McDavis, 1992) and cultural humility (Tervalon & Murray-García, 1998). Without seeking both ideals, we risk viewing our clients and their struggles from an ethnocentric perspective or relying on facile (and often harmful) stereotypes about groups of people.

Definitions of cultural competence vary somewhat, but here we follow The National Association of Social Workers Standards and Indicators (2015), which defines cultural competence as a:

> Process by which individuals and systems respond respectfully and effectively to people of all cultures, languages, classes, races, ethnic backgrounds, religions, spiritual traditions, immigration status, and other diversity factors in a manner that recognizes, affirms, and values the worth of individuals, families, and communities and protects and preserves the dignity of each.
>
> (p. 13)

This definition takes an affirmative stance towards difference, and frames cultural competence as a process rather than a static state of expertise. We particularly appreciate that this broad definition includes many facets of identity, (e.g., religion, race, and class) in its view of human difference, and we follow that broad understanding of human diversity here. However, critiques of cultural competence have suggested that the focus on acquiring knowledge about different cultural groups reinforces the problematic idea that the practitioner is the knowledgeable expert with mastery over cultural knowledge (Fisher-Borne, Cain, & Martin, 2014).

The more recent construct of cultural humility has been proposed as an alternative (Fisher-Borne, Cain, & Martin, 2014) or complement to cultural competence. Cultural humility shifts the source of cultural expertise from the practitioner to the client, acknowledging that he or she is always the resident expert on the world as it is experienced from his or her social location. Tervalon and Murray-García (1998) argue that cultural humility requires ongoing reflection and self-critique on the part of the practitioner and demands attention, not just to knowledge about diversity, but to the power differences present in the therapeutic relationship by virtue of inhabiting different social locations. We take the position that cultural competence and cultural humility might usefully be viewed as mutually sustaining projects. It is indeed useful to educate ourselves about how cultures differ in their worldviews and practices. It is also essential to defer to the cultural expertise of our clients and maintain a critically reflective stance (Kondrat, 1999) toward our own cultural points of view, because failing to do so positions us to unwittingly perpetuate injustice in our work.

For at least two reasons, it is particularly important to engage in culturally competent and humble practice when working with people who have lost a pet. First, in light of claims that pet keeping itself may be nearly universal (Serpell & Paul, 2011), it is important to remember that what companion animals mean to their humans and how their loss is experienced varies profoundly based on cultural and personal factors. It bears repeating that beliefs about the value, place, and grievability (Redmalm, 2015) of pets are not universal, nor are the practices that surround their lives and deaths (Herzog, 2014). Without an understanding of the cultural variation in pet keeping and pet loss, we risk pathologizing clients' experiences and practices when they differ from our own or missing opportunities to assist clients in resolving their grief.

Second, people who have lost a pet often experience disenfranchised grief – a loss that is not fully understood and acknowledged as important by others. According to Packman, et al. (2014), "Disenfranchised grief results when a person experiences a grief reaction, yet there is no social recognition or validation that the person has a right to grieve or a claim for social support" (p. 334). When working with bereaved pet owners whose culture differs from that of the practitioner, we must avoid contributing to the "disenfranchising circumstances" (Doka, 2008) that already surround grieving a pet by failing in cultural competence or humility. For example, a working class, White, Christian client who mourns her recently deceased dog by buying an $800 burial plot for his remains may already feel negatively judged by neighbors who find this expenditure extravagant for a woman who cannot always afford to pay her rent on time. If, from your cultural perspective, you do not find dogs to be person-like "significant others" (Haraway, 2003) worthy of such a burial, you may find yourself unwittingly joining the chorus of voices in your client's life who communicate to her that her grief and mourning are inappropriate. In this instance, knowing something about the history of pet interment in European American cultures might help you empathize with her decision, one which communicates how greatly she valued her relationship with her pet and how profoundly she experienced his loss. Simultaneously, beginning from the assumption that her decision to bury her dog in a pet cemetery makes sense *from her social location* may help us experience genuine empathy and invite us to learn more about how the world appears from her point of view. A commitment to cultural humility calls us to identify a failure of empathy during moments such as these as a time to invite the client – as an expert on her or his own cultural perspective – to educate the practitioner on the meanings of the experience and to question one's own culturally-based judgments.

Cultural Variation in Pet loss: What do We Know so Far?

Because all living things die, death, dying, grief, and loss have sometimes been approached as a universal experience. However, even the briefest engagement with anthropological literature on the end of life demonstrates that humans experience and respond to these events differently, more or less in line with the models and expectations provided by their culture. Indeed, cultures vary greatly in their expectations of how a loved one ought to be mourned, what performances of emotion are expected, tolerated, or discouraged, what counts as excessive or pathological grieving, and even in their understandings of who is dead and who is alive (Rosenblatt, 1993). Cultures also vary greatly in their distinctions between human and non-human animals, the appropriate forms of interaction between them, and the affective experiences that surround those relationships (Hurn, 2012). Yet very little scholarly literature addresses pet loss, grief, and mourning from a cultural perspective. Indeed, clinical literature on the human–animal bond has sometimes been ethnocentric, documenting trends in middle-class, North American pet keeping as if they were universal (Smith, 2018).[1] At this time, we lack a robust literature from which to draw generalizations about culturally specific patterns of grief and mourning resulting from the loss of a pet. However, a number of accounts exist that can serve as examples of how widely reactions to pet loss may vary by culture and in what ways they may be similar. We provide a review of some of them here.

Two recent accounts of contemporary Japan provide a portrait of changing beliefs and practices surrounding pet loss. Barbara Ambros (2010) argues that, like many in the US, contemporary Japanese pet owners "increasingly view their companion animals as family members" (p. 36). As such, their deaths are often mourned with ritual practices akin to those practiced at the death of a human family member. According to Ambros, the Buddhist belief that pets are fellow sentient beings who also experience reincarnation informs mourning practices. Several hundred pet cemeteries serve mourning pet owners in Japan, and specialized professionals officiate rituals specifically for pet death. Kenney (2004) describes a range of body-handling practices among Japanese pet owners. While many choose to bury a loved pet in a sacred or beautiful place, such as a garden or family burial plot, others keep pets' ashes at home or store them in a public "shelf grave" alongside memorials and offerings to other pets. Municipalities provide disposal services for the bodies of pets whose owners do not wish to or cannot bury or cremate them privately. However, according to Kenney, even these "most unsentimental" disposals are often accompanied by flowers and food offerings for the deceased animal, indicating recognition of the death as deserving of remembrance (p. 44). Funeral rites for Japanese pets share elements of human funerals and typically reflect a belief in reincarnation. The bereaved may attend communal memorial services, make food or incense offerings at a temple, visit the pet's grave as a part of ancestor worship, or purchase a *toba* (plaque) bearing the name of the pet and the wish that the pet achieve a higher state of being. Notably, Ambros (2010) states that Buddhism encourages reframing the sadness of pet loss as gratitude, because it saddens the "little ones" if their bereaved owners grieve for a long time and prevent their spirits from settling (p. 48). According to Ambros, "Once regarded as threatening, vengeful spirits, pet spirits have emerged as loving, faithful spiritual companions" (p. 35). Demonstrating the religious diversity of contemporary Japan, Buddhist traditions are often mixed with secular and Christian ideas about a joyful reunion with deceased pets in an afterlife much like the North American myth of the "Rainbow Bridge," which we will discuss later in this chapter.

Pagani, Robustelli, and Ascione (2007) have documented attitudes toward pets among youth in contemporary Italy. They found that pet ownership was common, as were fears of losing a pet through "un-natural" means, such as harm by another person or the pet being "given away" (p. 288), which accounted for 22% of the pet losses reported. Sixty-eight percent of participants reported that they "suffered a lot" when losing a pet, and 76% reported that they had been worried about pets in the past (p. 285). The authors suggest that a tendency in Italy to "take a pet without fully considering all the consequences of this choice for the pet and the family" (p. 290) contributes to young people's worries and experiences of pet loss.[2]

A recent documentary film on the street cats of Istanbul, Turkey suggests that many human residents of the city view these un-owned cats as a point of pride and interest for their city and a communal responsibility in both life and death (Torun, 2017). Residents feed, house, and provide veterinary care to thousands of cats that roam the city streets, allowing them into homes, shops, restaurants, and markets. In the midst of an interview for the film, a resident is presented with a severely injured kitten that was found near the market where he works. The man, clearly worried about the unknown kitten, listens for its breath, holding it delicately in his hands. When it finally moves a leg, he rushes it to a veterinary clinic in hopes of saving its life. Another participant in the film, who cares for a particularly hard-living street cat, says that many of his neighbors have running tabs at the veterinarian to provide care to sick or injured cats. Residents express deep sadness at the death of these cats, even though – from the perspective of many in the contemporary US – they do not "own" the cats. One Muslim resident describes having, as a child, buried and conducted funeral rituals for community cats, marking each grave with a wooden cross as he had seen in American Western films. The film expands notions of who ought to grieve the loss of which animals, suggesting that a profound bond and significant grief can exist even with animals that are communally stewarded, rather than privately owned.

Luiz Adrian and Stitt (2017) investigated complicated grief as a result of pet loss in the culturally diverse US state of Hawaii. Complicated grief is defined as a "maladaptive coping mechanism" including "persistent longing/yearning for the deceased; preoccupying thoughts of the deceased; trouble accepting the death in question; desire to die to be with the deceased; loneliness; bitterness; mistrust of others; emotional numbness" (p. 124). Their findings support those of studies of other cultural contexts, reporting that pet loss grief intensified when there had been prior trauma or loss of other loved ones, indicating pet loss can be a potential trigger for people with varying levels of PTSD. They theorize that reluctance to grieve the loss of a pet if one is highly attached to it may put the individual at increased risk for subclinical trauma and complicated grief. Social minimization, lack of empathy, and risk of ridicule by others may all contribute to a reluctance to grieve. Such responses should be avoided in therapeutic settings to minimize complicated grief. Interestingly, their study reported only one significant cultural difference in response to pet loss. Ethnically Filipino participants scored higher than other groups on measures of pet loss-related complicated grief.

Although not studies of culture explicitly, several studies of pet-related grief following 2005's Hurricane Katrina are relevant to our discussion of diversity because they address the role of socioeconomic status as well as race in the likelihood and experience of pet loss. As is well documented, African Americans and people with low socioeconomic status tended to fare more poorly than White and more affluent residents during and after the hurricane (Elliott & Pais, 2006). Lowe, Rhodes, Zwiebach, and Chan (2009) found that pet owners were more vulnerable to the negative impacts of pet loss if they had low levels of social support pre-hurricane. They also report that psychological distress was higher for individuals post-hurricane if they had lost a pet, and this finding was magnified for younger individuals. This finding is echoed by Hunt, Al-Awadi, and Johnson (2008), who posit that, as pets can mitigate psychological and physiological consequences of trauma and stress, losing them during a disaster can increase distress purely because a primary means of coping is now gone.

In her 2010 study on pet loss after Hurricane Katrina, Zottarelli found that pet loss resulted in depression, grief, and disruption of daily routine. Interestingly, this study found that complicated grief as a result of pet loss was most common among middle-aged white women with limited social networks. Findings suggest that pet loss caused by a disaster (versus other causes) can increase the risk of psychological problems (e.g., acute stress, dissociation, and symptoms of depression and PTSD). They also underscore that pet relationships during a disaster introduce human safety risks, exemplified in Hurricane Katrina by people attempting to save pets by either failing to evacuate effectively or reentering impact zones during the hurricane. Eighty percent of unauthorized entries into the evacuation zone were to rescue pets (Zottarelli, 2010). As people with lower socioeconomic status, and therefore less access to resources, have been found to experience higher levels of physical and psychological impacts of disasters in general and specifically Hurricane Katrina, it follows that people of lower socioeconomic status also were at greater risk for having additional trauma accompanying pet grief following Hurricane Katrina (Zottarelli, 2010).

It is important to note that during Hurricane Katrina – like many so-called "natural" disasters in the US (Squires & Hartman, 2013) – those with the means to evacuate comfortably with their pets were more likely to do so. Given the severe income inequality between Black and White residents of New Orleans and surrounding areas (Finch, Emrich, & Cutter, 2010), it stands to reason that Black residents were less likely than White residents to be able to evacuate with their pets. Viewed in this way, these experiences of pet loss may also reflect the long history of inequality, oppression, and violence against Blacks in the US.

Religion and spirituality, which vary within and across racial, ethnic, and class backgrounds, may shape how individuals experience pet loss and how they mourn and memorialize their lost pets. Faith traditions often dictate the proper relationships between humans and non-human animals and specify the place of non-human animals in hierarchies of being. Judaism, Christianity, and Islam have been described as highly anthropo-centric faith traditions, which tend to view humans as closer to God than other animals (Serpell, 2005). Beliefs about the nature and existence of an afterlife vary across cultures, and within cultures based on religion and spirituality, though not all faith traditions explicitly address the fate of non-human animals after death. Concern about whether the soul of a beloved pet can be expected to survive death and what form that afterlife will take may trouble clients who have lost a pet. Christian denominations disagree as to whether non-human animals have souls that transcend death, and only the Mormon faith clearly states that pets "go to heaven" (Royal, Kedrowicz, & Snyder, 2016). Judaism offers mixed views about animals in the afterlife (Royal et al., 2016). Chodrow (1998) writes of con-temporary Reform Judaism: "…our culture has no generally accepted rituals for dealing with pet loss," and reports on rabbinic responses ranging from a total lack of understanding or empathy to conducting a full funeral service (p. 1). Hinduism and Buddhism attribute an afterlife to both human and non-human animals in the form of reincarnation, yet reincarnation as a non-human animal is not typically viewed as a desirable transformation (Kenney, 2004; Royal et al., 2016). Islam makes clear that non-human animals have souls, but does not specify what becomes of them after death (Royal et al., 2016).

Perhaps the most comprehensive existing US cross-cultural comparison relevant to pet loss is Royal, Kedrowicz, and Snyder's (2016) investigation of beliefs about the animal afterlife by demographic groups across the country. The authors surveyed 800 US adults and found that a majority believed in an afterlife for animals. Buddhists, followed by American Indians/Alaska Natives, Blacks/African Americans, and southerners were the most likely to believe in an afterlife for animals. In general, those who believed in an afterlife for humans were more likely than others to believe in an afterlife for animals, and little distinction was made between the species or role (pet, non-pet) of the animal in terms of afterlife expectations. The authors stress that, though racial and ethnic differences in belief in pet afterlife existed, their effect sizes were quite small.

Dominant US Narratives and Practices Regarding Pet Loss

While it is clearly necessary to learn what we can about the range of ways humans understand and respond to the loss of a pet, cultural humility also calls us to critically examine the ways that the dominant culture (in this case, White, Christian, middle- or upper-class US American) makes sense of pet loss. This is important because the narratives and practices of the dominant group are often uncritically accepted, even by mental health professionals, as good, healthy, or morally right. We believe it is necessary for professionals in this field to consider some of these beliefs and practices, which may be familiar to many readers of this volume, *as culturally particular.* Understanding one's own cultural perspective as situated and one among many possible worldviews is necessary in order to avoid ethnocentrism.

More than half of US Americans now believe that the souls of pets live on in some form after death (Royal, Kedrowicz, & Snyder, 2016). Along with this belief has arisen a popular cultural myth about what that afterlife looks like. The "Rainbow Bridge" narrative, retold in various forms, reassures grieving pet owners that their deceased pet resides in a place between heaven and Earth, characterized by sunny green hills and meadows, where their illnesses and infirmities no longer trouble them. There, pets are said to romp together until they are each, one day, reunited with their human owner, with whom they finally enter heaven "across the Rainbow Bridge." Multiple websites using this name provide supportive materials for grieving pet owners, sell space to post obituaries and remembrances, and market visual representations of the Rainbow Bridge (e.g., www.rainbowsbridge.com; www.justovertherainbowbridge.com). Magliocco (2018) suggests that the origins of the myth are unknown, but argues that this vernacular ontology (p. 39) blends multiple religious and secular cosmologies and circumvents Victorian-era Christian teachings that left pets out of heaven. The myth of the Rainbow Bridge, which also has currency outside of North America, is certainly one dominant US cultural narrative about what happens when pets die, so much so that it is a common euphemism for pet death to say that an animal has "crossed the Rainbow Bridge" or is "waiting at the bridge."

US Americans memorialize their lost pets in many private and public ways, including painted portraits, jewelry bearing a paw print or made of a horse's hair, tattoos, social media elegies, and through practices surrounding burial or cremation. Brandes' (2009) study of pet cemetery gravestones suggests that Americans increasingly view their pets as rightful members of the family and memorialize them as such. The emergence of a pet mortuary industry in recent decades – providing burial, cremation, and funeral services – attests to the common contemporary US belief that the bodies of deceased pets should be treated in ways akin to the bodies of human family members. While we dispute Brandes' assertion that there are "no clear cut financial barriers, and certainly no class barriers, to pet cemetery interment" (p. 101), it is clear that it is now considered by many Americans inappropriate to dispose of a pet's body along with refuse.

Of course, not all pet losses in the US are due to death. US pet owners relinquish to animal welfare agencies more than 6 million pets each year (www.aspca.org) and countless others are abandoned or given away. This means that, despite significant advances in animal welfare and sheltering in the US, it remains a common, if not universally socially acceptable practice, to relinquish a pet. Surely, not all of these partings are experienced as losses, nor are they all grieved, but it is a mistake to view relinquishment as casual, unfeeling, or unconsidered. DiGiacomo, Arluke, and Patronek (1998) found that those who relinquished pets had often done so with great difficulty after exhausting other options. Although many Americans, including shelter workers (Frommer & Arluke, 1999), may harshly judge those who relinquish or abandon a pet, as mental health professionals we must remain sensitive to the possibility that such a decision might have been a difficult one and might result in distress, including disenfranchised grief. Finding empathy for those who have lost a pet through relinquishment may be easier when you consider that increasing income inequality in the US means that some pet owners have far greater resources than others for coping with challenges affecting pet ownership, including housing instability, the cost of veterinary care, spaying and neutering, feeding, fencing, and training.

Implications for Practice

Although a great deal more research is needed to more fully understand cultural diversity in regard to pet loss, we may still draw from this exploratory review some important implications for clinical practice. First, cultural beliefs and practices do, indeed, appear to differ across and within cultures, and these beliefs can change over time. Although pet keeping is very common around the world, how humans understand such relationships, how they experience their endings, and how they mark those endings are far from universal. Even within a single society, great within group variation exists. Such significant variation requires us, as mental health professionals, to remain culturally humble, viewing our clients as experts on their own lifeworlds, resisting relying on stereotypes and generalizations, and continuously reflecting on our own culturally shaped beliefs about pets and pet loss.

Because our own beliefs about pets, death, proper mourning, and what happens after death tend to be deeply, and sometimes uncritically, held, mental health professionals may struggle to empathize with clients whose responses to the loss of a pet are unfamiliar. This may occur when the depth of a client's pet-related grief seems to exceed what the practitioner views as socially acceptable, or it may occur when a client appears genuinely untroubled by a loss that the practitioner deems worthy of grief. We may find ourselves unintentionally contributing to the disenfranchisement of a client's grief through cultural misunderstandings about the grievabilty of animals or certain species of animals, ethnocentric assumptions about the personhood or family membership of pets, or unfamiliarity with particular cultural expectations (like prayer or food offerings) surrounding pet death.

Because of beliefs and practices around the loss of a pet are likely to be shaped by spirituality and religion, we must also become comfortable talking about these in our practice. Perhaps because most practitioners do not provide faith-based services and do not find it appropriate to bring their own spiritual or religious beliefs into the consulting room, we may be uncomfortable when our clients discuss religious beliefs about pet loss. We suggest that, when working with clients who have lost a pet, it may be useful to ask exploratory questions about how people in their family or community understand death and loss and respond to the loss of loved ones – human or animal. Such questions might include as appropriate: *Where do you believe your pet has gone now that (s)he has died? Are there ways that your relationship with your pet continues now that (s)he is gone? How have you and your family mourned the loss of loved ones in the past? Are there things about the way you mourned that might help you deal with this loss? What does your faith tradition have to say about the loss of pets? Are there people in your synagogue, church, mosque, temple, etc. who might be able to help you make sense of this loss?*

Given the tendency for pet loss to result in disenfranchised grief, when clients do not find support and understanding in their faith community or culture more broadly, it may be useful to work together to create and support desired rituals to mark the death and remember the life of the deceased pet. When clients do not find cultural recognition of their grief or community support for their mourning practices, psychotherapy may be a unique space in which to make peace with the loss of a pet. We believe that culturally competent and humble practice holds possibilities for profound comfort and transformation for people who have lost a pet. To that end, we close with two short practice scenarios and accompanying reflective questions designed to stimulate further thinking about the role of culture in the experience of pet loss and its treatment.

Case Scenarios

Case Scenario #1: The Case of Michaela and Timothy the Lesson Horse

Michaela is a 39-year-old White woman of Irish-American ancestry. She has been seeing her psychotherapist to address the anxiety that she attributes to financial troubles related to her horse boarding and training business. Her husband, Paul, who also works in their business, urged her to come to therapy after she experienced several panic attacks while teaching horseback riding lessons. During her panic attacks, her heart raced, she could not speak, and she could not pay attention to her students. Each time she felt as if she might die right there in the riding arena. After meeting for three weeks, Michaela seemed motivated to explore the cognitive and affective processes that triggered her anxiety, and she had reported no further panic attacks. However, in the fourth week, Michaela returns looking exhausted. She reports that she had decided the previous week to euthanize one of her elderly lesson horses, Timothy, who was no longer sound enough for riding. She explains that he "just cost too damn much to maintain, and I need space for a horse that can work." Indeed, in order to keep his arthritis at bay, she had been spending more than $150 per month on medications and health supplements. Because his old teeth were no longer good for chewing hay, she had to feed him expensive feed softened with water and kept from freezing in an electric bucket. All of this before she even added in his astonishing veterinary bills. "Oh, Michaela, what a difficult decision," her therapist said, hoping not to have assumed too much about the situation. Somehow, simultaneously teary-eyed and stern, she tells her therapist:

> He was the first horse I bought when we opened our business years ago. He was ugly as sin, but I loved him. He was a good lesson horse and took care of every kid I ever put on him. That's why we didn't send him through the auction – couldn't stand to think of him going to a meat buyer. It wasn't easy letting him go, but it was that or we couldn't afford preschool for our kid. What were we supposed to do?

She looks almost defiant and seems to expect her therapist to judge her harshly for her decision to euthanize the costly old horse.

Discussion Questions:

1. Do you find yourself making negative judgments about this client? If so, what?
2. How easy or difficult do you find it to empathize with Michaela at this moment?
3. Based on your own cultural beliefs, do you think of Timothy as a pet, livestock, or something else? Does this matter to the way you understand Michaela's situation?

4. What beliefs do you hold about euthanizing a horse under these circumstances? Where do you think those beliefs come from?
5. Why do you think Michaela may be concerned that her therapist may judge her actions harshly? Are there dominant cultural norms or narratives in the US that her actions might be thought to violate?
6. How do you understand her complex feelings of loss alongside her pragmatic explanation of the euthanasia decision?
7. What might you say next? Why?

Case Scenario #2: The Case of Hassan and Zipper

Hassan is a 30-year-old second-generation Pakistani-American client who has recently lost his dog to cancer. He sought therapy because the website for the practice indicated expertise in helping people with pet-related grief. Hassan appears in the office for his first session dressed in a perfectly tailored blue suit. He has hurried to the session after leaving his job in an advertising agency. He begins by telling the therapist the story of his deceased dog, Zipper. He is many times overcome by tears, each time covering his face with his hand and apologizing for "losing it." It is clear that Hassan is grieving quite profoundly for Zipper, whom he viewed as a member of his family. The dog's presence in his life had marked a turning point in his own identity development and individuation from his more observant Muslim parents, who believed that it was inappropriate to keep dogs in the house. He recalls buying a puppy for himself after graduating from college as a mark of his embrace of a more "American" lifestyle than his parents preferred – a lifestyle that also included dating. He described Zipper as his "wingman" for years, helping him strike up conversations with women on their long walks. Eventually, Zipper also became a companion to his wife, Aisha, and their two young children. Although his parents came to accept the dog to some extent and even sometimes came to let the dog out when he and Aisha worked long hours, they could not empathize with his love for it. When the dog died, they were not understanding. His older sister – who remained more observant than Hassan – even mocked him during a family dinner for being so "broken up about a *dog.*" He and Aisha and the children hung a clay mold of the dog's footprint (given to them by their veterinarian) in the hallway by the front door and had his body cremated. Hassan has found himself very worried about where the dog's ashes were being kept (they have not yet been returned by the vet), and he is troubled by intrusive thoughts of his friend being incinerated. For a while, Aisha was patient and understanding of his grief. She felt it, too. But now she is urging him to move on with life, and the children are asking to adopt a new dog. Hassan recognizes that he is experiencing prolonged and painful grief, but he is ashamed of how deeply the loss of Zipper has affected him.

Discussion Questions:

1. How difficult or easy do you find it to empathize with Hassan's grief? Why do you think that is?
2. How difficult or easy is it for you to empathize with his parents' and sister's point of view?
3. What, if anything, do you know about the experiences of second-generation Pakistani-Americans that might help you better understand Hassan's situation?
4. What would you like to know more about from Hassan to help you better understand the depth and persistence of his grief?
5. Would you consider talking with Hassan about disenfranchised grief? Why or why not?
6. Do you have any tentative ideas about how you might be able to help Hassan mourn and honor his beloved dog?

Dedication

This chapter is dedicated to my (Yvonne Smith's) beloved pit bull, Beatrice, who, despite a terminal brain tumor and a fetch-related torn cruciate, spent many days in the office "helping" to write this. When her life ends, I do not know where she will go or in what capacity she might somehow live on. I do know that, if there is a way that we might be together again, her tenacious and loyal soul will find it.

Notes

1. For an in-depth review of literature about cultural variation in pet keeping in general, see Smith, 2018.
2. Although their study was not comparative, it is important to point out that Italians are certainly not alone in relinquishing unwanted pets. More than 6 million are relinquished in the US annually (www.aspca.org).

References

Ambros, B. (2010). Vengeful spirits or loving spiritual companions? Changing views of animal spirits in contemporary Japan. *Asian Ethnology*, 69(1), 35–67.

ASPCA. (2018). Shelter Intake and Surrender. Retrieved from www.aspca.org/animal-homelessness/shelter-intake-and-surrender

Brandes, S (2009). The meaning of American pet cemetery gravestones. *Ethnology*, 48(2), 99–118.

Chodrow, R. E. (1998). A Jewish response to pet loss. *CCAR Journal: A Reform Jewish Quarterly*, 45, 23.

Cross, T., Bazron, T.J., Dennis, K., & Isaacs, M. (1989). *Towards a culturally competent system of care*. Washington, DC: CASSP Technical Assistance Center, Georgetown University.

DiGiacomo, N., Arluke, A., & Patronek, G. (1998). Surrendering pets to shelters: The relinquisher's perspective. *Anthrozoös*, 11(1), 41–51.

Doka, K. J. (2008). Disenfranchised grief in historical and cultural perspective. In M. S. Stroebe, R. O. Hansson, H. Schut, & W. Stroebe (Eds.), *Handbook of bereavement research and practice: Advances in theory and intervention* (pp. 223–240). Washington, DC: American Psychological Association.

Elliott, J. R., & Pais, J. (2006). Race, class, and Hurricane Katrina: Social differences in human responses to disaster. *Social Science Research, 35*(2), 295–321.

Finch, C., Emrich, C. T., & Cutter, S. L. (2010). Disaster disparities and differential recovery in New Orleans. *Population & Environment, 31*(4), 179–202.

Fisher-Borne, M., Cain, J.M., & Martin, S.L. (2014). From mastery to accountability: Cultural humility as an alternative to cultural competence. *Social Work Education, 34*(2), 165–181.

Frommer, S. S., & Arluke, A. A. (1999). Loving them to death: Blame-displacing strategies of animal shelter workers and surrenderers. *Society & Animals, 7*(1), 1–16.

Haraway, D. (2003). The companion species manifesto. Chicago, IL: Prickly Paradigm Press.

Herzog, H. A. (2014.) Biology, culture, & the origins of pet-keeping. *Animal Behavior & Cognition, 1*(3), 296–308.

Hunt, M., Al-Awadi, H., & Johnson, M. (2008). Psychological sequelae of pet loss following Hurricane Katrina. *Anthrozoös, 21*(2), 109–121.

Hurn, S. (2012). *Humans and other animals: Cross-cultural perspectives on human-animal interactions.* London: Pluto Press.

Just Over the Rainbow Bridge. Retrieved June 10, 2018, from www.justovertherainbowbridge.com

Kenney, E. (2004). Pet funerals and animal graves in Japan. *Mortality, 9*(1), 42–60.

Kondrat, M. E. (1999). Who is the self in self-awareness: Professional self-awareness from a critical theory perspective. *Social Service Review, 73*(4), 451–477.

Lowe, S. R., Rhodes, J. E., Zwiebach, L. & Chan, C. S. (2009). The impact of pet loss on the perceived social support and psychological distress of hurricane survivors. *Journal of Trauma Stress, 22*(3), 244–247.

Luiz Adrian, J. A., & Stitt, A. (2017). Pet loss, complicated grief, and post-traumatic Stress disorder in Hawaii. *Anthrozoös, 30*(1), 123–133.

Magliocco, S. (2018). Beyond the Rainbow Bridge: Vernacular ontologies of animal afterlives. *Journal of Folklore Research, 55*(2), 39–67.

National Association of Social Workers. (2015). *Standards and indicators for cultural competence in social work practice.* Washington, DC: NASW Press.

Packman, W., Carmack, B.J., Katz, R., Carlos, F., Field, N. P., & Landers, C. (2014). Online survey as empathic bridging for the disenfranchised grief of pet loss. *OMEGA, 69*(4), 333–356.

Pagani, C., Robustelli, F., & Ascione, F.R. (2007). Italian youths' attitudes toward, and concern for animals. *Anthrozoös, 20*(3), 275–293.

Rainbows Bridge: A pet loss grief support community. Retrieved June 10, 2018, from www.rainbowsbridge.com.

Redmalm, D. (2015). Pet grief: When is non-human life grievable? *The Sociological Review, 63,* 19–35.

Rosenblatt, P. C. (1993). Cross-cultural variation in the experience, expression, and understanding of grief. In D. P. Irish, K. E. Lundquist, & V. J. Nelsen, (Eds.), *Ethnic variations in dying, death, and grief* (pp. 13–19). Washington, DC: Taylor & Francis.

Royal, K. D., Kedrowicz, A. A., & Snyder, A. M. (2016). Do all dogs go to heaven? Investigating the association between demographic characteristics and beliefs about the animal afterlife. *Anthrozoös*, 29(3), 409–420.

Serpell, J. A. (2005). Animals & religion: Towards a unifying theory. In. F. H. de Jonge, & R. van den Bos (Eds.), *The human–animal relationship: Forever and a day* (pp. 9–22). Assen, The Netherlands: Royal van Gorcum.

Serpell, J. A., & Paul, E. S. (2011). Pets in the family: An evolutionary perspective. In C. Salmon, & T. Shackleford (Eds.), *The Oxford handbook of evolutionary family psychology* pp. 297–309. New York, NY: Oxford University Press.

Smith, Y. (2018). Pets and human diversity: Toward culturally competent, culturally humble psychotherapy. In L. Kogan, & C. Blazina (Eds.), *Clinician's guide to treating companion animal issues* (pp. 478–496). New York, NY: Elsevier.

Squires, G., & Hartman, C. (2013). There is no such thing as a natural disaster: Race, class, and Hurricane Katrina. New York, NY: Routledge.

Sue., D. W., Arredondo, P., & McDavis, R. J. (1992). Multicultural counseling competencies and standards: A call to the profession. *Journal of Counseling & Development*, 70(4), 477–486.

Sue, S., Zane, N., Nagayama Hall, G. C., & Berger, L. K. (2009). The case for cultural competency in psychotherapeutic interventions for cultural competency in psychotherapeutic interventions. *Annual Review of Psychology*, 60, 525–548.

Tervalon, M., & Murray-García, J. (1998). Cultural humility versus cultural competence: A critical distinction in defining physician training outcomes in multicultural education. *Journal of Health Care for the Poor and Underserved*, 9(2), 117–125.

Torun, C. (Director.) (2017). Kedi. [Motion Picture.] Turkey: Termite Films.

Zottarelli, L. K. (2010). Broken bond: An exploration of human factors associated with companion animal loss during Hurricane Katrina. *Sociological Forum*, 25(1), 110–122.

Part IV

Special Animal Populations

11 Grieving the Equine Companion

Implications for Mental Healthcare Practitioners

Katy Schroeder

Relationships among horses and humans date back thousands of years, with horses performing multifaceted roles in the lives of human beings. In today's society, horses occupy a unique space between working and companion animals. According to current estimates by the American Horse Council (AHC), there are over 7 million horses in the United States, and approximately 38 million American households either own horses, participate in horse activities, or attend horse-related events as spectators (AHC, 2018). While some individuals hold a more utilitarian or instrumental perspective about horses, far more people describe horses as their family members, companion animals, or best friends (AHP, 2015; Coulter, 2014). There are numerous subcultures within the equestrian world as well. For example, individuals involved in equestrian sports such as dressage, western reining, or show jumping, may identify as a competitor, trainer, groom (i.e., an equine caretaker), or horse owner.

Horses as a Way of Life

The horse industry provides an estimated 1 million direct jobs for human beings, while an estimated 537,261 horses make up the equine workforce (AHC, 2018). Horses are employed in a number of industries, including sports, police and military work, tourism and entertainment, ranch work, and healthcare services (e.g., equine-assisted therapy programs). Generally speaking, domesticated horses rely on human beings for their health and well-being; those who manage, train, or compete horses, will invest much time, energy, and money into caring for their equine partners. Horses also are highly social and very large prey animals. Regardless of their sociability, even the most docile young colt or filly needs desensitization, handling, and training in order to willingly accept human contact and leadership. Given a horse's size, strength, and speed, training them requires great skill and care in order to reduce the risks for serious accidents or injuries. Interestingly, while it is quite common for people to report feeling unconditional love from companion animals who dwell in the home, such as dogs or cats, Keaveney (2008) noted that some equestrians believe that horses do not provide their human companions with the same kind of unconditional love as other species. One respondent from Keaveney's qualitative investigation on this phenomenon commented, "My dog always loved me and my horse loves me providing I do everything 'right'" (p. 447).

Additionally, human beings can enter into an entirely different relationship with horses through riding astride their backs (Dashper, 2017; McGowan, Phillips, Hodgson, Perkins, & McGowan, 2012). Horseback riding is a unique, embodied experience; it involves all the senses and allows people to engage in various types of work or leisure activities that are not necessarily possible with other species (Dashper, 2017). For certain individuals, becoming a skilled rider is a learning process that they will devote their entire lives toward achieving. Relatedly, horse enthusiasts often experience joy, pride, and a sense of accomplishment from the process of gaining a horse's trust for the first time. This bonding experience is perceived to strengthen even more when people are able to teach their equine companions to overcome fearful responses to novel situations that are typical of prey animal species (Keaveney, 2008). In short, entering into relationships with horses can be full of incredible thrills and excitement, sometimes danger and injury, as well as extreme disappointments. For those of us who horseback ride, it often provides a felt sense of having a deeper relational connection with our equine companions.

Beyond individual human–horse relationships, horses are the heart and soul of equestrian communities. These communities sometimes appear to break down social barriers, as people seemly establish instant connections with their fellow equestrians, regardless of individual backgrounds or personal circumstances. This in turn fosters an important sense of belonging within the unique social microcosms of equestrian life (Keaveney, 2008). Whether a horse is viewed as a companion, employee, or teammate, when people devote themselves fully to equestrian pursuits; horses become a way of life and an integral part of a person's core identity (Dashper, 2017). This phenomenon produces noteworthy complexities when it comes to understanding the nature and depth of the horse–human emotional bond, as well as what the loss of a horse means to a human being.

Saying Goodbye to Equine Companions

Euthanasia Decision-Making

It is common for people involved with equestrian pursuits to create end-of-life plans for horses (USDA, 2016), and there are multiple factors horse owners consider during the euthanasia decision-making process (McGowan et al., 2012). Commonly reported decision criteria include the amount of pain and suffering a horse might be experiencing, a horse's likelihood of survival, the cost of medical treatment, a horses' ability to return to use, their length of recovery, and the insurance status (USDA, 2016). Other factors that have been deemed important by horse owners include veterinarian medical advice, an owner's relational bond with the horse and anticipated level of emotional distress, an owner's perception of the anticipated burden to other family members, and lastly, advice from friends and family (McGowan et al., 2012).

Veterinarians typically perform euthanasia procedures at a horse's stabling, or in a veterinary hospital. Acceptable methods for the humane euthanasia of horses include barbiturate overdose, gunshot, or use of a captive bolt device. Injection of a barbiturate by a veterinarian involves minimal discomfort to the horse and results in rapid loss of consciousness (Stull, 2013). However, the size of horses presents challenges for caregivers who would like to stand close to their equine companions and physically comfort them while the veterinarian administers euthanasia drugs. This is due to the possibility of a horse causing bodily harm to nearby humans when they collapse, as it can be difficult to predict in which direction they will fall to the ground. Additionally, horses may unexpectedly rear up, or strike out with their hooves during the process (Butler & Lagoni, 2006). Therefore, veterinarians usually instruct clients to stand well away from their horses. Once a horse is lying on the ground and loses consciousness, they may die quickly; however, they also could exhibit spastic leg movements, making gasping noises, defecate, or urinate, which can be distressing for a horse owner to witness (Corp-Minamiji, 2012).

The use of a gunshot or captive bolt has the advantage of providing a very quick and painless death for horses; however, someone with the proper training to handle the equipment must perform these types of procedures. There are some disadvantages to these methods too. For instance, there is a potential danger of ricochet when a gunshot is delivered to the horse's skull. When a captive bolt method is used, a horse must be restrained (Stull, 2013). This may increase the animal's distress prior to death, and also be upsetting for a horse owner to witness.

The Importance of the Client–Veterinarian Relationship

People who own horses often develop a close working relationship with veterinarians, and equestrians who manage show or sport horses may interact with their veterinarian team on a weekly basis. Horse owners primarily rely on veterinarian advice during the euthanasia decision-making process, and one national survey suggests it is much rarer for a horse owner to seek support from a professional counselor prior to the death of their equine companion (USDA, 2016). Consequently, the strength of the horse owner–veterinarian relationship plays an important role in the horse owner's experience (Edenburg, Kirpensteijn, & Sanders, 1999), and could be a protective factor mitigating the potential for complicated or unresolved grief reactions to surface later down the road. Veterinarians who provided horse owners with a detailed description of what to expect during the euthanasia process, demonstrate warmth and compassion, and follow-up, help clients to feel at peace with the decision, as well as the euthanasia process itself (Edenburg et al., 1999).

Caring for the Equine Body After Death

Equestrians have unique logistical issues to navigate regarding the removal or burial of an equine companion's body. In order to protect public health, as well as wildlife, and water supplies, state and local authorities tightly regulate large animal carcass burials. Obtaining the proper depth for an equine burial site requires special digging equipment (e.g., backhoe). If a horse dies in the winter, burial may not be possible because of the frozen ground. Rendering is another option; however, the number of rendering facilities in the United States that can take horses has decreased dramatically. In some counties, landfills will accept horse carcasses. In either case, the removal of the carcass can be upsetting for a horse owner to witness. If not properly prepared, a person may be startled and distressed when watching their horse being lifted by a winch system and placed into a rendering truck box. Cremation is another option if a facility is located nearby, and composting an equine body is possible provided the proper space and resources are available at the horse owner's property. The sudden, unexpected death of a horse can complicate caretaking plans. In which case, a grieving owner has little time to process the events unfolding and will need to find a suitable option for carcass disposal as quickly as possible. This may be emotionally disturbing on many levels, especially if a horse owner was not able to say goodbye, or provide the dignified death process they had envisioned for their equine companion.

Memorializing Horses

Countless equestrians, from owners of famous racehorses, to young adults mourning the loss of their first show ponies, memorialize their equine companions during the bereavement process. There are a number of common practices within the equestrian world such as planting trees at a horse's burial site, or creating a specific space in the home to display favorite objects associated with a special horse (e.g., horseshoes, or halters). Some people create jewelry from locks of their horses' mane and tail hairs.

Client Considerations for Mental Healthcare Practitioners

Working with horses brings a profound sense of personal accomplishment, enjoyment, and feelings of comradery for equestrians; however, they also must face the stark reality of horses' physical fragility. While the life expectancy of a horse (typically 25 to 30 years) is much longer than some companion animal species (Parker, 2012), domesticated horses are also prone to a number of injuries and illnesses that may drastically shorten their lifespan. Currently, there is very little empirical literature available on how human beings experience the loss of their equine companions. Furthermore, research studies tend to be composed primarily of female respondents (Adrian & Stitt, 2017; Davies & James, 2018; Edenburg et al., 1999; Gilbert, 2008; McGowen et al., 2012). While this information mirrors equestrian demographics in the United States, more literature is needed to understand men's grief responses (Chur-Hansen, 2010), and how people from diverse backgrounds experience the loss of equine companions.

Grief responses of horse owners will vary based on a number of contextual factors, including personality, culture, religious orientation, perceived emotional bond with horses, as well as other social and economic influences. This is why it is critical for mental healthcare practitioners to examine their own assumptions and personal beliefs about grief and loss of companion animals, as well as to conduct a thorough case history with the client (Chur-Hansen, 2010). For example, when listening to a client describe the death of their horse, a counsellor might find the details of the euthanasia process unsettling and assume the client is experiencing distress from the event itself. Whereas the client might actually be more distressed about losing an important part of their identity, or the major disruption to their social life (Robinson, 1999). For some people who care for horses as an occupation, the death of horse also could mean a major loss of routine and their primary source of life purpose and financial stability (Helmer, 1999).

It is important to note that there are particular values associated within a number of equestrian subcultures, to include mental toughness, grit, determination and perseverance, hard work, stoicism, pragmatism, and even detachment. Decorated jockey, Victor Prado, captured some of these values well when he stated that racehorse jockeys learn to, "get on them, get off them, and move on" (Prado, 2009, p. 148). Sometimes though, despite attempts to minimize emotional attachment, people develop special relationships with particular horses. For Prado, this was Barbaro, the famous racehorse who died tragically following complications from a catastrophic injury that occurred at the 2006 Preakness Stakes:

> I couldn't just get on Barbaro, get off him, and move on. I loved him too much. It wasn't just that he had done so much for me. It was the way he came to me when saw me, ears pricked, anxious to communicate. It was the warm look in his eyes when he heard my voice. It was his sense of humor, the way he teased me when I fed him a baby carrot, looking away and then swooping back in with a gulp.
>
> (Prado, 2009, p. 149)

As mentioned at the beginning of this chapter, horses could be considered working animals, companions, or could occupy both roles at the same time. Consequently, some people's attitudes toward horses may seem paradoxical, as their perspectives could contain elements of both emotionality and instrumentality whereby they develop a close relationship caring for a horse on a day-to-day basis, while accepting that the horse is essentially, a living commodity who will be bought/sold for breeding, sport, or leisure purposes (Helmer, 1991; Schuurman, 2014). As such, equestrians may take more of a pragmatic perspective regarding a loss, whether it is loss of use, death, or the sale of a horse to another person. Sometimes this perspective stems from familial norms, especially if someone grew up on a farm with livestock animals, or their family managed equine breeding or sale operations. Although some attachment to animals in these contexts is appropriate for safe handling and welfare practices, too much attachment can lead to emotional complications and moral dilemmas, especially for young children and adolescents who will need to let these animals go later (Ellis & Irvine, 2010).

It is also vital for mental health practitioners to understand the ways in which the loss of an equine companion may occur. Although a good number of horses die of natural causes (e.g., old age), it is very common for horse involved in sport, showing, or recreational activities to experience exercise-related injuries, such as tendon/ligament or back and neck injuries (Davies & James, 2018). Horses are also extremely prone to experiencing colic. Colic is a broad term for abdominal pain caused by gastrointestinal problems, and it is the leading cause of mortality in adult horses (Scantlebury, Perkins, Pinchbeck, Archer, & Christley, 2014). Colic episodes are usually medical emergencies that require immediate veterinary care. During an episode, a horse's pain may subside for a brief period, only to return later, with more intensity. This can be a very distressing for a horse owner to witness, as horses with a severe episode of colic tend to repeatedly drop to the ground, roll, grunt, and sweat profusely in response to belly pain.

Nonsurgical treatment of colic may last over several days, sometimes requiring a person to stay with their horse and monitor symptoms around the clock. This could include walking the horse to encourage normal digestive processes, monitoring IV fluids, giving pain medications, and assisting the veterinarian with procedures. Many equestrians can attest to the significant emotional and financial costs of treating colic. Some types of colic require surgery to increase a horse's chances of survival, and because symptoms of colic may present without warning, horse owners could find themselves under great duress to make a quick life or death decision for their equine companions.

If a horse is a good candidate for colic surgery, an owner can expect to pay between $5,000–10,000 for the procedure, in addition to expenses associated with pre and post-operative care. This creates additional stressors, especially if a person does not have the financial means to pay for surgery. An equine caregiver may experience a great deal of guilt surrounding the decision to opt out of surgery and have the horse euthanized. Other people may rationalize the decision to euthanize a horse as the most practical or kind option given personal finances, the risks associated with surgery, the utility of the horse, or the horse's age (Scantlebury et al., 2014).

Disenfranchised Grief

Loss of an equine partner can occur due to life circumstances that require individuals to sell or otherwise relinquish a horse, such as during divorce, relocation, financial hardships, or even because of a personal injury. In one qualitative study on children's experiences of grief and loss, a young person recalls feelings anguish after selling a beloved horse:

> I remember when I left to go to the States, to go to college, and I was going to have to sell my horse. That really, really was very upsetting for me, even though I knew that was what had to happen. But it was, that was really disturbing, and I think I had nightmares about it and stuff – wondering if he was being taken care of all right.
>
> (Gilbert, 2008, p. 101).

While selling or rehoming horses are normal and accepted practices for many equestrians, individuals may struggle with the decision, and if other people minimize their grief, this could lead to feelings of disenfranchisement, especially if outward displays of grief or mourning for the loss of a horse are not recognized or accepted by family members, peers, or colleagues.

For equestrians who have built their entire livelihood around competition, the equestrian world can be a source of community and strong support during times of grief and loss. Coulter (2014) aptly described horse show life as "nomadic" – competitors, owners, trainers, and other stable staff can be on the road weeks or even months at a time with a string of show horses. This type of milieu naturally creates close-knit and family-like relationships. Unfortunately, the other reality of horse shows is that there exists a chance that a horse will suffer a catastrophic injury, or even sudden death, during an event. While some elite riders who have lost a horse during competition reported they felt understood and supported by their fellow equestrians, others find themselves exposed to criticism and judgment from the public (Davies & James, 2018). Media coverage exacerbates negative publicity, with social media in particular presenting significant challenges for grieving riders who compete on the national or international stage (for examples of riders' experiences of social media backlash see Keogh, 2015; Young, 2010).

Horse owners are not the only ones who experience grief around the loss of a horse. Barn support staff, such as trainers, instructors, managers, and grooms, often have close relational bonds with the horses they work with on a daily basis. In busy boarding and training stables, grooms are most often horses' primary caregivers, administering to their physical and emotional needs 24/7 (Helmer, 1991). A groom's relationship with the horses under their care is a very close bond indeed. However, grooms may have less control over important decisions made about their equine charges, and there is potential for an individual's grief to be minimized or forgotten when a horse dies, suffers a career-ending injury, or is sold. The amount of attention given to stable staffs' grieving processes may be a function of a barn's culture and social hierarchy. For instance, grooms may not be able to have any input on how a horse is memorialized, nor be given time off work to grieve. Alternatively, they may receive a great deal of social support, as well as care and concern, from their employers and a horse's owner.

Complicated Grief

Equestrians' experiences of complicated or prolonged grief have yet to be fully explored in clinical practice or scientific literature. Adrian and Stitt's (2017) study on complicated grief (CG) and companion animal loss is noteworthy, as results indicated horse owners in particular might represent a subgroup at risk for developing symptoms of CG and post-traumatic stress. Though the number of horse owners in the study's sample was small, all four respondents scored high on the PTSD checklist (PCL; Weathers, Litz, Herman, Huska, & Keane, 1993), with three out of four respondents meeting criteria for a probable diagnosis of PTSD. These results suggest more research is needed to understand factors that could contribute to higher levels of distress in equestrians.

The grief process could also be complicated when an individual not only has a significant attachment to their horse, but also to the barn setting and daily routines (e.g., riding, barn chores) as well. When a horse becomes injured, he or she may not be able to occupy the same a role in a person's life. For equestrians who compete, their equine partner's injuries can take on heightened significance. For example, riders may experience symptoms associated with vicarious trauma such as depression and helplessness, similar to what human athletes might experience when losing a teammate due to injury (Davies, Collins, & Ennis, 2015). A survey of 308 amateur riders indicated that experiences of shock and emptiness were most salient for riders whose horses had a career-ending injury or needed to be euthanized (Davies & James, 2018). The loss of access to riding can also be problematic, since riding might be central to a person's feelings of belongingness in their equestrian communities. Individuals may struggle with the change in their daily routine, or feel disconnected from their fellow riders. Indeed, research indicates riders who have lost their horses to injury appear to feel more iso-lated from others (Davies & James, 2018). Another sort of loss that can occur is when equestrians are no longer able to access equine sport or leisure activ-ities due to personal injuries or illnesses. In Sparkes' (1998) case study on athlete identity construction, "Rachael" described just how difficult life could be for someone who devoted her entire life to horses:

> I feel like I have lost my identity. I was a horse rider through and through, and I felt so at home when I was competing ... I lived, ate, and breathed horses. Anything could go wrong and it just didn't seem to matter so long as I had the horse "on the road." ... I do wish I could feel grateful for my lot, but I don't. It's no use pretending that life goes on, and there is more to life than horses because in my opinion, there isn't.
>
> (p. 647)

Grief complications also may arise during the euthanasia decision-making process. What makes this decision more difficult? Researchers suggest gender and personality could influence decision-making, as well as how individuals rate the acceptability of the procedures used to euthanize their horses (McGowan et al., 2012). For instance, researchers in Australia con-ducted a survey of 111 horse owners and found that female horse owners who scored higher in neuroticism (e.g., exhibiting more worry, frustra-tion, anger, or guilt) had a greater likelihood of perceiving the decision process as "more difficult" (McGowan et al., 2012). Thus, when talking with a client about the euthanasia process, it is important to listen for their beliefs about the acceptability of the method used, as well as their experi-ence of working with the attending veterinarian. If a person perceived the euthanasia method as less acceptable, or felt unsupported by their veteri-narian, they may experience more intense feelings of distress, such as anger, anguish, guilt, or remorse (Dickinson & Hoffman, 2017; McGowan et al., 2012). The experience of anticipatory grief may also be relevant in these situations, as the possibility of an impending loss may result in a horse's caregiver experiencing an internal conflict accompanied by strong feelings of fear or anxiety. These feelings may contribute to a person delaying the euthanasia decision-making process, which in turn could potentially prolong a horse's suffering.

Conclusion

The strength of the horse–human bond is influenced by a number of factors, especially considering the variety of roles horses occupy in the lives of human beings. Due to the myriad ways in which people define their relationships with horses, it is critical for mental healthcare practitioners to draw out information from clients about the nature of their bonds with equine companions. Helpful lines of inquiry might include asking a client how long a horse was with them, if the horse was a recreational or sports partner, the amount of time they spent with their horse each day, whether the horse lived at home or a boarding stable, and if most of the people in their social circles were equestrian enthusiasts too. Lastly given that a horse could be in a person's life for 20 years or more, it might also be helpful to gather historical information to determine in what ways the client's relationship with an equine companion was connected with other important relationships in their lives, significant life events, developmental milestones, and major life transitions.

Case Scenarios

Case Scenario #1:

Jen is a 30-year-old female horse trainer who is seeking counseling support for a troubling issue that occurred at her workplace. Jen reports that last Saturday, a 6-year-old quarter horse gelding she has been training for the last 4 years suffered a severe colic episode and was euthanized. She recounts how she arrived at the stable on Monday morning to find that the horse's stall was empty, and no one was on the premises to explain his whereabouts. She was finally able to get a hold of the stable manager who explained that the owner of the horse, who is also Jen's employer, decided to have the gelding euthanized due to the expense and risks associated with colic surgery.

Jen stops talking, and you notice she is trying to hold back tears. After a few moments of silence, Jen admonishes herself for crying and states to you that she understood why the horse's owner did not want to risk surgery. When you redirect her to share more about her sadness, she mentions feeling heartbroken that she did not get to say goodbye to the gelding, but quickly wipes away her tears and says to you, "I don't know why I am so upset right now; he wasn't my horse." After another moment of silence, you inquire if she has spoken to the owner yet. She shares with you that she has been feeling extremely irritable with the gelding's owner. Although she has other horses to train for this person, she is struggling to find the motivation to go to the stable every morning. She even went so far as to rearrange her schedule so she could exercise horses when her employer was not on the premises.

Discussion Questions:

1. What factors might be contributing to Jen's feelings of ambivalence about the death of this particular horse?
2. Describe why it is important to ask Jen about her relationship with the horse, as well as her relationship with the horse's owner.

3. How might broader equestrian cultural norms influence Jen's grieving process, and how might you support her in acknowledging and validating her own grief experience?

4. What special considerations related to non-horse owners and the concept of disenfranchised grief might be relevant in this case scenario?

5. What circumstances surrounding the horse's death could be contributing to Jen's need to seek out counseling, and what clues in her narrative point to the potential for her to experience complicated grief?

Case Scenario #2:

Sarah is a single, 48-year-old female client who owns a small horse ranch, and she is seeking counseling because of a distressing conversation she had with a veterinarian regarding her horse Bonnie's health. Bonnie is Sarah's 22-year-old mare who recently suffered an acute laminitic episode, which caused damage to the internal structures of her hoof, resulting in severe pain and lameness. Currently, Bonnie is unable to walk without pain, so she is confined to stall rest. Sarah tells you that since this was Bonnie's third episode of laminitis to happen over a short amount of time, the veterinarian strongly recommended to her that she have her horse humanely euthanized. Sarah is sobbing now, and tells you that she is angry with the vet for "giving up" on Bonnie, and she thinks there is still a chance that her mare will be able to live a comfortable life. She also says that she felt that the vet was judging her negatively for not immediately agreeing to have Bonnie euthanized. She felt ashamed for disagreeing with him. You reflect to Sarah that you can see how distressed she is right now, and you ask if she has ever had to think about a decision like this before. Sarah shakes her head to indicate "no," and tells you that she cannot imagine choosing to end Bonnie's life, and she wants Bonnie to go on her own terms someday. Sarah purchased Bonnie as a 2-year-old, and they have been inseparable ever since. Sarah then describes how Bonnie bounced back from the last two episodes of laminitis, so she feels hopeful that there is something that can be done this time too. Sarah also reports that she has not been able to sleep since she talked with the vet, and she starts crying every time she goes out to feed Bonnie in the morning. She states that yesterday, she noticed Bonnie had not eaten her evening meal from the night before, and this worries her. As Sarah shares this information, she begins crying and says, "I don't know what to do!"

Discussion Questions:

1. Could anticipatory grief be a relevant issue in this case? If so, describe how you might approach this topic with Sarah.

2. Is there any evidence that Sarah might be experiencing a moral dilemma surrounding the euthanasia decision-making process? What questions might you ask to explore this with Sarah?

3. Describe why it is important to talk with Sarah about her experience with the veterinarian. What questions could you ask her in order to increase your understanding of their working relationship, as well as her perceptions about the vet's behavior?
4. Bonnie has been in Sarah's life for 20 years. She uses the word "insep-arable" to describe her relationship with Bonnie, and you have noted that Sarah is single. How might these factors contribute to Sarah's dif-ficulty making a decision about Bonnie's health, and what questions should you ask in order to assess Sarah's current level of social support beyond her relationship with Bonnie?
5. How might your own beliefs and feelings about euthanasia, and eutha-nizing companion animals, influence the counseling process with Sarah? Describe potential ethical issues and ways you can address these issues in accordance with best practices in ethical decision-making and client care.

References

Adrian, J. A. L., & Stitt, A. (2017). Pet loss, complicated grief, and post-traumatic stress disorder in Hawaii. *Anthrozoös, 30*(1), 123–133.

American Horse Council (AHC) (2018). *Economic impact of the US horse industry.* Washington, DC: American Horse Council Foundation.

American Horse Publications (AHP) (July, 2015). *2015 AHP Equine Industry Survey.* South Daytona, FL: American Horse Publications.

Butler, C., & Lagoni, L. (2006). Euthanasia and grief support in an equine bond-centered practice. In J. J. Bertone (Ed.), *Equine geriatric medicine and surgery* (pp. 241–243). St. Louis, MO: Saunders Elsevier.

Chur-Hansen, A. (2010). Grief and bereavement issues and the loss of a compan-ion animal: People living with a companion animal, owners of livestock, and animal support workers. *Clinical Psychologist, 14*(1), 14–21.

Corp-Minamiji, C. (2012, August). Euthanasia and what comes next. *The Horse.* Retrieved from https://thehorse.com/117879/euthanasia-and-what-comes-next/

Coulter, K. (2014). Herds and hierarchies: Class, nature, and the social construc-tion of horses in equestrian culture. *Animals & Society, 22,* 135–152.

Dashper, K. (2017). Listening to horses: Developing attentive interspecies relation-ships through sport and leisure. *Society & Animals, 25*(3), 207–224.

Davies, E., & James, S. (2018). The psychological responses of amateur riders to their horses' injuries. *Comparative Exercise Physiology, 14*(2), 135–142.

Davies, E., Collins, R., & Ennis, J. (2015). Psychological and emotional responses of elite riders to the injury of their equine partners. Poster session presented at Division of Sport and Exercise Psychology Conference 2016, Leeds, UK.

Dickinson, G. E., & Hoffmann, H. C. (2017). Saying Goodbye to Family. *Society & Animals, 25*(5), 490–507.

Edenburg, N., Kirpensteijn, J., & Sanders, N. (1999). Equine euthanasia: The vet-erinarian's role in providing owner support. *Anthrozoös, 12*(3), 138–141. doi: 10.2752/089279399787000219

Ellis, C., & Irvine, L. (2010). Reproducing dominion: Emotional apprenticeship in the 4-H youth livestock program. *Society & Animals, 18*(1), 21–39.

Gilbert, K. R. (2008). Loss and grief between and among cultures: The experience of third culture kids. *Illness, Crisis, and Loss*, 16(2), 93–109.

Helmer, J. (1991). The horse in backstretch culture. *Qualitative Sociology*, 14(2), 175–195.

Keaveney, S. M. (2008). Equines and their human companions. *Journal of business research*, 61(5), 444–454.

Keogh, F. (2015, July). Kauto Star: Rider Laura Collett hurt by "lies" over horse's death. Retrieved from www.bbc.com/sport/horse-racing/33400764

McGowan, T. W., Phillips, C. J., Hodgson, D. R., Perkins, N., & McGowan, C. M. (2012). Euthanasia in aged horses: relationship between the owner's personality and their opinions on, and experience of, euthanasia of horses. *Anthrozoös*, 25(3), 261–275.

Parker, R. (2012). *Equine science* (4th ed.). Clifton Park, NY: Delmar.

Prado, E. (2009). *My guy Barbaro: A jockey's journey through love, triumph, and heartbreak*. New York, NY: Harper.

Robinson, I. H. (1999). The human-horse relationship: how much do we know? *Equine Veterinary Journal*, 31(S28), 42–45.

Scantlebury, C. E., Perkins, E., Pinchbeck, G. L., Archer, D. C., & Christley, R. M. (2014). Could it be colic? Horse-owner decision making and practices in response to equine colic. *BMC Veterinary Research*, 10(1), S1.

Schuurman, N. (2014). "I Throw Them Out of Here": The horse trade as phronetic Action. *Anthrozoös*, 27(4), 591–602.

Sparkes, A. C. (1998). Athletic identity: An Achilles' heel to the survival of self. *Qualitative Health Research*, 8(5), 644–664.

Stull, C. L. (2013). Death and euthanasia as contemporary topics in equine curricula. *Journal of Equine Veterinary Science*, 33(5), 309–314.

USDA (2016). *Baseline reference of equine health and management in the United States, 2015 (Report no. 718.1216)*. Fort Collins, CO: USDA–APHIS–VS–CEAH–NAHMS.

Weathers, F., Litz, B., Herman, D., Huska, J., & Keane, T. (October, 1993). The PTSD Checklist (PCL): Reliability, validity, and diagnostic utility. Paper presented at the annual meeting of the International Society for Traumatic Stress Studies, Chicago, IL.

Young, C. (2010, August). Three Days Three Ways Interviews Laine Ashker. *The Chronicle of the Horse*. Retrieved from www.chronofhorse.com/article/three-days-three-ways- interviews-laine-ashker

12 Separation from Assistance Dogs

The Complicated Psychological Burden During Loss of the Relationship

Mariko Yamamoto and Lynette A. Hart

Introduction

Many studies have focused on people experiencing the loss of their pets, but there are very few studies that have focused on similar losses of people living with assistance dogs. In recent decades, assistance dogs have greatly expanded in both their numbers and their varied roles (Walther et al., 2017). Assistance dogs enrich their partners' lives and are prominent among the working dogs in the world. Therefore, it is essential to understand the psychological challenges that assistance dog partners may experience when their partnership ends. Assistance dogs are important family members, but they also have working roles in assisting with their partners' disabilities. Thus, they differ from pet dogs, and these differences can cause unique psychological distress among assistance dog partners when these working relationships end. This chapter introduces some of the differences between assistance dogs and pet dogs and describes the experiences of assistance dog partners that frequently result when their working relationships end.

Characteristics of Assistance Dogs

Assistance dogs are specially trained to perform tasks that support their partners who have disabilities. Guide dogs for people with visual impairments, hearing dogs for people with hearing impairments, and service dogs for people with other types of disabilities, including but not limited to orthopedic disabilities, psychiatric disabilities, or autism, are all assistance dogs (Assistance Dogs International, 2018). "Service Animal" is another term used under the US Americans with Disabilities Act (ADA) and has the same meaning as an assistance dog, except that the US Department of Justice (DOJ) regulations implementing the ADA include miniature horses as assistance animals (US Department of Justice, 2011). The ADA requires "reasonable accommodation" for people with disabilities. The DOJ regulations specify that people living with assistance dogs are allowed to have access with their dogs to all places/facilities used by the general public. Similar laws and/or regulations exist in many other countries, allowing assistance dog partners to spend most of the day accompanied by their dogs.

Assistance dogs can assure more independent lives for their partners. They provide assistance by performing various tasks. Some studies have shown that acquisition of assistance dogs facilitates partners going to school or starting a new job (Sachs-Ericsson, Hansen, & Fitzgerald, 2002). Assistance dogs may also provide psychological support as well as physical support: increased confidence, self-esteem, and sense of safety. Decreased loneliness and anxiety are often reported after partners acquire assistance dogs (Davis, Nattrass, O'Brien, Patronek, & MacCollin, 2004; Fairman & Huebner, 2001; Hart, Zasloff, & Benfatto, 1996; Rintala, Sachs-Ericsson, & Hart, 2002; Whitmarsh, 2005). Assistance dogs and the tasks that they provide are essential for their partners, but they also are associated with specific difficulties that assistance dog partners can experience at the end of the partnership, as discussed later in this chapter.

The US Department of Transportation (DOT) and the US Department of Housing and Urban Development (HUD) have broader definitions of assistance dogs in their regulations, including "Emotional Support Animals" (ESAs) (US Department of Housing and Urban Development, 2004; US Department of Transportation, 2008). The DOT and HUD provide reasonable accommodations to persons with disabilities and assure that such persons can spend more time with their animals. Unlike assistance dogs, ESAs are not required to perform tasks related to assisting an owner with a disability. Unfortunately, the very broad definition of disabilities and the confusion over these various laws have increased the lack of enforcement and the number of fraudulent assistance dogs in the US (American Veterinary Medical Association, 2017). Particularly with ESAs, the American Veterinary Medical Association is offering leadership (Fine et al., 2019). Various other efforts to make some regulatory improvements in legislation, regulations, and/or policies by legislators, airlines and others are currently underway (Burr, 2018; Canine Companions for Independence, 2016; Edelman, 2018; US Department of Transportation, 2018). This chapter primarily focuses on assistance dogs as described in the DOJ regulations and does not include ESAs, yet, clearly, partners with ESAs rely greatly on their animals and also experience severe grief at their loss. Losing an assistance dog means not only losing the companionship of the dog, but also losing assistance in tasks the dog provides. This contrasts with people losing an ESA, where the dog's main role is for support and companionship. Yet, just as with losing an assistance dog, losing an ESA causes a great impact on the partner's life. Therefore, many of the comments in this chapter related to assistance dog partners also pertain to ESA partners, which are specifically addressed at the end of this chapter.

Defining Assistance Dogs

Clarifying the unique lifestyle of assistance dogs facilitates understanding the specific difficulties that assistance dog partners experience at the end of the partnership. In this section, we will discuss the life, from birth through training, of a typical assistance dog that is trained by an Assistance Dog International (ADI)-accredited facility.

Birth to Puppy Raiser

Procedures in raising assistance dogs vary among training organizations, but typically guide and mobility dogs at ADI-accredited facilities begin life through a careful selection process for a desirable sire and dams. The breeds typically used, especially with guide dogs, are primarily purpose-bred Labrador Retrievers, Golden Retrievers, and German Shepherds (Contreras, 2003; Walther et al., 2017). Young puppies usually stay with their mother until they are eight weeks old. During this period, they are socialized to various stimuli that assistance dogs typically might encounter as an adult. When puppies reach around eight weeks of age, they are assigned to a family with whom they live until about 12 months old. During this puppy-raising period, they are exposed to various environmental experiences and also receive basic training in living with, and being around, different people.

Training and Team Training

When puppies reach around 12 months of age, they are returned to the training facility for several months to be assessed for their potential as an assistance dog. If deemed acceptable, they undergo the next phase of training, and if qualified by exhibiting the appropriate skills and temperament to be an assistance dog, they are paired with a future partner. At this time, the team receives additional training. During this team training, the future partner learns to live and work with the dog.

Working and Retirement

Once dogs are fully trained, they and their partners begin living together and receive periodic follow-ups. Unless problems arise, dogs can usually work until they reach 8 to 12 years of age (Wenthold & Savage, 2007). Once they retire, dogs shift to a pet role. For example, a partner may keep the dog as a pet. The dog may also be adopted by a family member, friend, or a volunteer family chosen by the training program. This lifestyle sharply contrasts with the lifestyle of a typical companion dog that spends its entire life with one family until its death. It's possible if the assistance dog was adopted out to another family, the partner of the dog may have lost contact with the dog by the time it approaches death, and the partner actually experienced the separation long before. Some of these more complicated but typical outcomes of human-assistance dog partnerships are depicted in Figure 12.1. The partner typically needs to deal with the loss of a working relationship with one dog and at the same time prepare to work with a new dog.

Personally Trained Assistance Dogs

In some cases, as allowed in the US, people may choose to train their own assistance dogs with or without guidance from trainers. Others may ask a professional dog trainer to train their assistance dogs. In these cases, the sources of dogs vary with some training programs given suitable puppies or adult dogs from breeders, dog owners, and shelters. Team training is not always provided at these training programs; it sometimes is given within the partners' home environment.

Dealing with Separations from Assistance Dogs

As with companion dogs, partners cannot avoid separation from assistance dogs. However, assistance dog partners may experience several different

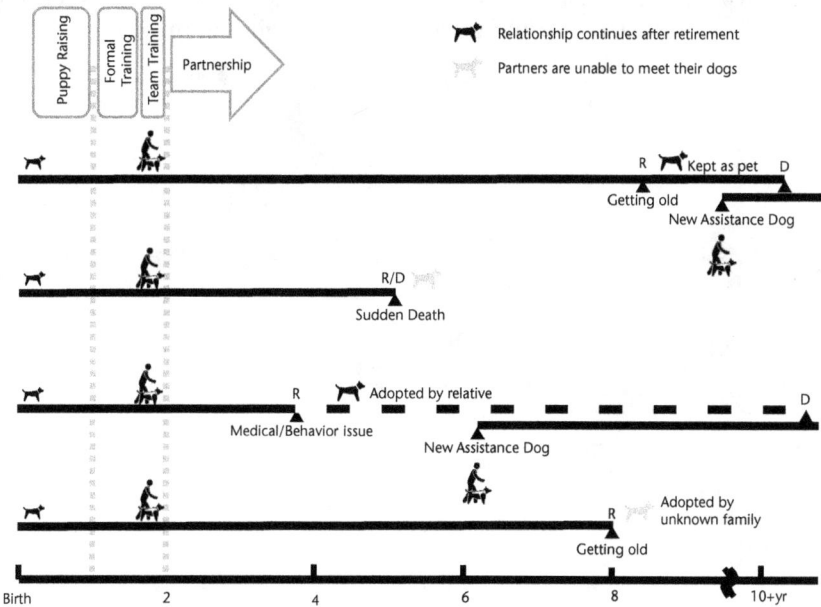

Figure 12.1 Outcomes of Human-Assistance Dog Partnerships. Partners Lose Assistance from their Dogs at Various Times and are Separated from their Dogs in Numerous Ways. Partners are often not with the Dog at the Time of its Death.

types of separation from their partnership that differ from that of a typical companion dog owner. When assistance dog partners are able to live with their retired dogs, or a family or friend adopts these dogs, then the assistance dog partners can maintain contact with their dogs. In these situations, the actual final separation does not occur until their dogs die. However, in other circumstances, the separation happens when families unknown to the partners adopt the dog. Some partnerships end before one would expect, due to the dog's early retirement. These unforeseen retirements occur when the dogs can no longer perform their required tasks, such as when they develop health or behavior problems, or suffer untreatable injuries. Moxon, Whiteside, and England (2016) reported that there were some cases where guide dogs had to retire because they experienced dog bites by other dogs, causing injury or distress – precluding them from continuing to work as a guide dog. Another study found that 43 out of 118 guide dogs experienced early retirement (Lloyd, Budge, La Grow, & Stafford, 2016). Examples of early retirements identified by Contreras (2003) are shown in Figure 12.2; these early retirements end the working partnership and require that the partner make plans to move on with a new dog.

The working success rate 1-year post training from some facilities was as low as 13%, but varies among organizations (Batt, Batt, Baguley, & McGreevy, 2010). Whelan (2017) found that 15–20% of guide dogs retired within 3 years after graduating from their training programs. Thus,

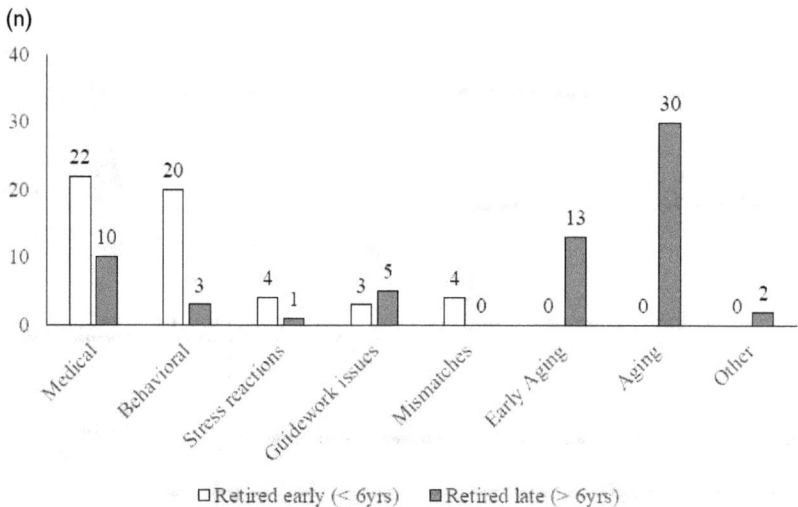

Figure 12.2 Final Outcomes for Causes for Retirement of Guide Dogs. Early Retirement is Usually Due to Medical or Behavior Problems, whereas Later Retirement is Associated with Problems of Aging.

Source: Data from Lena Contreras, 2003. © Yamamoto & Hart, 2018.

frequently assistance dog partners experience early retirements requiring that partners experience early separations from their dogs.

A study by Contreras (2003) on the causes for guide dogs retiring, either before or after 6 years of age, found that medical and behavior problems were the primary causes for early retirement before 6 years of age. After 6 years of age, problems related to aging were the primary cause of retirement. In the case of guide dogs, Contreras (2003) found that a large proportion of dogs retire from working before they have a terminal disease; hence, only a small fraction of guide dogs are euthanized at the instruction of their partners, as shown in Figure 12.3. The separation that occurs at the end of the working dog partnership can create major grieving and loss for guide dog partners: often equivalent to the grief experienced from the actual death of the dog.

An example of the frequent early retirements of dogs is illustrated by Lena Contreras' experience (personal communication, 2018). A guide dog partner, Lena's experiences with past guide dogs reflect the difficulties related to separating from guide dogs. Lena currently has her sixth guide dog. She had her first guide, Liza, until Liza was 10, when Liza died of a hemorrhage while still a working guide. After Liza, Lena had Maggie, but had to have her euthanized after 4 years, due to a brain tumor. Her next dog, Baltic, retired from work at the age of 9, and then lived with Lena's mother until she was euthanized at the age of 14. Alden was Lena's first male dog, and he worked with her for 4 years but then had to stop due to inflammatory bowel disease. Alden's puppy raiser then adopted him and gives updates to Lena regarding his health. Next, Lena had Jasper. Just as they were developing their partnership, he was

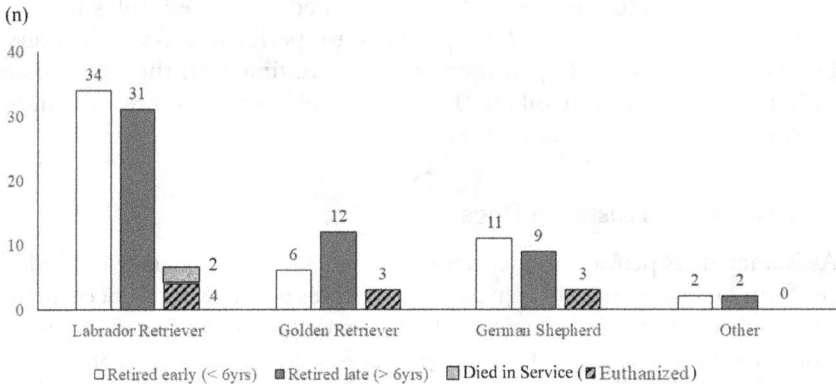

Figure 12.3 Final Outcomes for the Working Lives of Guide Dogs. Most Guide Dogs Retire from Guide Work, whether Early, before 6 Years of Age, or Late, after 6 Years of Age. Few Dogs Die in Service, and even Fewer have Euthanasia Arranged by their Partners.

Source: Data from Lena Contreras, 2003. © Yamamoto & Hart, 2018.

repeatedly attacked by other dogs. The final attack frightened him to such an extent that he lost the confidence he needed to work. Finally, Lena's current dog, Elora, has been her partner for 3 years. For Lena, the greatest loss was with Jasper. She was expecting to work with him for 6–8 years and she felt robbed of the partnership with him when it ended so early. When she returned him to the facility from which she obtained him, they transferred him to another facility to become a service dog to assist someone with post-traumatic stress disorder. Although Lena sent information to the new owner, she has not received any news on how Jasper is doing, which exacerbates her feeling of loss. This experience with Jasper has been the hardest, despite being the shortest duration of time she spent with a guide dog.

Duration of Partnership with Assistance Dogs

Assistance dogs take a different life course from companion dogs while filling their special roles. Dogs raised by assistance dog programs are paired with assistance dog partners to form a team when the dogs are around 2 years old. The partnership can then continue for 6 to 10 years, until ideally the dog retires when it is around 8 to 12 years old (Wenthold & Savage, 2007). Therefore, assistance dog partners often experience repeated separations from successive dogs. When people choose not to adopt their retired dogs, the duration of these relationships are shorter than those of companion dogs that usually continue until the dog dies. While the partnership duration with assistance dogs often is shorter than that of companion dogs, assistance dog partners spend a great amount of time with their assistance dogs. The dogs accompany their partners to places where companion dogs are not allowed, and their roles include being physically close to their partners to perform tasks as needed. Frequently, assistance dog partners spend more time with their dogs than with any other family members. This strong relationship cannot be measured simply by the years of partnership.

Benefits from Assistance Dogs

Assistance dogs provide tremendous benefits. They are specially trained to perform tasks to support their partners with disabilities, and indeed many studies describe partners' increased independence as a result of having an assistance dog (Lloyd, La Grow, Stafford, & Budge, 2008a, 2008b; Valentine, Kiddoo, & LaFleur, 1993). However, these tasks are only a part of the benefits brought by assistance dogs. They can assure safety for their partners by assisting with mobility (Audrestch et al., 2015; Burrow, Adams, & Spiers, 2008; Sachs-Ericsson et al., 2002; Valentine et al., 1993). These dogs provide socializing effects (Davis et al., 2004; Hart, Hart, & Bergin, 1987; Hart et al., 1996; Wiggett-Bartnard & Steel, 2008) and offer their partners a sense of social integration (Guest, Collis, & McNicholas, 2006; Lane, McNicholas, & Collis, 1998; Refson, Jackson, Dusoir, & Archer, 1999). Through the dogs' assistance, partners may become more independent, have less anxiety about going outside of the house, have more confidence, and become more active. All of these changes lead to increased sociability and social integration. People with disabilities often experience social stigma and discrimination (Bedini, 2000; Green, Davis, Karshmer, Marsh, & Straight, 2005), but when they are with their assistance dogs, the dogs facilitate social interaction with strangers and shift people's attention away from their disabilities (Hart et al., 1987). In addition, handling a well-trained dog reveals to the public that the person can control the dog, thus increasing the person's self-esteem and confidence. Assistance dogs also help with loneliness since they are almost always present.

Besides receiving benefits from these dogs, assistance dog partners also provide nurturing and care for their dogs, assuming responsibility for the dogs and devoting their efforts to maintaining their dogs' physical and mental well-being. Daily affectionate interactions, grooming, feeding, and exercising, and medical care are some examples of dogs' requirements. While partners cannot directly provide some aspects of care, they can arrange for other people to provide the necessary care. Providing such care and making these arrangements might seem troublesome, but these responsibilities actually are additional benefits from assistance dogs, giving partners a sense of purpose and a feeling of being needed. Managing a planned schedule and consistent daily life for their dogs is also necessary. Accompanying a dog in public is like bringing along a small child, whereby the partner must assure that everything is acceptable for the dog.

Partners may experience negative reactions from others, such as not being allowed to enter a public facility. In such circumstances, the partner may have to educate the proprietor on the importance of assistance dogs and the law, sometimes leading to partners gaining new skills and becoming more assertive (Valentine et al., 1993; Wiggett-Barnard & Steel, 2008). Kwong and Bartholomew (2011) reported that assistance dog partners learn how to control their own emotions so that their emotional changes do not negatively affect their dogs. All these elements of daily life with assistance dogs can enhance a person's development. Kwong and Bartholomew (2011) mention that this reciprocal caregiving, in which dogs assist with tasks for their partners and partners provide care for the dogs, is a very important element of this relationship. The strong attachment between assistance dog partners and their dogs is developed through their unique relationship. Therefore, assistance dogs are not just providing tasks. Their existence provides synergetic effects in various aspects of the lives of their partners.

The Meaning for Partners of Losing the Partnership with an Assistance Dog

Although assistance dogs differ from companion dogs, assistance dogs are considered as important family members and the impact of separation from assistance dogs shares some similar aspects as separation from companion dogs. However, assistance dogs often provide a stronger impact on partners' lives than companion dogs do. Separation from assistance dogs can also mean losing many of the synergetic benefits that assistance dogs provide. Some people say that assistance dogs are like a part of their body. Nicholson and her colleagues found that 35–42% of guide dog partners felt like they lost their sight again at the end of the partnership (Nicholson, Kemp-Wheeler, & Griffiths, 1995). This section examines some of the outcomes of ending the unique relationship between assistance dog partners and their dogs.

Schneider (2005) described three phases of good-byes in the loss of a guide dog. The first goodbye is when people decide to retire their dogs; the second goodbye is when the dogs retire; and the third goodbye is when the dogs dies (also see Figure 12.1). People may think about their dog's retirement when they start showing signs of getting older and/or have difficulties performing some tasks. In her own experiences, Allen (2006) mentioned that as her guide dog was getting older with a deteriorating physical condition, Allen's autonomy was gradually taken from her and even her freedom began to vanish. As her experience indicates, assistance dog partners may start feeling some loss of the gained benefits from their assistance dogs even before a true separation or retirement occurs. Therefore, people often worry about the time when their dogs will retire long before the actual retirement (Contreras, 2003; Nicholson et al., 1995).

When assistance dogs retire, some partners choose to keep living with their retired dogs. In this case, it is not a true separation from their dogs. However, retiring assistance dogs does mean that the relationship between the assistance dogs and their partners fundamentally changes. Retired dogs no longer perform the same tasks as before, especially outside of the house, since they do not always accompany their partners as assistance dogs do. Losing the assistance provided by these dogs may require their partners to re-acknowledge their disabilities. Social participation and independence that had been facilitated by assistance dogs can deteriorate following the retirement of a dog. Retiring assistance dogs means that partners have to adjust to a life without the dog's assistance. Additionally, keeping a retired dog at home can provide challenges when people begin applying for a new assistance dog. They may have no accredited facilities nearby, for despite numerous facilities in the US, 18 states lack an accredited facility; this presents particular geographic challenges when acquiring a new dog (Walter, Yamamoto, Thigpen, Willits, & Hart, 2017). Some people prefer not to leave an old dog at home while they are taking team training lessons at a facility (Allen, 2006), and others worry that their old dogs will be upset seeing them with a new dog (Schneider, 2005). Additionally, older dogs may require more medical costs. For all these reasons, assistance dog partners may feel increasing conflict during this time of transition.

At the time of the dog's death, assistance dog partners express feelings similar to those experiencing the loss of a close relationship or a best friend (Kwong & Bartholomew, 2011). Some people even feel that the loss is more difficult than with a significant other such as a family member (Kwong & Bartholomew, 2011). This death is a final separation for partners who were able to keep their retired dogs close to them.

On the other hand, people who give up living near their dogs are faced with experiencing two losses at the same time: a separation from their dogs and loss of assistance from their dogs. This often creates a significant burden. As discussed previously, even if this relationship was short, they typically have a strong attachment to their dogs and often feel guilt, shock, and even anger for their dogs' early retirements and death (Kwong & Bartholomew, 2011; Whelan, 2017).

The End of Life of an Assistance Dog

The more fulfilling life an owner has had with his/her dog, the more difficult it is to say goodbye. Knowing that the dog's death is coming soon and then deciding how to end the dog's life is extremely difficult. People who live with retired assistance dogs also face these difficulties. Euthanasia is a common way to end a dog's life (Kemp, Jacobs, & Stewart, 2016), while others choose a natural death for their dog. Still, other dogs die unexpectedly (e.g., accident or sudden terminal illness). The partners' grief may be somewhat relieved if they can choose a satisfactory and acceptable measure for ending their dogs' life. Indeed, if owners are conflicted about a decision for euthanasia, or feel that appropriate care was not provided, they often feel guilty. This is a frequent component of the grief (Messam & Hart, 2018). Having sought veterinary care for their dog can reduce the grief experienced by the partner, but the amount of time spent actively caring for a dog after they become ill is negatively associated with coming to terms with the loss.

In the near future, hospice care may increasingly provide supportive and convenient strategies for owners with retired assistance dogs. Recently, hospice care is becoming more available (Cooney, 2015; Goldberg, 2016). Hospice care focuses on a patient's comfort rather than treatment when a cure no longer can be expected. Therefore, the goal of hospice care is to maintain the animal's well-being, comfort, and dignity at the end of its life (Cooney, 2015). Hospice care involves taking a team approach, similar to hospice for humans (Cooney, 2015). However, people with disabilities likely would require additional support for the hospice care of their dogs. For example, elderly dogs, especially large breeds, may experience mobility issues, with more physical assistance required for them. If partners cannot provide such care, hiring pet-sitters, or requesting help from family members or friends may be an alternative choice. The financial costs for pet-sitters and hospice care are certainly considerations for many. Preparing well in advance for the physical support and the financial burdens associated with ailing dogs is important, rather than avoiding the subject and delaying the formation of a viable plan for their dog's impending death. This preparation heightens the chance that partners can choose a satisfactory measure when ending their dog's life.

Situational Features of Assistance Dogs Influencing Grief

The stronger the attachment people feel to their pets, the more likely they are to experience severe grief (Field, Orsini, Gavish, & Packman, 2009; Wrobel & Dye, 2003). Partners spend long periods of time with their assistance dogs throughout each day, often more than the time spent with their family members. Not surprisingly, they consider their assistance dogs as family members and develop strong attachments to their dogs. Hence, they experience a big impact when they lose their dogs. On the other hand, the timing and types of separation they experience from their assistance dogs also affect the impact that their partners experience. Nicholson and her colleagues found that when assistance dog partners or their family member or a friend can adopt their retired dogs, their experienced grief, distress, and scores on the General Health Questionnaire are less than those whose retired dogs were adopted by unknown families through training organizations (Nicholson et al., 1995). Apparently, if people can continue having contact with their former assistance dogs, they feel less grief than people who cannot maintain contact with their dogs. Knowing their dogs are being cared for also helps to relieve their grief. Most assistance dog partners experience strong grief after separation from their dogs, likely due to the loss of the caregiving relationship (Kwong and Bartholomew, 2011). The reciprocal caregiving between assistance dog partners and their dogs is a core relationship dynamic and essential to establishing the synergetic effects in the relationship.

Early retirement causes a different type of loss. It might be thought that early retirement causes less grief for their partners than death. However, this is not true. Instead, such separation can cause greater psychological distress for people who had to give up their relationship much earlier than expected, as highlighted by Lena Contreras (private communication, 2018). Considering service dogs for children with autism, Burrows and her colleagues (2008) noted one mother who had a hard time returning their service dog even though the dog developed behavior problems. Although it was a short relationship and the dog did not fulfill the originally defined role, the dog had already become an important family member, making it difficult to return the dog when it was not adequately performing tasks. Whelan (2017) conducted interviews with guide dog partners who experienced an early retirement. Four out of nine interviewees reported that they had a good relationship with their dogs as pets. As with companion dogs, assistance dogs require care from the first day of partnering. Becoming a working partner in a new relationship is a new special role for the assistance dog, and this gradually develops as the team spends more time together. Therefore, even with assistance dogs that do not fulfill their roles of assisting with disabilities, people may experience significant grief from an early retirement.

In interviews conducted by Whelan (2017), guide dog partners experienced strain and suffering from their dogs' behavior problems, going through significant difficulties when making the decision to return their dogs and thereby also losing their partners. Further, such people have to wait until their next guide dog is trained, and these people worry that they might experience an early retirement again with the upcoming dog. As Nicholson and her colleagues (1995) found, knowing their dogs are given good care relieved their partners. But without such knowledge, people developed considerable worry. Assistance dog partners usually make the decision for early retirement, and they tend to blame themselves, and feel guilt, doubt, and confusion for this decision.

Assistance dogs are designed to provide assisting tasks, and at the same time they are important companions – two different roles. Assistance dog partners face a dilemma when deciding to return their dogs while at the same time having a good relationship with their dogs as companions. Partners often question the decision they have made, and worry about the future after their dogs have been returned to a school or training facility. Whelan (2017) mentioned that early retirements cause "ambiguous loss" and "disenfranchised grief." Early retirement happens suddenly and assistance dog partners do not have enough time to understand the situation well before separating from their dogs. Also, it is hard for them to receive the kind of understanding that they need from people. The "ambiguous loss" and "disenfranchised grief" complicate partners' psychological distress. Thus, even though their relationships with their assistance dogs were short, such unique separations may cause great burdens. An early retirement comes suddenly and can be classified as a traumatic loss and cause further symptoms for partners.

Grief becomes even more severe when people are already experiencing adverse events in their lives besides the loss of their assistance dog (Nicholson et al., 1995). These people are especially vulnerable and require more care. A training organization of assistance dogs can play an important role for people experiencing a difficult time when losing a dog. Training organizations that offer little information and communication, and insufficient support for the decision-making of retirement, can lead to increased grief (Nicholson et al., 1995). On the other hand, assistance dog partners experience less grief when they feel they have support from their organization. Living alone can be another risk factor for greater grief. Among pet dog owners, it is reported that people living alone experienced greater grief (Field et al., 2009). Some studies reported that people living alone are more likely to show strong attachments to their pets (Amiot & Bastian, 2015; Brown, 2006), and those strongly attached to their pets experience severe grief (Field et al., 2009; Wrobel & Dye, 2003). It is not surprising that assistance dog partners living alone experience greater grief, similar to pet dog owners living alone, than those living with their family members. Isolation and loneliness are added to missing the companionship and assistance of the dog. How people prepare for their separation from dogs as well as the timing and types of dogs' retirement affect the grief reactions of partners.

Even assistance dog partners who keep their retired dogs as pets may experience unique difficulties. With a retired dog at home, partners worry about welcoming in a new assistance dog. Some people refuse to welcome a new dog because of this and sacrifice their freedom or independence because of this concern. Thus, the retirement of assistance dogs affects their partners' daily life. Partners are often in this situation when their first assistance dog retires – a phase sometimes called the "second dog syndrome" (Allen, 2006; Schneider, 2005). Being emotionally attached to their previous dog sometimes makes it difficult for partners to build a relationship with a new dog, which can be a burden for both the dogs and the person. Similar to pet dog owners, assistance dog partners who are open with their feelings are more likely to manage their grief compared to people who are not open about their emotions to others (Allen, 2006; Dunn, Mehler, & Greenberg, 2008). Therefore, whether the person has access to resources, such as family or friends, where they can disclose their grief or whether the person's personality allows them to disclose their emotions, are other factors affecting the impact of losing assistance dogs. Reactions to losing assistance dogs vary depending on the situation of partners and it is important to provide care with an understanding of those situations.

Supporting People During their Loss of Assistance Dogs

Losing important relationships is hard for anyone. However, there is more than one way to support people who have lost their assistance dogs, depending on the relationships with their dogs. Therefore, support with understanding is required in each different situation. When psychological care is required for such people, the support strategies suggested for pet dogs (Cordaro, 2012) may be helpful. However, because the relationship with an assistance dog is special; the useful support strategies for companion dogs may not be sufficient for assistance dog partners. Therefore, understanding the unique features of the partnership between assistance dogs and their partners is important. Psychological distress may be caused by dramatic changes in the person's life as well as by a loss of the assistance dog. Additional support for their disabilities may be required, perhaps provided by human welfare services, medical professionals, or family members. Programs that train assistance dogs are another important resource. Some people abandon applying for another assistance dog because their retired dog requires care or because of concern for the effects on the retired dog. Team training in a home environment may be more feasible for such people.

Among companion dog owners, understanding and acceptance provided by friends and family can help relieve the grief over the loss of their pet (Kemp et al., 2016). Ritual ceremonies also help some people process their loss (Chur-Hansen, 2010; Kemp et al., 2016). Similar support and activities may also help assistance dog partners, especially when losing their first dog. Again, assistance dog organizations can play an essential role in this process. Having good communication with assistance dog organizations, being well-prepared for retirement in advance, having trust in assistance dog organizations, and feeling supported in difficult decisions, all offer relief for people who have lost their assistance dogs (Nicholas et al., 1995). Counselors and social workers should be available at all training schools, not only at the stage of loss (grief counseling) but also in preparing for retirement (Allen, 2006).

But not all assistance dog partners have access to assistance dog programs because people acquire their assistance dogs in various ways. For those lacking access to such programs and requiring some psychological support, local mental health professionals may be an answer. However, understanding the special characteristics of relationships between assistance dogs and their partners is important. Mental health professionals who are knowledgeable can be helpful, and counselors and social workers working with assistance dog programs may be a good resource, as well as some grief counseling teams who are knowledgeable in this area (for example, Assistance Dog Loss Committee of the International Association of Assistance Dog Partners).

Experiencing grief at losing assistance dogs not only affects adults, but also children who live with assistance dogs. Service dogs for children with autism are increasing rapidly (Walther et al., 2017), and for these children special instruction should be available about separation or loss, presented in a developmentally appropriate way. This information can be provided even before a service dog is introduced to a child. Professionals working with children who have autism can also provide support.

Psychological distress is something assistance dog partners cannot avoid. Some people may even develop serious psychological problems that require support from medical professionals, a possibility for people with any type of disability. Therefore, human health professionals working closely with clients who consider acquiring an assistance dog are advised to carefully assess with clients as to whether an assistance dog is the best choice for them and the possible impact of losing that dog in the future. Therefore, human health professionals should be well-educated about both the positive and negative aspects of assistance dogs.

Distress Arising for Family and Friends During the Loss of Assistance Dogs

Family members and friends are also affected by the loss of assistance dogs. A friend of the authors, Paul Knott, mentioned that his colleagues at work also grieved when his assistance dog passed away (personal communication, 2018). Paul's assistance dog accompanied him to work; for his colleagues, the dog was a member of their office environment. The loss of Paul's assistance dog had a big impact on his co-workers. Assistance dogs accompany their partners to places where companion dogs are not allowed; hence, they usually interact with more people than do companion dogs. These people may also experience some psychological impact upon the loss of a dog, just as Paul's colleagues did.

In a study of people who adopted retired assistance dogs, it was reported that they also felt grief and had to overcome difficulties associated with the dog's death (Ogura, Tsunoda, & Yoshikawa, 2010). For these people, support from their family members, friends, neighbors, and veterinarians was useful. Furthermore, support and understanding from an assistance dog program helped relieve their psychological distress. People adopting retired dogs may feel a great responsibility so that they can fulfill the expectations of the dogs' partners and assistance dog programs as well as the dogs' needs. People adopting retired dogs may understand that their time living with retired senior dogs is limited and build a unique relationship with retired assistance dogs. Sufficient support for such populations is also essential to prepare them well.

Emotional Support Animals and their Partners' Grief

Emotional Support Animals (ESAs) should be distinguished from assistance dogs. ESAs are not required to be specially trained to do tasks related to the disability; simply their presence itself is important for their partners. Therefore, it is not possible to differentiate them from pet dogs except that their partners have a disability and for reasonable accommodation the animals are permitted greater access to housing and transportation than pets. However, for those who require support from ESAs, these animals can provide psychological stability at home and when traveling.

Many studies have demonstrated the value of companion animals for people's health and well-being. Unfortunately, however, studies specifically on ESAs are scarce, though their benefits would be similar to companion animals; the primary difference is that the partner with a disability is assured more contact with the animal at home and when traveling. For example, some research has shown that petting animals can reduce anxiety (Crossman, Kazdin, & Knudson, 2015; Shiloh, Sorek, & Terkel, 2003). Also, it is reported that pets play a role in disease recovery or reduction of symptoms among people with mental illness (Stern et al., 2013; Wisdom, Saedi, & Green, 2009). Although the increased number of people violating the laws and regulations surrounding ESAs creates a negative image for these animals, for people with disabilities, the ESAs provide great value, and such people can suffer from a severe grief when they lose their ESAs.

ESAs have less broad public access than assistance dogs, but people still spend more time with their ESAs compared to pet dogs. Losing such close company can have a great impact on the lives of their partners, especially for those who cannot even leave their house without their ESAs. Some psychological and physical difficulties caused by losing ESAs may be similar to those of losing assistance dogs. However, ESAs are similar to pets and the partners are less likely to have contact with assistance dog organizations or private trainers. Assistance dog organizations and trainers can assume important roles to support people losing assistance dogs. Veterinarians may be additional sources of guidance and support (Fine et al., 2019). Partners of ESAs may also require special support, but supportive organizations are less available. On the other hand, under the regulations by DOT and HUD, partners accompanying or living with ESAs can be asked to show documentation from a human health professional that shows the person's need for an ESA. Therefore, people who require support from their ESAs may already have a connection to human health professionals even before they start living with ESAs or considering their pet dogs to be ESAs. This is an important resource for them. Professionals working closely with people living with or trying to acquire ESAs should understand the positive and negative aspects of ESAs.

Summary

Although assistance dogs and companion dogs differ in some specific ways, the research conducted on pet loss experienced by pet dog owners can be informative for people with assistance dogs. Additional understanding of the characteristics of assistance dogs and the unique relationship between those dogs and their partners may help to support partners experiencing psychological/physical distress from the loss of their assistance dogs. While several studies describe grief experienced by guide dog partners, few studies address the grief of other types of assistance dog or ESA partners. Disabilities of assistance dog partners differ, and their challenges with grief and loss of the dog likely also differ from one another. Therefore, further studies on partners of other types of assistance dogs and ESAs could clarify the impact of their loss of partnership and the effects of the separation from their dogs. People can best support assistance dog partners by noting and attending to their specific individual needs.

Case Scenarios

Case Scenario #1:

William has been using a wheelchair after a car accident caused a permanent spinal cord injury at the age of 35. He had never had a dog before, but decided to obtain a service dog, a large Labrador retriever named Bella. He had much to learn about dogs and their care, and there were initial challenges, but after a short period of time, Bella became an essential life partner for William. He could even go back to work again because of Bella. Five years later, when Bella was 7 years old, she was still a happy and cheerful girl without any sign of health problems. But she had grown some gray hairs on her face and William has begun thinking about her retirement, even though this won't happen for another few years. William wants to keep Bella after her retirement, but his wife has severe back problems and it does not seem feasible for them to care for a large aging dog.

Discussion Questions:

1. What are the possible difficulties William may face before and after the retirement of Bella?
2. What kind of preparations can he take to mitigate these possible difficulties?
3. If William can choose where Bella goes after her retirement, which option is most likely to minimize his grief?

Case Scenario #2:

Sarah is a veteran suffering from PTSD. After she learned about psychiatric service dogs, she decided, with the help of a professional pet dog trainer, to train her own dog to be a service dog. She chose this option because there were no service dog programs close to where she lived. A beautiful Cavalier King Charles Spaniel puppy, Bobby grew into a perfect psychiatric service dog for Sarah with her training efforts. Bobby reminded her to take medications and alerted her to upcoming panic attacks. Because of Bobby's service, Sarah was able to go outside of her house as often as she had before developing PTSD. Bobby accompanied Sarah everywhere and her PTSD symptoms were under control. However, one morning, Bobby looked "off" so Sarah brought him to her veterinarian. The veterinarian told her that Bobby had a severe heart problem and he would not be able to continue his work. Sarah has felt lost since then.

Discussion Questions:

1. Sarah had been meeting with her mental health professional regularly. What risks should the mental health professional have mentioned as possibilities before Sarah started to train her own service dog?
2. What kinds of support can be offered or advised for Sarah who has no connection to a service dog training program?

References

Allen, D. M. (2006). Letting go of the harness for the last time: A descriptive realism approach to exploring the ending of working relationships with guide dogs. *McNair Scholars Research Journal*, 2, 7–13. Retrieved July 25, 2018, from https://scholarworks. boisestate.edu/cgi/viewcontent.cgi?referer=https://scholar.google.co.jp/&httpsre dir=1&article=1046&context=mcnair_journal

American Veterinary Medical Association. (2017). Assistance animals: Rights of access and the problem of fraud. Retrieved November 23, 2018, from www.avma. org/KB/Resources/Reports/Pages/Assistance-Animals-Rights-of-Access-and-the-Problem-of-Fraud.aspx

Amiot, C. E., & Bastian, B. (2015). Toward a psychology of human-animal relations. *Psychological Bulletin*, 141, 6–47. doi: 10.1037/a0038147

Assistance Dogs International (ADI). (2018). Types of assistance dogs. Retrieved July 26, 2018, from www.assistancedogsinternational.org/about-us/types-of-assistance-dogs/

Audrestch H. M., Whelan, C. T., Grice, D., Asher, L., England, G. C. W., & Freeman, S. L. (2015). Recognizing the value of assistance dogs in society. *Disability and Health Journal*, 8, 469–474. doi: 10.1016/j.dhjo.2015.07.001

Batt, L., Batt, M., Baguley, J., & McGreevy, P. (2010). Relationships between puppy management practices and reported measures of success in guide dog training. *Journal of Veterinary Behavior Clinical Applications and Research*, 5, 240–246. doi: 10.1016/j.jveb.2010.02.004

Bedini, L. A. (2000). Just sit down so we can talk: Perceived stigma and the pursuit of community recreation for people with disabilities. *Therapeutic Recreation Journal*, 34, 55–68. Retrieved July 25, 2018, from http://libres.uncg.edu/ir/uncg/f/L_Bedini_Just_2000.pdf

Brown, K. (2006). Pastoral concern in relation to the psychological stress caused by the death of an animal companion. *Mental Health, Religion and Culture*, 9, 411–422. doi: 10.1080/13694670500212208

Burr, R. (2018). Senator Burr introduces bill to strengthen airline service animal procedures. Retrieved November 25, 2018, from www.burr.senate.gov/press/releases/senator-burr-introduces-bill-to_strengthen-airline-service-animal-procedures

Burrows, K. E., Adams, C. L., & Spiers, J. (2008). Sentinels of safety: Service dogs ensure safety and enhance freedom and well-being for families with autistic children. *Qualitative Health Research*, 18, 1642–1649. doi: 10.1177/10497323 08327088

Canine Companions for Independence. (2016). Legislative win for legitimate assistance dogs. Retrieved November 25, 2018, from www.cci.org/news-media/latest-news/legislative-win-for.html

Chur-Hansen, A. (2010). Grief and bereavement issues and the loss of a companion animal: People living with a companion animal, owners of livestock, and animal support workers. *Clinical Psychologist*, 14, 14–21. doi: 10.1080/13284201003662800

Contreras, L. T. (2003). *Paws for thoughts: the beginning and ending of a partnership.* (Unpublished Master's Thesis). University of California, Davis.

Cooney, K. (2015). Offering hospice care for pets. *Vet Record Careers*, 177, 1–2. doi: 10.1136/vr.h4921

Cordaro, M. (2012). Pet loss and disenfranchised grief: Implications for mental health counseling practice. *Journal of Mental Health Counseling*, 34, 283–294. doi: 10.17744/mehc.34.4.41q0248450t98072

Crossman, M. K., Kazdin, A. E., & Knudson, K. (2015). Brief unstructured interaction with a dog reduces distress. *Anthrozoös*, 28, 649–659. doi: 10.1080/0892 7936.2015.1070008

Davis, B. W., Nattrass, K., O'Brien, S., Patronek, G., & MacCollin, M. (2004). Assistance dog placement in the pediatric population: benefits, risks, and recommendations for future application. *Anthrozoös*, 7, 130–145. doi: 10.2752/089279304786991765

Dunn, K. L., Mehler, S. J., & Greenberg, H. S. (2008). Social work with a pet loss support group in a university veterinary hospital, MSW, ACSW. *Social Work in Health Care*, 41, 59–70. doi: 10.1300/J010v41n02_04

Edelman, A. (2018). Collared: New laws crack down on fake service dogs. *NBC News*. Retrieved November 25, 2018, from www.nbcnews.com/politics/politics-news/collared-new-laws-crack-down-fake-service-dogs-n871541

Fairman, S. K., & Huebner, R. A. (2001). Service dogs: A compensatory resource to improve function. *Occupational Therapy in Health Care*, 13, 41–52. doi: 10.1080/J003v13n02_03

Field, N. P., Orsini, L., Gavish, R., & Packman, W. (2009). Role of attachment in response to pet loss. *Death Studies*, 33, 334–355. doi: 10.1080/07481180802705783

Fine, A., Knesl, O., Hart, B., Hart, L., Ng, Z., Patterson-Kane, E., Hoy-Gerlach, J., & Feldman, S. (2019). The role of veterinarians in assisting clients identify and care for emotional support animals. *Journal of the American Veterinary Medical Association*, 254(2), 199–202.

Goldberg, K. J. (2016). Veterinary hospice and palliative care: a comprehensive review of the literature. *Veterinary Record*, 178, 369–374. doi: 10.1136/vr.103459

Green, S., Davis, C., Karshmer, E., Marsh, P., & Straight, B. (2005). Living stigma: The impact of labeling, stereotyping, separation, status loss, and discrimination in the lives of individuals with disabilities and their families. *Sociological Inquiry*, 75, 197–215. doi: 10.1111/j.1475-682X.2005.00119.x

Guest, C. M., Collis, G. M., & McNicholas, J. (2006). Hearing dogs: A longitudinal study of social and psychological effects on deaf and hard-of-hearing recipients. *Journal of Deaf Studies and Deaf Education*, 11, 252–261. doi: 10.1093/deafed/enj028

Hart, L. A., Hart, B. L., & Bergin, B. (1987). Socializing effects of service dogs for people with disabilities. *Anthrozoös*, 1, 41–44. doi: 10.2752/089279388787058696

Hart, L. A., Zasloff, R. L., & Benfatto, A. M. (1996). The socializing role of hearing dogs. *Applied Animal Behavior Science*, 47, 7–15. doi:10.1016/0168-1591(95)01006-8

Kemp, H. R., Jacobs, N., & Stewrt, S. (2016). The lived experience of companion-animal loss: A systematic review of qualitative studies. *Anthrozoös*, 29, 533–557. doi: 10.1080/08927936.2016.1228772

Kwong, M. J., & Bartholomew, K. (2011). "Not just a dog": an attachment perspective on relationships with assistance dogs. *Attachment & Human Development*, 13, 421–436. doi: 10.1080/14616734.2011.584410

Lane, D. R., McNicholas, J., & Collis, G. M. (1998). Dogs for the disabled: benefits to recipients and welfare of the dog. *Applied Animal Behaviour Science*, 59, 49–60. doi: 10.1016/S0168-1591(98)00120-8

Lloyd, J. K. F., La Grow, S., Stafford, K. J., & Budge, R. C. (2008a). The guide dog as a mobility aid part 1: perceived effectiveness on travel performance. *International Journal of Orientation & Mobility*, 1, 17–33.

Lloyd, J. K. F., La Grow, S., Stafford, K. J., & Budge, R. C. (2008b). The guide dog as a mobility aid Part 2: perceived changes to travel habits. *International Journal of Orientation & Mobility*, 1, (2008), 34–45.

Lloyd, J., Budge, C., La Grow, S., & Stafford, K. (2016). An investigation of the complexities of successful and unsuccessful guide dog matching and partnerships. *Frontiers in Veterinary Science*, 3, 1–15. doi: 10.3389/fvets.2016.00114

Messam, L. L. M., & Hart, L. A. (2018). Persons experiencing prolonged grief after the loss of a pet. In L. Kogan (Ed.), *Clinician's guide to treating companion animal issues* (pp. 267–280). Amsterdam: Elsevier.

Moxon, R., Whiteside, H., & England, G. C. W. (2016). Incidence and impact of dog attacks on guide dogs in the UK: An update. *Veterinary Record*, 178, 1–17. Retrieved July 25, 2018, from http://eprints.nottingham.ac.uk/38873/

Nicholson, J., Kemp-Wheeler, S., & Griffiths, D. (1995). Distress arising from the end of a guide dog partnership. *Anthrozoös*, 8, 100–110. doi: 10.2752/08927939 5787156419

Ogura, K., Tsunoda, Y., & Yoshikawa, A. (2010). Considering support and encouragement for the activities of volunteer handlers of retired guide dogs: From a qualitative analysis of the experiences of volunteer handlers. *Journal of Service Dog Research*, 4, 22–30. doi: 10.3373/jssdr.4.22

Refson, K., Jackson, A. J., Dusoir, A. E., & Archer, D. B. (1999). The health and social status of guide dog owners and other visually impaired adults in Scotland. *Visual Impairment Research*, 1, 95–109. doi: 10.1076/vimr.1.2.95.4411

Rintala, D. H., Sachs-Ericsson, N., & Hart, K. A. (2002). The effects of service dogs on the lives of persons with mobility impairments: A pre-post study design. *SCI Psychosocial Process*, 15, 65, 70–82.

Sachs-Ericsson, N., Hansen, N. K., & Fitzgerald, S. (2002). Benefits of assistance dogs: a review. *Rehabilitation Psychology*, 47, 251–277. doi: 10.1037/0090-5550.47.3.251

Schneider, K. S. (2005). The winding valley of grief: When a dog guide retires or dies. *Journal of Visual Impairment and Blindness*, 99, 368–370.

Shiloh, S., Sorek, G., & Terkel, J. (2003). Reduction of state-anxiety by petting animals in a controlled laboratory experiment. *Anxiety, Stress, and Coping*, 16, 387–395. doi: 10.1080/1061580031000091582

Stern, S. L., Donahue, D. A., Allison, S., Hatch, J. P., Lancaster, C. L., Benson, T. A., Johnson, A. L., Jeffreys, M. D., Pride, D., Moreno, C., & Peterson, A. L. (2013). Potential benefits of canine companionship for military veterans with posttraumatic stress disorder (PTSD). *Society and Animals*, 21, 568–581. doi: 10.1163/15685306-12341286

US Department of Housing and Urban Development. Office of Fair Housing and Equal Opportunity. (2004). Joint Statement of the Department of Housing and Urban Development and the Department of Justice. Reasonable accommodations under the Fair Housing Act. 42 U.S.C. § 3604(f)(3)(B). Retrieved July 26, 2018, from www.justice.gov/sites/default/files/crt/legacy/2010/12/14/joint_statement_ra.pdf

US Department of Justice. (2011). ADA 2010 revised requirements. Service animals. Retrieved July 26, 2018, from www.ada.gov/service_animals_2010.htm

US Department of Transportation. (2008). 14 CFR Part 382. Nondiscrimination on the Basis of Disability in Air Travel. Retrieved July 26, 2018, from www.transportation.gov/sites/dot.gov/files/docs/Part%20382-2008_1.pdf

US Department of Transportation. (2018). Advance Notice of Proposed Rulemaking. Retrieved December 9, 2018, from www.transportation.gov/sites/dot.gov/files/docs/resources/individuals/aviation-consumer-protection/310476/service-animal-anprm-final.pdf.

Valentine, D. P., Kiddoo, M., & LaFleur, B. (1993). Psychosocial implications of service dog ownership for people who have mobility or hearing impairments. *Social Work in Health Care*, 19, 109–125. doi: 10.1300/J010v19n01_07

Walther, S., Yamamoto, M., Thigpen, A. P., Garcia, A., Willits, N. H., & Hart, L. A. (2017). Assistance dogs: Historic patterns and roles of dogs placed by ADI or IGDF accredited facilities and by non-accredited US facilities. *Frontiers in Veterinary Science*, 4, 1–14. doi: 10.3389/fvets.2017.00001

Wenthold, N., & Savage, T. A. (2007). Ethical issues with service animals. *Topics In Stroke Rehabilitation*, 14, 68–74. doi: 10.1310/tsr1402-68

Whelan, C. (2017). *The complexities of guide dog partnerships: why some go wrong and the impact of a failed relationship on the owner.* (PhD Thesis). University of Nottingham. Retrieved May 14, 2018, from http://eprints.nottingham.ac.uk/41785/1/Chantelle%20Whelan%20PhD%20thesis.pdf

Whitmarsh, L. (2005). The benefits of guide dog ownership. *Visual Impairment Research*, 7, 27–42. doi: 10.1080/13882350590956439

Wiggett-Barnard, C., & Steel, H. (2008). The experience of owning a guide dog. *Disability and Rehabilitation*, 30, 1014–1026. doi: 10.1080/09638280701466517

Wisdom, J. P., Saedi, G. A., & Green, C. A. (2009). Another breed of "service" animals: STARS study findings about pet ownership and recovery from serious mental illness. *American Journal of Orthopsychiatry*, 79, 430–436. doi: 10.1037/a0016812

Wrobel, T. A., & Dye, A. L. (2003). Grieving pet death: Normative, gender, and attachment issues. *Journal of Death & Dying*, 47, 385–393. doi: 10.2190/QYV5-LLJ1-T043-U0F9

13 Supporting Bereaved Clients after the Death of an Assistance Dog

Cara A. Miller

Introduction

Variable measures make it difficult to estimate the number of Americans with disabilities, but recent estimates are 37–57 million people, or approximately 12.8% of the US population in 2016 (Kraus et al., 2018). A subset of this population has chosen to enlist the skills of trained assistance dogs[1] for increased daily independence and quality of life (Eames & Eames, 2001).

Assistance dog partnerships present extraordinary opportunities to realize the deepest and most mutually fulfilling potential of the human–animal bond. However, the death of an assistance dog subsequently ushers in the ending of a human–canine partnership uniquely colored by love, constant companionship, increased safety, and enhanced independence.

The Unique Nature of Assistance Dog Partnerships

While trained dogs have accompanied and assisted humans for years in various capacities through pursuits such as hunting, tracking, protection, and detection, in the last century dogs' roles have expanded to include those of assistance providers to people with disabilities. Since the establishment of the first domestic guide dog school, The Seeing Eye™, in New Jersey in 1929, the number of assistance dog organizations and guide dog schools in the United States has steadily increased (Walther et al., 2017). In the decades since, the canine assistant concept has expanded and evolved to include dogs trained to assist people with a variety of disabilities in addition to those impacting mobility and vision. Today, a number of assistance dog organizations specialize in the breeding, training, and placement of highly-skilled assistance dogs to partner with children and adults with physical, neurological, and developmental disabilities. Assistance Dogs International, Inc. (ADI), founded in 1986, is a worldwide coalition of non-profit programs that train and place assistance dogs and is a leading authority in promoting standards of excellence in all areas of assistance dog training and partnership. Similarly, the International Guide

Dog Federation (IGDF) is an industry-elected body with international oversight of guide dog training and placement standards among approximately 90 guide dog schools throughout the world (IGDF, 2018).

The Americans with Disabilities Act (ADA), through the United States Department of Justice, defines and articulates the qualifications of service animals. In 2011, the DOJ instructed through its regulations that only dogs (and in some cases, miniature horses) may be considered qualified service animals. Minimum criteria for qualification include substantial individual training in tasks that directly assist the disabled partner through mitigating the effects of disability on activities of daily living. Historically, such tasks have contributed to the rise of training and placement categories, including dogs guiding individuals who are blind or have vision impairments (guide dogs); dogs alerting deaf and hard of hearing individuals to sounds (hearing dogs); and dogs retrieving dropped items, opening and closing doors and drawers, turning lights on and off, and pulling wheelchairs (service dogs), among others. Within the latter category, additional aspects of task training may informally categorize service dogs that specialize in mobility and balance assistance for partners with mobility impairments and paralysis (as may be experienced with conditions such as muscular dystrophy, cerebral palsy, spina bifida, bone, and arthritic conditions, spinal cord injuries, etc.). Similarly, medical alert service dogs may be trained to detect, respond to, and assist disabled partners with symptom mitigation resulting from conditions including epilepsy, diabetes, narcolepsy, and cardiovascular and respiratory diseases, among other conditions.

While the DOJ provisions exclude from the "service animal" definition those dogs that provide only emotional support or comfort for their owners, in recent years the concept of the psychiatric service dog has expanded to include dogs specially trained in tasks to mitigate the symptoms of partners' psychological disabilities. Most recently, dogs trained to serve veterans with disabling post-traumatic stress disorder (PTSD) resulting from combat trauma and military sexual trauma have been trained to perform mitigating tasks such as nightmare interruptions, perimeter searches, and direct pressure behaviors in response to anxious cues demonstrated by the handler. As many veterans may have physical and cognitive disabilities stemming from traumatic brain injuries, blast injuries, and other wounds sustained during service, PTSD service dogs may perform a variety of additional assistive tasks (O'Haire, Guérin, & Kirkham, 2015; O'Haire & Rodriguez, 2018).

ADA Titles II and III allow disabled handlers to be accompanied by qualified service dogs in most public facilities and transportation, with additional specific public access rights conferred by the Air Carrier Access Act (ACAA) and Fair Housing Act (FHA). The protections afforded by these laws typically enable disabled handlers to be accompanied by their assistance dogs in various settings including shared residential buildings, schools, businesses, places of employment, and public transportation and other public facilities. As a result, many assistance dog teams work side by side on a 24/7 basis, 365 days per year, for much of the duration of the partnership.

Functional Impact of Assistance Dogs

Assistance dogs support their partners in attaining and enjoying independence in daily functioning. These dogs may function in the stead of, or as complementary supports for, technological and other adaptive aids as well as paid and unpaid human caregiving and labor (Winkle, Crowe, & Hendrix, 2012). Similarly, assistance dogs may offer support with activities essential to communication, including alerting deaf and hard of hearing partners to name calls, doorbell rings, or knocks at the door; retrieving and delivering communication devices; conveying messages to human companions or personal care assistants, and including signaling when help is needed, among other tasks. In a personal testimonial, assistance dogs are frequently compared to crucial appendages, extensions of the human partner's body, or independence-enhancing mobility aids. Among guide dog partners, it is sometimes said that partnership with guide dogs may surpass the freedom offered by white canes.

Research suggests that assistance dogs may enhance the emotional and physical health of their human partners in ways similar to, and in others thematically or ontologically different from, those benefits conferred to pet owners through companion animal ownership (Collins et al., 2006; Fairman & Huebner, 2001; Guest, Collis, & McNicholas, 2006; Julius, Beetz, Kotrschal, Turner, & Uvnas-Moberg, 2013; Lane, McNicholas, & Collis, 1998; Mowry, Carnahan, & Watson, 1994; Sachs-Ericsson, Hansen, & Fitzgerald, 2002; Valentine, Kiddoo, & LaFleur, 1993). For persons with disabilities impacting mobility and balance, service dog partnership may reduce reliance on human assistance in activities of daily living including getting around home and community, dressing and grooming, bathing, eating and feeding self and family, and more (Fairman & Huebner, 2001). Whitmarsh (2005) found that increased mobility and independence are oft-reported benefits of guide dog partnership. Similarly, assistance dog partnerships across all categories of training and disability may be seen to facilitate improved community integration, school attendance, daily independence, and employment among partners (Allen & Blascovich, 1996; Eddy, Hart, & Boltz, 1988; Fairman & Huebner, 2001; Hart, Zasloff, & Benfatto, 1996). As a result, an assistance dog's support in enhancing the partner's ability to manage activities of daily living may subsequently reduce the need for hours of caregiving by others (Fairman & Huebner, 2001; Merbitz & Sachs-Ericcson, 2009; Rintala, Matamoros, & Seitz, 2008).

In addition to the functional benefits facilitating completion of daily living activities, assistance dog partnership may also confer direct and indirect psychological benefits. In a study of service dog owners with severe ambulatory disabilities, self-reported improvements following a partnership with a service dog included increased self-esteem and internal locus of control, and enhanced psychological well-being (Allen & Blascovich, 1996). Hearing dog partners report feelings of improved independence, and greater safety and security within and outside their home (Valentine et al., 1993; Pang, 1999). Among a sample of adults with progressive health conditions who used wheelchairs or scooters, a subset reported symptoms of clinical depression; of that subset, those partnered with service dogs demonstrated significantly higher positive affect than those not partnered with service dogs (Collins et al., 2006). Finally, guide dog partners report improved confidence and social interaction following guide dog placement (Whitmarsh, 2009).

Notably, such psychological benefits may be conferred both directly and indirectly. Service dog partners report increased social integration and psychological support (Lane et al., 1998); reduced loneliness (Valentine et al., 1993); improved confidence and increased sense of control in their lives (Fairman & Huebner, 2001; Roth, 1992); reductions in tension, anxiety, and depression (Guest et al., 2006); and higher levels of both self-esteem and assertiveness (Valentine et al., 1993). Finally, in one of the first studies to examine the functional impacts of service dogs specifically trained to assist veterans with PTSD, findings included significant reductions in PTSD, depression, and anxiety symptoms, and reduced absenteeism from work due to health issues following service dog placement (O'Haire & Rodriguez, 2018).

Identity, Attachment, and Assistance Dog Partnerships

While research has increasingly explored the functional benefits conferred by assistance dog partnership, researchers are more recently investigating the psychosocial aspects of such partnerships and ways in which partners' identities and experiences may transform before, during, and after the loss of an assistance dog.

Importantly, for many people, partnership with an assistance dog can be a powerful catalyst for greater self-acceptance, and an impetus for reorganizing one's self-concept in relation to one's disability. Assistance dog partnership may lead to increased consolidation and pride in one's identity as an assistance dog partner and as such, may serve as a vehicle for improved self-acceptance and self-advocacy; indeed, Eames and Eames (2001) suggest that assistance dog partnership is, for many people with disabilities, a "transformational experience in which the individual's self-concept is enhanced and feelings of empowerment gained" through advocating for public access (p. 60). Transformation of personal identity to encompass one's assistance dog as a part of one's self is a finding also reported by Miller (2011) and Sanders (2000).

Marcie Davis, a paraplegic manual wheelchair user, writes of developing chronic shoulder problems from long-term wheelchair use, as well as significant spasticity stemming from a spinal cord cyst. Describing how increased discomfort and functional limitations prompt her to quit driving and consider switching to a power wheelchair, Davis writes:

> I didn't realize how limited I had become until I got [service dog] Ramona. ... With Ramona, I had assistance and backup. She was a furry, four-legged adaptive helper. Ramona helped me to accept the idea that adaptive equipment made me more independent.
>
> (Davis cited in Vogel, 2011, para. 5)

After training and establishing a working partnership with Ramona, Davis did begin using a power wheelchair, and also obtained an accessible van which enabled her to resume driving. "Ramona opened up my world – when I didn't know it had closed in" (in Vogel, 2011, para. 5).

Similarly, recent studies of the assistance dog–partner relationship have attempted to illuminate, understand, and describe the close bonds commonly reported by assistance dog partners. Relevant and salient factors in the formation of these deep, affectionate relationships may include the nature of the attachment bond, the degree of interdependence, and the affordance of opportunities and independence enjoyed by the assistance dog partner and dog alike (White, Mills, & Hall, 2017). Olson (2002) reports that the relationship between blind guide dog partners and their working guide dogs are frequently "referred to as the gold standard for the human–animal bond ... involving a 24/7 relationship whereby mobility is enhanced for the blind person and enjoyable work is performed by the guide dog" (p. 353). Similarly, as service dog partner Davis attests, the bond between the service dog and human partner:

> ... cannot be described or defined. My love and adoration for all of my service dogs knows no limits. It is a feeling and a loyalty that has no bounds. We simply take care of one another. It is a lifetime commitment.
>
> (Davis cited in Vogel, 2011)

Interestingly, research by White et al. (2017) suggests that anxious attachment to pets as reported by pet owners may reflect owners' feelings of fear and worry about the pet's health, safety, or behavior. Comparatively, among a sample of assistance dog partners, self-reported anxious attachment to the assistance dog was found to be a significant predictor of one's self-reported quality of life. Accordingly, the researchers suggest that the partner's attachment to their assistance dog "reflects the degree to which the assistance dog supports the individual to lead a fulfilling and independent life" (p. 663). Similarly, Kwong and Bartholomew (2011) suggest that the presence of a high level of interdependence between an assistance dog and human partner underscores the unique attachment bond undergirding assistance dog partnerships.

Anticipatory Grief and Assistance Dog Retirement

> If Old Dog worked well for you, it was a life changer for you, kind of like first love. Now you've come to expect that level of dignity and independence in a functioning service/assistance dog. New Dog has big shoes to fill. If Old Dog didn't work out well, you've got a million ideas of what you and New Dog need to do differently this time.
>
> (Schneider cited in Davis, 2012, para. 6)

Eames and Eames (2001) describe the process of retiring an assistance dog as an unwanted rite of passage awaiting all assistance dog partners. Inevitably, as an assistance dog ages, the nature, speed, and efficacy of its work will change as well: efficiency, confidence, motivation, and skill are all subject to the influences of changing health and situational factors on the part of both human and canine. With partnership success and longevity a driving goal in the breeding, training, and placement of assistance dogs, retirement may be a complex and difficult process for many assistance dog partners. Furthermore, early or premature retirement of an assistance dog is sometimes necessitated by circumstances beyond the aging or developing health issues that interfere with its work.

Indeed, the assistance dog's retirement is in itself commonly experienced as change or loss, with the precipitating and ensuing circumstances typically coloring the human partner's experience of that loss. In "The Winding Valley of Grief: When a Dog Guide Retires or Dies," Schneider (2005) suggests that three significant farewells transpire in the process of concluding one's partnership with an assistance dog: (1) the "decision-making goodbye," (2) the "working relationship goodbye," and (3) "the goodbye of death" (para. 3).

Schneider (2005) describes the initial "decision-making goodbye" as the bittersweet process of coming to recognize the nearing time for a dog's retirement, as evidenced by increasing changes in the dog's ability and/or motivation to work, frequently offset by compensatory adjustments on the part of the human partner for as long as is possible. Such a process may be uniquely marked by anticipatory grief as well as remembrances of the partnership in times past. Partners may reflect on the circumstances of their disability onset and/or progression as related to the impetus for originally pursuing a partnership with an assistance dog. Similarly, partners may reflect upon their shifting identities and self-concepts in relation to their disability, functioning, and independence vis-a-vis the partnership with the assistance dog. Additional reflection may include recalling the team's developing maturation and deepening trust over time, from the earliest days as a newly-minted pair to the highs, lows, and mundane details of years of life together.

The second goodbye, according to Schneider (2005), effectively concludes the working relationship with the newly-retired assistance dog. Again, working partnerships may be concluded for a tremendous variety of reasons, including but not limited to the dog's deteriorating health, late-onset behavioral issues impairing the dog's ability to work, and/or progression of a partner's illness, among other factors. When possible, many partners retiring an assistance dog will elect to keep the retired dog in their home as a pet, where it may remain the only dog, become one of a number of companion animals, and/or be joined eventually by the partner's successor assistance dog.

Upon the assistance dog's retirement, partners must often negotiate emergent challenges to their previously-enjoyed independence of movement, access to communication, and freedom of functioning. In "Letting Go of the Harness for the Last Time," guide dog partner Deborah Allen writes:

> ... as [guide dog] Lily's physical condition deteriorates, my autonomy is gradually being taken from me. The freedom I once took for granted is vanishing. No longer can I just walk to and from the store if I need something, nor can I walk to the campus if I miss the bus, or the buses are not running. I must depend more and more on others to provide transportation for me.
>
> (Allen, 2006, p. 7)

For Allen, Davis, and many other assistance dog partners, increased reliance on other people due to the assistance dog's inability to work may emerge as an economically fraught and psychologically complex change. As institutional challenges and societal stigma frequently impede opportunities for gainful employment by individuals with disabilities, consequential financial constraints can impact treatment decisions related to veterinary and follow-up care and options for paid caregiving to compensate for an assistance dog's incapacitation due to illness. Indeed, costs associated with veterinary expenses in an assistance dog's illness and death; those resulting from interruptions to gainful employment; incurred from increased reliance on caregivers or adaptive equipment; and finally, costs incurred for travel to and from an assistance dog school for placement with a successor dog and follow-up support may be potentially prohibitive expenditures and additional sources of stress on the grieving disabled partner. As two-thirds of Americans with disabilities are unemployed or underemployed, and many live on federal Supplemental Security Income programs, the costs of caring for a chronically ill dog (either alone or along with one's successor assistance dog), may be financially infeasible (Kraus et al., 2018).

Assistance dog organizations and guide dog schools invest significant funds to maintain and continue improvement of quality breeding, training, and placement support the success of healthy and long-lived partnerships. Many schools offer financial support to defray partners' fiduciary responsibilities stemming from degenerative or congenitally-related health problems in some assistance dogs. Yet, functional and logistical constraints sometimes stemming from disability-related challenges, financial limitations, and other factors can necessitate rehoming the retired assistance dog with family, friends, or puppy-raisers who are bonded with the dog. As a retired assistance dog legally no longer meets ADA/DOJ criteria defining a qualified service animal, an assistance dog partner may not be permitted to keep the retired assistance dog in the home if residing in shared housing with pet animal prohibitions – also potentially a complicating aspect of grief.

Those partners who are able to keep their retired assistance dog must frequently contend with significant and ongoing transitional factors. Complicating elements include feelings of loss engendered by terminating the active working relationship with the retiring dog; assisting the dog in adjusting to retirement; determining circumstances for initiating successor assistance dog partnerships, if at all; arranging logistics of successor assistance dog training; acclimating to the successor dog while negotiating thoughts and feelings about the new and old partnership; assisting the retired dog in relinquishing its working role to the successor dog; acclimating the successor dog to its new home and partnership, etc. The aforementioned processes are furthermore influenced by factors including one's health and psychological readiness, status of relationship to the assistance dog organization, available support systems, and numerous other factors. Finally, well-meant support and encouragement from family, friends, puppy-raisers, communities, and/or assistance dog organization staff may unintentionally contribute to a partner's sense of expected urgency to expedite grieving and transitional processes, an aspect of bereavement that surely merits further research.

The end of an assistance dog partnership through retirement may engender feelings of grief similar, if not exact in nature, to those arising after an assistance dog's death. Following the end of a partnership, according to Schneider (2005), the newly single partner's "… self-esteem, sense of safety, comfort in moving around, and joy in facing a new day may be decreased markedly" (para. 9). After her first service dog's health issues necessitated her dog's abrupt and unforeseen early retirement at age 7, Davis recalls:

> I felt like someone had punched me in the stomach. I also felt like I had become disabled all over again. I was lost. How could I go out at night without her? Would I be safe? Would it be OK?
>
> (Davis in Vogel, 2011, para. 14)

Navigating the home, venturing solo into public spaces, and negotiating previously-surmounted scenarios without an assistance dog's support, may indeed exacerbate a partner's underlying anxiety, depression, or adjustment-related challenges (Contreras, 2003; Davis, 2010, 2012; Ogden, 1992).

Notably, many assistance dog organizations and guide dog schools retain legal ownership of their assistance dogs for the duration of the team's working partnership; they may contribute follow-up and fiduciary support for veterinary care and/or retraining in the event of catastrophic illness or unforeseen adverse circumstances. Accordingly, such organizations and schools often constitute a significant support system throughout partners' retirement and bereavement processes by way of guidance, consultation, and resource referrals, among other supports offered. As such, many partners elect to return to the same organizations or schools for successor assistance dog training and placement, with consideration to factors such as geography, timing, training duration, availability of eligible canine candidates, and of course health, career, and family-related circumstances. Additionally, organizations and schools commonly offer education and advocacy support to partners' families, employers, and communities around issues of access, etiquette, training, and more. As such, the relationship between an assistance dog partner and their training organization or school may exert a significant role in support and guidance available during the ending of an assistance dog partnership.

Indeed, a review of the literature yields some testimonial from assistance dog partners about the importance of their training organizations helping to prepare them for the end of the working relationship with their dogs (Allen, 2006). Most notable supports include phone, email, and in-person follow-up; provision of retirement-related information early and often; and in some cases, recommendations or referrals made for supportive counselors to assist grieving partners upon the retirement or death of an assistance dog (Schneider, 2005).

The successor assistance dog partnership may differ significantly from one's initial partnership in various ways. One's disability, and related functional and adaptive needs, goals, and even self-concept, may have evolved from the start and end periods of the initial assistance dog partnership. Additionally, as successor training may necessitate travel and on-site residency at the training school for a period of 2–4 weeks, such an undertaking often entails significant financial expenditures as well as time away from family, work, and other responsibilities. Although training and placement with a successor dog is often a much-anticipated event, it is very often a complicated and bittersweet process involving the initial stages of a discrete phase of grief that may overlap with grief processes following the previous assistance dog's retirement or death. Indeed, schools and organizations quite often work collaboratively with partners in assessing interest in and readiness for initiation of successor partnerships following the retirement or eventual death of the working assistance dog.

For the duration of time without one's dog, "the days or weeks between dogs may seem unreal, with feelings that part of one is missing" (Schneider, 2005, para. 10). Accordingly, friends, family, colleagues, and community may do well to "treat [retirement] as seriously as they would a death or divorce" (Schneider, 2005, para. 14). Finally, writes Schneider:

> ... a few empathic souls "get it" that working dogs are very different from pets and do the right things like listening and showing up to help with the transition or just bringing a dish ... but [perhaps] more would if they realized this dog is my best friend, my eyes and my key to safe transportation.
>
> (Schneider cited in Davis, 2012, para. 4)

Schneider (2005) offers the following advice to supportive persons for consideration before, during, and after the retirement process: sharing gentle, honest feedback about changes noted in the working partnership; directly discussing, rather than avoiding, the subject of retirement with indicated openness to hearing about the partner's experience; welcoming the arrival of a successor dog with reminders of the time needed to adjust to a new dog, and avoiding comparisons between the retired dog and successor dog.

Acute Grief and Assistance Dog Death

> Consider what it must be like if an animal companion had also been one's lifeline to the outside world – and served as an extra pair of eyes, ears, or limbs, providing courage and stability, reassurance, protection and constant attention. Ironically, being dependent also ultimately provides independence, enhanced self-esteem, and restored dignity. This special kind of relationship also opens new doors of communication, acceptance, and social education.
>
> (Association for Pet Loss and Bereavement, 2007, para. 2)

Recognizing and considering the many factors that impact and mediate grief experiences following an assistance dog's death is important for clinicians, caretakers, family members, and peers supporting the bereaved partner. While recent research continues to qualify individual experiences following the loss or death of a companion dog and other animal pets, there is little in the way of published, peer-reviewed literature about bereaved assistance dog partners or on the particular grief uniquely engendered through assistance dog death (Contreras, 2003).

Bereaved partners may experience symptoms of acute and prolonged grief similar to and in sometimes felt to exceed those experienced by bereaved pet owners and survivors mourning loved ones. Such symptoms may include those aspects named in the Grief Experience Inventory (GEI) such as despair, guilt, hostility, anger, social isolation, somatization, depersonalization, rumination, loss of control, and death anxiety (Sanders, Mauger, & Strong, 1985). Like bereaved pet owners, bereaved assistance dog partners may experience symptoms like tearfulness, depression, pain, loss of appetite, increased loneliness, and preoccupation with memories of their deceased canine partner, with grief experiences as unique as the various persons, dogs, and partnerships themselves (Rémillard, 2014; Sherman, 2017; Wrobel & Dye, 2003).

Of particular note, Nicholson, Kemp-Wheeler, and Griffiths, in their 1995 study of a sample of guide dog partners grieving the end of the partnership, found that partners reported high levels of self-blame in their assistance dog's death. Feelings of anger and guilt were reported by more than half of partners whose guide dogs had died within the previous year, at rates equaling or surpassing those reported by participants whose partnerships ended through retirement or removal of the dog by the training school. Such results suggest that schools and organizations as well as mental health professionals supporting bereaved partners might make additional support available to partners particularly in circumstances in which voluntary euthanasia is necessitated.

After the Assistance Dog's Death

> I think that night we realized how completely we had depended not only on our eyes but on Lox's ears. His vigilance was our safety measure and without it our sleep was very fitful indeed … It wasn't until after his death that we discovered how much Lox had really done for our peace of mind. Now the phone would ring, the doorbell would buzz, strangers and friends would knock on the front or back door, people would wander through our front yard, cats would shoot into our backyard and begin to fight, the smoke alarm would go off in response to burning food in the frying pan, and visitors would actually open the door and peer around it, then venture into the house....
>
> (Ogden, 1992, p. 27)

The published literature on disability includes notable themes of continuous adjustment and ongoing adaptation required to manage functional inhibitions related to physical impairments, particularly within many progressive disabilities. Assistance dog partners have pointed out how the assistance dog's absence is sharply felt in the emergence of new challenges previously mitigated with the assistance dog's support. Wachsler (2010) reflects such a sentiment:

> I think this is a typical part of living with a disability – we become habituated to our limitations and therefore don't realize just how

much pain, exhaustion, isolation, or limitation we are dealing with, until something (a medication, a piece of medical equipment, a personal assistant) eases the difficulty.

(para. 30)

As such, relying upon others for caregiving, assistance, and support with activities of daily living that were previously eased by one's assistance dog may engender renewed feelings of guilt, anger, and frustration. To the degree that the end of a partnership involves renegotiating interpersonal and functional roles relative to caregiving and assistance with activities of daily living, partners may encounter a variety of feelings including guilt, shame, embarrassment, and anger at the reliance on human supports. Feelings may relate to the perception of the assistance dog's aid as willingly and freely given, absent the complications of accepting support from caring friends and family or paid caregivers.

Importantly, loss of the canine partner and grief for the partnership may be experienced in ways similar to those following the loss of a spouse in the sense of grieving the "we" comprised by the 24/7 companionship with an assistance dog. For many assistance dog partners, identity may be conceptualized or experienced as deeply or inextricably bound up with the dog or partnership. Indeed, Zee (1983) found that as guide dog partnerships progress, partners report an emerging and newly developed sense of self into which the guide dog is incorporated. Similarly, guide dog partners who report also owning pet dogs describe a comparatively closer bond with their guide dog than with their pet (Zee, 1983).

Wachsler (2010) articulates the feelings of grief accompanying changes in her identity as a service dog partner following the death of her second service dog:

> How can I even put into words what Gadget meant to me, how inextricably he was entwined in my life, how he was a part of my body, mind, and soul? It's a struggle I have every day now, as the anniversary of his death descends on me, and my grief at his loss feels overwhelming ... The Sharon partnered with Gadget is gone forever. A piece of me died when my partner breathed his last.
>
> (Wachsler, 2010, para. 30)

Similarly, she describes a scenario in which friends encourage her to purchase a wireless doorbell to facilitate in-home communication with her partner and caregivers, a task for which her deceased service dog was previously responsible.

> My friends said, "You're not replacing him. You loved Gadget. He was so special. That can never be replaced with a doorbell," but it felt like they were talking about the loss of love, the heart-dog loss. I wasn't just

talking about that. I was talking about that *and* the Gadget who was my arms and legs and voice. I didn't know how to explain the wholeness of Gadget as *my partner,* and the essentialness of that partnership beyond finding a solution for anyone task – my longing not to *make do* in life any more than was strictly necessary.

(2010, para. 12)

Here, Wachsler touches on the effect of a service dog's assistance and supportive, independence-enhancing presence as well as the immensity of the remnant void – felt in terms of functional well-being and psychosocial identity.

Contextual Factors in the Grieving Process

Studies have consistently indicated that level of attachment to a beloved deceased animal is one of the most important elements impacting grief processes (Wrobel & Dye, 2003). Other factors shown to influence grief include suddenness of loss and living arrangements, with living alone being particularly salient in terms of acute grief impact (Archer & Winchester, 1994). Similarly, Gosse and Barnes (1994) indicate that the level of perceived support from others, and other stressful events leading up to the death are factors most greatly impacting the intensity of grief.

While the aforementioned studies have highlighted variables that may mediate grief processes following companion animal death, few studies have looked specifically into factors that may impact assistance dog partner bereavement experiences. Notably, factors may include the particular significance of the partnership; major milestones accomplished together; the suddenness of the dog's death; and whether death was preceded by retirement and/or rehoming. Finally, the influence and impact of a partner's disability or multiple disabilities upon their cognitive, physical, emotional, or psychosocial functioning, may additionally impact the grief process.

Cohen (2002) outlines nine themes that may indicate an individual's risk for complicated grief following the loss of a human–animal bond. Cohen's thematic risk factors include: spending 14 or more hours per day with the animal; living alone; whether the animal is a partner's first (service) dog or most recent (service) dog; sharing a significant life event or events with the dog; when the dog's presence ties the bereaved partner to another person; identification with the dog; the presence of other recent losses; whether the dog was procured through rescue; and feelings of blame or guilt about the dog's death. Such themes suggest that individual grief experiences, while differing greatly from person to person, are likely further mediated by various factors that influence the bereavement experience (Cohen, 2002).

In one of the first of few studies examining salient factors that arise at the end of assistance dog partnerships, Nicholson, Kemp-Wheeler, and

Griffiths (1995) collaborated with Guide Dogs for the Blind Association (GDBA); they administered grief and emotional distress measures to guide dog owners whose partnerships had ended within the previous year due to the dog's death or retirement. Notably, among subgroups of partners who reported no additional distressing events or losses occurring around the same time their partnerships ended, significant differences were seen. Particularly high distress levels were self-reported by those whose dogs had died, as well as those whose dogs were withdrawn from the partnership and/or rehomed through GDBA. Comparatively lower distress levels were reported by those whose dogs retired and continued to live with them, as well as those whose retired dogs had then been rehomed into a home of their choosing. Finally, particularly high levels of distress at the end of guide dog partnership were also reported by partners who experienced additional, concurrent adverse events around the time that the partnership ended, regardless of the reasons for the ending or its outcomes (Nicholson, Kemp-Wheeler, & Griffiths, 1995).

Furthermore, the GDBA study participants indicated that the end of the partnership with their guide dog was likely to be particularly painful in specific circumstances. Partners reported significantly higher levels of distress if the partnership was the individual's first with a guide dog; if the dog had particularly special significance; if the partnership ended abruptly; or if the partner's relationship with the training school of origin (GDBA) was experienced as poor or strained. Such findings corroborate certain factors named by Cohen (2002) as predictive for increased complicated grief risk as well as increased distress following the end of the partnership.

Importantly, Nicholson, Kemp-Wheeler, and Griffiths (1995) suggest that emotions engendered by the end of a partnership do vary among partners for different reasons. In particular, the specialness of a first partnership forged with one's assistance dog and fortified by significant amounts of time together, and dog's presence throughout significant lifetime milestones, may contribute to particularly complex grief. Indeed, the first assistance dog partnership is frequently transformative in that partnership facilitates achievement or reclaiming of anticipated or previously-enjoyed levels of independent functioning and freedom of choice. The independence and confidence bequeathed by first partnerships is frequently so transformative as to generate new opportunities and expand vocational, functional, and relational aspirations. As such, grief following the death of the meaningful first assistance dog may be exceptionally difficult, sorrowful, or poignant for the partner as well as their family and community. Corroborating this, among guide dog owners who participated in Nicholson, Kemp-Wheeler, and Griffiths' study, those who had had several guide dog partnerships frequently looked back upon the ending of their first partnership as "especially painful" (1995, p. 108).

Grieving partners may be particularly impacted by the death of an assistance dog with special significance. For example, few stories are as gripping as that of Michael Hingson and his guide dog Roselle, who led her partner and other evacuees down 78 floors out of Tower One of the World Trade Center in New York City on September 11, 2001. In his 2011 book, *Thunder Dog*, Hingson details his upbringing, life's journey, and advocacy for improved public awareness about vision impairment and guide dogs. As graduates of Guide Dogs for the Blind™, Hingson and Roselle traveled internationally to lecture and advocate on the subjects of "trust and teamwork, guide dogs, and blindness in general" (Hingson & Flory, 2011). In *Thunder Dog*, Hingson, who has partnered with a number of guide dogs both before and after Roselle, admits that Roselle is missed more than any of his previous dogs.

As noted above, the loss of the canine partner – whether through retirement or death – poses practical challenges along with the painful and distressing feelings engendered by bereavement. While the assistance dog's retirement is typically, ideally followed by a transitional period during which the first assistance dog's retirement overlaps with or is followed smoothly by the successor dog partnership, a dog's sudden or unexpected death is very often traumatic, disorienting, and furthermore functionally disabling.

Among guide dog partners, particular distress is consistently attributed to abrupt endings; partners often compare the sudden loss of the guide dog to the initial loss of one's sight (Nicholson, Kemp-Wheeler, & Griffith, 1995). In the published literature there is a dearth of information on assistance dog partners grieving the death of the dog under tragic circumstances (e.g., perishing in vehicular accidents; getting loose and disappearing; being attacked and killed by other dogs, etc.). However, available research on guide dog partners whose partnerships ended subsequent to attacks by other dogs, resulting in early retirement and/or rehoming of a guide dog, suggests that such events are particularly distressing. Losing a canine partner in such circumstances is essentially upending for bereaved partners, as well as their family, community, and extended support networks (Clements, Benasutti, & Carmone, 2003).

Adverse Life Events and Impacts on Grief

Even at the prime of assistance dog partnership, disability-related sequelae may include progressively declining health, underemployment or chronic unemployment, health and stress-related family challenges, and other stressors. Such factors may be felt with particular salience when an assistance dog dies.

Grieving processes may be further complicated in the context of a challenging relationship with the assistance dog organization or school. Among partners with whom a relationship with an assistance dog is prematurely terminated – whether due to early retirement or after many successful years of partnership – efficacious communication and abundant, appropriate support from the training organization or school is particularly helpful. According to Nicolson, Kemp-Wheeler, and Griffiths, "lack of understanding, lack of information and communication, and lack of involvement in making decisions related to retirement and retraining" were most commonly described as distressing factors by guide dog partners whose working partnerships had ended prematurely (1995, p. 108). Indeed, bereaved partners reporting such experiences were "likely to be among those most in need of support irrespective of why the partnership ended or what subsequently happened to the dog" (1995, p. 108). As such, mental health professionals supporting clients grieving the loss of an assistance dog are encouraged to support partners in exploring feelings and thoughts relevant to the end of the partnership; renegotiating relationship to the deceased canine partner; and increasing embodied capacity for grief, longing, and love. It is also suggested that issues related to renegotiating the constellation of relationships impacted by the end of an assistance dog partnership – to self, dog, school, and others – also be given ample attention.

Supporting the Bereaved Assistance Dog Partner

> Sometimes it is even hard to get support from others who have lost service dogs. There are groups for assistance-dog partners who are grieving, but they may be small or inactive. My guess is that unless one is in the midst of grieving, it is too painful to be exposed to the topic. That emotional wound could reopen at any time, because – if we're fortunate – we will outlive our assistance dogs, again and again. The choice to be a life-long service dog partner is as Kafkaesque as it is fulfilling. Few who have escaped the black hole of that loss want to be reminded of staring into the abyss again.
>
> (Wachsler, 2010)

Review of the literature yields no published research on the specific nature of assistance partner bereavement as related to grief disenfranchisement. Of the extant research that importantly examines grief disenfranchisement and contributing factors, the significant majority focuses on pet owners grieving for deceased companion animals. The existing literature on human–companion animal bonds – both personal and peer-reviewed – emphasizes the likelihood that the bereaved will experience disenfranchised grief due to social factors including invalidation, minimization, or even shaming by others (Clements, Benasutti, & Carmone, 2003; Doka, 2002; Miller, 2017).

As assistance dogs routinely, often necessarily accompany and support their partners in activities of daily living at home, work, school, while commuting, and in other leisurely activities, the dog's presence extends broadly and its absence is often widely felt. For grieving partners who turn to pet loss hotlines or elect to participate in pet loss support groups, such resources may sometimes fail to understand, address, or seemingly approach the totality of the grief experience. However, the same factors which make grieving for the deceased assistance dog a most acute and poignant process may also serve to somewhat buttress partners against disenfranchised grief experiences. That is, when others in one's home, school, work, or communities recognize the absence and loss of the assistance dog, through subsequently inquiring after the well-being of the bereaved partner, one's grief reactions and processes may be affirmed and validated in ways not always afforded to companion animal owners following the death of pet dogs.

However, the reverse corollary is that bereaved assistance dog partners are very likely to encounter numerous, unending reminders of their loss while out and about, in part due to such inquiries from others accustomed to seeing person and dog together outside of the home and in spaces where pets are typically not permitted. Additionally, as indicated in the previous testimonial earlier in this chapter, the increased challenge of activities of daily living without the dog's support, and resultant feelings of frustration and vulnerability, may serve as a constant, compounding reminder of loss.

The Role of the Assistance Dog Support Network

Grieving processes may be experienced differently by assistance dog partners who pursued training and placement through regional or national assistance dog organizations and schools, and by those who trained their own dogs or worked privately with professional trainers. Other factors that may impact grief processes include the strength and amicability of relationship to instructors or training staff; connection with extended grief support communities of assistance dog partners and program staff and/or volunteers; and access to such aforementioned and other grief support communities.

The staff and volunteers of affiliate assistance dog organizations and guide dog schools may be among the most significant supports for many bereaved partners, having sometimes uniquely witnessed and fostered the team's growth over the course of years. The relationship to one's school of origin may span years, from the first partnership through successive partnerships, evolving health challenges related to progressive disabilities, and resultant changes in psychological, psychosocial, and occupational functioning. As such, these supporters may be among those to whom the grieving partner first turns for support. Additionally, support may be solicited from other assistance dog partners, such as other members of one's graduating cohort as well as other graduates from the same school or organization. Among schools and organizations that utilize volunteer efforts (for puppy whelping, raising, fundraising, etc.), volunteers may also play a significant role in supporting bereaved assistance dog partners. In particular, a close and enduring relationship with one's assistance dog's puppy raiser or trainer can sometimes serve as a wellspring of validation and a source of great comfort, particularly through shared memories, stories, and photographs. Anecdotally, a number of assistance dog partners state that gestures of support from others in the assistance dog world, such as heartfelt handwritten cards, social media posts, memorial plaques or brick purchases on campuses, and other gestures are tremendously meaningful.

Interestingly, Nicholson, Kemp-Wheeler, and Griffiths (1995) did not find a relationship between the intensity of grief reactions and available levels of social support among bereaved guide dog partners. That is, available social support does not necessarily serve as a moderating influence for the intensity of grief following an assistance dog's death, as varying sources of social support may exert variable influence at different stages after a loss. Of note, bereaved guide dog partners consistently named other guide dog users as their most helpful supports in that these persons were considered best equipped to "fully understand" grief reactions following a guide dog's death. One partner suggested, "no matter how hard you try, you cannot get a non-[guide dog owner] to understand the feelings about a relationship with a guide dog" (1995, p. 108). Such perceptions may be further influenced by the nature of the partner's disability or disabilities, such as functional limitations on mobility and communication that may serve to facilitate access to existing grief support resources and inhibit access to others. On the other hand, as Wachsler (2010) states above, engaging the support of other assistance dog partners can be bittersweet, in that interactions may further underscore the deceased dog's absence, potentially generate anxiety or apprehension in others about the longevity of their own partnership, and increase the bereaved partner's desire to grieve somehow most "appropriately."

Wachsler (2010) suggests that those who can offer especially meaningful support through grief companionship to bereaved assistance dog partners include relatives, friends, training staff, veterinary staff, and mental health professionals. In particular, veterinary care professionals, especially those with whom longstanding, trusting, and collaborative working relationships are held and valued by the partner, may be among the key witnesses to a partner's most acute grief reactions as well as those that unfold over time.

Wider Pet Loss/Bereavement Support Resources

Regrettably, there are few consolidated, widely-known, or widely-reaching extant resources geared especially to grieving assistance dog partners. The US-based Association for Pet Loss and Bereavement

(APLB) for some time operated a Service Dogs Committee dedicated to "providing empathy insight, advocacy, and direction with resource information and referrals for those grieving or anticipating the loss of the unique partnership with a service/guide dog or assistance animal" (Association for Pet Loss and Bereavement, 2007, para. 6). APLB Committee Chair Cheryl Nahas writes:

> The loss of a faithful and dedicated companion is complicated by having to reenter society with a new service animal. Readjustment around issues of trust, independence, socialization, and caretaking need to be made. For others, waiting to be paired with a new service animal can leave a void. This can complicate the bereavement process.
>
> (Association for Pet Loss and Bereavement, 2007, para. 11)

While regrettably now defunct, resources previously offered by APLB included an online chat feature and website subsection on issues uniquely associated with assistance dog bereavement.

The International Association of Assistance Dog Partners (IAADP), a non-profit, cross-disability organization representing partnerships across all categories of disability and training, offers a monthly conference call for partners who have recently lost or are facing the loss of their assistance dog. However, utilization of such supports is often contingent on one's ability and resources for successfully accessing and optimizing conferencing technology as well as one's comfort in doing so; for example, hearing dog partners may have difficulty participating in phone calls or be reluctant to utilize third-party technologies to participate.

Nahas (Association for Pet Loss and Bereavement, 2007) advocates for greater assistance dog partner grief awareness among the lay public and support professionals alike. Citing deficits in grief support resources within and affiliated with assistance dog organizations, Nahas also encourages schools and organizations to continue improving grief-related resources and bereavement supports for partners and families. For example, schools might refer particularly-distressed bereaved partners to trained bereavement professionals familiar with assistance dog loss and grief reactions unique to assistance dog partnership, which includes understanding ways in which grief processes may be uniquely influenced by disability-related neurocognitive, psychosocial, and health issues. Additionally, Nahas emphasizes the importance of empowering all assistance dog partners through improved access to grief psychoeducation and bereavement resources, in turn enabling partners to provide grief support and education to other grieving partners.

To-date, there are no published, evidence-based best mental health practices outlining recommended supports for clients grieving the death of their assistance dog. Such practices would make a much-needed contribution to the mental health literature, and would be a boon for assistance dog organizations looking to improve support resources for bereaved clients and their families.

Putting it into Practice

Competencies Relative to Working with Clients with Disabilities

As previously indicated, public health and rehabilitation research indicates that people with disabilities may universally face barriers to housing, employment, and leisure and recreation activities as well as constraints on access to social opportunities because of stigma, discrimination, and physical and communication inaccessibility. A decidedly heterogeneous client population, individuals with disabilities typically present in mental health settings with tremendous variation in presenting concerns, sociocultural identities, psychosocial issues, and treatment needs (Artman & Daniels, 2010; Lantican, Birdwell, & Harrell, 1994).

The abundance of relevant, extant mental health literature has focused on supporting clients' psychosocial adjustment to disability to the exclusion of exploring and establishing best practices for serving such clients in mental health contexts (Artman & Daniels, 2010; Olkin & Pledger, 2003). Guidelines for assessment of and intervention with people with disabilities are nascent in the psychological literature, and have been newly adopted by major psychiatric, psychological, and counseling accrediting bodies only in the last decade (American Psychological Association, 2012). Mental health professionals working with such clients are strongly urged to gain familiarity with ethical guidelines for working with clients with disabilities, and are encouraged to seek out current information on pertinent therapeutic and cultural issues, including those perhaps most relevant to clients partnered with assistance animals (Artman & Daniels, 2010).

Even more regrettably, there is a dearth of psychological scholarship on demographic and sociocultural variables impacting, intersecting, influencing, and influenced by disabilities in the clinical context – such as race, ethnicity, gender identity, sexual orientation, socioeconomic status, educational background, language use, and other such fundamental identity factors. Relative to assistance dogs, there is in particular a lacuna in the psychological research on supporting children and young adult clients with disabilities in grief processes following assistance dog loss. While critical, such work is beyond the scope of this chapter and certainly bears further research, particularly as families increasingly seek out and invest time, finances, and energies into assistance dog partnerships to support children with activities of daily living and improved psychosocial and socioemotional functioning.

Clinical practice issues are best conceptualized in light of factors relative to but not limited to disability. That is, among other presenting issues, clients with disabilities may present with concerns sometimes related to, stemming from, or exacerbated by issues relevant to achieving or maintaining autonomy and freedom of choice in the face of systemic, institutional, and physiological barriers. Among the many themes that may warrant attention in mental health contexts are issues of personal agency, self- and other advocacy, self-determination in living, occupational, and social contexts, and negotiation of physical and attitudinal barriers to access (Artman & Daniels, 2010; Iezzoni & Long-Bellil, 2012; Lantican et al., 1994). It is necessary as well to understand that at variable times and contexts, disability may be one of the less or least relevant factors to the presenting concerns, and while considered, should not necessarily be fore-grounded in clinical contexts (American Psychological Association, 2012).

Diagnostically and clinically, mental health professionals should use judgment in considering disability-related factors relevant to the selection, norming, administration, and interpretation of assessment instruments including grief inventories and other functioning measures (American Psychological Association, 2012; Olkin, 1999; Olkin & Taliaferro, 2006). For example, in grief symptom rating measures, bereaved assistance dog partners may endorse items positive for physical illness, fatigue, or somatic concerns that reflect complexly-intertwined organic components of dis-ability and grief processes. Relatedly, deaf and hard of hearing clients grieving the death of their hearing dogs may endorse increased anxiety symptoms and safety concerns that uniquely underscore the acuity of a sense of lost security as well as an intensified grief reaction. Mental health professionals would also do well to consider such factors relevant to case conceptualization and treatment planning.

Cornish et al. (2008) propose aspirational suggestions for ethical practice and competency with clients with disabilities. These include recognizing dis-ability as a multicultural factor; improving understanding of culturally-variable disability subgroups and communities; learning about various disability models and relevant developmental considerations; supporting disability-related advocacy and social justice issues; and seeking specialized consultation and clinical supervision to ensure competent care. In particular, mental health providers especially wanting to grow their foundation of know-ledge in assistance dog-related matters might consider undertaking disability awareness trainings; pursuing opportunities to tour guide and assistance dog schools; attending assistance dog/partner graduation and matriculation events when available; supporting assistance dog coalitions and organiza-tions; offering bereavement psychoeducation workshops to schools and members; and working with local and national assistance dog organizations and guide dog schools to establish referral networks.

In working with bereaved assistance dog partners, it is especially recom-mended that mental health professionals consider disability as a relevant but not necessarily most salient factor among the array of complexly-intertwined aspects of the client's life (Olkin, 1999). Certainly, such aspects may assume increased salience in light of an assistance dog's illness or death, and may be less salient in the exploration of other themes and experiences. Explorations of client affective states might appropriately include considerations of the following themes: available support networks; establishing a meaningful narrative of the loss experience; consolidating and embodying felt sense memories of the deceased canine partner; and negotiating disability-related factors such as the affective impacts of stigma, discrimination, and access barriers, particularly those that may be felt more acutely without one's canine partner by one's side.

Case Scenarios

Case Scenario #1:

Jen, a 23-year-old, White, bisexual woman with cerebral palsy who uses a power wheelchair, just graduated from college accompanied by her service dog Wade, a 7-year-old black Labrador-Golden Retriever cross. Jen is seeking therapy to help her deal with anxiety and adjustment issues post-graduation. Since graduating with Jen 5 years ago, Wade has been by Jen's side through her last year of high school, all of college, and her first year as a young, emerging professional. Wade has regularly accompanied Jen to her weekly psychotherapy sessions in the last six months, during which Jen has discussed her challenges finding gainful employment post-graduation.

Her face drawn and looking ashen, Jen comes in for therapy today without Wade, whom she tearfully reports she had to "put down" early last week following a rapid onset illness and deterioration. Jen describes how Wade became increasingly ill at home and began to refuse food, necessitating a city paratransit ride to the veterinary hospital for a thorough work-up where examination, tests, and abdominal ultrasound resulted in a diagnosis of acute pancreatitis.

Jen describes how the staff at the veterinary hospital aided her in transferring in and out of her wheelchair in order to sit on the floor with Wade during treatments leading up to his rapid deterioration from acute liver failure during his final hours. Due to Wade's increasingly unmanageable pain levels and lack of response to aggressive treatment, the veterinarian suggested that Jen consider euthanasia as the kindest option.

After many phone calls with the staff and veterinary clinic at her training assistance dog organization, Jen elected to proceed with euthanasia, and held Wade's head in her lap as he took his last breaths. Jen says that she felt numb during her ride home via paratransit that evening, and tells the therapist that since arriving home, she has stayed in bed and cried on and off during her waking hours, "senseless with grief." She tearfully describes feeling bereft without Wade beside her at every waking moment of her day, and explains that family members living on the other side of the country are helping her arrange for temporary short-term personal care assistants to assist her with tasks that Wade used to do. Jen tells her therapist that she is "not sure how to live without Wade."

Case Scenario #2:

Martin is a 47-year-old Latino man who resides with his wife and two young daughters. After sustaining a minor heart attack four months ago, Martin presents for therapy at the behest of his wife, who is worried about his health and stress levels. He explains that his heart attack occurred shortly after the death of his 12-year-old German Shepherd guide dog, Eloise, with whom he had been partnered for nearly 10 years.

During intake, Martin explains that at age 35 he was diagnosed with bilateral retinitis pigmentosa (RP), a degenerative hereditary eye disease, following ongoing complaints of decreased vision at night. Martin recalls how each advancement of his RP, and its associated, accompanying vision loss contributed to his increased caution and trepidation in the world around him. Seeking greater mobility and independence, at the suggestion of his mobility and orientation specialist he elected to pursue a partnership with a guide dog. Martin and Eloise graduated from a large guide dog school in the US Northeast, and in her swift and surefooted way, she supported his increased independence through work, business school, and becoming a parent two young children. "Next to my wife and kids, she's been the most amazing thing to happen to me," Martin says.

Last year, Martin learned that Eloise had a fast-growing, incurable cancer. Concerned about his daughters' reaction, and not yet ready to say goodbye, Martin opted to let Eloise continue her guiding work daily until she indicated that she was no longer interested in working due to increased pain. In the days and weeks following euthanasia, Martin says, "I cried like a baby." He explains that in the months since, he has been feeling exceedingly hopeless, irritable, and sometimes inexplicably angry; he notes that he is staying home much more frequently, and these days only goes out when needed since "getting around is so much more work all of a sudden." He says that his wife, while understanding and supportive, has encouraged him to return to guide dog school for a successor dog as soon as possible, but he is just not ready, and does not know when he will be. Additionally, he recognizes that his wife and daughters are missing Eloise as well, and is struggling to support them while negotiating his own distress at her absence.

Discussion Questions:

1. How might your own perceptions of and reactions to disability, and attendant beliefs and attitudes, impact your work with Jen or Martin?

2.   What are the potential social and psychological aspects of Jen's and Martin's grief processes as people with disabilities who have chosen to partner with assistance dogs?
3.   How might you explore attachment and/or developmental issues with Jen or Martin in light of how their partnerships with their assistance dogs may contribute to particularly acute grief experiences?
4.   What resources might you consider utilizing in your work with Jen or Martin?

Acknowledgments

For their assistance in conceptualizing and organizing information relative to this topic, the author wishes to thank Anna Benham; Deborah Dodson Craft, DVM; Ray Craft, DVM; Joan E. Heller Miller, M.Ed.; and Sarah Birman and Becky Miller of Canine Companions for Independence®. Gratitude to Morgane Vincent for research support.

Note

1. This chapter uses the term "assistance dog" as the favored nomenclature for the varying categories of service dogs specially trained to assist their disabled partners. Within the assistance dog industry there are a number of different terms denoting various categories of assistance dogs, including guide dogs for blind and visually impaired persons; hearing dogs assisting deaf and hard of hearing people; and service dogs assisting people with disabilities other than blindness and deafness. Substantial training to mitigate the human partner's disability is but one of a number of criteria required for a dog to meet the legal definition of a "service animal" as described in the Americans with Disabilities Act (ADA).

References

Allen, D. (2006). Letting go of the harness for the last time: A descriptive realism approach to exploring the ending of working relationships with guide dogs. *McNair Scholars Research Journal*, 2(1), 5.

Allen, K., & Blascovich, J. (1996). The value of service dogs for people with severe ambulatory disabilities. *Journal of the American Medical Association*, 275, 1001–1006.

American Psychological Association. (2012). Guidelines for assessment of and intervention with persons with disabilities. *The American Psychologist*, 67(1), 43.

Archer, J., & Winchester, G. (1994). Bereavement following death of a pet. British *Journal of Psychology*, 85, 259–271.

Artman, L. K., & Daniels, J. A. (2010). Disability and psychotherapy practice: Cultural competency and practical tips. *Professional Psychology: Research and Practice*, 41(5), 442–448.

Association for Pet Loss and Bereavement (2007). Bereavement for service dogs. Retrieved October 28, 2018, from http://web.archive.org/web/20070513154612/www.aplb.org/services/service_dogs.html

Cohen, S. P. (2002). Can pets function as family members? *Western Journal of Nursing Research*, 24(6), 621–638.

Collins, D. M., Fitzgerald, S. G., Sachs-Ericsson, N., Scherer, M., Cooper, R. A., & Boninger, M. L. (2006). Psychosocial well-being and community participation of service dog partners. *Disability and Rehabilitation: Assistive Technology*, 1(1–2), 41–48.

Cornish, J. A. E., Gorgens, K. A., Monson, S. P., Olkin, R., Palombi, B. J., & Abels, A. V. (2008). Perspectives on ethical practice with people who have disabilities. *Professional Psychology: Research and Practice*, 39(5), 488a.

Clements, P. T., Benasutti, K. M., & Carmone, A. (2003). Support for bereaved owners of pets. *Perspectives in psychiatric care*, 39(2), 49–54.

Contreras, L. (2003). *Paws for thought: The beginning and end of a partnership.* (Unpublished Master's Thesis). University of California, Davis.

Davis, M. (2012). What I know for sure after 39 years of being a guide dog handler. Guest Post by Schneider, K.S. Retrieved October 28, 2018, from https://working-likedogs.com/what-i-know-for-sure-after-39-years-of-being-a-guide-dog-handler/

Davis, M. (2010). The journey of 2010 begins. Retrieved October 28, 2018, from https://workinglikedogs.com/the-journey-of-2010-begins/

Doka, K. J. (2002). *Disenfranchised grief: New directions, challenges, and strategies for practice* (pp. 187–198). Champaign, IL: Research Press.

Eames, E., & Eames, T. (2001). Bridging differences within the disability community: The assistance dog movement. *Disability Studies Quarterly*, 21(3), 55–66.

Eddy, J., Hart, L. A., & Boltz, R. P. (1988). The effects of service dogs on social acknowledgments of people in wheelchairs. *The Journal of Psychology*, 122(1), 39–45.

Fairman, S. K., & Huebner, R. A. (2001). Service dogs: A compensatory resource to improve function. *Occupational Therapy in Health Care*, 13(2), 41–52.

Gosse, G. H., & Barnes, M. J. (1994). Human grief resulting from the death of a pet. *Anthrozoös*, 7(2), 103-112.

Guest, C. M., Collis, G. M., & McNicholas, J. (2006). Hearing dogs: A longitudinal study of social and psychological effects on deaf and hard-of-hearing recipients. *Journal of Deaf Studies and Deaf Education*, 11(2), 252–261.

Hart, L. A., Zasloff, R. L., & Benfatto, A. M. (1996). The socializing role of hearing dogs. *Applied Animal Behaviour Science*, 47(1), 7–15.

Hingson, M., & Flory, S. (2011). *Thunder Dog: The true story of a blind man, his guide dog, and the triumph of trust at ground zero.* London: Harper Collins.

Iezzoni, L. I., & Long-Bellil, L. M. (2012). Training physicians about caring for persons with disabilities: "Nothing about us without us!" *Disability and Health Journal*, 5(3), 136–139.

International Guide Dog Federation. (2018). Retrieved June 16, 2019, from https://www.igdf.org.uk.

Julius, H., Beetz, A., Kotrschal, K., Turner, D., & Uvnas-Moberg, K. (2013). *Attachment to pets: An integrative view of human–animal relationships with implications for therapeutic practice.* Cambridge, MA: Hogrefe Publishing.

Kraus, L., Lauer, E., Coleman, R., & Houtenville, A. (2018). 2017 Disability Statistics Annual Report. Durham, NH: University of New Hampshire.

Kwong, M. J., & Bartholomew, K. (2011). "Not just a dog": An attachment perspective on relationships with assistance dogs. *Attachment & Human Development*, 13(5), 421–436.

Lane, D. R., McNicholas, J., & Collis, G. M. (1998). Dogs for the disabled: Benefits to recipients and welfare of the dog. *Applied Animal Behaviour Science*, 59(1–3), 49–60.

Lantican, S. M., Birdwell, C. N., & Harrell, R. T. (1994). Physically handicapped individuals in psychotherapy: Some empirical data, *Issues in Mental Health Nursing*, 15(1), 73–84.

Merbitz, N. H., & Sachs-Ericcson, N. (2009). Benefits of animal contact and assistance dogs for individuals with disabilities. *Canine Ergonomics*, 10(15), 301–324.

Miller, C. (2011). *Relationship between deaf identities and D/deaf and hard of hearing individuals' attitudes toward hearing dog partnership.* UMI # 3467392. (Unpublished Doctoral Dissertation). Gallaudet University, Washington, DC.

Miller, J. (2017, March 23) Things I wish I had known when my dog died. *Pet City.* Retrieved November 13, 2018, from www.nytimes.com/2017/03/23/nyregion/things-i-wish-i-had-known-when-my-dog-died.html

Mowry, R. L., Carnahan, S., & Watson, D. (1994). *A national study on the training, selection and placement of hearing dogs.* Fayetteville, AR: University of Arkansas Rehabilitation Research and Training Center for Persons who are Deaf or Hard of Hearing.

Nicholson, J., Kemp-Wheeler, S., & Griffiths, D. (1995). Distress arising from the end of a guide dog partnership. *Anthrozoös*, 8(2), 100–110.

Ogden, P. (1992). *Chelsea: The story of a signal dog.* Boston, MA: Little, Brown and Company.

O'Haire, M. E., Guérin, N. A., & Kirkham, A. C. (2015). Animal-assisted intervention for trauma: A systematic literature review. *Frontiers in Psychology*, 6, 1121.

O'Haire, M. E., & Rodriguez, K. E. (2018). Preliminary efficacy of service dogs as a complementary treatment for posttraumatic stress disorder in military members and veterans. *Journal of Consulting and Clinical Psychology*, 86(2), 179.

Olkin, R. (1999). *What psychotherapists should know about disability.* New York, NY: Guilford Press.

Olkin, R., & Pledger, C. (2003). Can disability studies and psychology join hands? *American Psychologist*, 58(4), 296–304.

Olkin, R., & Taliaferro, G. (2006). Evidence-based practices have ignored people with disabilities. Evidence-based practices in mental health: Debate and dialogue on the fundamental questions, 353–359.

Olson, P. N. (2002). The modern working dog – A call for interdisciplinary collaboration. *Journal of the American Veterinary Medical Association*, 221(3), 352–355.

Pang, P. E. I. (1999). *Hearing dogs: Enhancing human adaptability.* (Doctoral Dissertation). ProQuest Information & Learning.

Rémillard, L. W. (2014). *Exploring the grief experience among bereaved pet owners.* (Unpublished Master's Thesis). University of Guelph.

Rintala, D. H., Matamoros, R., & Seitz, L. L. (2008). Effects of assistance dogs on persons with mobility or hearing impairments: a pilot study. *Journal of Rehabilitation Research & Development*, 45(4).

Roth, S. (1992). The effects of service dogs on the occupational performance and life satisfaction of individuals with spinal cord injuries. (Unpublished Master's thesis.) Rush College.

Sachs-Ericsson, N., Hansen, N. K., & Fitzgerald, S. (2002). Benefits of assistance dogs: A review. *Rehabilitation Psychology*, 47(3), 251.

Sanders, C. M., Mauger, P. A., & Strong, P. A. (1985). *A manual for the grief experience inventory.* Palo Alto, CA: Consulting Psychologists Press.

Sanders, C. R. (2000). The impact of guide dogs on the identity of people with visual impairments. *Anthrozoös*, 13(3), 131–139.

Schneider, K. S. (2005). The winding valley of grief: When a dog guide retires or dies. *Journal of Visual Impairment and Blindness*, 99(6), 368–370.

Sherman, S. G. (2017). *Grief counseling for adult pet loss: A primer for mental health professionals*. (Unpublished Master's Thesis). University of Alaska Fairbanks.

Valentine, D., Kiddoo, M., & LaFleur, B. (1993). Psychosocial implications of service dog ownership for people who have mobility or hearing impairments. *Social Work in Health Care*, 19(1), 109–125.

Vogel, B. (2011, August). Service dogs: Making the grade. *New Mobility: The Magazine for Active Wheelchair Users*. Retrieved November 12, 2018, from www.newmobility.com/2011/08/service-dogs-making-the-grade/

Wachsler, S. (2010, September 18). Without Gadget, who am I? A SD-less service dog partner's identity. *After Gadget*. Retrieved November 11, 2018, from https://aftergadget.wordpress.com/2010/09/18/without-gadget-who-am-i-a-sd-less-service-dog-partners-identity/

Walther, S., Yamamoto, M., Thigpen, A. P., Garcia, A., Willits, N. H., & Hart, L. A (2017). Assistance dogs: historic patterns and roles of dogs placed by ADI or IGDF accredited facilities and by non-accredited US facilities. *Frontiers of Veterinary Science*, 4(1), 1–11.

White, N., Mills, D., & Hall, S. (2017). Attachment style is related to quality of life for assistance dog owners. *International Journal of Environmental Research and Public Health*, 14(6), 658.

Whitmarsh, L. (2005). The benefits of guide dog ownership. *Visual Impairment Research*, 7(1), 27–42.

Winkle, M., Crowe, T. K., & Hendrix, I. (2012). Service dogs and people with physical disabilities partnerships: A systematic review. *Occupational Therapy International*, 19(1), 54–66.

Wrobel, T. A., & Dye, A. L. (2003). Grieving pet death: Normative, gender, and attachment issues. *Omega*, 47(4), 385–393.

Zee, A. (1983). Guide dogs and their owners: assistance and friendship. In A. H. Katcher, & A. M. Beck (Eds.), *New Perspectives on our lives with companion animals* (pp. 472–483). Philadelphia, PA: University of Pennsylvania Press.

14 Helping Clients Cope with Grief Associated with Euthanasia for Behavior Problems

Emma K. Grigg and Tammy McCormick Donaldson

Introduction: Euthanasia for Behavior Problems and its Impacts

Loss of a valued companion animal is always difficult, as is making the decision to euthanize a pet, even when the reason for euthanasia is illness, old age, or physical suffering of the pet. The euthanasia of a pet for reasons of severe behavioral problems is likely to be an even more challenging experience, given that in all other respects the pet may be healthy, and much of the time may be a happy, loving companion to his human family. Most pet owners experience deeply conflicted emotions when considering euthanasia for behavioral reasons. It is highly unlikely they have come to this decision lightly and have probably experienced significant stress and anxiety over the behavior of their pet. They may feel isolated, not knowing where to turn for help. Lack of societal understanding and support for grief over pet loss in general can make owners unwilling to share their feelings or seek grief counseling (Winch, 2018). This lack of societal support may be more marked for owners who have had to euthanize their pet for behavioral reasons. Many owners fear the criticism and judgment of other owners and of pet enthusiasts who may blame the owners for the problem, and/or who claim they themselves would "never" euthanize a pet for behavioral reasons (Summerfield, 2017). Many of these owners express feelings of guilt or shame for not being able to help their pet resolve their behavior issues. On the other hand, some owners may fear criticism for keeping the ("dangerous," "destructive," etc.) pet in their homes for as long as they did. Even some companion animal professionals may sometimes be too quick to recommend euthanizing pets based on limited information (Summerfield, 2017). All members of the owner's own household may not agree with the decision, adding to the overall stress associated with this procedure. In some cases, euthanasia may not even be the choice of the owner, but a court mandate, with the owners facing criminal charges if they do not comply. Owners euthanizing for behavior may be more at risk for slow recovery from grief than owners losing pets to other causes, due to the increased complexity of emotions (e.g., grief, shame, anger, guilt, regret, and perhaps relief) that they experience, exacerbated by the preceding stressful experience of living with the pet while attempting to address the behavior problem. The purpose of this chapter is to shed light on this issue for clinicians working with human clients going through this experience, and provide strategies and discussion topics to help these clients cope with this complicated and often heartbreaking issue.

Background: The Positive and Negative Impacts of Life with a Companion Animal

The bond between owners and their companion animals can be a profound and important one, and the magnitude and relevance of this bond may surpass that of the bond between humans (Ross & Baron-Sorensen, 1998). In the daily lives of many owners and caretakers, pets provide significant emotional and social support, as is described in detail elsewhere in this volume. Publications abound on the potential benefits of pet ownership to health and quality of life for humans. These benefits include improvements in cardiovascular health and better survival rates after heart attack (Allen, Shykoff, & Izzo, et al., 2001; Friedmann, Katcher, Lynch, & Thomas, 1980; Levine et al., 2013); improvements in mental health such as reduced feelings of loneliness, stress and depression (El-Alayli, Lystad, Webb, Hollingsworth, & Ciolli, 2006; McConnell, Brown, Shoda, Stayton, & Martin, 2011); and increased levels of physical exercise, with the health benefits that often accompany these increased levels (Christian et al., 2013; Schofield, Mummery, & Steele, 2005). Arguably the most convincing body of literature on how pets benefit their human companions concerns pets providing their human companions with social support. This is the finding of numerous studies (e.g., McConnell et al., 2011), and makes intuitive sense to anyone who has lived with and loved a companion animal. When the human–animal bond is intact, pets may assist in mediating the long-term effects of stress by providing a buffer between life's often unavoidable stressors and our physical and emotional health (Friedmann & Son, 2009; Grigg & Donaldson, 2017).

For the most part, we now accept that a companion animal in the household can have significant and varied beneficial effects on the health, mental well-being, and quality of life of the human members of that household, even if we do not yet fully understand the mechanisms of this effect. However, the effects of companion animals may not always be unequivocally positive (Simon, 1984). Presence of a behavior problem in the pet (whether the behavior is truly abnormal, or whether the behavior is species-normal but is considered unacceptable by the owner) can have a detrimental effect on the human–animal bond (Landsberg, Hunthausen, & Ackerman, 2013; Seksel, 1997; Spencer,

1993). Behavior problems in companion animals are not uncommon: more animals may suffer from behavior problems (or, behaviors considered unacceptable by their human caretakers) than from any other medical issue (Hammerle et al., 2015). Like humans, non-human animals can suffer from emotional and mental disorders, and these companion animals are often treated with the same medications (antidepressants, anxiolytics, anti-seizure drugs) used to treat these conditions in humans. If the behavior problem persists, it can result in declines in the quality of life and even the welfare of all members of the household. This is particularly true if the behavior represents a safety risk for humans or other non-human animals (aggression, for example), or jeopardizes the owner's living situation (destruction of property and excessive barking due to separation anxiety, or persistent housesoiling, for example). Anyone who has worked with clients seeking help for behavior problems exhibited by their pets has witnessed the stress, frustration, and anxiety that can be caused by these issues.

Serious canine aggression, in particular, can be very challenging to treat, and highly stressful for owners (Reisner, 2003). Dog bite-related human fatalities are relatively rare in the US (31 in 2016, within a human population of 320+ million and a canine population estimated at 70 million or more), and reported dog bites have dramatically decreased across the country since the 1970s, according to the National Canine Research Council (NCRC, 2018). Nonetheless, living with an aggressive animal is highly stressful and potentially dangerous, both physically, legally (given owner liability for the actions of their pet), and socially. In some instances, behavior problems can be extremely persistent, and may continue for weeks, months, and even years before the owners are able to successfully modify the behavior, or until they decide that they can no longer maintain the pet in their home.

When the behavior problem cannot be remedied to the owner's (or, society's) satisfaction, the consequences for the pet can be fatal. Although shelter outcomes are improving in the US, the staggering numbers of companion animals surrendered to shelters each year, and the significant proportion of those animals that are euthanized, represent stark evidence that the relationship between owner and companion animal does not always go smoothly. A breakdown in this relationship can have very serious consequences for the animals involved (Arkow & Dow, 1984). Reasons why owners relinquish animals to shelters and rescue organizations vary (Salman, et al., 1998). Sometimes the reasons are logistical or financial (e.g., a change in the lifestyle, health or living situation of the owners, resulting in the owner being unable or unwilling to continue caring for the pet). Another major reason for shelter relinquishments, however, is the behavior of the individual pet (Salman et al., 1998, Salman et al., 2000). The National Council on Pet Population Study and Policy (NCPPSP) Regional Shelter Study assessed

12 shelters, in four regions of the US, over a 1-year period, and found that "behavioral problems, including aggression toward people or companion animals, were the most frequently given reasons for canine relinquishment and the second most frequently given reasons for feline relinquishment" (Salman et al., 2000; p. 93). As early as 1988, McKeown and Luescher noted that "undesirable behavior is one of the most common fatal diseases of pet animals" (p. 74). Some North American studies suggest that more companion animals are euthanized for behavioral reasons than for all medical reasons combined (Landsberg et al., 2013). Although our understanding of companion animals has grown exponentially in the last 20 years, thanks to recent dramatic increases in research on companion animal behavior, training, and cognition (see Grigg & Donaldson, 2017, for an overview), the issue of problematic behavior in our animal companions remains.

Complicating this issue is the possibility that owners may not know where to obtain qualified help for behavior problems in their pets, or may not be able to easily access or afford what help is available. Many owners, when faced with a question or concern about their pets, will first approach their veterinarian. Unfortunately, numerous studies have now noted the lack of behavior services offered by many veterinarians, perhaps due to the minimal training many veterinary students receive in the diagnosis and treatment of behavior problems, resulting in a lack of clinician confidence in treating these cases (Calder, Albright, & Koch, 2017; Grigg, Kogan, van Haaften, & Kolus, 2018; Golden & Hanlon, 2018; Kogan, Hellyer, Rishniw, & Schoenfeld-Tacher, in press; Roshier & McBride, 2013). In one study, 70% of dogs and 50% of cats relinquished to 12 US shelters had seen a veterinarian prior to relinquishment, but the problems that led to their eventual relinquishment were either not addressed or not resolved (Salman et al., 2000). Many owners of companion animals may have only a limited understanding of companion animal behavior. They often rely on sources other than veterinarians (Hammerle et al., 2015) or Certified Applied Animal Behaviorists for behavioral advice for their pets and the quality of the advice they receive varies. Given that there is currently no single, required certification process for companion animal trainers or behaviorists, owners may inadvertently choose a trainer or "behaviourist" who uses harsh, punishment-based approaches which have been shown to make the problems worse, not better (Herron, Shofer, &, Reisner, 2009). Suggestions for referring clients to qualified help for their pets will be reviewed in the section on "Best Practices," below.

Some of the most common companion animal behavior problems resulting in consultation for behavior advice from a veterinarian or applied animal behavior professional, and/or in relinquishment or euthanasia of the pet, are as follows (Landsberg et al., 2013; New et al., 2000; Salman et al., 2000):

Common Behavior Problems in Companion Animals

Dogs:

- Aggression (towards humans or other non-human animals, particularly when the behavior represented a real safety risk)*
- Fears/phobias
- Separation Anxiety
- Housesoiling
- Excitability/unruliness
- Destructiveness

Cats:

- Housesoiling (elimination disorders and/or marking behaviors)*
- Aggression (towards humans or other non-human animals)
- Excessive vocalization/nighttime activity
- Destructiveness (esp. scratching furniture)

Another significant way that bringing a companion animal into the home can add to human emotional distress involves the eventual (and inevitable) death of the pet, whether due to illness, trauma, old age, or euthanasia for behavioral reasons. The loss of a beloved family pet can be a significant source of grief for pet owners and can also represent a critical loss of emotional and social support for these owners, as is described elsewhere in this volume. Winch (2018) points out the severity of grief following the death of a pet, which can be acute for months and persist up to a full year or more (Wrobel & Dye, 2003), and which has been associated with "Broken Heart Syndrome," in which a person's response to grief is so severe that they exhibit symptoms resembling a heart attack (Maiti & Dhoble, 2017). Pets provide companionship, reduce loneliness and depression, and can help reduce anxiety. Therefore, whether task-trained or not, all pets function as therapy or emotional support animals to some extent; their loss can constitute a significant emotional challenge for owners (Winch, 2018). The loss of a companion animal can cause feelings of grief that may equal or exceed grief associated with the loss of a family member (Hart, Hart, & Mader, 1990; Sife, 1993).

Complicating the recovery from grief following pet loss is the fact that, as noted earlier, much of society does not recognize the death of a pet as a legitimate reason to experience grief. Friends, co-workers and even other family members may take the attitude that "it's just a dog," or "you can just get another cat," effectively trivializing or dismissing the pet owner's feelings of grief. This in turn can make sufferers hesitant to discuss their feelings with others, and may impede the recovery process (Winch, 2018). Pet owners who experience a lack of societal recognition for their loss are likely to experience what is known as disenfranchised grief (Doka, 1989; Adams, Bonnett, & Meek, 2000; Cordaro, 2012; Packman et al., 2014), and pet owners experiencing disenfranchised grief are at a greater risk of excessive or complicated grief reactions (Adams et al., 2000; Tzivian & Friger, 2014). Complicated grief has been associated with negative health outcomes, such as social isolation, emotional withdrawal, and inability to work (Prigerson et al., 1995). Lack of social support has been associated with more intense grief, and lower quality of life, following pet loss (Planchon & Templer, 1996; Tzivian, Friger, & Kushnir, 2015). In addition, social support is often identified as an important component of grief recovery, and may be protective against the development of complicated grief (King & Werner, 2011; Vanderwerker & Prigerson, 2004). Perceived social support (i.e., the perception that social support will be available when needed) may be particularly important (Sherbourne & Stewart, 1991; Wågø, Byrkjedal, Sinnes, Hystad, & Dyregrov, 2017). In a recent analysis of 75 calls to a pet loss support hotline (Rémillard, Meehan, Kelton, & Coe, 2017), 23% of callers reported that they had no one to rely on for emotional support, corroborating the conclusion that pet loss is still not widely viewed as an acceptable form of grief by mainstream society.

Euthanasia in particular may represent ethical and emotional challenges for pet owners, and can intensify the emotional distress associated with pet loss and complicate the recovery process. Rémillard et al. (2017), in comparing grief experienced following loss of a pet to that following loss of another human, noted that the ethical dilemma of euthanasia "may complicate pet owners' grief and does not often exist in relation to human death" (p. 150; citing Adams et al., 2000; Quackenbush & Glickman, 1983). After the euthanasia procedure, owners often continue to dwell on their decision. Rémillard et al. (2017) reported that 33% of callers to a pet loss hotline reported having significant difficulty making the decision to euthanize their pet, and 40% of callers expressed lingering concerns about their decision. Guilt and uncertainty following the loss of a pet are frequently reported in studies of grief associated with pet loss (Hart et al., 1990; Kirby-Madden, Shreyer, Nielsen, & Herron, 2014; McCutcheon and Fleming, 2002). Having to consciously make the decision to end the pet's life (even when the reasons are humane, such as providing an end to the pet's suffering) is often accompanied by guilt, feeling responsible for the death, and other negative emotions (Fogle, 1981; Quackenbush & Glickman, 1983).

There is an extensive body of literature documenting the serious emotional impacts of conducting or being associated with euthanasia among veterinarians, animal shelter staff, and animal rescue workers. Working in these fields, where euthanasia is performed frequently and may be seen as an unavoidable necessity, can erode the mental and physical well-being of staff, leading to compassion fatigue, burnout, and overall stress (Baran et al., 2009; Figley & Roop, 2006; Lovell & Lee, 2013; Scotney, McLaughlin,

& Keates, 2015). While the average pet owner does not, of course, deal with euthanasia on the same scale as veterinarians or shelter staff, the ethical issues associated with making the decision to end the life of a companion animal remain. For owners, the strong bond they have with their own pet can make the grief associated with the resulting loss more intense, and the greater the attachment to the pet the more intense the feelings of loss may be (Gosse & Barnes, 1994; Planchon et al., 2002). The circumstances surrounding the pet's death may make the grief experience worse, as has been noted for human deaths (Planchon et al., 2002). Interestingly, studies which have compared owner's grief reactions following the euthanasia versus accidental or natural death of their pet tend to report more intense and/or more lasting grief associated with accidental or natural death than with euthanasia (McCutcheon & Fleming, 2002; Planchon, Templer, Stokes, & Keller, 2002). Authors of these studies have suggested that the observed greater levels of grief may be related to factors such as the unanticipated nature of the death, and thus the inability to prepare for the loss; a feeling of lack of control; and/or having the watch the pet suffer, in the case of death due to illness or old age. However, it is important to note that these studies do not distinguish between euthanasia performed due to illness, injury, or old age, and euthanasia performed because of serious behavioral issues. In our experience (and as others have noted) there is a distinct difference in these two situations. In the case of euthanasia for behavior, the pet is often physically healthy, may be young, and can be happy, loving, and loyal the vast majority of the time. It is the memory of the incident (or incidents) of unacceptable behavior, and the ever-present fear of the behavior reoccurring (and what the consequences of reoccurrence might be), that can be a significant and chronic source of stress and anxiety for these owners. Shame (feeling that they caused the problem, or for failing to fix it) and fear of judgment by others only exacerbate the stress these owners experience.

The Most Difficult Decision: Euthanasia for Behavior Problems

As noted at the start of this chapter, euthanasia of a pet due to severe behavioral problems is a difficult and highly emotional topic. It is not often discussed in the literature, beyond studies reporting statistics on reasons for relinquishment and/or euthanasia of companion animals. In many cases, owners who have had to euthanize their pet for behavioral reasons may have a more difficult time coping with the loss than owners who have lost a pet for other reasons. The lack of societal understanding and support over pet loss is likely more marked for these owners, as they may fear the criticism and judgment of others about their choice. In some cases, the choice may not be that of the owner. State laws vary in their "dangerous dog laws," but in general, any dog that is deemed a risk for injury to another domestic

animal or person may be declared a dangerous dog and ordered euthanized. Many owners feel immense guilt, and blame themselves for causing
the problem in the first place, and/or for not doing enough to fix the
problem once identified. There is a perception in the minds of many dog
owners, exemplified in the famous phrase of the British trainer Barbara
Woodhouse, that "there are no bad dogs, only inexperienced owners"
(Woodhouse, 1982). Although dogs with behavior problems may not be
"bad" dogs, and while it is true that many (if not most) behavior problems
can be successfully treated with qualified help, there are certainly behavior
problems that are caused by physiological and/or mental imbalances or
deficiencies, and which have not been caused by the owner. The sad fact is,
not all behavior problems can be solved (certainly not by the average pet
owner). The section on "Best Practices," below, includes some useful documents for clients faced with this decision, primarily recommendations
written for owners facing these issues (where to seek help, what to consider
when making the decision, etc.), and for the veterinary community (to assist
clients in making these decisions).

Prior to addressing these issues with a client who is dealing with euthanasia of a pet for behavioral reasons, it is worth taking the time to read
through some of the personal accounts of this experience available online
(from both owners, and from behavioral professionals working with these
owners); some examples are listed below. The lengths to which some
owners will go to keep the pet in their home, and to try and help their
pets overcome their challenges, and the intensity of the owners' reactions
to the loss of these pets (including reports of clinical depression and
PTSD-like symptoms), is highly informative and sometimes heartbreaking.
Many writers describe their grief following the loss of their pet in deeply
personal terms: "Even though I knew we made the right decision, I felt as
though I had murdered my dog" (Lodge, 2013). As one veterinarian notes
of owners struggling with this decision, "The biggest battle these families
face is not with the pet, however; it's with themselves" (McVety, 2015).
Below is a list of sites available at the time of publication which describe
this experience in detail. In addition, two case studies (detailing the
history of the problem, outcome, owner's emotional reactions, and recommendations for addressing owner grief) will be described in the
"Scenarios" section, later in this chapter.

Stories of Pet Loss Due to Euthanasia for Behavioral Reasons Available Online

Lodge, M. (2013) Please don't hate me for this: I had to euthanize my
aggressive dog. Available from www.dogster.com/lifestyle

London, K. B. (2015) Considering euthanasia because of aggression. Available from www.thebark.com

McConnell, P. (2015) When is it time to put down a dog who is aggressive to people? Available from www.patriciamcconnell.com/theotherendoftheleash

McVety, D. (2015) The unfair necessity of euthanizing an aggressive dog. Available from www.drandyroark.com

Stremming, S. (2017) We need to talk about behavioral euthanasia. Available from www.thecognitivecanine.com

Summerfield, J. (2017) Harsh truths and difficult choices: the reality of behavioral euthanasia. Available from www.drjensdogblog.com

Wylie, K. (2015) Making the decision to euthanize our problem behavior dog. Available from www.karenwylie.wordpress.com

Best Practices – Helping Clients Facing Serious Pet Behavior Issues

The nature of recommendations for helping clients dealing with these issues will depend largely on what stage of the process the client is in – are they currently living with a pet with a serious behavior problem, and struggling with how best to deal with it? Or, have they reached the point where they are unable or unwilling to live with the problem behavior any longer, and are seeking advice and perhaps reassurance as to how to make a very difficult decision about euthanizing their pet? Or finally, have they recently been through the very challenging experience of euthanizing a pet for behavioral reasons, and are struggling to deal with the impacts of this experience and loss?

Helping Clients Dealing with an Existing Behavior Problem:

Recommendations for helping clients dealing with behavior problems in their pets are summarized below. These are covered in detail elsewhere (Grigg, 2018). It is important to consider, when working with a client who lives with a pet exhibiting problematic or dangerous behaviors, both the value of the human–animal bond (including the client's emotional attachment to the animal, and the social support that animal provides for that client) *and* the potential stressors caused by the pet's behavior problem (and how these stressors might impact their lives and recovery). Do not assume, because the pet is exhibiting severe behavior problems (even in cases of aggression towards the client), that your client no longer has a strong bond with his or her pet. These issues can do significant damage to the human–animal bond, but as the personal accounts referenced in the previous section reveal, many owners still feel a deep affection and strong sense of responsibility towards their pet, which actually contributes to their emotional conflict. Your clients may not know how to effectively address a companion animal behavior problem and may be faced with a confusing variety of often contradictory recommendations on how to treat these issues. In addition, it is likely that they have already tried (perhaps repeatedly) to address the problem without success, leading to feelings of frustration and helplessness.

Recommended Steps that Clients Can Take When Dealing with an Ongoing Behavioral Problem (Adapted from Grigg, 2018):

If the safety of the client (or any members of the client's household) appears to be at risk due to the pet's behavior, in the case of aggression, for example, urge the client to immediately put household management measures in place to ensure the safety of all concerned. The behavior professionals listed below ("Resources for Clients Seeking Expert Help") can help with specific recommendations tailored to the client's situation, and detailed client handouts are available in veterinary behavior textbooks (e.g., Horwitz & Neilson, 2007) and in the scientific literature (e.g., Reisner, 2003). Initial safety recommendations (for aggression) often include:

- Learn to recognize the body language that indicates when the pet is becoming fearful, defensive or tense, and respect these warnings. All interaction with the animal should be discontinued until the animal is calm (Horwitz & Neilson, 2007). For dogs, these warnings could include body tensing/stiffening, intense/hard stare, growling, snarling (lifting the lip and showing teeth), lunging, and snapping. For cats, warnings could include tail rapidly flicking, ears pinned back, hissing, growling, swatting.
- Avoid situations and specific triggers that are known to cause the pet to become stressed and/or aggressive; a calm animal is a safer animal.
- Never leave the pet alone with children, or with anyone unwilling or unable to heed the pet's warning signs and react appropriately. Unless the pet can be closely (and actively) supervised by an adult trained in the pet's warning signs, the pet should be confined safely in a crate or carrier. For dogs, basket muzzles may also be useful in these situations.
- Do not physically punish the pet (for example, by hitting, scruffing, or forcibly holding the animal down); these confrontational approaches put the person administering them at risk, and tend to intensify rather than reduce the behavioral problem (Herron et al., 2009).

Once safety measures are in place (if applicable), the next step for problems involving companion animals would be to take the animal to a veterinarian for a comprehensive examination, to ensure that the animal is physically healthy. Some behavioral issues may be symptoms of an underlying medical condition. In these cases, once the medical issue is resolved, the behavioral issue usually improves or disappears. For example, inappropriate elimination in cats and aggression in dogs are two problems often linked to pain and other underlying medical causes. Veterinarians with sufficient training in behavioral medicine may be able to effectively treat the behavior problem themselves. If not, they can usually provide referrals to a boarded veterinary behaviorist, other behavior professionals, or qualified trainers in the area for more minor issues.

If the client has consulted a veterinarian, but the problem remains, the best practice is to promptly refer the client to an animal behavior professional for expert help. Resources available to clients to help them locate a professional qualified to treat behavior problems in companion animals, as well as for general training help, are shown below. Individual trainers will vary in their methods and experience; we always recommend that owners ask any potential trainers about their education, certifications, and experience with the species to be trained.

Resources for Clients Seeking Expert Help in Effectively Treating Unwanted Behaviors in their Pets.

Professional Behavior Consultants:

- Diplomates of the American College of Veterinary Behavior (ACVB) are veterinarians who have completed a residency in behavioral medicine, and passed a comprehensive board exam – www.dacvb.org/resources/for-the-public/
- Certified Applied Animal Behaviorists (CAAB) are board certified by the Animal Behavior Society, a national academic and resource organization. CAABs are required to have a PhD in animal behavior, plus at least 3 years of clinical experience in treating behavior problems – www.animal behaviorsociety.org/web/applied-behavior-caab-directory.php
- Certified dog (or cat) behavior consultants (CDBC dogs, CCBC cats): The International Association of Animal Behavior Consultants (IAABC) certifies behavior consultants who have extensive experience (3 years/ 500 hours) treating behavior cases – https://iaabc.org/consultants

Trainers:

- The American Veterinary Society of Animal Behavior (AVSAB) has a very helpful handout to help owners identify a qualified trainer, available online at https://avsab.org/resources/position-statements/
- Karen Pryor Academy graduates – www.karenpryoracademy.com/find-a-trainer
- The Association of Pet Dog Trainers (APDT) – https://apdt.com/about/trainer-search/

- The Certification Council for Professional Dog Trainers (look for "Knowledge Assessed" after the trainer's certification level) – www. ccpdt.org/dog-owners/certified-dog-trainer-directory/
- Victoria Stillwell's Positively dog trainers – https://positively.com/ dog-training/find-a-trainer/find-a-vspdt-trainer/

Helping Clients Struggling with Whether or Not to Euthanize their Pet for Behavioral Concerns:

In the case of severely emotionally compromised or truly dangerous animals, when all attempts to modify the behavior or resolve the problem have failed, owners may be faced with the most difficult decision of all – whether euthanasia may be the only remaining option for their pet. While it is sadly true that these decisions are sometimes made more lightly than we would like and some pets are euthanized for reasons of human convenience, the majority of owners facing this decision are fiercely dedicated to their pets and find the experience highly stressful and even heartbreaking (McConnell, 2015; Grigg & Donaldson, 2017). The decision to euthanize a companion animal is a highly personal and permanent one, and should never be recommended lightly (Haug, 2011). By the same token, it should always be the owner's decision to make, as they are the one who will live with the emotional consequences of the decision (McConnell, 2015; Summerfield, 2017).

As Haug (2011) notes, owners of pets with serious behavior problems are faced with four possible options: continue to live with the problem as is; rehome the pet to a more suitable situation; rehabilitate the pet by modifying the behavior to a safe and acceptable level; or euthanize the pet. Continuing to live with a serious behavior problem is not a particularly satisfying solution, and can be physically and emotionally dangerous for other members of the household. Chances are if your client has reached the point of considering euthanasia, they have already realized that they can no longer live with the behavior. They are struggling with a difficult and painful decision, while simultaneously coping with the physical and emotional strain of living with and caring for a pet with a serious behavior problem (Durkin, 2009; Ross & Baron-Sorensen, 1998). Many times these clients have reached the point where they are seeking permission, approval, or support for their decision to euthanize, or affirmation that they are not responsible for the pet's behavior issue. Clients often express relief or an outpouring of emotion when they are counseled that it is not their fault, and when they are informed that others have had to make similar decisions for behavioral euthanasia.

Rehoming animals with serious behavior problems is problematic at best, and involves significant ethical and legal considerations (Haug, 2011; Kirby-Madden et al., 2014). In the case of less severe issues (such as a cat who begins to urinate outside the litterbox when another cat is added to the household, or a young, active dog who is left alone for long periods by busy owners and consequently destroys furniture and other household items out of boredom and frustration), placement in a more suitable home may resolve the problem, or allow it to be managed to an acceptable level. However, anyone rehoming an animal with a known behavior problem is ethically and legally obligated to inform the new owners of the pet's behavioral history (Kirby-Madden et al., 2014). Many shelters and rescues will not accept dogs with a known bite history, for example, and those that do may require that the dog be euthanized rather than rehomed because of the legal liabilities involved if the dog bites again following rehoming. There are sanctuaries that exist to allow animals with severe behavioral issues to live out their lives in relative comfort, but space in these with good reputations is limited. Owners must be very careful to screen any individuals or organizations offering to take on "problem pets" prior to relinquishing their pet to them, to ensure that the pet will continue to maintain a good quality of life in the new situation. And, as McConnell (2015) notes, even though there may be, out there somewhere, the perfect person to resolve the behavioral issue, or the perfect home for the pet, there simply aren't enough of these people and homes available. The number of pets who need a new home far exceeds the number of suitable homes available to them (McConnell, 2015).

Recommendations for rehabilitating the pet by obtaining qualified, humane help with modifying the pet's behavior are covered earlier in this chapter. Whenever possible, an owner should seek the advice or assistance of a trained behavior professional prior to making a decision as final as euthanizing their pet. These professionals can assist with a better understanding of the pet's behavior; with developing a management, behavioral modification and training plan; and (in the case of veterinary behavior professionals) with medication recommendations to assist the client in treating this issue. In many cases, even serious behavior problems can be resolved with proper treatment and a committed owner.

Nonetheless, treating behavior problems can sometimes be challenging, frustrating, and expensive for owners, and may pose significant physical and legal risks for the owners and others. In some cases, the behavioral issues cannot be resolved, even despite the very best efforts of owners and behavior professionals. In some situations, the risks are too great, and euthanasia may be the only safe option. Haug (2011) presents a summary of critical factors that veterinarians and owners should consider when deciding how to proceed regarding a pet with serious behavior problems. These factors are many, and depending on the individual case, may relate to the owner themselves (e.g., an owner unable or unwilling to do the work needed to change the behavior); to the animal itself (e.g., genetic predisposition, early life experiences); to the animal's environment (e.g., a living situation that cannot be changed or managed for safety); and to the nature of the behavior in question (e.g., how predictable is the behavior? Does the behavior pose a physical danger to anyone in the household, including the pet?). Realistically, not all owners and households will be able to safely manage the behavior, and/or succeed at a training or behavioral modification program. In cases of serious behavior problems, owners may risk financial losses, loss of homeowners' insurance or rate increases, and legal consequences.

To help clients think more objectively about the situation, it may be beneficial to ask the client to compile two lists (with your help if they wish) – one listing positive indicators for eventual resolution of the problem, and one listing negative indicators that do not bode well for the successful resolution (van Haaften cited in Grigg, 2018). Have the client then consider the four possible options listed above for addressing the problem – do nothing, work to modify the behavior, rehome the pet, or euthanasia. What would it take (logistically, financially, emotionally, etc.) for each of these options to be successful for the pet, and acceptable to the owner? Again, an experienced behavioral professional can assist in identifying these factors and suggesting a prognosis for each case, but if necessary, owners should be allowed to consider the necessity of euthanasia without judgment (Haug, 2011).

Behavioral Issues and Quality of Life

It is often helpful for these clients to acknowledge that severe behavior problems (e.g., abnormally high levels of anxiety, intense compulsive behaviors, intense aggression) can be a quality of life issue, not just for the human members of the household, but also for the pet. Dogs who feel the need to constantly defend themselves, for example, or cats who live in a constant state of fear, may be living very restricted, troubled lives, especially when they must be intensively and continuously managed or confined for safety. Because a pet is physically healthy does not always mean that that pet is mentally healthy; chronic stress and mental suffering may not be as obvious as physical suffering, but can significantly detract from quality of life (Kirby-Madden et al., 2014). It may be helpful for the owner to assess the current quality of life of their pet, using methods similar to those used by owners of ill or aging pets (see Neilson, 2013, for a sample Quality of Life scale for companion animals). While physical declines may not be seen in pets suffering from behavior problems, other aspects of quality of life may be significantly impacted. For example, the owner can ask:

1. Is the pet still enjoying the "Five Freedoms"? These guidelines are considered the most basic needs of any animal, and the minimum required for a good quality of life (Farm Animal Welfare Council, 2009):

    1. Freedom from hunger and thirst (by providing fresh water and a healthy diet)

2. Freedom from discomfort (by providing shelter and a comfortable place to rest)
3. Freedom from pain, injury, and disease (by prevention and rapid diagnosis and treatment when necessary)
4. Freedom to express normal behavior (by providing sufficient space, proper facilities, and company of the animal's own kind)
5. Freedom from fear and distress (by ensuring conditions and treatment which avoid mental suffering)

2. Some negative experiences are inevitable in life, but overall, is the pet having more good days than bad?

- Mellor (2016) suggests that we need to move beyond the Five Freedoms model to ensure animal well-being, noting that for animals to have "lives worth living," we should continually strive to minimize their negative experiences while providing the animals with frequent opportunities to have positive experiences. Is it feasible or reasonable that the owner can ensure that the pet's experiences are primarily positive ones?
- Can the pet still enjoy his or her favorite activities?
- Can the pet still spend time with his or her favorite people, or does he/she need to be frequently isolated to prevent the behavior from reoccurring?

As certain types of behavior problems can progress and worsen over time, it may be helpful for the owner to think back to the pet's behavior and quality of life a year or two ago and ask whether the pet's quality of life is the same, better or worse than it was in the past. Ideally, if the human household consists of multiple individuals, each of these will contribute to the discussion about quality of life, in order to facilitate communication about this difficult decision. Ask the client to consider what the pet's future quality of life will look like, in whatever scenario they are considering (Grigg, 2018) and whether it will be better, or worse, if the client needs to severely limit the pet's freedom and daily activities in order to increase the safety of others. What about if the pet is relinquished to a shelter, or rehomed? If we are truly unable to help the pet and resolve these problems in a way that will guarantee not only quality of life for the human household, but of the pet as well, as responsible pet owners we may need to consider euthanasia to humanely end mental suffering.

Given that severe behavioral issues in the pet can negatively impact the quality of life of the human household, the owner(s) may wish to complete a quality of life scale for themselves as well, in order to better understand the toll the issue is taking on their lives (Grigg & Donaldson, 2017). While painful, it is important to consider the "what if's" – what if something goes wrong with the management plan? What if the problem behavior occurs again? What will this mean for other members of the household (including, if applicable, other pets living in the household)? As McConnell (2015) writes, of owners living with dogs exhibiting serious aggression towards people:

> No one begins a conversation about whether their dog should be put down for aggressive behavior if there haven't been several incidents (or one horrifically serious one). And every dog owner has to know that if "it," the aggression, happened once, it might happen again. This is true even if the dog is carefully managed and the owners work hard on a treatment plan. The question is, what is "it"? What are the consequences if "it" happens again?

For some owners, it may be comforting for them to plan a "best last day" for the pet, providing him or her with abundant attention and affection, his very favorite foods, special treats, and activities. If the owner wishes (and if appropriate, given the nature of the behavior problem involved), this could include visits from the pet's favorite people, which gives friends and family who have known the pet a chance to say goodbye, and can provide social support for the owner during this difficult time. Other owners may wish to spend their time alone with their pet.

Finally, it may be helpful for some clients to understand what happens during a euthanasia procedure. Descriptions of what happens during this final visit with the veterinarian can be found in the American Humane Association's "Euthanasia: Making the Decision" document, available online at www.americanhumane.org, and in Grigg and Donaldson (2017). Grigg and Donaldson (2017) also provide information to help clients locate veterinarians who will perform in-home euthanasia, for owners who prefer that option. Reassure the client that they can request time alone with their pet, before and/or after the procedure, to grieve and say a last goodbye. Many veterinarians will offer this time as a regular part of the euthanasia procedure.

Helping Clients who Have Euthanized a Pet for Behavioral Reasons

Recommendations for helping clients dealing with grief due to loss of a pet are covered in detail elsewhere in this volume. This section will revisit a few important points to remember, but will primarily focus on specific recommendations for those clients who are struggling with their decision to euthanize a pet for serious behavioral concerns, and the emotions surrounding this loss.

Coping with the Grief of Losing a Pet

Many, if not all, pet owners will experience some form of grief due to pet loss at some point in their lives. It is imperative that society at large be aware of the intensity and longevity of this grief, and acknowledge it as a legitimate experience (Rémillard et al., 2017; Winch, 2018). If the pet owner is hesitant to discuss their feelings because of a lack of social acceptance, it is important to normalize this experience for the grieving owner. Grief due to pet loss is a well-recognized, normal human reaction to the loss of an important social companion. In discussions with clients coping with pet loss, avoid devaluing the owner's relationship with their pet with statements like, "it's only a dog," or, "why don't you just get another cat?" (Durkin, 2009; Winch, 2018). The vast majority of owners will benefit from being provided with a safe, supportive, and sympathetic environment, and given the chance to talk about their pet and their experiences (Morris, 2012). Many clients may seek reassurance from their veterinarian or behavior professional that the decision they made was the right one. Pet owners often benefit from interactions with other emotionally supportive pet owners and professionals who can help them discuss these feelings and share coping strategies, for example by calling a pet loss hotline, joining a pet loss support group (often offered by local veterinary clinics, veterinary schools, or rescue organizations), or by reading pet loss support literature and/or the accounts of other owners who have gone through this experience. Note that some owners who have euthanized their pet for behavioral reasons may feel isolated and may not feel that these resources "apply to them." Reassuring these owners that others have gone through this difficult experience, and that these resources are relevant for them, may help them benefit from the widest range of help available. Shown below is a brief list of recommended reading for clients dealing with pet loss. Grieving owners may find it helpful to remember and formally memorialize their pet in some way, such as by holding a small memorial ceremony, planting a special plant or placing a small memorial stone in their garden, or by donating to an animal welfare charity in the pet's name (Durkin, 2009; Rémillard et al., 2017; Hart et al., 1990).

Recommended Resources for Dealing with Pet Loss (Adapted from Grigg & Donaldson, 2017)

Carmack, B. (2003). *Grieving the death of a pet.* Augsburg: Augsburg Publishers.

Donaldson, T. M. (2017). Too short lives: quality of life and end-of-life decisions for your dog. In Grigg, E. K. & Donaldson, T. M., *The science behind a happy dog.* Sheffield: 5m Publishing.

Friedman, R., James, C., & James, J. W. (2014). *The grief recovery handbook for pet loss.* Lanham, MA: Taylor Trade Publishing.

Nieburg, H. A., & Fischer, A. (1982). *Pet loss: A thoughtful guide for adults and children.* London: Harper & Row Publishing.

Sife, W. (2014). *The loss of a pet: A guide to coping with the grieving process when a pet dies.* London: Howell Book House.

In addition, as Winch (2018) notes, losing a pet can result in significant disruptions to routines that provide owners with structure and comfort. Recovering from pet loss also requires that owners acknowledge the changes to their lives caused by loss of a pet (e.g., decreased exercise and/or social interactions; loss of their identity as a "pet parent") (Winch, 2018). In order to fill these voids and avoid losing the mental and physical benefits gained from living with a companion animal, owners need to seek support from those who will understand and sympathize with this experience, and avoid or ignore those who judge them callously or too harshly. They will need to find ways to meet the needs formerly met with the help of their pet, by ensuring that they continue to engage in regular physical exercise, by seeking out opportunities for social interactions (take a class in a topic of interest, join a neighborhood sports team, a book group or yoga class; etc.), and by maintaining friendly interactions with neighbors and acquaintances that knew them as "Jake's mom" or "Bella's dad."

Coping with Euthanasia for Behavioral Problems

In addition to the strategies listed above for making this difficult decision, and for coping with pet loss in general, it may be helpful for those clients who are struggling with euthanizing a pet for reasons of serious behavior issues to share with them the statistics listed earlier in this chapter as to how often this situation occurs. This can help normalize this experience for these owners, and help them realize that they are not alone in experiencing these complex and distressing emotions. These clients may also benefit from being made aware of potential sources of support from those who have gone through a similar experience (see the list of "Stories of Pet Loss Due to Euthanasia," above).

Euthanizing a companion animal for behavior problems, even more so than euthanasia for old age or illness, can put owners at risk of disapproval and censure by others who have not gone through this experience. This is an extremely difficult, often painful, and very personal decision. As Kirby-Madden et al. (2014) note, owners must remember that they are the ones having to live with the behavior and the pet; they are the ones taking on the risks that living with the pet entails; they are the ones with a strong enough bond with their pet to thoroughly consider all the options for the pet; and they are the ones who, in the end, will make the decision that works best for them, for their family, and for the pet for which they are ultimately responsible. Questioning the decision after the fact is normal. It is important to remind the owner that they made the best decision they could at the time, given the information available and the factors present at that time. Emphasize that the pet is now at peace and experiencing no more anxiety or fear, no more need to aggress, no more risk of punishment, relinquishment, or removal from the home. In addition to feeling guilty, some owners may feel a sense of relief after the procedure, which in turn may trigger further feelings of guilt. This also is a normal emotional response and does not mean that the choice that they made was the wrong one (Kirby-Madden et al., 2014).

Case Scenarios

This section will include two sample scenarios, each including:

- behavioral history and diagnosis that led owners to the decision to euthanize;
- actors considered in making the decision, including both veterinarian/behaviorist recommendations of points to consider in making this decision, and the individual issues considered by owners/guardians in this case; and
- emotional responses of owner/guardians to this event, drawn from personal descriptions from owner/guardians going through this experience.

Case Scenario #1: Erin and Hannah

Erin was a veterinary technician in an emergency veterinary clinic as well as a graduate student. Erin had purchased a new home with a large yard and wanted to rescue a dog as a companion to her and her 3-year-old spayed female American Bull Dog mix, Maya. Erin obtained Hannah, a 3-year-old spayed female American Pit Bull Terrier from a local county animal shelter. She was originally looking for a black male bully type breed dog either older or younger than Maya because she was concerned about dog aggression issues in dogs of similar sex, breed, and size, and was trying to avoid having these issues. Hannah caught her eye since she was sweet and calm but appeared forlorn and resigned to her fate at the shelter given that she was there 35 days (a long stay for a high kill shelter). After adoption, Hannah was initially cute and cuddly, played well with Maya, and loved playing with her ball. At some point, Erin reported that Hannah had a personality shift that she described as a "second puppyhood" in which she was more energetic and playful and seemed happy. The aggression appeared to come "out of nowhere." The first incident of aggression occurred within the first year while the Erin was away from home. The attack resulted in Maya receiving four puncture wounds, which were treated by Erin. There were five to six incidences of dog aggression with Maya over the 5 years that Erin had Hannah. Erin took precautions and separated the dogs when she was not at home, but incidences continued to occur both when Erin was at home and while she was away. Erin enlisted the help of a dog trainer that used electronic shock collars as part of his training approach. He had been successful in working with her other dog that had a history of running away and Erin thought he could assist in Hannah's case. The trainer taught commands to help gain short-term control over situations but did not treat the specific dog aggression behavior issue. Hannah did not like the trainer according to Erin. Hannah responded to him with fear and avoidance and Erin discontinued using his services. Erin did try using the shock collar one time during a fight but it had no effect.

The last incident prior to behavioral euthanasia was an attack on the neighbor's younger female intact dog. Hannah had a history of fence fighting with the neighbor's dogs (a mother-daughter pair of female intact Chesapeake Bay Retrievers). Erin was playing with Hannah off leash in the front yard. The neighbor walked by with her younger dog on leash and Hannah immediately ran out into the street and attacked the dog. Hannah delivered a bite to the thoracic/abdominal area of the neighbor's dog that resulted in tearing of the thoracic muscles. Erin could not release Hannah's bite. The neighbor claimed that the dog had also bitten her thumb but Erin disputed this. Another neighbor witnessing the attack contacted animal control and the police. Erin consulted a veterinary behaviorist who helped her come to the decision to euthanize Hannah.

Erin faced a number of legal and financial consequences. Erin was issued with a citation and was required to appear in court. Erin was sued by her neighbor for damages and loss of wages. Erin agreed to pay the dog's vet bills of over $5,000. She also paid a $1,500 retainer to obtain a lawyer. Hannah was euthanized prior to the court date but the judge charged Erin with a misdemeanor and fine totaling approximately $500–700. Erin issued no statement and pleaded guilty. The incident was reported to her insurance and her rates increased. The incident happened in August; Erin sold her home in November of that year; the incident was partially responsible for the move.

After the incident, Erin withdrew from friends and she lost a longtime friend over the issue. She reported that she did not tell anybody the entire story of her experience with Hannah. She conveyed that she experienced guilt, shame and regret for not being able to do more for Hannah. She felt that she (an experienced veterinary technician) "should be better." Erin described her experience as devastating. Contributing to her personal sense of guilt was the belief that she was perpetuating the pit bull bad reputation and that her dog was another statistic. When asked how the experience impacted her, she said that she "doesn't trust herself," in selecting her next dog. Erin further described her experience as traumatizing. Five years after the euthanasia, she was still experiencing grief. She stated that the experience resulted in her self-isolating. She reported feeling a fear of judgment and not wanting to face questions from friends, especially those that were veterinarians or veterinary technicians and not wanting to have to tell the whole story. When asked about resources, she related that she did not know of resources because she felt her grief was "personal." When asked what would have been helpful, Erin said that it would have been helpful to know the statistics, that she wasn't alone.

Discussion Questions:

1. How might Erin's experience of grief be different from others who grieve over the loss of a pet euthanized for medical reasons?
2. Erin felt that the usual pet loss resources were not appropriate for her. What resources might she find helpful?
3. What resources might you use to help Erin?
4. Erin described feelings of self-isolation due to shame and fear of judgment. How might you help Erin find social support given these sensitivities and perceptions of public opinion on euthanasia for behavior reasons?

Case Scenario #2: Lynn and Sara

Lynn was a highly regarded dog trainer and behavior consultant, specializing in complex dog behavior issues including aggression, holding professional certifications from three internationally recognized organizations. Lynn was referred to and contacted by a municipal animal shelter to consult on a dog that they had in their care. Sara, a female spayed Pit Bull, was approximately 18 months old at that time. At the shelter, Sara displayed atypical behavior, uncoordinated movements, and balance problems that the shelter had not previously seen and was not equipped to handle. Upon meeting Sara, Lynn thought that she was bright, responsive, sweet, and playful. The shelter had reported that Sara did not have any issues with other dogs and Lynn did not observe any issues with dogs while at the shelter. Lynn liked Sara immediately and brought her home the same day. Sara displayed atypical seizure type activity and was diagnosed by a veterinary neurologist with cerebellar hypoplasia (a congenital neurological condition in which the cerebellum is smaller than usual or not completely developed) confirmed by MRI. Lynn was aware that Sara would have ongoing issues and a shorter life span but she wanted to give her a happy life, even if short.

Lynn lived with her spouse and four other dogs that included a 6-year-old neutered male American Pit Bull Terrier, 5-year-old neutered male black Labrador Retriever, 5-year-old female spay Border Collie, and a mature 5 lb. neutered male Chihuahua. Sara got along with all of the dogs, but the Chihuahua especially loved Sara. The household was well equipped for the multiple dogs, exceeding recommendations for multiple dog households, with extra bedding/sleeping locations, feeding locations and various toys/items for environmental enrichment. The dogs had open access to a fenced yard and home. While Lynn was away from home, Sara was confined to a separate room for safety from her balance issues. Sara enjoyed advanced training with Lynn and was able to respond to numerous commands. Sara was taken to a number of small advanced seminars for dog trainers and used in demonstrations for teaching trainers how to adapt to different learning rates and styles.

At approximately 2.5-years of age, Sara began to display aggressive threat behavior over a variety of resources, commonly referred to as Resource Guarding with multiple triggers. Her triggers included but were not limited to bedding, doorways, food, and odor trails from food. Sara's arousal and loss of balance would trigger seizures that heightened her response and start a cascade of behaviors not seen outside of the seizure activity including a hard eye, stiffening, freezing, prolonged snarling, lunging and attacks. Sara also exhibited this behavior during body-handling, including hugging, or when examining her facial features. Lynn had experience treating Resource Guarding in dogs and used the most up-to-date, humane training practices such as classical conditioning, operant conditioning, trades, etc. Lynn had discussed Sara's quality of life with her longtime trusted veterinarian. Given Lynn's advanced training, education, and experience, there were no professionals that were able to offer additional training recommendations. She presented Sara to other colleagues and they offered encouragement but no further insight.

The event that precipitated the decision to euthanize Sara was one in which the Lynn was in the kitchen at the back of the house and all the dogs were in the front of the house in the living room. Lynn knew that something was amiss when all of the dogs came to her in the kitchen and placed themselves behind her in the corner of the kitchen. Sara entered the kitchen in a predatory stalk (body low to the ground, hard set eye) trapping them all in the corner of the kitchen. The dog was unresponsive to her name or commands. Lynn was a retired large metro police officer and felt similarly to when she was in dangerous situations on the job. She felt afraid. Lynn was able to throw a large phone book on the ground in front of Sara, effectively stopping Sara's seizure-like activity and aggression. This allowed Lynn to gather her and take her to the veterinarian. Lynn ultimately decided that the welfare and safety of her other dogs, herself, and her spouse was at risk with Sara and that she should be euthanized. The veterinarian agreed that euthanasia was the best decision for the welfare of Sara and the family.

Lynn had experienced having to euthanize a dog for medical reasons in the past, but this was her first experience of euthanizing a dog for behavior reasons. Lynn reported that she felt out of her depth with Sara and that she was truly afraid of her in the end. Lynn reported that everyone in her household felt in peril. Lynn knew the decision was best for Sara, but she felt that she delayed the decision for too long because she kept wanting to try to remedy her behavior.

Lynn had a great emotional conflict during her grieving process. She loved Sara deeply because when she was well, she was "so much fun," but when she was not well Lynn was truly afraid of Sara. Lynn described feeling guilty for not being able to do more. She conveyed that when, in professional meetings, speakers advised professional trainers that, "If we were only better, we could save more dogs' lives" this only reinforced her feelings of guilt. Another way in which this experience differed greatly from other pet loss was that the Lynn felt deep compassion fatigue and experienced a sense of relief with Sara's passing. She experienced guilt at feeling relief and reported that this made her grieving process different and more complex. The grieving process was also different in that the other dogs in the household did not respond as they typically would at the loss of a housemate (e.g., they didn't mope or sniff around or try to find her). This reinforced Lynn's feeling that the household's welfare was compromised with Sara.

Lynn said that there was excellent support among her colleagues and friends who were primarily dog professionals; she never felt judged. She also had the support of a very compassionate and caring veterinarian. When asked if there were resources that she found helpful in coping with her grief she stated that there were only a few websites at the time and they seemed too maudlin for her and her relationship with Sara. When asked what would have been helpful, Lynn responded that more advances in science and behavioral pharmacology could have benefited Sara. Lynn did report that given the same situation, she would do it all again.

Discussion Questions:

1. How did Lynn's sense of compassion fatigue, relief, and resulting guilt complicate her grieving experience?
2. How did Lynn's support system impact her decision to euthanize her dog for behavior reasons?
3. Are there questions you would like to ask or further information you would like to gather before prior to intervening?
4. What resources can you use to help Lynn?

Discussion Questions:

The following discussion questions are suggested in order to help clients talk about behavior problems in their pets, to assist them in considering the decision about whether or not to euthanize their pet, and to accept this decision once it has been made. Which questions to raise will depend on the client's unique situation. These questions are drawn from sources in the veterinary and popular literature focused on these issues (e.g., Grigg & Donaldson, 2017; Hart et al., 1990; Neilson, 2013). Questions should of course be raised and discussed in a compassionate, respectful, and non-judgmental manner.

1. How has living with this pet affected your daily quality of life? What are the good things about living with this pet? What are the bad (stressful, unpleasant) things about living with this pet? What kind of changes have you had to make in your life, in order to maintain this pet in your home?

2. How do other members of the household feel about this pet and this behavior? How has the presence of this pet impacted their lives, and what changes have they had to make to continue living with this pet? (It may be that marked differences of opinion exist between household members about how the situation should be resolved. It is important, if possible, to engage all members of the household in this discussion, so that each person's concerns and feelings can be heard and addressed.)

3. Have you seen behaviors that indicate that family members or others may be at risk of harm from (pet's name)? What steps are you currently taking, or could you take, to ensure that everyone is safe?

4. Does the pet's behavior put him/her at risk of punishment or retaliation by anyone in the household? If so, can you put measures in place to prevent the pet from causing further trouble, until help with changing his/her behavior has been obtained?

5. Walk your client through the four possible options listed earlier for responding to a serious behavior problem: continue to live with the problem; rehome the pet (remembering the ethical and legal obligations to inform the shelter or new home of the pet's behavior problem); seek professional help and attempt to modify the behavior; and euthanasia. What would be required (of the client, of the household) in each case, and what factors argue for and against each choice? What are the foreseeable risks and benefits of each option? What might the outcome of each choice be for the client/household? (van Haaften in Grigg, 2017).

6. Compile, with your client's help, two lists: one listing "positive signs" for the eventual resolution of the problem, and one listing "negative signs" that do not bode well for a successful outcome. This activity can help clients be more objective about the situation and probable outcomes (van Haaften, in Grigg, 2017).

7. Note that changing behavior (in pets, as in humans) is rarely a quick fix. The work of behavioral modification can take months or even years, may involve medication and other interventions, and may incur costs associated with repeated visits to the veterinarian, behaviorist, and/or trainer. Are you committed to taking the time and doing the work necessary to help your pet improve?

8. What is the pet's current quality of life? Is he/she still able to engage in activities that, in the past, made him happiest? What do you see as the future quality of life for your pet, if you have to severely limit his/her life in order to increase the safety of others?

9. What are your best memories of your pet? Is there a way that you could honor your pet's memory that would resonate with you (such as a small memorial service with friends and/or family, planting a special tree in your garden, or making a donation in the pet's name to a local animal charity)?

Note

* These were the most common reasons given when relinquishing a pet specifically for euthanasia, in the NCPPSP Regional Shelter Study (Kass et al., 2001).

References

Adams, C. L., Bonnett, B. N., & Meek, A. H. (2000). Predictors of owner response to companion animal death in 177 clients from 14 practices in Ontario. *Journal of the American Veterinary Medical Association, 217*, 303–309.

Allen, K., Shykoff, B. E., & Izzo, J. L. (2001). Pet ownership, but not ACE inhibitor therapy, blunts home blood pressure responses to mental stress. *Hypertension, 38*, 815–820.

Arkow, P. S., & Dow, S. (1984). The ties that do not bind: A study of the human–animal bonds that fail. In R. K. Anderson, B. L. Hart, L. A. Hart, (Eds.), *The Pet Connection* (pp. 348–354). Minneapolis, MN: University of Minnesota.

Baran B. E., Allen J. A., Rogelberg S. G., Spitzmüller C., Digiacomo N. A., Webb J. B. B, Carter, N. T., Clark, O., Teeter, L. A., &Walker, A. G. (2009). Euthanasia-related strain and coping strategies in animal shelter employees. *Journal of the American Veterinary Medical Association, 235*, 83–88.

Calder, C. D., Albright, J. D., & Koch, C. (2017). Evaluating graduating veterinary students' perception of preparedness in clinical veterinary behavior for "Day-1" of practice and the factors which influence that perception: a questionnaire-based survey. *Journal of Veterinary Behavior, 20*, 116–120.

Carmack, B. (2003). *Grieving the death of a pet.* Augsburg: Augsburg Publishers.

Christian, H. E., Westgarth, C., Bauman, A., Richards, E. A., Rhodes, R. E., Evenson, K. R., Mayer, J. A., & Thorpe, Jr., R. J. (2013). Dog ownership and physical activity: A review of the evidence. *Journal of Physical Activity and Health, 10*, 750–759.

Cordaro, M. (2012). Pet Loss and disenfranchised grief: Implications for mental health counseling practice. *Journal of Mental Health Counseling, 34*, 283–294.

Doka, K. J. (1989). *Disenfranchised grief: Recognizing hidden sorrow.* Lanham, MD: Lexington Books.

Donaldson, T. M. (2017). Too short lives: quality of life and end-of-life decisions for your dog. In Grigg, E. K. & Donaldson, T. M., *The science behind a happy dog.* Sheffield: 5m Publishing.

Durkin, A. (2009). Loss of a companion animal: Understanding and helping the bereaved. *Journal of Psychosocial Nursing, 47*, 26–31.

El-Alayli, A., Lystad, A. L. Webb, S. R., Hollingsworth, S. L., & Ciolli, J. L. (2006). Reigning cats and dogs: A pet-enhancement bias and its link to pet attachment pet-self similarity, self-enhancement and well-being. *Basic and Applied Social Psychology*, 28, 131–143.

Farm Animal Welfare Council (2009). *Farm animal welfare in Great Britain: Past, present and future.* London, pp. 243–254.

Figley, C. R., & Roop, R. G. (2006). *Compassion fatigue in the animal-care community.* Washington, DC: Humane Society Press.

Fogle, B. (1981). Attachment – euthanasia – grieving. In B. Fogle (Ed.), *Interrelations between people and pets* (pp. 331–343). Springfield, IL: Charles C. Thomas, Publisher.

Friedman, R., James, C., & James, J. W. (2014). *The grief recovery handbook for pet loss.* Lanham, MA: Taylor Trade Publishing.

Friedmann, E., & Son, H. (2009). The human-companion animal bond: How humans benefit. *Veterinary Clinics of North America: Small Animal Practice*, 39, 293–326.

Friedmann, E., Katcher, A., Lynch, J., & Thomas, S. (1980). Animal companions and one-year survival of patients after discharge from a coronary care unit. *Public Health Reports*, 95, 307–312.

Golden, O., & Hanlon, A. J. (2018). Towards the development of day one competences in veterinary behaviour medicine: survey of veterinary professionals' experience in companion animal practice in Ireland. *Irish Veterinary Journal*, 71, 12.

Gosse, G. H., & Barnes, M. J. (1994). Human grief resulting from the death of a pet. *Anthrozoös*, 7, 103–112.

Grigg, E. K. (2018). Helping clients facing behavior problems in their companion animals. In L. Kogan, & C. Blazina (Eds.), *Clinician's guide to treating companion animal issues: Addressing human-animal interaction* (1st ed., pp. 281–317). London, UK: Elsevier.

Grigg, E. K., & Donaldson, T. M. (2017). *The science behind a happy dog.* Sheffield, UK: 5M Publishing House.

Grigg, E. K., Kogan, L., van Haaften, K., & Kolus, C. (2018). Cat owners' perceptions of psychoactive medications, supplements and pheromones for the treatment of feline behavior problems. *Journal of Feline Medicine and Surgery*, doi: 10.1177/1098612X18807783

Hammerle, M., Horst, C., Levine, E., Overall, K., Radosta, L., Rafter-Ritchie, M., & Yin, S. (2015). 2015 AAHA canine and feline behavior management guidelines. *Journal of the American Animal Hospital Association*, 51, 205–221.

Hart, L. A., Hart, B. L., & Mader, B. (1990). Humane euthanasia and companion animal death: Caring for the animal, the client, and the veterinarian. *Journal of the American Veterinary Medical Association*, 197, 1292–1299.

Haug, L. I. (2011, November). Treat or euthanize? Helping owners make critical decisions regarding pets with behavior problems. Retrieved June 4, 2018, from Veterinarymedicine.dvm360.com

Herron, M. E., Shofer, F. S., & Reisner, I. R. (2009). Survey of the use and outcome of confrontational and non-confrontational training methods in client-owned dogs showing undesirable behaviors. *Applied Animal Behaviour Science*, 117, 47–54.

Horwitz, D. F., & Neilson, J. C. (2007). *Blackwell's five-minute veterinary consult clinical companion: Canine & feline behavior.* Ames, IA: Blackwell Publishing.

Kass, P. H., New Jr., J. C., Scarlett, J. M., & Salman M. D. (2001). Understanding animal companion surplus in the United States: Relinquishment of nonadoptables to animal shelters for euthanasia. *Journal of Applied Animal Welfare Science*, 4(4), 237–248. doi: 10.1207/S15327604JAWS0404_01

King L. C., & Werner P. D. (2011). Attachment, social support, and responses following the death of a companion animal. *Omega* (Westport), 64, 119–141.

Kirby-Madden, T., Shreyer, T., Nielsen, J., & Herron, M. (2014). Euthanasia for behavioral issues: A complicated and difficult decision. Client handout from The Ohio State University (OSU) Veterinary Medical Center. Retrieved June 1, 2018, from https://vet.osu.edu/vmc/companion/our-services/honoring-bond-support-animal-owners

Kogan, L. R., Hellyer, P. W., Rishniw, M., & Schoenfeld-Tacher R. (in press). Animal behavior – Veterinarian training, comfort level and intervention techniques. *Journal of Veterinary Medical Education*.

Landsberg, G., Hunthausen, W., & Ackerman, L. (2013). *Handbook of behavior problems of the dog and cat* (3rd ed.). New York, NY: Elsevier.

Levine, G. N., Allen, K. Braun, L. T., Christian, H. E., Friedmann, E., Taubert, K. A., Thomas, S. A., Wells, D. L., & Lange, R. A. (2013). Pet ownership and cardiovascular risk: A scientific statement from the American Heart Association. *Circulation*, 127. doi: 10.1161/CIR.0b013e31829201e1

Lodge, M. (2013). Please don't hate me for this: I had to euthanize my aggressive dog. Retrieved June 6, 2018, from dogster.com/lifestyle

London, K.B. (2015). Considering euthanasia because of aggression. Retrieved June 4, 2018, from www.thebark.com

Lovell, B., & Lee R. (2013). Burnout and health promotion in veterinary medicine. *Canadian Veterinary Journal*, 54, 790–791.

Maiti, A., & Dhoble, A. (2017). Images in clinical medicine: Takotsubo cardiomyopathy. *New England Journal of Medicine*, 377, e24.

McConnell, A. R., Brown, C. M., Shoda, T. M., Stayton, L. E., & Martin, C. E. (2011). Friends with benefits: On the positive consequences of pet ownership. *Journal of Personality and Social Psychology*, 101, 1239–1252.

McConnell, P. (2015). When is it time to put down a dog who is aggressive to people? Retrieved June 4, 2018, from www.PatriciaMcConnell.com/theother endoftheleash

McCutcheon, M. A., & Fleming, S. J. (2002). Grief resulting from euthanasia and natural death of companion animals. *Omega*, 44, 169–188.

McKeown, D., & Luescher, A. (1988). A case for companion animal behavior in the veterinary practice. *Canadian Veterinary Journal*, 29, 74–75.

McVety, D. (2015). The unfair necessity of euthanizing an aggressive dog. Retrieved June 4, 2018, from DrAndyRoark.com.

Mellor, D. J. (2016). Updating animal welfare thinking: Moving beyond the "Five Freedoms" towards "a life worth living." *Animals*, 6, 1–20.

Morris, P. (2012). Managing pet owners' guilt and grief in veterinary euthanasia encounters. *Journal of Contemporary Ethnography*, 41, 337–365.

National Canine Research Council. (2018). Final report on dog bite-related fatalities. 2016. Retrieved June 4, 2018, from www.nationalcanineresearchcouncil. com/sites/default/files/Final-Report-on-Dog-Bite-Related-Fatalities-2016.pdf

Neilson, J. (2013). How do I know when it's time? Assessing quality of life for your companion animals and making end-of-life decisions. Client handout from The Ohio State University Veterinary Medical Center. Retrieved June 4, 2018, from vet.osu.edu/honoringthebond.

New, J. C., Salman, M. D., King, M., Scarlett, J. M., Kass, P. H., & Hutchison, J. M. (2000). Characteristics of shelter-relinquished animals and their owners compared with animals and their owners in US pet-owning households. *Journal of Applied Animal Welfare Science* 3, 179–201.

Nieburg, H. A., & Fischer, A. (1982). *Pet loss: A thoughtful guide for adults and children*. London: Harper & Row Publishing.

Packman W., Carmack B. J., Katz R., Carlos F., Field N.P., & Landers C. (2014). Online survey as empathic bridging for the disenfranchised grief of pet loss. *Omega* (Westport), 69, 333–356.

Planchon, L. A., & Templer, D. I. (1996). The correlates of grief after death of a pet. *Anthrozoös*, 9, 107–113.

Planchon, L. A., Templer, D. K., Stokes, S., & Keller, J. (2002). Death of a companion cat or dog and human bereavement: Psychosocial variables. *Society & Animals*, 10, 93–105.

Prigerson, H., Maciejewski, P., Reynolds, C., Bierhals, A., Newsom, J., Fasiczka, A., Frank, E., Doman, J., & Miller, M. (1995). Inventory of complicated grief: A scale to measure maladaptive symptoms of loss. *Psychiatry Review*, 59, 65–79.

Quackenbush, J., & Glickman, L. (1983). Social work services for bereaved pet owners: A retrospective case study in a veterinary teaching hospital. In A. Katcher, & A. Beck (Eds.), *New perspectives on our lives with companion animals* (pp. 377–389). Philadelphia, PA: University of Pennsylvania Press.

Reisner, I. R. (2003). Differential diagnosis and management of human-directed aggression in dogs. *Veterinary Clinics of North America: Small Animal Practice*, 33, 303–320.

Rémillard, L. W., Meehan, M. P., Kelton, D. F., & Coe, J. B. (2017). Exploring the grief experience among callers to a pet loss support hotline, *Anthrozoös*, 30:1, 149–161. doi: 10.1080/08927936.2017.1270600

Roshier, A. L., & McBride, E. A. (2013). Canine behavior problems: discussions between veterinarians and dog owners during annual booster consultations. *Veterinary Record Open*, March 2, 2013. doi: 10.1136/vt.101125

Ross, C. B. & Baron-Sorensen, J. (1998). *Pet loss and human emotion: Guiding clients through grief*. Philadelphia, PA: Accelerated Development.

Salman, J. M., Hutchison, J., Ruch-Gallie, R., Kogan, L. R., New, J. C., Kass, P. H., & Scarlett, J. M. (2000). Behavioral reasons for relinquishment of dogs and cats to 12 shelters. *Journal of Applied Animal Welfare Science*, 3(2), 93–106.

Salman, M. D., New, Jr., J., Scarlett, J. M., Kass, P. M., Ruch-Gallie, R., & Hetts, S. (1998). Human and animal factors related to relinquishment of dogs and cats in 12 selected animal shelters in the United States, *Journal of Applied Animal Welfare Science*, 1(3), 207–226. doi: 10.1207/s15327604jaws0103_2

Schofield, G., Mummery, K., & Steele, R. (2005). Dog ownership and human health-related physical activity: An epidemiological study. *Health Promotion Journal of Australia*, 16, 15–19.

Scotney, R. L., McLaughlin, D., & Keates, H. L. (2015). A systematic review of the effects of euthanasia and occupational stress in personnel working with animals in animal shelters, veterinary clinics, and biomedical research facilities. *Journal of the American Veterinary Medical Association*, 247, 1121–1130.

Seksel, K. (1997). Puppy socialization classes. *Veterinary Clinics of North America – Small Animal Practice*, 27, 465–477.

Sherbourne, C. D., & Stewart, A. L. (1991). The MOS social support survey. *Social Science & Medicine*, 32(6), 705–714.

Sife, W. (1993). *The loss of a pet*. New York, NY: Howell Book House.

Sife, W. (2014). *The loss of a pet: A guide to coping with the grieving process when a pet dies.* London: Howell Book House.

Simon, L. (1984). The pet trap: Negative effects of pet ownership on families and individuals. In: R. K. Anderson, B. L. Hart, L. A. Hart (Eds.), *The pet connection* (pp. 226–240). Minneapolis, MN: University of Minnesota.

Spencer, L. (1993). Behavioral services in a practice lead to quality relationships. *Journal of the American Veterinary Medical Association,* 203, 940–941.

Stremming, S. (2017). We need to talk about behavioural euthanasia. Retrieved June 4, 2018, from www.thecognitivecanine.com

Summerfield, J. (2017) Harsh truths and difficult choices: the reality of behavioral euthanasia. Retrieved June 4, 2018, from DrJensDogBlog.com

Tzivian, L., & Friger, M. (2014). Grief and bereavement of Israeli dog owners: Exploring short-term phases pre- and post-euthanization. *Death Studies,* 38, 109–117.

Tzivian, L., Friger, M., & Kushnir, T. (2015) Associations between stress and quality of life: Differences between owners keeping a living dog or losing a dog by euthanasia. *PLoS ONE* 10(3), e0121081. doi:10.1371/journal.pone.0121081

Vanderwerker, L. C. & H. G. Prigerson (2004). Social support and technological connectedness as protective factors in bereavement. *Journal of Loss and Trauma,* 9(1), 45–57.

Wågø, S. S., Byrkjedal, I. K., Sinnes, H. M., Hystad, S. W., & Dyregrov, K. (2017). Social support and complicated grief: A longitudinal study on bereaved parents after the Utøya terror attack in Norway. *Scandinavian Psychologist,* 4, e10.

Winch, G. (2018, May 22). Why we need to take pet loss seriously. *Scientific American.*

Woodhouse, B. (1982). *No bad dogs: The Woodhouse Way.* New York, NY: Fireside/ Simon&Schuster Books.

Wrobel, T., & Dye, A. (2003). Grieving pet death: normative, gender and attachment issues. *Omega,* 47, 385–393.

Wylie, K. (2015) Making the decision to euthanize our problem behavior dog. Retrieved June 4, 2018, from www.karenwylie.wordpress.com.

Part V

Special Topics

15 Grieving Pet Loss

The Unique Experience of Bereaved Pet Owners

Phyllis Erdman and Kathleen Ruby

Introduction

As mortals, loss is inevitable. Although we accept this reality in theory, how it actually plays out in our lives is often a bitter pill to swallow. As social beings, we long for connection and closeness, seeking it with other people and the companion animals who share our lives. Relatively recent societal changes in many countries have contributed to pets' evolving roles in our lives. Families are smaller and relatives no longer live in close proximity. Working couples struggle to balance work and family, let alone social lives outside of the home. The elderly are living longer, but may spend more of their later years alone. Pets often fill the voids left by these collective changes (Cohen, 2002). Rather than merely acting as substitutes for human–human relationships, the attachments that people form with their pets are as valid, meaningful, and enduring as those they form with other people (Durkin, 2009).

We demonstrate our love and care in numerous ways, including special food, treats, toys, as well as dog daycares – complete with outdoor playgrounds and participant birthday parties. Others take their pets to pet spas or restaurants that are designed to include our four-footed family members. Many companion animals are seen as children by their "pet parents" and enjoy a mutually beneficial relationship. Pets work with us, play with us, exercise with us, and travel with us (Volshe, 2019).

According to a 2017–2018 national survey, 68% of US homes have pets (APPA, 2017–2018). Most pet owners experience pet loss at some point and many of these owners will experience such severe grief over the loss that they seek mental health services to help with the grief (Kemp, Jacobs, & Stewart, 2016; Messam & Hart, 2019). The evolving human–animal bond (HAB) described in this introduction illustrates why it is imperative that mental health practitioners become familiar with the current ways people relate to their pets and the resulting implications for mental health care (Kemp, Jacobs, & Stewart, 2016; Morley & Fook, 2005; Walsh, 2009). Even though many people now view their pets, as their "children" there are very few resources to help mental health practitioners understand the lived experience of animal loss (Kemp, Jacobs, & Stewart, 2016). Many issues make the bereavement of a companion animal a unique challenge. In this chapter, we will explore the grief experience of those who share their lives with companion animals, familiarize practitioners with this phenomenon, and provide a framework to guide care, support, and treatment.

Conceptual Frameworks for Grief

Although grief is a universal phenomenon, our understanding of how people grieve is not. There are several theories related to grief, from Freud's early attempt at quantification (Freud, 1917), to Kübler-Ross's stage theory (1969) or Worden's (2002) process of mourning that involves movement through four tasks associated with the loss.

In his seminal work on grief, Sigmund Freud suggested that although grief was a natural response to loss, the griever needed to actively confront the loss, fully feel its anguish and completely separate from the lost individual in order to recover (Freud, 1917). It was his sense that if life was to move on unimpeded, the griever must severe all emotional attachment with the deceased.

Later theorists, although they subscribed to the idea that grief must be acknowledged and processed, suggested that some degree of continued attachment of deceased loved ones was normal and expected. For many years, Kübler-Ross's (1969) stages of grief was the model that most researchers and clinicians referenced to explain how people navigate through grief. In actuality, Kübler-Ross set out to capture the experience of dying people as they approached their impending death when she designed her model, rather than the experiences of those left behind, but the stage theory became the gold standard for guiding grief work for many decades. Her five-stage model included denial, anger, bargaining, depression, and acceptance. Each was seen as a potential, linear step in the grieving process, through which a griever would proceed, reconciling the emotions specific to each phase.

More recently, Worden (2002) proposed that the process of mourning requires completing four tasks to reestablish a sense of equilibrium. He makes it clear that these tasks do not have to be completed in any particular order; however, the completion of some tasks presuppose completion of another task. He emphasized that grief is not linear, and that it is difficult to determine a timeline for completing the grief tasks. He identified the tasks as accepting the reality of the loss, working through the pain of grief, adjusting to an environment in which the deceased is missing, and finding an enduring connection with the deceased while embarking on a new life.

All of these models, although helpful in offering a theoretical understanding of the grief experience, have also been criticized as simplifying an immensely complex, individualistic human process (Neimeyer & Jordan, 2002). Grief is now seen through a broader, more fluid lens – one that acknowledges its nature as a highly individualized experience. People process grief as they need to, and healing occurs in a myriad of ways that include a variety of healthy responses to loss, based on an individual's unique circumstances. Furthermore, we cannot assume that grief experienced with the death of a human is the same, or very similar, to that experienced with the death of a companion animal (Lavorgna & Hutton, 2018; Reisbig, Hafen, Drake, Girard, & Breunig, 2017). It is therefore recommended that mental health practitioners adopt guiding therapeutic models that address the social milieu in which a client resides, as well as their personal circumstances, beliefs, and challenges (Doughty, Wissel, & Glorfield, 2011).

A study by Adams, Bonnett, and Meek (1999) sheds light on some common challenges among those who have lost companion animals. The premise is that grief for a pet does indeed differ in numerous ways from the grief resulting from the loss of a person. Although much of the literature on human loss and grief can be relevant, it should be approached with the caveat that there may be differences when working with pet loss, due to both the distinctive way society views such losses, as well as intrapersonal experiences of the pet owner (Kidd & Kidd, 1987; Reisbig, Hafen, Drake, Girard, & Breunig, 2017). The grief experienced by bereaved pet owners is also influenced not only by societal expectations of what is acceptable when grieving for a pet, but by how the owner's veterinarian guided end of life decisions and care (Masterson, Kogan, & Erdman, 2018). How the veterinarian communicates about the dying process, how the actual death is handled, and how the body is cared for after death are all important components that can impact owners' grief process. Clients indicate they appreciate a veterinarian who recognizes the significance of the dying process and subsequent death, and are distressed by a lack of appropriate support or attention to details by the veterinarian or the veterinary team (Rémillard, Meehan, Kelton, & Coe, 2017).

The Grief Experience

Although grief, over the loss of a human or animal companion, is a universal experience, it is essential that we begin this exploration with an operational definition of the term. Kübler-Ross and Kessler (2007) suggest that grief is a common physical, emotional, spiritual, cognitive, and social response to any form of loss. The National Cancer Institute defines grief as "the primarily emotional/affective process of reacting to the loss of a loved one through death." Normal or common reactions to loss may include numbness or disbelief, anxiety from the distress of separation, depression, and eventual recovery (PDQ Cancer Information Summary, 2017).

Although everyone experiences grief, people respond to it in a myriad of ways. The loss of a beloved companion animal, however, includes some unique dynamics that may impact the type, duration, or severity of the grief experienced by their bereaved owners. In spite of the increasingly significant role that pets play in our lives today, we are still often at a loss on how to process the grief associated with a pet's death.

It is widely agreed that grief over the loss of a pet companion can best be understood within the context of attachment theory (Sable, 2013; Zilcha-Mano, Mikulincer, & Shaver, 2011). Field, Orsini, Gavish, and Packman (2009) found that closeness to the deceased pet is the strongest predictor of grief severity – a finding also validated in later studies (Eckerd, Barnett, & Jeff-Dias, 2016). In working with clients, it is often helpful to explore their subjective closeness level with their dying or deceased pets, to better prepare them for the depth of their potential grief experience. Rather than approach this topic directly, a narrative approach may be more fruitful (Neimeyer, 1999). For example, one might ask the client to describe a day with their pet, or talk about activities they most enjoyed together. Attachment and degree of closeness will be apparent through the stories they tell. This technique has the benefit of being thera-peutic as well as instructive, as sharing these narratives can be validating for the client.

Complicating Factors in Pet Loss

Today's veterinary colleges and specialty animal hospitals rival most human hospitals in terms of highly trained medical professionals, services, and technologies. Having innovative medical science available to animals as well as people is a blessing and a curse. While it is wonderful, for example, that pets can now get the same level of oncology care, joint replacement or neurological assessment afforded the rest of the (human) family, this care can be prohibitively expensive and time-consuming. Not all households are willing or able to take advantage of such advanced care. The resultant quandaries of how much care is too much, too expensive, or when to stop care, can result in guilt and remorse. The next section of this chapter will examine some issues unique to pet loss that can confound and complicate the grief process.

Disenfranchised Grief

I knew I could not go to work and be effective. Jake had been my best friend, my buddy. Seeing him hit by that car, suffer terribly, and die in my arms practically killed me, too. I can't sleep. I can't eat. I know I just can't fake being okay with my co-workers. But what will they think? I need a bereavement week off because my dog died? They'll think I'm crazy.

Doka (1989) defined disenfranchised grief as "the grief that persons experience when they incur a loss that is not or cannot be openly acknowledged, publicly mourned, or socially supported" (p. 4). He further identified five categories of disenfranchised loss: when the relationship is not recognized, when the loss is not acknowledged, when the griever is excluded, circumstances around the death, and ways that the individual grieves (Doka, 2002). Any of these categories could obviously apply to the grief experienced from a pet. Essentially, when a person suffers such an unsanctioned loss, the care, concern, and compassion offered to most grievers is absent. An example of this kind of grief might be seen when an elderly parent dies, and rather than tend to the grief of the middle-aged orphaned child, people comment on the long life the elder parent experienced. It can happen when someone commits suicide and people are not able to acknowledge the death because they are uncomfortable with the type of death. In both examples, those who are grieving do not receive validation and acknowledgment of their suffering. In the case of our pets, who are often perceived as family members or children, their death can seem inconsequential to those who do not understand or value such relationships. It is not uncommon for most companies to have bereavement leave for close human family members, but not for animal family members, leaving those suffering this type of loss without support for, and validation of, the pain they are experiencing.

Traumatic or sudden loss is understandably a life-changing event when it involves a human family member or friend. But what about when that friend is "only an animal" in the eyes of many? Societally, or individually, the death of a companion animal may not be viewed as a compelling loss, worthy of the same attention or care as the loss of a human. The discordance between what a grieving owner is experiencing and the societal response can be shattering and leave owners without a socially acceptable framework to navigate through the experience.

The key to counseling disenfranchised grievers is to help them recognize what is essentially an empathic failure (Neimeyer & Jordan, 2002). The counselor can assist the client in understanding the disenfranchisement and where it originates. Sometimes, this disenfranchisement can be internal. Some owners may be embarrassed or ashamed of the grief they are experiencing because it does not fit his/her sense of what is appropriate or acceptable. The clinical task in this case is to assist the client in recognizing this block, and learn to accept that the love they shared with their animal companion can result in very real and valid grief over the loss. The mental health practitioner can support and validate these clients through a variety of effective interventions including ongoing counseling support, referral to a grief group or online forum, bibliotherapy, the creation of a grief narrative that conveys the depth of the client's grief, or the therapeutic use of ritual.

Anticipatory Grief

> The cancer diagnosis we got scares me to death. What will it mean for the family? How will it progress? How can we all watch Sammy go downhill, suffer, die? How can I cope with a dying animal at home and still care for my kids? How will we ever say goodbye? I can't stand the thought of watching him become more incapacitated each day. I've heard cancer can be a terrible way to die. What if I can't do it, be what he needs? What if I fall apart? Or, cause him more pain? I can't even imagine saying goodbye at this point. I keep picturing the end in my head, over and over.

Rando (1986) defines anticipatory grief as:

> The phenomenon encompassing the processes of mourning, coping, interaction, planning, and psychosocial reorganization that are stimulated, and begun in part, in response to the awareness of the impending loss of a loved one and in the recognition of associated losses in the past, present, and future.
>
> (p. 24)

Unlike people with terminal illnesses, pet owners have the option of euthanasia when a pet is terminally ill or very old, which means they often face a difficult decision over terminating the pet's life or prolonging their suffering. Working through this decision-making process can be confusing and onerous. Yet, caring for a dying family member can also be a grueling and time-consuming task. It is not surprising that many caregivers feel resentful and frustrated, especially when they have inadequate support (D'Antonio, 2014). Supporting a dying loved one does not involve a smooth, steady progression of letting go as they are sliding towards death, but rather an episodic and ongoing reflection process that involves recognizing the emotional, physical, and spiritual losses that occur with death.

There has been ongoing controversy regarding anticipatory grief in the literature, as it was at first seen as a positive adaptive response that could diminish post-death grief. Whether or not it does so has been the subject of many studies over the past two decades, and there is no clear evidence that experiencing anticipatory grief increases or decreases distress after death (Kehl, 2005). The bottom line is that it is a common phenomenon and clients need to understand it so they can better recognize and label their experience. Without this knowledge, anticipatory grieving may inhibit their ability to fully appreciate their last weeks and days with their pet. Owners may experience guilt as they note their own premature physical or emotional withdrawal, or suffer censure from others, including veterinary professionals, for what appears to be a lack of caring (Sweeting & Gilhooly, 1990). They need to understand their anticipatory grieving is a normal dimension of accompanying a loved one as they transition from life to death, and be aware of the potential for premature emotional or physical withdrawal when left unmonitored or unchecked.

Lack of Home Medical Support

> I knew Moog was going to die, but hoped I still had some time with him beforehand. But, giving him that time means giving him twice the day fluids, lifting him in and out of the house to relieve himself and weekly visits to the veterinary office. I can't leave the house in case he needs me, or needs to go outside. I love him dearly, but don't know how much longer I can do this all by myself.

When a human family member is stricken with a terminal illness, or is actively dying, it is common to have a great deal of formal and informal support. Home health, hospice, and an array of palliative services have evolved to assist with these transitions. Family and friends often step forward to help carry the load of supporting human loved ones through the dying process. When a death occurs, funeral professionals assist the bereaved in planning and executing a meaningful goodbye celebration or funeral. Unfortunately, none of this is true for most animal family members. Although the veterinary profession is in the early stages of helping veterinary practices develop palliative care guidelines and hospice-like care (Bishop et al., 2016), such assistance is not available in most areas. Clients with dying animals often make major life sacrifices to care for their pet through their final life stages. In addition, once the pet passes, there are typically no funeral professionals, loving rituals, or traditional support from neighbors or friends to ease the pain of the loss. It is not unusual to hear of clients who keep the loss private, or only share with those few who will understand. When we lose human family members, our mailboxes fill with cards, our refrigerators fill with food, and people fill the house to ease the pain of the sudden void. With the death of a pet, often there is only the void. The poignancy of this experience was expressed by a client who, upon euthanizing her beloved dog, described arriving home from the veterinary hospital, alone.

> As I walked in the door, I was struck by the quiet. No happy creature almost knocked me over with joy, or trilled hello. There was no food bowl to fill or water to replenish. Her leash and harness hung limp by the door, awaiting a walk that would never happen again. I realized this was it. This was my new life. Without her.

Euthanasia

> The vet said I'd know when it was time. Samantha, our baby, our first kid purchased right after we got married, is now 14. She's incredibly old for a boxer. Her arthritis has her crippled and she no longer wants to eat or play. But she still smiles when I walk into the room and wags her tail when it's time to go outside. How can I make the decision to say her life is over? How can I bring myself to say goodbye?

> It's over. It was awful. Oh, I don't mean the vet did a bad job, but it was a terrible experience. And the decision! I had to decide to have my dog killed. I never thought I'd be in that position. How do I shake this overwhelming feeling of guilt?

Perhaps one of the most difficult realities of pet ownership is the specter of euthanasia for ailing or elderly pets. Although euthanasia literally means "good death," deciding to end the life of a beloved companion animal is anything but easy. Most clients struggle with when "it is time" (Lagoni, 2011). Although fairly common, the decision to euthanize often includes conflicted feelings and guilt. In most of today's veterinary practices, owners can choose to be present while their pet is being euthanized. While this allows transparency and a degree of intimacy at the end, it is a daunting and difficult event for most people. Adequate education and preparation can aid in demystifying the process and help prepare the client for the sights, sounds, and realities of an owner-present euthanasia. Since most people have not watched another living being die, learning in advance what to expect can ease the shock of the experience (Lagoni, 2011). Some veterinary clinics employ counselors and social workers to help clients make the decision to euthanize as well as prepare for a family-present euthanasia. Helpful interventions include providing clients with a means to quantify their pet's quality of life and to invite them to explore the meaning of a "good death" for their pet. One example of an instrument to quantify quality of life is the HHHHHMM Quality of Life Scale (Villalobos, 2011). This is a well-established method used by many veterinarians to help guide difficult decisions and ease the fear of subjective assessment (Wojciechowska & Hewson, 2005). Clients who have experienced the difficulty of watching the prolonged process of a terminally ill human family member or friend recognize the value of protecting their pet from such suffering. The goal of both pre-euthanasia decision-making and post-euthanasia processing is to keep the context of the pet's death firmly centered on what is best for the ailing pet rather than on the difficulty of the decision, the shock of the death, or guilt over the decision to euthanize.

Complicated Grief

A more atypical response to loss is complicated or traumatic grief. It is imperative that this more intractable and debilitating response to loss is discovered early and that treatment begins as soon as it is suspected.

> In the past two years, my mother and brother both died, and I struggled with breast cancer. I was going through radiation treatment at the same time that I had to coordinate two funerals. It was an awful time. I ended up inheriting my mom's elderly dog, Peaches, who was a great comfort to me through those terrible days. I had to have her euthanized 8 months ago. I just can't recover. I want to sleep all the time. I've stopped returning calls from friends. I can hardly drag myself to the grocery store when I run out of food. All I can think about is how alone I am. How sad I am. I keep thinking about all that I've lost. Sometimes, the ache I feel inside seems so intensely physical, I'm sure my heart is literally breaking in two. I can't imagine ever feeling good again.

In the first few months of grief, most people experience some amount of pain, rumination over the loss, social withdrawal, and exhaustion. The acute adjustment to a major loss is a time of anguished challenge. Sometimes, however, grief symptoms become protracted and chronic. Complicated grief is grief that lingers, or even gets worse, as time goes on. In a recent review of a decade of research, Lombardo et al. (2014) sought to identify where, on the spectrum of grief, complicated bereavement starts. They state that although most people experience acute grief many times over a lifetime, a small number of sufferers experience more prolonged and intractable symptoms. Research indicates that sudden or traumatic death can exacerbate the potential of co-morbid disorders such as post-traumatic stress disorder or major depressive disorder. Additionally, the recovery trajectory from grief symptoms as a result of sudden or traumatic death appear to be slower. Given this potential, clients who have experienced such deaths may require different interventions to assist in recovery (Kristensen, Weisaeth, & Heir, 2012).

In terms of the potential for a complicated grief response, companion animals not only provide friendship and affection; they can also act as "bridges" to other important relationships. For example, a widow may be left alone with their shared pet when her husband dies, making her connection to that pet a link to her deceased spouse. Or parents who have become empty nesters may transfer some of the attention and care they lavished on their children onto the family pet. These losses can take on additional meaning and carry the risk of complicated grief.

Many other factors can contribute to complicated grief specific to companion animal loss. One of the most common of these pertains to the euthanasia process. Although euthanasia is usually a pain-free, peaceful process, it can go wrong, or be traumatic for the pet owner who remains present during the procedure. This is especially true for owners who were not adequately prepared. Observing the animal's physical responses to the procedure can trigger many emotional responses from the owner who is not prepared. In a recent study by Masterson et al. (2018), clients were asked about their experiences with euthanasia. The results suggested that pet owners want to be prepared; they want their opinions and ideas included in the process, and want follow-up resources offered. They noted that these are key variables in contributing to a positive euthanasia experience.

Sufferers of prolonged grief disorder have intrusive thoughts and images of the deceased, and a painful yearning for his/her presence. They may also express feeling extreme aloneness and the desire to die themselves. Individuals who are diagnosed with complicated grief 6 to 12 months after a death have a substantially higher risk of mental and functional impairment and may experience intense intrusive thoughts, pangs of severe emotion, distressing yearnings, feeling excessively alone and empty, excessively avoiding tasks reminiscent of the deceased, unusual sleep disturbance and maladaptive levels of loss of interest in personal activities (Horowitz et al., 1997).

Those at higher risk for complicated bereavement include women, those with pre-existing trauma, prior losses, insecure attachment, pre-existing mood and anxiety disorders, and a complicated relationship with the deceased. In addition to the trauma of sudden or violent death as a precursor, so too is being in a caretaker role at the time of a loved one's death. Complicated grief can also be exacerbated by a lack of social support or resources, alcohol or drug dependence, a lack of understanding about the cause of death, and an inability to experience usual grieving practices (Simon, 2013).

Treatment for complicated grief depends on early identification of those with risk factors, careful diagnosis, as well as targeted psychotherapy which explore specific risk factors. Prigerson et al. (2013) proposed a diagnostic process to help identify people who are at risk for experiencing complicated grief and ensuring they receive appropriate, timely intervention, while avoiding pathologizing normal grief. Interventions include psychoeducation about complicated grief and exploring the issues or behaviors that may contribute to factors.

Conclusion

We will all experience grief. Yet, how we process that grief is unique to each of us. Over the years, there has been significant research describing the process of grief and providing theories for helping us to understand the grieving process. Unfortunately, very little of that research has been conducted within the context of human–animal relationships. Since animals are increasingly becoming more like family members, it is imperative that we, as mental health providers, understand the intensity of the grief that accompanies the loss of these relationships and encourage our clients to express it in therapeutically helpful ways. We need to hear their stories, validate their pain, and legitimize their feelings. It is also essential we find ways to network with veterinarians and help everyone better understand the role that each plays in acknowledging and supporting grieving pet owners.

The scenarios below describe clients experiencing many of the issues we have discussed above. As you read through the scenarios, consider some of the complexities we have described in this chapter and how you, as a mental health provider, can help these clients.

Case Scenarios

Case Scenario #1:

Samantha is a 67-year-old client who recently experienced the death of her husband from brain cancer. The last two weeks of his life were spent in hospice care, and Samantha slowly watched the cancer take over his body. Six months after his death, her dog was terminally ill and she chose to have him euthanized. She reported to her counselor:

> It was horrible. I had no idea what to expect from euthanasia, but I certainly had no idea my dog would writhe and scream in pain. It was hard for me to decide to attend the euthanasia, but I felt I owed it to him to be there. I wanted his last sense to be me, holding him and petting him. Instead, his scream shocked me so much that I jerked away. I was shaking so badly afterwards, that I'm sure I was anything but comforting to him as he died. I can't get that scream out of my mind. I hear it over and over, and it's been almost a year now. All I can think about is my husband lying there wasting away and I couldn't do anything to help him, and then when I did what I thought was best for my dog, I couldn't even be there to comfort him like I should have. The idea that someone else I love might die, or I might have to watch them die, haunts me.

Discussion Questions:

1. What are some of the complications surrounding grief and loss that are contributing to Samantha's pain?
2. What are some of the feeling that you can help her identify and the source of those feelings?
3. What might be some helpful interventions to help her begin a healing process?
4. How might her experiences be different had she not lost her husband to cancer?

5. How could the veterinarian have assisted her to better prepare her for the euthanasia?

Case Scenario #2:

Jeff is a 35-year-old construction worker. He adopted Buddy, a rescue dog, 6 years ago and the two have been inseparable, even on hiking and camping trips. Two weeks ago, he went hiking with Buddy, and Buddy got into a major fight with another dog on the trail. Buddy was injured very severely and after a week of treatment at the vet, he was faced with either euthanizing him or possible amputation of one of his legs. Jeff has struggled with making the right decision and it's affecting his work. His co-workers say he is unfocused and can't understand how an issue such as this could impact his work. Jeff is divorced and lives alone and has no one to help him with his decision. He asked his counselor:

> What should I do? How do I know I'm making the best decision, and is it more about me or Buddy? No one understands what I'm struggling with and I don't have anyone to talk to. The guys at work make fun of me and call me "Mr. Whimp" because I actually cry at work when I think about Buddy laying there waiting on me to determine his fate. They say I should "man up" and get over it. What if I make the wrong decision? I just can't stand to think of coming home to an empty house without my Buddy to greet me, but how about if he isn't happy with just three legs to hop around on? I have to make this decision soon and I'm just lost. I'm just stuck!

Discussion Questions:

1. What are some of the issues that make it so difficult for Jeff to make his decision?
2. What are some of the feelings that you can help him identify and the source of those feelings?
3. What might be some helpful interventions to guide him in his decision-making?
4. How might his experiences be different if he had someone to talk to about this?
5. Could you suggest ways that Jeff might include his veterinarian in this decision? What would those be?

References

Adams, C. L., Bonnett, B. N., & Meek, A. H. (1999). Owner response to companion animal death: development of a theory and practical implications. *Canadian Veterinary Journal*, 40, 33–39.

American Pet Products Association. (2017–2018). APPA national pet owners survey. Retrieved on 22 January 2018, from www.americanpetproducts.org.

Bishop, G., Cooney, K., Cox, S., Downing, R., Mitchener, K., Shanan, A., Soares, N., Stevens, B., & Wynn, T. (2016). AAHA/IAAHPC End-of-life care guidelines. *Journal of the American Animal Hospital Association*, 52(6), 341–356.

Cohen, S. J. (2002). Can pets function as family members? *Western Journal of Nursing Research*, 24(6), 621–638.

D'Antonio, J. (2014). Caregiver grief and anticipatory mourning. *Journal of Hospice and Palliative Nursing*, 16(2), 99–104.

Doka, K. J. (1989). Disenfranchised grief. In K. J. Doka (Ed.), *Disenfranchised grief: Recognizing hidden sorrow* (pp. 3–23). Lexington, MA: Lexington Books.

Doka, K. J. (2002). Introduction. In K. J. Doka (Ed.). *Disenfranchised grief: New directions, challenges, and strategies for practice* (pp. 5–22). Champaign, IL: Research Press.

Doughty, E. A., Wissel, A., & Glorfield, C. (2011). Current trends in grief counseling. Unpublished presentation. American Counseling Association Conference and Exposition. March 23–27, 2011, New Orleans, LA.

Durkin, A. (2009). Loss of a companion animal: understanding and helping the bereaved. *Journal Of Psychosocial Nursing and Mental Health Services*, 47(7), 26.

Eckerd, L. M., Barnett, J. E., & Jeff-Dias, L. (2016). Grief following pet and human loss: Closeness is key. *Death Studies*, 40(5), 275–282.

Field, N. P., Orsini, L., Gavish, R., & Packman, W. (2009). Role of attachment in response to pet loss. *Death Studies*, 33(4), 334–355.

Freud, S. (1917). Mourning and melancholia. In J. Strachey (Ed. & Trans.), *The standard edition of the complete psychological works of Sigmund Freud* (Vol 14, pp. 237–260). London: Hogarth

Horowitz, M. J., Siegel, B., Holen, A., Bonanno, G. A., Milbrath, C., & Stinson, C. H. (1997). Diagnostic Criteria for complicated grief disorder. *American Journal of Psychiatry*, 154(7), 904–910

Kehl, K. A. (2005). Recognition and support of anticipatory mourning. *Journal of Hospice & Palliative Nursing*, 7(4), 206–211.

Kemp, H. R., Jacobs, N., & Stewart, S. (2016). The lived experience of companion-animal loss: A systematic review of qualitative studies. *Anthrozoös*, 20(4), 533–557.

Kidd, A. H., & Kidd, R. M. (1987). Seeking a theory of the human/companion animal bond. *Anthrozoös*, 1, 140–157

Kristensen, P., Weisaeth, L., & Heir, T. (2012) Bereavement and mental health after sudden and violent losses: A review. *Psychiatry*, 75(1),76–97

Kübler-Ross, E. (1969). *On death and dying*. NY: The Macmillan Co.

Kübler-Ross, E., & Kessler, D. (2007). *On grief and grieving: Finding the meaning of grief through the five stages of loss*. New York, NY: Scribner.

Lagoni, L. (2011). Family-present euthanasia: Protocols for planning and preparing clients for the death of a pet. In C. Blazina, G. Boyraz, & D. Shen-Miller (Eds.), *The psychology of the human–animal bond: A resource for clinicians and researchers* (pp. 181–202). New York, NY: Springer.

Lavorgna, B. F., & Hutton, V. E. (2018) Grief severity: A comparison between human and companion animal death, *Death Studies*, doi: 10.1080/07481187.2018.1491485

Lombardo, L., Lai, C., Luciani, M., Morelli, E., Buttinelli, E., Aceto, P., Lai, S., D'Onofrio, M., Falli, F., & Penco, I. (2014). Bereavement and complicated grief: towards a definition of prolonged grief. *Rivista. Psichiatria*, 49(3), 106–114.

Masterson, H. E., Kogan, L., & Erdman, P. (2018) Animal loss and grief experience of pet owners: How to prepare pet owners for the end of life process. Poster session. APA conference, San Francisco, CA.

Messam, L. L., & Hart, L. A. (2019). Persons experiencing prolonged grief after the loss of a pet. In L. Kogan, & C. Blazina (Eds.), *Clinicians' guide to treating companion animal issues* (pp. 267–280). London: Elsevier.

Morley, C., & Fook, J. (2005). The importance of pet loss and some implications for services. *Mortality*, 10(2), 127–143.

Neimeyer, R. A. (1999). Narrative strategies in grief therapy. *Journal of Constructivist Psychology*, 12, 65–85.

Neimeyer, R. A., & Jordan, J. (2002). Disenfranchisement as empathic failure: Grief therapy and the co-construction of meaning. In K. J. Doka, (Ed.), *Disenfranchised grief: New directives, challenges and strategies for practice* (pp. 95–117). Champaign, IL: Research Press.

PDQ Supportive and Palliative Care Editorial Board. (2017). Grief, bereavement, and coping with loss. Health professional version. April 20, 2017. National Cancer Institute.

Prigerson, H. G., Horowitz, M. J., Jacobs, S. C., Parkes, C. M., Aslan, M., & Goodkin, K. (2013). Prolonged grief disorder: psychometric validation of criteria proposed for DSM-V and ICD-11. *Plos Med*, 10(12). doi: 10.1371/annotation/a1d91e0d-981f-4674-926c-0fbd2463b5ea

Rando, T. A. (1986). A comprehensive analysis of anticipatory grief: perspectives, processes, promises, and problems. In T. Rando (Ed.), *Loss and anticipatory grief* (pp. 1–37). New York, NY: Lexington Books.

Reisbig, A. M. J., Hafen, M., Drake, A. A. S., Girard, D., & Breunig, Z. B. (2017). Companion animal death: A qualitative analysis of relationship quality, loss, and coping. *Journal of Death and Dying*, 75(2), 124–150.

Rémillard, L. W., Meehan, M. P., Kelton, D. K., & Coe, J. B. (2017). Exploring the grief experience among callers to a pet loss support hotline. *Anthrozoös*, 30(1), 140–161.

Sable, P. (2013). The pet connection: an attachment perspective. *Clinical Social Work Journal*, 41, 93–99.

Simon, N. M. (2013). Treating complicated grief. *The Journal of the American Medical Association*, 310(4), 416–423.

Sweeting, H. N. Gilhooly, M. L. (1990). Anticipatory grief: a review. *Social Science Medicine*, 30 (10), 1073–1080.

Villalobos, A. E. (2011). Quality-of-life Assessment Techniques for Veterinarians. *Veterinary Clinics: Small Animal Practice*, 41(3), 519–521.

Volsche, S. (2019). Understanding cross-species parenting: A case for pets as children. In L. Kogan, & C. Blazina, (Eds.), *Clinician's guide to treating companion animal issues* (pp. 129–142). London: Elsevier.

Walsh, F. (2009). Human–animal bonds 1: The relational significance of companion animals. *Family Process*, 48(4), 462–480.

Wojciechowska, J., & Hewson, C. J. (2005). Quality-of-life assessment in pet dogs. *Journal of the American Veterinary Medical Association*, 226(5), 722–728.

Worden, J. W. (2002). *Grief counseling and grief therapy. A handbook for the mental health practitioner* (3rd ed.). New York, NY: Springer Publishing Company

Zilcha-Mano, S., Mikulincer, M., & Shaver, P. R. (2011). An attachment perspective on human–pet relationships: Conceptualization and assessment of pet attachment orientations. *Journal of Research in Personality*, 45(4), 345–357.

16 Helping Clients Prepare for Pet Loss

Erin Allen and Maria Gore

When working with pet owners, at some point, they will face the impending loss or actively process the death of their pet. As a mental health professional, you can help them prepare cognitively and emotionally for experiencing the loss of a pet.

According to the 2017–2018 National Pet Owners Survey, conducted by the American Pet Products Association (2019), 68% of American households have pets. Of those households, over 80% reported that their animals are a source of affection and they feel an unconditional love for their pet. Pets fill many roles within a family system. Many people consider pets as family members, caring for them physically and emotionally as they would a human, even choosing to have pets before or instead of children (Walsh, 2009). These animals often provide an emotional link to a previous period of life or individual who may be gone. The presence of the "unconditional love" shared with pets provides unwavering support to individuals through life challenges, often acting as the "glue" of the family (Cain, 1983). Due to their unyielding love and supportive role in one's life, the loss of a pet can often be felt as profoundly as or even more so than the loss of a human friend or family member. The depth of the grief felt by the pet's owner may reflect the importance of the pet's role in his or her life. This grief process is also impacted by societal belief systems that can minimize and disenfranchise the grief of losing a pet, due to a generalized lack of acknowledgment, understanding, and support in relation to a pet's death (Cordero, 2012). Without familiar recognitions, rituals, and memorializations, as often experienced with a human loss, grief from losing a pet can seem overwhelming and isolating. Pet owners may also be surprised and caught unaware by the depth of their emotions, thus compounding their grief experience.

Grief for a pet is not only felt after death; it can occur at the onset or diagnosis of a terminal illness – in anticipation of the approaching loss. Acknowledging the loss of a pet prior to its occurrence can impact an owner's grief process. Rando (1986, p. 24) defines anticipatory grief as:

The phenomenon encompassing the processes of mourning, coping, interaction, planning, and psychosocial reorganization that are stimulated and begun in part in response to the awareness of the impending loss of a loved one (death) and in the recognition of associated losses in the past, present, and future.

It creates an opportunity to prepare oneself, identify the changes that are to come and develop some resolution of unresolved concerns. Helping your client reflect on the remaining time they have with their pet can help them focus on what is meaningful. Social workers and mental health professionals who understand the importance pets have in their clients' lives can be valuable sources of support for those who are anticipating the loss of a pet.

Preparing Yourself

When a client is facing the impending loss of a pet, as the mental health professional, you can help them prepare emotionally, cognitively, and physically for what is to come each step of the way. The first step to consider is your own emotional preparedness to address the client's process. As with any emotionally heightened subject matter, identifying personal triggers in preparation for counseling a pet owner is important.

Consider:

- Have you lost pets before? What species/breeds?
- How did you lose them?
- How is this similar or different from what your client is dealing with currently?

Your own relationships with personal companion animals may be similar or very different than those of your clients, yet regardless, may lead to some personal triggers that can impede your ability to counsel impartially. Maintaining awareness of personal bias and judgment surrounding human/animal relationships is essential to creating and maintaining a neutral and supportive therapeutic role.

Normalizing their Experience

In recognizing that grief over the impending loss or death of a pet is not generally socially supported, creating a safe space for your client to evaluate and process their emotions is essential. Normalizing their grief emotions, including their intensity, as an expected potential experience not unlike many other pet owners can help alter the negative self-perspectives often experienced by grieving pet owners. The loss of an animal companion is a significant loss and can be expected to be grieved as one.

Who is on their Side?

Another area that is helpful to evaluate is the client's personal support system.

- Who is involved with the decision-making for the pet?
- Who does the client turn to for support in difficult times?

Though some families consider pets as members of the family, this perspective can vary, even within a single family unit. It is not uncommon for each family member to have a unique relationship with the pet, at an individual level of intensity. For example, one partner might work from home, staying with the pet all day while the other partner might travel and is home infrequently, thus creating different levels of connection with the animal. These differences can impact each person's grief process, which in turn can affect the interpersonal relationships within the family system. The client you counsel may have a strong family system but it may not be supportive for this event, given the personal and unique relationships each family member has with the pet. Helping your client identify who understands the bond they share with the pet, who is able to provide support without judgment, and who "gets it," can help your client create a supportive network. It can also help them understand why some individuals whom they may expect to be supportive, are not, thus reducing the impact of unmet expectations.

Loss History

As you counsel your client in preparation for the loss of a pet, assessing their loss history is beneficial. Through the process of anticipatory grieving, the strong emotions associated with grief can be experienced. Anticipatory grieving can also trigger past losses and reminders of those experiences. Evaluating past losses helps your client identify what worked well before, and reminds them how they approached strong emotions in the past. If, historically, the client has lost pets, have them evaluate the similarities and differences between those experiences and the current one.

- When you lost your last dog, Bo, what has stuck with you the most about his passing?
- When you decided that it was time to euthanize Cricket, how did you approach that decision?

Explore how they made decisions and the lessons learned from previous pets. Guidance through previous losses provides valuable insight into the current situation.

As you help clients assess their past loss history, you are also opening the door to examine how particular influences in their life, such as religion, beliefs, and morals will impact their experience through a pet's illness process and eventual death. It can be beneficial to help them evaluate exactly how those influences play a part in the decision-making for the pet's medical care. Some religions and individual moral objections do not support euthanasia as an option during a pet's dying process. It is good to identify these beliefs so the client can communicate clearly with their veterinarian to develop an appropriate end-of-life plan for natural death. Identifying these beliefs early will open channels for communicating about the client's wishes and identifying the next steps for their pet.

End of Life Preparation

As you are helping a client examine their pet's health process and impending decline, they may ask you a big question:

- Client: How will I know it's time?

This is a question that will not have an absolute and clear answer without further examination. If they have asked this of friends and family, they may have received a classic response of "You'll just know" which, to some may be true but to others may add undue pressure about their abilities to read their pet's experience. You can help them approach this sensitive subject in an objective, step-wise manner.

Learning What to Expect

First, encourage your client to talk with their veterinarian to learn exactly what to expect as their pet's disease progresses. Their veterinarian can help create a plan identifying what can be done to support the pet medically. Sometimes there is not a specific disease but rather a general decline in physical and mental abilities of the pet. It is important for a pet owner to assess basic bodily functioning needs, such as eating, drinking, elimination, and movement. These are life-sustaining and if they are faltering, a veterinarian should be consulted as the pet may be in or near distress.

If the pet is stable medically but declining due to age or disease, help your client define quality. Quality of life is having quality not only in the days but in the moments that make up the days of the pet's life. Quality is going to look different to each pet owner based on that particular pet. Help your client define quality as it pertains to their pet.

- What makes Marley's days enjoyable?
- What specific things does he do that make him happy?

- What does quality look like for Marley?
- If quality were to diminish, what would that look like?

Pain Versus Suffering

Oftentimes people state they simply do not want their pet to be in pain or suffer. Again, it is helpful to take that declaration a step further and examine what exactly that means for their pet. Pain is a negative physical experience a pet may experience. Suffering can encompass the overall quality and enjoyment of life.

Pain

Pain is a physical and emotional sensation that can be complicated to assess. Keep in mind, a pet's reaction to pain is dependent upon its personality and the degree of pain it's experiencing. The following signs might indicate that their pet is in some degree of pain:

- Trembling or shaking
- Panting
- Slow to rise
- Whining or lack of vocalization (no greeting bark or noise)
- Decreasing or absent appetite
- Acting out of character
- Being restless or unable to get comfortable
- Sitting or lying abnormally
- Bearing no or partial weight on the affected limb
- Hesitant to be touched in a painful area
- Change in energy level

Suffering

Suffering is more than physical attributes, and it involves assessing a pet's quality of life. These are the "qualities" that make the pet who he or she is and are often part of the daily routine. If these characteristics are no longer present, then it might be considered suffering.

Here are some questions you might ask your clients to help assess their pet's quality of life:

- Is your pet eating and drinking well?
- Is your pet able to relieve himself on his own?
- Is your pet able to move on her own?
- Is your pet playful?
- Is your pet affectionate with you?
- Is your pet interested in activities going on around him?

- Is your pet tired much of the time?
- Is your pet withdrawn much of the time?
- Is your pet sleeping comfortably?

(Argus Institute, 2015)

Sometimes pets can experience some amount of pain, perhaps general age pains like arthritis, and their owner is comfortable with allowing it if they perceive their pet as happy and not suffering. Creating a distinction between pain and suffering is important in identifying the specific details that make the pet unique.

- How does Marley experience pain now?
- What would suffering look like for Marley?
- How would you define suffering?
- What would it look like if Marley were starting to suffer?

Assisting a client to determine the answers to questions like these can help the client begin to comprehend what their pet's quality of life looks like in order to objectively measure it. After your client has decided what attributes are meaningful in their pet's life, they can use those parameters to objectively measure quality. Some tools for tracking quality in a pet's life are as follows:

- *Joy list* – The idea is to create a list of specifics (i.e., playing fetch, getting treats, cuddling on the couch, affectionate with family, etc.) that the pet enjoys. This list will resemble the qualities defined earlier. By bringing a log of the pet's joys to attention, they can be more easily monitored when those joys begin to diminish as quality of life does.
- *Calendar* – This method is a simple way to objectively monitor quality of life. The pet owner can create a list of things that bring quality to their pet's life. Each day, they can assess whether the day was a "Good Day" or "Bad Day" and mark it on a calendar. This can be a good method for families with children, allowing each person to participate in evaluating the day. This provides an impartial perspective across a span of time and can aid in maintaining an objective perspective.
- *Marble jar* – This simple method resembles the calendar method. Instead of maintaining a written record of each day, a specifically colored marble or stone is placed in a jar. One color for good days and one color for bad. A visual representation of the pet's quality is easily evident in a short period of time.
- *Journaling* – This tool can be helpful for those accustomed to writing. It is a good way to process the pet's days, by writing it all down and reviewing it after a period of time. Sometimes details can be diminished mentally but a written record can help highlight key points of consideration when assessing a pet's quality of life when reviewed.

Any of these tools or a combination can help your client develop an unbiased perception of how their pet is experiencing its life. These perspectives can also help your client assess their own quality of life. Caring for a terminally ill or aged pet can be very taxing psychologically and physically. Maintaining an awareness of how they are handling the stress is an important consideration in this decision-making process.

As your client is assessing quality of life for their pet, an additional impartial resource that may be helpful is a pet hospice provider. In this way, a veterinary professional can help assist the owner in gauging changes in the pet's quality of life as well as provide services when the time for euthanasia comes.

Making an End of Life Plan for a Pet

Although no amount of preparation will eliminate the pain of losing a pet, planning ahead for the loss allows the owner to regain some control over the situation and develop a sense of acceptance. One helpful approach when your client is beginning to evaluate end of life decisions for their pet is to help them identify what regrets certain decisions or actions may leave them with.

- If you could look at this experience from a future perspective, what would cause you regret?
- What would your biggest regrets be when you looked back at this time with Max?

Regret negatively impacts a person's grieving process. Helping clients identify potential regrets early can benefit them after the loss of their pet.

Deciding Euthanasia or Natural Death

The first step in preparing for the end of a pet's life is to focus on whether euthanasia is the right choice. The word *euthanasia* comes from the Greek "*eu*" *goodly or well* and "*Thanatos,*" *death = the good death.* In some ways, it can be considered as a way to protect the pet's quality of death when the quality of life has diminished. Often a person's perception of the act of euthanasia is influenced by their historical pet loss experiences, religious beliefs, and personal morals. If someone has never faced the decision to euthanize a pet, they may have fear and uncertainty about what exactly the process looks like or have heard scary recollections from others. Encouraging them to discuss the details of the euthanasia procedure and the medical technique with their veterinarian is important. Identifying what they can expect to experience helps alleviate some of the fear. This can also help your client decide if euthanasia is the right choice for their pet. The alternative, a natural death, looks very different. Getting information about what that would look like from a veterinarian who is familiar with the pet's disease process is important as well. Broaching these subjects opens an opportunity for a dialogue about your client's wishes.

- How would you like to remember Bella's last day?
- How would deciding euthanasia play a part in this?
- If she were to die naturally, what are your biggest concerns?

Some considerations for you to examine with your client surrounding a natural dying process involve the control of the event. A natural death is unpredictable in its duration and severity of physical experiences. It can be smooth and peaceful but it can also last for an extended duration and involve some physical observations that can be troubling for some people to see.

- What would you like Bella's last moments to look like?
- How would it affect you if Bella were to die when you were out of the house?
- How would you take care of Bella's body if she were to die at home?

It can help to explore your client's perspectives on quality of life as compared with the veterinarian's advice of what to expect from a disease process. This supports them in deciding if a natural, unassisted death is what they wish for their pet.

Creating a Plan

If your client feels that euthanasia is appropriate, deciding the details beforehand helps to simplify the process when the actual event occurs. This can be done in two lines of thought – creating Plan A and Plan B. Plan A would be a planned, controlled experience that looks as they imagine. Plan B would be an emergent situation, hurried but still thought out. Having both of these plans developed ahead of time can greatly ease the stress of having to make emotional decisions during such a difficult time, allowing your client to focus more on themselves and their pets in the last moments together.

In Plan A, one important decision is whether or not they going to stay with their pet through the euthanasia process. Some choose to stay and some do not. While it is truly acceptable not to wish to witness the death of a pet, it may be beneficial to help your client evaluate the reasons not to be present to identify any potential regrets of "walking away" from their pet in the last moments.

- What is compelling you to not be present?
- Will you feel any regret for not being present?
- What flexibility is there to be present for only part of the process?

Another decision is determining the physical details of the euthanasia. Some pet owners wish for their pet to be euthanized at home while others wish for it to occur at the veterinary hospital. If it is to occur at the veterinary hospital, what are the location options? Can it occur outdoors or in a special private room?

- What do you want this day to look like?
- How will you create some special time for yourself during this process? What will you need?

Have your client consider whom they wish to perform the euthanasia. Some may have a special relationship with a veterinarian that makes it meaningful for that doctor to be the one present. Planning the euthanasia around a specific veterinarian will affect the scheduling of a euthanasia appointment so encourage your client to gather that information ahead of time. It is also important information to determine anyone else, such as family or friends, your client wishes to be present for the euthanasia, to make sure they are available for that day.

Creating a special ambiance surrounding the euthanasia is important to some people. This may include certain religious rituals, special readings, music, photos, and anything that would be helpful to your client. It's important to normalize these wishes as, again, pet loss is not typically recognized as important as a human loss. Therefore, helping your client feel comfortable in asking for specifics such as these is very helpful.

If the pet's disease process is unpredictable, or hastens more quickly than expected, Plan B may be necessary. It will help to have this planned out ahead of time so that decisions do not need to be made under extreme emotional duress. Plan B is for an emergent situation. Helping your client identify the resources for this scenario is important.

- What close emergency hospital can you take Duke to?
- Whom would you call if he isn't able to walk? How would you manage to get him there?
- What would it be like for you if there was an emergency with Duke?

Evaluating how the emergency Plan B would impact your client is beneficial as it can sometimes clarify a client's concerns, aiding in some decision-making regarding a planned euthanasia appointment.

Body Care Decisions

Another consideration for your client is how they wish to have their pet's body cared for after its death. Depending on the circumstances surrounding the death of the pet, there may be lingering questions for the family. Some veterinary hospitals offer a postmortem study of the body, a necropsy, similar to an autopsy in human medicine. This examination can sometimes provide insight into a disease process or sudden death. Your client could talk with his/her veterinarian to determine if this option is available to them. This step may influence their choice of final body care.

In regard to caring for the body, options to consider include burial or cremation. If your client is considering burying their pet's body, it is important to discuss how a possible necropsy study may negate this option, based on hospital policies of releasing a body afterwards. Also, it is crucial to know the local ordinances as well as regulations about burying a euthanized pet. Even in urban areas, wildlife can cause considerable damage to a gravesite as well as a body. Additionally, euthanasia medications can negatively impact wildlife. It is important to evaluate these details with clients.

- If you are planning to bury at home, who will help you with that?
- With Duke's large size, how will you be able to go about digging a grave and lifting his body?
- How will it be for you to have to move and maneuver Duke's body after he's deceased?

Some pet cemeteries can facilitate burials for pets in specialized locations. This could be an option for families who wish to bury but cannot do so on their own property.

Cremation is an option in many places. If your client is considering this, encourage them to decide if they would like the cremains returned to them. Some facilities will offer a communal cremation where individual ashes are not returned to the owner. Also important to note is if their veterinarian will facilitate the transportation of the animal's body to the crematorium.

Keepsakes and Memorializing

Sometimes people wish to have keepsakes as additional reminders of their beloved pets. These can include ink or clay prints of the pet's paws, hair clippings, collars and leashes, toys, and more. You can help your client identify what is important for them to have so that they can communicate their wishes with their veterinary team.

Memorializing a pet can be a sensitive subject to contemplate. Again, as pet loss is not typically recognized as widely as human loss, you may find your client surprised that memorialization is something they can do for themselves. Normalizing this as part of their process is helpful for your client to allow themselves to choose meaningful activities to benefit their grief process.

Some ideas for memorialization are:

- Having a memorial service for the pet. This can be tailored to whatever your client envisions. They can hold it alone or they can invite friends and family to share stories, read readings, play music, and celebrate the life of their pet.
- Write and/or send an obituary for the pet. This is especially helpful when the pet is known across a community of people, alleviating the need for your client to repeatedly share the news.
- Plant a tree or bush in memory of the pet. This reminder of life and beauty can have deep meaning as the plant blooms.
- Create a memory box. Some people place mementos such as paw prints, collars, hair clippings into a shadow box as a collection of special items to keep their pet's memory close.
- Create something from the cremains. There are several options for jewelry keepsakes and lockets that will allow your client to keep a portion of their pet's ashes close to them always. There are also glass artists that can incorporate the ashes into a piece of art.
- Donate to a favorite cause in the pet's honor. Many pets are rescues and donating back to the organization or a breed-specific cause can help the pet's legacy live on.

There are many other personal choices that your client may wish to do to memorialize their pet. Acknowledging that each person will go about the loss of a pet differently and that each individual way is normal to that person will help them to develop a greater comfort level for asking what their needs are.

Creating these plans and making these many decisions ahead of time can help your clients organize their thoughts in a time before they may be overcome with emotions. This can help ensure they are able to do what they need to do for themselves emotionally when they are saying goodbye to their pets, reducing regrets later. Taking the time to evaluate these many considerations is a great service to your clients.

Case Scenarios

Case Scenario #1:

Susan Novak is a client you've seen only twice up until today's appointment. She came in today with some upsetting news. Her 8-year-old Golden Retriever, "Luke," has been diagnosed with an aggressive form of cancer. This dog means the world to Susan and her husband who consider "Luke" their "child," as they do not have human offspring. They plan their daily lives and vacations around "Luke," who goes to work with Susan and travels with them on every trip. Susan is quite distraught in your office and is not sure what to do for her family and "Luke."

Discussion Questions:

1. What strategies can you utilize to assist Susan in her anticipatory grief?
2. How can you best help Susan with quality of life concerns for "Luke"?
3. What other issues may Susan confront while making decisions for "Luke"?

Case Scenario #2:

Mark Thomas is a new client who recently lost his cat "Cricket" in a traumatic accident. "Cricket" was hit by a car after bolting from the front door of the house as Mark and his partner left for work. They rushed her to an emergency clinic, but "Cricket's" injuries were severe and would have required expensive medical interventions that Mark could not afford. The choice was made to humanely euthanize "Cricket" and end her suffering. For Mark, the guilt is crippling, and he feels that he failed "Cricket" and blames himself for her death.

Discussion Questions:

1. How can you help Mark with his acute grief?
2. What strategies can you utilize to help Mark with his feelings of guilt?
3. What other concerns would you assess that Mark may be experiencing?

References

American Pet Products Association, Inc. (2019). 2017–2018. APPA National Pet Owners Survey. Retrieved May 24, 2018, from www.americanpetproducts.org/press_industrytrends.asp

Argus Institute, College of Veterinary Medicine and Biomedical Sciences (2015). *Making decisions when your companion animal is sick* (2nd ed.). Fort Collins, CO: Colorado State University.

Cain, A. (1983). A study of pets in the family system. In A. Katcher, & A. Beck (Eds.), *New perspectives on our lives with companion animals* (pp. 72–81). Philadelphia, PA: University of Pennsylvania Press.

Cordaro, M. (2012). Pet loss and disenfranchised grief: Implications for mental health counseling practice. *Journal of Mental Health Counseling*, 34(4), 283–294. Retrieved from doi: 10.17744/mehc.34.4.41q0248450t98072

Rando, T. A. (1986). A comprehensive analysis of anticipatory grief: Perspectives, processes, promises, and problems. In T. Rando (Ed.), *Loss and anticipatory grief* (pp. 1–36). New York, NY: Lexington Books.

Walsh, F. (2009). Human–animal bonds I: The relational significance of companion animals. *Family Process*, 48(4), 462–480. Retrieved from doi: 10.1111/j.1545-5300. 2009.01296.x

17 Palliative Medicine and End of Life Care for Pets

A Primer for Mental Health Professionals

Katherine Goldberg

The death of a pet is a universal experience for those who share their lives with animals. In parallel with a rising interest in palliative medicine, hospice care, and advance-care planning within *human* medicine, increasing attention is currently being given to these issues within veterinary medicine. Given the potential for misalignment between client expectations and the marketing of services and delivery of services – particularly for vulnerable clients, accurate characterization of these services, as well as discernment between what level of care may be expected from various providers, is important.

What is Hospice?

Hospice is the philosophy of care that regards death as a natural process, prioritizes comfort and quality of life over quantity of life as death draws near. It supports the cultural and spiritual aspects of dying. Hospice, simply defined, is palliative care at the end-of-life. (Goldberg, 2016)

What is Veterinary Hospice?

There is not one single definition of veterinary hospice care, though many variations have been proposed. I use the broad definition outlined above as a framework for treatment planning within a veterinary setting and am committed to upholding it as a standard of care. It is the veterinarian's job to utilize exemplary pain and symptom management techniques to address the effects of both serious illness and its treatment. It is the mental health professional's job to attend to the human needs that arise over the course of veterinary treatment, for both clients and veterinary professionals. More important than determining *is this, or is this not "hospice,"* is a dedication to optimizing care for both animals and their human caregivers as time runs short. Most people have experienced the loss of a pet, and have had to make difficult decisions on an animal's behalf prior to and leading up to death – whether via euthanasia or unassisted death. Because euthanasia is deeply integrated into the end of life care for animals, veterinary hospice care is distinct from its human counterpart. Similarities exist in the overall philosophy of hospice, that is, respect for the family unit as "patient" in addition to the dying individual, acceptance that additional medical interventions are unlikely to change the outcome of a disease, a desire to alleviate pain and emotional suffering, and a focus on comfort and quality of life rather than aggressive treatment to extend it. Utilization of an interdisciplinary care team is also a common feature within both human and veterinary hospice. Most notably, this includes mental health professionals.

Veterinary hospice care can include some, or all, of the following:

- Goals of care conversations
- Education regarding death and the dying process
- Individualized medical care as death draws near
- Regularly scheduled home visits with the provision of pain medications and nursing care
- Provision of palliative care within a veterinary hospital
- Palliated but not intentionally hastened death
- Personalized euthanasia services (often in-home)
- Body care and ritual
- Memorialization and bereavement support
- Supportive counseling for clients provided by licensed mental health professionals

Hospice is not:

- Unassisted dying for companion animals in the name of "natural" death
- Mobile euthanasia services in the absence of other supports
- "Rescue" of geriatric animals at risk of euthanasia in shelters

Sanctuary-based care of seriously ill or geriatric companion animals, i.e., caring for many animals in one location, such as occurs with various "rescue" and non-profit animal-related organizations, must also be evaluated critically. While there are some high-quality organizations doing the work of caring for seriously ill and/or geriatric animals, many others have become overwhelmed by the financial, emotional, and time commitment involved, and still others have been subject to animal cruelty and neglect investigations. Mental health professionals who are becoming involved in this area of work need to recognize the many challenges associated with hospice for animals and decide where and how they can best contribute their expertise. Familiarity with animal-related grief and bereavement, animal neglect and abuse, the link between violence against people and animals, and compassion fatigue and conflict management are highly recommended since the overlap among these domains is significant when dealing with end of life care.

What is Palliative Care?

Palliative care, which may be provided at any time over the course of an illness for patients of any age, is a growing medical specialty that provides relief from the symptoms, pain, and stress of serious illness as well as emotional support and help navigating the healthcare system for patients and families (Goldberg, 2016). While palliative care is commonly associated with hospice, these terms are not synonymous.

What is Veterinary Palliative Care?

Palliative care as a discipline within veterinary practice is still emerging; however, principles and philosophy of care are identical to those in human medicine. Many veterinarians are already providing palliative care on a regular basis for their patients and clients and may choose to further develop this area of their practice. Others are cultivating independent practices or services within larger hospital systems dedicated solely to palliative medicine (Goldberg, 2018). Veterinarians who are currently providing exemplary palliative care include oncologists, anesthesiologists/pain specialists, sports medicine and rehabilitation veterinarians, credentialed integrative care providers (such as certified veterinary acupuncturists), and those focused on geriatric care. Social workers and other mental health professionals are important members of palliative care teams. Palliative care may be delivered at any time and is not limited to end of life situations. In a veterinary setting, palliative care may be provided to stable patients of any age, as well as seriously and chronically ill patients. Given the legal availability of euthanasia for animals, delineating "hospice" from palliative care, and/or determining which illnesses are "terminal" in patients whose lives can be ended at any time, is murky at best. It is for these reasons that thoughtful and rigorous discourse is critical (Goldberg, 2018).

What is the Current State of the Art for Veterinary Hospice and Palliative Care?

While veterinarians have historically provided many of the defining elements of hospice and palliative care, the establishment of hospice and palliative care as distinct areas of veterinary practice is a relatively recent phenomenon (Goldberg, 2016). Overall, increased attention is currently being given to end of life issues in veterinary medicine. In parallel, pet owners are increasingly seeking hospice and palliative care for their companion animals (Bishop, Long, Carlsten, Kennedy, & Shaw, 2008; Jarolim, 2014; Rich-Kern, 2015; Richtel, 2013). However, there has been limited scholarly research in these areas to date. A recent review concludes that veterinary hospice and palliative care is currently hindered by an inadequate amount of scholarly research to guide clinicians (Goldberg, 2016).

Despite this gap in the scholarly literature, there are several resources available for clients and practicing veterinarians. Currently, all end of life care provided by veterinarians falls under the jurisdiction of the American Veterinary Medical Association's (AVMA) Guidelines for Hospice Care (2011), now called (as of 2017) the Veterinary End-of-Life Care policy. Additional guidelines and position statements have been developed by other organizations (American Association of Feline Practitioners, 2014; American Association of Human Animal Bond Veterinarians, 2014; International Association for Animal Hospice and Palliative Care, 2013), and most recently, the American Animal Hospital Association in collaboration with the International Association for Animal Hospice and Palliative Care (Bishop et al., 2016). These documents outline the standards of care which should be upheld by providers of these services, and expected by clients who utilize them. Of particular note for readers is that the AVMA guidelines state, "The veterinary hospice team should be prepared to recommend that clients contact licensed mental health professionals who are trained and experienced in grief and bereavement" (AVMA, 2011).

Professional Guidelines and Training

All team members, whether veterinary or mental health professionals, should be familiar with the AVMA policy, which is under review as of this writing. Key elements of the policy include an acknowledgment that "clients facing terminal illness in companion animals may desire veterinary end-of-life care for their animals" as well as two statements with particular relevance for mental health professionals. They are: (1) "Maximizing the benefits of veterinary end-of-life care requires that any family/household members attached to the animal participate in the care of the patient," and (2) "The respectful closure of each unique human–animal bond through end-of-life services can be time-consuming for the veterinarian with regard to the medical needs of the patient and emotional needs of the client, and not all veterinarians are in a position to offer these services" (AVMA, 2011). These statements highlight the importance of client care (i.e., human support in the delivery of veterinary hospice services). Additionally, the statement regarding client participation in patient care is unique among veterinary disciplines. While client participation is desirable in all aspects of veterinary care, it is not a stated "requirement" for optimal veterinary care. Mental health professionals are in a good position to contribute their expertise and experience to this unique aspect of veterinary service provision.

It is my belief that comprehensive hospice and palliative care (for people or animals) simply cannot take place without the involvement of mental health professionals. Minimally, this occurs in veterinary medicine via referral to licensed professionals who have agreed to take referrals from the veterinary practice, *and* are skilled in the field of human–animal relationships. In its most progressive form, licensed mental health professionals are integrated into veterinary practices in the way social workers are integrated into human hospital systems. Due to the positive impact that veterinary social workers have had, programs have been established in a handful of large referral hospitals and the development of additional programs is underway. The model which is currently the standard of care for private practice social work program implementation, as well as supervision and training of masters-level social work interns in these settings, was developed by Sandra Brackenridge, LCSW. Among licensed mental health professionals, social workers have particular training and expertise in macro-level interventions, program development, organizational leadership, community organizing, and program evaluation – all of which have the potential to benefit veterinary hospice and palliative care services immensely.

Mental health professionals are encouraged to pursue as much high-quality continuing education as possible in relevant areas to enhance their understanding of the issues that arise in veterinary hospice and palliative care settings. This includes presentations at social work, medical, and veterinary conferences, as well as self-study of relevant literature. Given that these areas are continuing to emerge, it is important to be resourceful in pursuit of additional learning opportunities. A top recommendation for gaining familiarity and training in hospice care delivery is to become a trained human hospice volunteer. Part of the Medicare Hospice Benefit of 1982, the expansion of Medicare that provided for hospice services, is a mandate for volunteer hours in hospice organizations, which means that these organizations are providing comprehensive training for community members who wish to become volunteers. Volunteers obtain training in the philosophy and delivery of hospice care, and gain comfort working with the interdisciplinary care team. This is step one. Familiarity with veterinary practice settings is the second step, with knowledge and skills obtained in the human hospice environment being judiciously applied to animal patients and their caregivers. This includes recognizing the essential differences between human and veterinary hospice care and developing a keen ability to discern between interventions that may *not* be appropriate for both settings.

Unique to the Veterinary Profession: Euthanasia, Responsibility, and Judgment

Arguably, the most fundamental difference between human death and companion animal death is the intentional ending of our companion animals' lives via euthanasia. Precise statistics regarding euthanasia versus natural death for companion animals are unknown; however, veterinarians will tell you that euthanasia is the mode of death for the vast majority of their patients. Even among hospice veterinarians, who are comfortable facilitating palliated dying experiences without the use of euthanasia, "natural" dying is the exception rather than the rule. The dominant paradigm of death and dying within veterinary medicine is via euthanasia (Dickinson, Roof, & Roof, 2010, 2011; Epstein et al., 2005; Hart, Hart, & Mader, 1990; Hartnack, Springer, Pittavino, & Grimm, 2016; Lagoni, 2011; Leary, Underwood, Anthony, & Cartner, 2013; Manette, 2004; McMullen, Clark, & Robertson, 2001; Morris, 2012; Patricia Morris, 2009, 2012; Rollin, 2009, 2011; Sanders, 1995; Schneider, 1996; Stull, 2013; Villalobos & Kaplan, 2008; Yeates, 2010). The impact of this reality on client experiences cannot be overstated.

No discussion of veterinary hospice and palliative care is complete, therefore, without acknowledgment that companion animal loss is most likely a loss in which we humans have a great responsibility. Euthanasia is covered in depth elsewhere in this book; however, a brief discussion will follow here in the context of hospice and palliative care provision.

Many veterinary clients are not opposed to their pet dying, per se, but rather their role and responsibility in the death. A common phrase from clients is some version of the following, "*I just wish I would come downstairs one morning and find her dead. It would be sad, but at least I wouldn't have to make the decision.*" For people who have accepted that the end of their pet's life is coming, it is often the decision-making process surrounding euthanasia that is most distressing. Certainly, arriving at acceptance is often its own challenge, but the process of determining the time and manner of death is significant. This process is itself a significant part of hospice and palliative care for animals. Social workers and other licensed mental health professionals can utilize their skills to help facilitate this.

Euthanasia has been identified as an "important and disturbing issue for many pet owners" (Adams, Bonnett, & Meek, 2000, p. 1308). The commonly asked question, "*When is it time?*" itself implies that there is a "right" (and therefore, also a "wrong") time to end a pet's life. We do not intentionally end the lives of human family members as a routine part of their medical care. To do so for our beloved pets is often wrought with confusion, anxiety, guilt and stress unlike anything we have experienced before (Adams et al., 2000; Carmack, 1985; Cordaro, 2012; Cowles, 1985; Fernandez-Mehler, Gloor, Sager, Lewis, & Glaus, 2013; Gosse & Barnes, 1994; P. Morris, 2012; Tzivian, Friger, & Kushnir, 2014; Wrobel & Dye, 2003). It is important for mental health professionals to appreciate this unique aspect of pet death so they can understand their clients' grief experiences (which are sometimes confusing and surprising even to the client), and provide appropriate support.

Clients who have *not* chosen euthanasia as a mode of dying for their pet may be experiencing their own particular struggle, in that they may be facing judgment for the fact that they did not euthanize. This occurs more commonly in "hospice" settings, wherein clients may not choose euthanasia in the time-frame which has been recommended by the veterinarian, or not choose it at all. A common myth of veterinary hospice is that euthanasia is withheld, contributing to animal suffering. This is certainly not the case with hospice done *well*, but it is a risk that must be acknowledged and addressed.

Many clients will comment on the calm, peaceful quality of dying following a good euthanasia experience for a pet and say something along the lines of, "*I wish we had this for people.*" The distinctions between euthanasia for people (illegal throughout the United States) and physician-assisted dying (legal in a handful of states and steadily increasing) *must* be front and center in any discussion regarding end of life care for both people and animals. Physician-assisted dying is currently limited to patients who are mentally competent, decisionally capable, and can self-administer life-ending medication. This is hardly a description of euthanasia for companion animals. It is essential to recognize that while the "pleasant" death experience for animal patients (and human witnesses) may be internalized by clients as a possible model of care for people, no other aspects of the veterinary euthanasia experience have an equivalent in human medicine. It is an understatement to say that the ethical, legal, and financial issues are quite distinct. Suffice it to say, assisted death is complicated, and beliefs about it take many forms. The veterinary profession is slowly acknowledging that it cannot expect all clients to conform to its dominant belief system regarding euthanasia as the only acceptable standard of care for companion animal death.

Euthanasia is a tool and is often the best way to alleviate suffering in animals, when appropriate. But it is not the only way for animals to die humanely. Mental health professionals are well-served to know that veterinarians have minimal, if any, training in attending to animal deaths other than those facilitated by euthanasia (Bittel & Armer, 2011; Christiansen, Kristensen, Lassen, & Sandøe, 2016; Dickinson & Paul, 2014; Dickinson et al., 2011; Goldberg, 2015, 2016; Villalobos & Kaplan, 2008). Most have had limited exposure to reflective practice regarding their own beliefs regarding end of life issues in veterinary school. Therefore, it may be the case that the client–veterinarian relationship becomes strained during end of life decision-making if goals and values do not align.

Clients may also experience relational strain with family members and friends, who actively or passively disagree with the decisions that were made on behalf of the pet. It is often the case that clients who do not euthanize their pets are judged harshly for "letting them suffer." This experience may further isolate clients and complicate their grief experience. Mental health professionals can provide support by simply bringing awareness of this issue into the therapeutic relationship, as well as asking open-ended questions regarding the client's experience with family, friends, and colleagues following the death of a pet.

Goals of Care Conversations

Palliative care providers know that the likelihood of patients and families receiving care that is consistent with their preferences depends on whether a Goals of Care (GOC) conversation occurs with their health care team. They also know that this conversation should not wait until the last days or hours of life to take place. GOC conversations are essential, considering the evidence from human medicine suggesting that patients not only receive care inconsistent with their goals and values at the end of life, but also care that does not address, and may actually result in, considerable suffering (Gawande, 2016; Institute of Medicine, 2015; Singer et al., 2015). Similar concerns are now emerging in veterinary practice.

Research in human medicine regarding end of life preferences consistently demonstrates positive outcomes from early GOC discussions (Bernacki & Block, 2013, 2014; Bernacki, Block, & American College of Physicians High Value Care Task Force, 2014; You et al., 2015). However, deficits in the content and timing of these discussions have been identified (Bernacki, Hutchings, & Vick, 2015). Deficits relevant to veterinary practice include conversations occurring too late, occurring when patients are in crisis, or when clinicians who know the patient are not available. Additionally, physicians tend to focus on choices regarding procedures (i.e., resuscitation code status, mechanical ventilation) rather than on goals and values (Bernacki et al., 2015). Finally, "clinicians are underprepared and undertrained to conduct high-quality end of life conversations and tend to avoid them" (Block, 2002; Buss et al., 2011 cited in Bernacki et al., 2015). Learning from the human medical profession regarding serious illness communication is essential if we are to provide high-quality veterinary care in a goal-concordant way. Support *following* the death of a pet is important, but it is not the only opportunity to support clients as they face the final phase of their pets' lives. Variables found to increase the intensity of both uncomplicated and complicated grief reactions following pet loss include an attachment to the pet, level of social support, and preferences regarding means of death/euthanasia (McCutcheon, 2004). These would all be explored in a GOC conversation.

The Serious Illness Conversation Guide (SICG) is a tool designed to help optimize GOC conversations. Developed by Ariadne Labs, under the leadership of Drs. Susan Block, Rachelle Bernacki, Atul Gawande, and others, the guide is currently in use and has been the focus of a recent cluster randomized controlled trial (Bernacki et al., 2015). The SICG has been modified for veterinary use (Goldberg, 2015). This user-friendly scalable tool provides veterinarians and their teams with a guide to help with some of the most difficult conversations that arise in practice. It provides a basic framework that may be used in a variety of settings to help facilitate serious illness and end of life conversations for veterinary patients. Understanding the nuances of client beliefs and preferences enables clinicians to provide care that is concordant with individual goals and values. Goal-concordant care is vital in veterinary medicine, specifically as relates to end of life choices, since it has been shown that reactions to pet death are more likely to be associated with variables related to the client than with factors related to the pet (Adams et al., 2000). Certainly, increased palliative care training for veterinarians is essential, but utilizing an interprofessional care team will increase the likelihood of success. Mental health professionals' involvement in GOC conversations in the veterinary setting has the potential to transform pet loss support and pet-related bereavement.

Future Directions

Hospice and palliative care, whether for human or animal patients, needs mental health professionals as part of the team. Whether this occurs via referral, or integrated partnerships, the benefits of interprofessional collaboration cannot be overstated. People are seeking comprehensive serious illness and end of life care for their companion animals in ways increasingly similar to corresponding care for people. The landscape of this trend is in flux, but interest is increasing steadily. Mental health professionals are sure to find a role, if not in a veterinary hospital directly, then in their own practice settings as they support people who are experiencing challenges associated with end of life issues for their pets.

Case Scenarios

Case Scenario #1: Polly

Polly, a 5-year-old spayed female Golden Retriever, presented to the emergency room (ER) with acute collapse and was diagnosed with metastatic hemangiosarcoma, an aggressive cancer, within minutes of evaluation. Euthanasia was recommended by the ER veterinarian. This recommendation was very poorly received by Patti's owners, who felt "bullied" into euthanasia and judged by the veterinary care team for refusing. They report that no options other than euthanasia were presented.

Polly's owners are a White, married, heterosexual couple in their mid-40s. The husband is an ER physician. One year prior to presentation with Polly, their other dog was hit by a car and hospitalized in the Intensive Care Unit for several weeks, including being on a ventilator for several days, from which he was successfully weaned and discharged from the hospital. This care was provided at the same referral hospital where they brought Polly, and the clients were disappointed that the staff did not recall the prolonged and expensive care that they had pursued previously. They felt "insulted" by the recommendation for immediate euthanasia and brought Polly home for hospice care.

Palliative support was initiated following a hospice intake evaluation, which included Western medications and Chinese herbs for pain, nausea, and regulation of coagulation, a comprehensive Goals of Care conversation, establishment of a crisis/emergency plan, emotional support for clients, discussion regarding clients' preferred death plan, and communication with the clients' family veterinarian. Acupuncture was also initiated and continued at regular intervals dictated by symptom burden. Polly maintained an excellent quality of life for six weeks following her diagnosis. A hospice-assisted death was achieved in-home, without euthanasia. The clients were immensely grateful for their experience. They have since become vocal advocates for this type of care and have shared their experience with their family veterinarian and veterinary students in a palliative care course at a veterinary teaching institution.

Discussion Questions:

1. What steps would you need to take to facilitate this kind of experience for clients?
2. What information would you need to optimize the support that you, as a mental health professional, can provide, and how can you obtain it?
3. If you are communicating with a veterinarian (or working in a veterinary hospital), how much information can you share with her/him? How much information can the veterinarian share with you?
4. How does prior experience with human and animal illness and death affect current decision-making?
5. What role did client participation in the veterinary school course play (for the clients), and how is this similar/different from pet loss support groups?
6. How does the information in this chapter help you understand a case like this?

Case Scenario #2: Olivia

Olivia is a 13-year-old spayed female Great Dane mix. She has a combination of osteoarthritis (inflammatory joint disease) and degenerative myelopathy (a progressive neurologic condition) which causes her pain with poor mobility. Her neurologic function is variable but is declining over time. Due to her large size, poor mobility is particularly life-limiting and creates significant caregiving issues.

Olivia's owner is a single, White female in her mid-50s with generalized anxiety and a complex trauma history, most recently including a physically and emotionally abusive marriage. She left this relationship with Olivia, who has been her constant companion ever since. Because she lives alone, Olivia's owner is concerned about being able to manage her care if her mobility declines significantly, or if another crisis occurs. Additionally, Olivia is protective of her and has been aggressive to people when they have attempted to care for Olivia. This became an issue recently, when the client was hospitalized and Olivia bit the neighbor who was taking care of her.

A palliative care consultation was sought to onboard in-home care, and establish a relationship with the palliative care veterinarian proactively. Pain management and Goals of Care conversations, as well as emotional support for the client, were the mainstays of palliative management for greater than 1 year; Olivia was euthanized in-home when her mobility worsened and the client recognized that avoiding a crisis was more important for her than making sure that she did not euthanize "when Olivia still had more time to live."

Discussion Questions:

1. What impact do you think this client's trauma history had on her relationship with Olivia?
2. How can you, as a mental health professional, help veterinarians provide trauma-informed care?
3. If you were this client's therapist, working outside of the veterinary profession, how might you help her cope with the impending loss of Olivia?
4. What do you need to know about Olivia's medical situation to be helpful in this case?
5. What do you make of the euthanasia decision around crisis avoidance versus maximizing length of life?

References

Adams, C. L., Bonnett, B. N., & Meek, A. H. (2000). Predictors of owner response to companion animal death in 177 clients from 14 practices in Ontario. *Journal of the American Veterinary Medical Association*, 217(9), 1303–1309. doi: 10.2460/javma.2000.217.1303

American Association of Feline Practitioners. (2014). AAFP position statement: Hospice care for cats. Retrieved from http://ac.els-cdn.com/S1098612X10002573/1-s2.0-S1098612X10002573-main.pdf?_tid=a4ee3bc0-a804-11e5-89a4-00000aacb35f&acdnat=1450717540_bb2437618b0d47d7de4c0ccfd2381142

American Association of Human Animal Bond Veterinarians. (2014). Position Statement: End of life hospice care. Retrieved from http://aahabv.org/end-of-life-hospice-care/

AVMA. (2011). Guidelines for veterinary hospice care. Retrieved from www.avma.org/KB/Policies/Pages/Guidelines-for-Veterinary-Hospice-Care.aspx

Bernacki, R. E., & Block, S. D. (2013). Serious illness communications checklist. *AMA Journal of Ethics*, 15(12), 1045–1049. doi: 10.1001/virtualmentor.2013.15.12.stas1-1312

Bernacki, R. E., & Block, S. D. (2014). Communication about serious illness care goals. *JAMA Internal Medicine*, 174(12), 1994. doi: 10.1001/jamainternmed.2014.5271

Bernacki, R. E., Block, S. D., & American College of Physicians High Value Care Task Force. (2014). Communication about serious illness care goals: a review and synthesis of best practices. *JAMA Internal Medicine*, 174(12), 1994–2003. doi: 10.1001/jamainternmed.2014.5271

Bernacki, R., Hutchings, M., Vick, J. (2015). Development of the Serious Illness Care Program: a randomised controlled trial of a palliative care communication intervention. *BMJ Open*, 5, e009032. doi: 10.1136/bmjopen-2015-009032

Bishop, G. A., Cooney, K., Cox, S., Downing, R., Mitchener, K. L., Shanan, A., Soares, N., Stevens, B., & Wynn, T. (2016). AAHA/IAAHPC End-of-life care guidelines for dogs and cats. *Journal of the American Animal Hospital Association*, 52(6), 341–356. Retrieved from www.aaha.org/graphics/original/professional/resources/guidelines/eolc/iteolc_toolkit.pdf

Bishop, G. A., Long, C. C., Carlsten, K. S., Kennedy, K. C., & Shaw, J. R. (2008). The Colorado State University Pet Hospice Program: End-of-life care for pets and their families. *Journal of Veterinary Medical Education*, 35(4), 525–531. doi: 10.3138/jvme.35.4.525

Bittel, E., & Armer, J. (2011). When is end of life care for animals truly hospice? *The Latham Letter*, (Fall), 221–234. Retrieved from www.Latham.org

Block, S. D. (2002). Medical education in end-of-life care: The status of reform. *Journal of Palliative Medicine*, 5(2), 243–248. doi: 10.1089/109662102753641214

Buss, M. K., Lessen, D. S., Sullivan, A. M., Von Roenn, J., Arnold, R. M., & Block, S. D. (2011). Hematology/oncology fellows' training in palliative care. *Cancer*, 117(18), 4304–4311. doi: 10.1002/cncr.25952

Carmack, B. J. (1985). The effects on family members and functioning after the death of a pet. *Marriage & Family Review*, 8, 149–161. doi: 10.1300/J002v08n03_11

Christiansen, S. B., Kristensen, A. T., Lassen, J., & Sandøe, P. (2016). Veterinarians' role in clients' decision-making regarding seriously ill companion animal patients. *Acta Veterinaria Scandinavica*, 58(1), 30. doi: 10.1186/s13028-016-0211-x

Cordaro, M. (2012). Pet loss and disenfranchised grief: Implications for mental health counseling practice. *Journal of Mental Health Counseling*, 34, 283–294. Retrieved from http://search.ebscohost.com/login.aspx?direct=true&db=a9h&AN=82398411&site=ehost-live

Cowles, K. V. (1985). The death of a pet: Human responses to the breaking of the bond. *Marriage & Family Review*, 8(3–4), 135–148. doi: /10.1300/J002v08n03_10

Dickinson, G. E., & Paul, E. S. (2014). UK veterinary schools: Emphasis on end-of-life issues. *The Veterinary Record*, 174(7), 170. doi: 10.1136/vr.102152

Dickinson, G. E., Roof, P. D., & Roof, K. W. (2010). End of life issues in United States veterinary medicine schools. *Society and Animals*, 18, 152–162. doi: 10.1163/156853010X492006

Dickinson, G. E., Roof, P. D., & Roof, K. W. (2011). A survey of veterinarians in the US: Euthanasia and other end-of-life issues. *Anthrozoös*, 24(2), 167–174. doi: 10.2752/175303711X12998632257666

Epstein, M., Kuehn, N. F., Landsberg, G., Lascelles, B. D. X., Marks, S. L., Schaedler, J. M., & Tuzio, H. (2005). AAHA senior care guidelines for dogs and cats. *Journal of the American Animal Hospital Association*, 41(6), 81–91. doi: 41/2/81 [pii]

Fernandez-Mehler, P., Gloor, P., Sager, E., Lewis, F. I., & Glaus, T. M. (2013). Veterinarians' role for pet owners facing pet loss. *Veterinary Record*, 172(21), 555. doi: 10.1136/vr.101154

Gawande, A. (2016). Quantity and Quality of Life. *JAMA*, 315(3), 267. doi: 10.1001/jama.2015.19206

Goldberg, K. J. (2015). Letter to the editor: In-home euthanasia versus hospice. *Journal of the American Veterinary Medical Association*, 246(4), 401–402. doi: 10.1016/0002-9610(92)90118-B

Goldberg K. J. (2015). *Serious Veterinary Illness Conversation Guide 2015*. Modified from the *Serious Illness Conversation Guide*, © Ariadne Labs: A Joint Center for Health Systems Innovation (www.ariadnelabs.org) at Brigham and Women's Hospital and the Harvard T.H. Chan School of Public Health, in collaboration with Dana-Farber Cancer Institute. Licensed under the Creative Commons Attribution – NonCommercial-ShareAlike 4.0 International License, http://creativecommons.org/licenses/by-nc-sa/4.0/

Goldberg, K. J. (2016). Veterinary hospice and palliative care: a comprehensive review of the literature. *Veterinary Record*, 178(15), 369–374. doi: 10.1136/vr.103459

Goldberg, K. J. (2018, June). Palliative care in veterinary practice: Principles and practical tools. Proceedings for the American College of Veterinary Internal Medicine Forum, Seattle, WA.

Gosse, G. H., & Barnes, M. J. (1994). Human grief resulting from the death of a pet. *Anthrozoös*, 7(2), 103–112. doi: 10.2752/089279394787001970

Hart, L. A., Hart, B. L., & Mader, B. (1990). Humane euthanasia and companion animal death: caring for the animal, the client, and the veterinarian. *Journal of the American Veterinary Medical Association*, 197(10), 1292–1299.

Hartnack, S., Springer, S., Pittavino, M., & Grimm, H. (2016). Attitudes of Austrian veterinarians towards euthanasia in small animal practice: impacts of age and gender on views on euthanasia. *BMC Veterinary Research*. doi: 10.1186/s12917-016-0649-0

Institute of Medicine. (2015). Dying in America: Improving quality and honoring individual preferences near the end of life. Washington, DC: The National Academies Press. doi: 10.17226/18748

International Association for Animal Hospice and Palliative Care. (2013). Animal hospice and palliative care guidelines. Retrieved from www.iaahpc.org/images/IAAHPCGUIDELINESMarch14.pdf

Jarolim, E. (2014, May). AAHA trends: Spreading the word on hospice care. *American Animal Hospital Association (AAHA), Trends Magazine*, (May), 39–42.

Lagoni, L. (2011). Family-present euthanasia: Protocols for planning and preparing clients for the death of a pet. In C. Blazina (Ed.), *The psychology of the human–animal bond* (pp. 181–202). New York, NY: Springer Science+Business Media, LLC. doi: 10.1007/978-1-4419-9761-6

Leary, S., Underwood, W., Anthony, R., & Cartner, S. (2013). AVMA guidelines for the euthanasia of animals: 2013 edition. American Veterinary Medical Association. Retrieved from www.avma.org/kb/policies/documents/euthanasia.pdf

Manette, C. S. (2004). JAVMA Commentary: A reflection on the ways veterinarians cope with the death, euthanasia, and slaughter of animals. *Journal of the American Veterinary Medical Association*, 225(1), 34–38. doi: 10.2460/javma.2004.225.34

McCutcheon, K. A. (2004). Predictors of complicated and uncomplicated grief after the death of a companion animal. York University. Retrieved from http://search.proquest.com.proxy.library.cornell.edu/docview/305111891?pq-origsite=summon&accountid=10267

McMullen, S. L., Clark, W. T., & Robertson, I. D. (2001). Reasons for the euthanasia of dogs and cats in veterinary practices. *Australian Veterinary Practitioner*, 31(2), 80–84. doi: 10.1136/vr.143.4.114

Morris, P. (2009). Encounters with "death work" in veterinary medicine: An ethnographic exploration of the medical practice of euthanasia. Retrieved from http://ezproxy.nottingham.ac.uk/login??url=http://search.proquest.com/docview/304966158?accountid=8018%5Cnhttp://sfx.nottingham.ac.uk/sfx_local/?url_ver=Z39.88-2004&rft_val_fmt=info:ofi/fmt:kev:mtx:dissertation&genre=dissertations+&+theses&sid=ProQ:ProQuest

Morris, P. (2012). Blue Juice: Euthanasia in veterinary medicine. Temple University Press. Retrieved from https://books.google.com/books?hl=en&lr=&id=7TwpBO0ugNMC&pgis=1

Morris, P. (2012). Managing pet owners' guilt and grief in veterinary euthanasia encounters. *Journal of Contemporary Ethnography*, 41(3), 337–365. doi: 10.1177/0891241611435099

Rich-Kern, S. (2015, April 17). Peaceful passings: hospice, palliative care for pets grows in demand. *New Hampshire Business Review*. Retrieved from http://bi.galegroup.com.proxy.library.cornell.edu/essentials/article/GALE%7CA412555672?u=nysl_sc_cornl&sid=summon&userGroup=nysl_sc_cornl

Richtel, M. (2013). All dogs may go to heaven. These days, some go to hospice. *The New York Times*. Retrieved from www.nytimes.com/2013/12/01/business/all-dogs-may-go-to-heaven-these-days-some-go-to-hospice.html?_r=0

Rollin, B. E. (2009). Ethics and euthanasia. *The Canadian Veterinary Journal. La Revue Vétérinaire Canadienne*, 50(10), 1081–1086. Retrieved from www.pubmedcentral.nih.gov/articlerender.fcgi?artid=2748292&tool=pmcentrez&rendertype=abstract

Rollin, B. E. (2011). Euthanasia, moral stress, and chronic Illness in veterinary medicine. *Veterinary Clinics of North America – Small Animal Practice*, 41(3), 651–659. doi: 10.1016/j.cvsm.2011.03.005

Sanders, C. R. (1995). Killing with kindness: Veterinary euthanasia and the social construction of personhood. *Sociological Forum*, 10(2), 195–214. doi: 10.1007/BF02095958

Schneider, B. J. (1996). Euthanasia and the veterinarian. *The Canadian Veterinary Journal. La Revue Vétérinaire Canadienne*, 37(4), 217–218. Retrieved from www.pubmedcentral.nih.gov/articlerender.fcgi?artid=1576349&tool=pmcentrez&rendertype=abstract

Singer, A. E., Meeker, D., Teno, J. M., Lynn, J., Lunney, J. R., & Lorenz, K. A. (2015). Symptom trends in the last year of life from 1998 to 2010: A cohort study. *Annals of Internal Medicine*, 162(3), 175–183.

Stull, C. L. (2013). Death and euthanasia as contemporary topics in equine curricula. *Journal of Equine Veterinary Science*, 33(5), 309–314. doi: 10.1016/j.jevs.2013.03.183

Tzivian, L., Friger, M., & Kushnir, T. (2014). Grief and bereavement of Israeli dog owners: exploring short-term phases pre- and post-euthanization. *Death Studies*, 38(1–5). doi: 10.1080/07481187.2012.738764

Villalobos, A., & Kaplan, L. (2008). *Canine and feline geriatric oncology: Honoring the human–animal bond*. Oxford, UK: Blackwell Publishing, Ltd. doi: 10.1002/9780470344446

Wrobel, T. A., & Dye, A. L. (2003). Grieving pet death: Normative, gender, and attachment issues. *OMEGA: The Journal of Death and Dying*, 47(4), 385–393. doi: 10.2190/QYV5-LLJ1-T043-U0F9

Yeates, J. (2010). Ethical aspects of euthanasia of owned animals. *Practice*, 32(2), 70–73. doi: 10.1136/inp.c516

You, J. J., Downar, J., Fowler, R. A., Lamontagne, F., Ma, I. W. Y., Jayaraman, D., Kryworuchko, J., Strachan, P. H., Ilan, R., Nijjar, A. P., Neary, J., Shik, J., Brazil, K., Patel, A., Wiebe, K., Albert, M., Palepu, A., Nouvet, E., des Ordons, A. R., Sharma, N., Abdul-Razzak, A, Jiang, X., Day, A., & Heyland, D. K. (2015). Barriers to goals of care discussions with seriously ill hospitalized patients and their families. *JAMA Internal Medicine*, 175(4), 549. doi: .1001/jamainternmed.2014.7732

18 Therapeutic Continuing Bond Interventions with Bereaved Companion Animal Owners

Cori Bussolari and Wendy Packman

Introduction

The death of a companion animal (CA)[1] can be a heartbreaking experience, similar to the death of a human. In our clinical practice, we hear bereaved CA owners say things like, "I'm in such pain because of the loss that I can hardly function." "The loss of Ringo has been the hardest experience of my life," or, in regard to veterinary euthanasia, "I feel so terrible and hate myself because I couldn't do anything for them." Continuing bonds (CB) (i.e., dreams, fond memories, rituals, memorials) can be an adaptive means of coping and grief processing following the loss of a beloved attachment relationship. In this chapter, we examine how CB can be a source of positive coping after the death of a CA and a means for bereaved owners to stay connected to their CA in a healthy way. This will include a discussion about the human–animal bond and grief, disenfranchised grief, social constraints, and CB. We will then discuss clinical intervention strategies, as well as provide pet bereavement vignettes.

Human–Companion Animal Bond and Grief

Many authors have written about the strength and meaning of human–CA relationships (e.g., Carmack, 2003; Toray, 2004). The depth of responses to CA loss is often based on the strength and longevity of relationships individuals had with their pets. In the case of CA loss, many people may not perceive the death of a CA as a cause for intense grief, yet research has clearly demonstrated strong ties between pets and humans and profound reactions to loss (Archer & Winchester, 1994; Carmack, 2003). CAs are described as having the ability to elicit an emotional response from humans. They are described as family members by a large percentage of CA owners (Cowles, 1985; Toray, 2004) and even as a surrogate child (Vevver, 2008). Moreover, humans tend to interpret CAs as having unconditional positive regard for them (Archer, 1997). Recent studies have shown that when humans interact with their dogs, their oxytocin levels increase, mimicking the bonding that occurs between mother and baby (Nagasawa, Mogi, & Kikusui, 2009).

People become emotionally close to their CAs, accept responsibility for them, and grieve deeply when their CA dies (Field, Orsini, Gavish, & Packman, 2009). Research has consistently demonstrated that the grief following the death of a CA can equal or exceed the loss of a beloved human (Field, et al., 2009; Gerwolls & Labott, 1994; Habarth et al., 2017; Packman, Field, Carmack, & Ronan, 2011). Carmack (2003) described several features of CA owner grief: anger, often directed towards the veterinarian; difficulties with concentration; and avoidance of painful reminders. Weissman (1990–1991) noted that the extent of grief in bereaved CA owners may approach clinical proportions, especially in individuals who "valued their pets more than friends or relatives" (p. 246).

Indeed, the grief following the death of a CA manifests itself in similar ways to that experienced after human loss in terms of sleep disruption, and social and psychological challenges (Archer & Winchester, 1994; Habarth et al., 2017; Packman et al., 2011). In one study, Gerwolls and Labott (1994) assessed whether the loss of a CA was different from the loss of a human companion (parent, child, or spouse). At two and eight weeks post-loss, the grief score (Grief Experiences Inventory) of those who had lost a CA were similar to those who had lost a human companion. Importantly, at six months post-loss, there were no statistically significant differences in grief scores between the two groups. In our more recent CA loss research, we have also found scores well above the mean on a measure of complicated grief (ICG; Prigerson & Jacobs, 2001), comparable to human loss (Packman, Field, Carmack, & Ronen, 2011). However, in the case of CA loss, many people may not perceive the death of a CA as a cause for intense grief. Yet, research has clearly demonstrated strong ties between CAs and humans and profound reactions to the loss (Archer & Winchester, 1994; Carmack, 2003).

Disenfranchised Grief and Social Constraints

Disenfranchised grief occurs when a death is not validated or acknowledged by our social connections. Thus, when a person experiences a grief reaction, yet there is no social recognition or validation that the person has a right to grieve or a claim for social support (Doka, 2008), their experience is disenfranchised. Doka (2008) has proposed several categories of disenfranchised grief. Certain circumstances surrounding the death may disenfranchise grief or the ways a person grieves may not be recognized (Doka, 2008). This perspective has been described in relation to CA loss (Packman, et al., 2011; Packman, Carmack, & Ronen, 2012). Packman, et al., (2012) write that the death of a CA may not be fully recognized or validated as a significant loss, resulting in grievers feeling isolated and lacking in support. Statements such as "You can always get another one" or "it's just an animal" add to bereaved CA owners' experiences of isolation and distress (Toray, 2004). In fact, encouraging pet owners to get a new CA soon after a death is commonplace (Podrazik, Shackford, Becker, & Heckert, 2000) and, in most cases, inappropriate.

Disenfranchised grief has been identified as a complicating factor in bereavement (Rando, 1993). Disenfranchised grief usually precludes social support – thus, although the griever has experienced a profound loss, the "grief may have to remain private" (Doka, 2008, p. 235). The bereaved may not be entitled to time off from work nor receive sympathy from others, and therapeutic rituals may be unavailable (Doka, 2008). Neimeyer and Jordan (2002) relate the concept of disenfranchised grief within a broader pattern of empathic failure. They describe such a failure as one that "subtly or obviously invalidates the bereaved person, family, or community's distinctive narrative of the loss" (p. 95). Empathic failure frequently occurs within the social support systems of those grieving the death of a CA. Empathic failure, or "the failure of one part of a system to understand the meaning and experience of another" (Neimeyer & Jordan, 2002, p. 96), exists in which people do not understand the depth of the human–CA relationship. Their social system also fails to understand the meaning and nature of the human–pet relationship which is typically based on unconditional love, continuing presence, support and consistent companionship.

The authors have observed that social constraints are a key component of disenfranchisement within the CA loss experience (Habarth et al., 2017; Packman et al., 2011), even though the frequency of CA deaths is high (Hewson, 2014). Juth, Smyth, Carey, and Lepore (2015) indicate that social constraints reflect the perceived ability of those in one's social network to provide support, and not solely the number of contacts in one's network. To our knowledge, Packman et al., 2011 and Habarth et al., 2017 were the first to explore social constraints in a CA loss sample. Their findings suggest that social constraints are associated with negative psychosocial outcomes such as depression, anxiety, somatization and functional impairment. In addition, it appears that self-compassion buffers the effects of perceived lack of support on depression symptoms.

The Concept of Continuing Bonds with Bereaved CA Owners

The bereavement literature has recently focused on the function of a "continuing bond" in relation to coping (Field & Friedrichs, 2004; Field, Gao, & Paderna, 2005; Stroebe, Gergen, Gergen & Stroebe, 1992) and adaptation following the death of a loved one (Klass, Silverman, & Nickman, 1996). Studies suggest that an emotional connection can be sustained, even though death brings about permanent physical separation (Field, Nichols, Holen, & Horowitz, 1999). According to Field (2008), the resolution of grief involves "a reorganization of the relationship with the deceased" (p. 115) while acknowledging that the loved one has died. The

CB theory (Klass, et al., 1996) is in contrast to the Freudian notion that resolution of grief involves a detachment or termination of the relationship with the deceased (Freud, 1917/1957). Thus, resolving grief does not necessarily involve ending a relationship, but instead involves a restructuring which can continue throughout a lifetime (Field, 2008).

The use of CB theory regarding CA loss was not reported in the professional literature until 2009. Field, Orsini, Gavish, and Packman (2009) were the first to investigate the role of CB in CA loss. They identified four CB expressions (fond memories, sharing of those memories, legacy of the deceased, and use of photographs of the deceased), all of which underscored that an attachment to a CA continues after the death, in a similar way to that found in human loss. In a later CA loss study, Packman et al. (2011) examined and quantified 12 types of CB expressions that occur among bereaved CA owners:

- A continuing connection (sense of deceased CA's presence)
- Belongings (use of deceased pet's belongings)
- Associated places (drawn to places associated with deceased CA)
- Focus on fond memories
- Dreams involving CA
- Thoughts of being reunited with CA
- Living up to ideals or wishes of CA
- Making everyday decisions based on CA's preferences
- Reminiscing with others about CA
- Memorials and rituals (Organizing special events to commemorate CA
- Intrusive thoughts (mistaking other sounds or sights for CAs)
- Lessons learned from CA (positive lasting influence of CA)

Participants reported a tendency to experience CB as more comforting than distressing (Packman et al., 2011). The extent to which they endorsed each of the CB expressions was comparable to that found in a spousal loss sample (Field & Frederichs, 2004). The results of the pilot study confirmed that individuals experienced dimensions of CB following the death of their CA and emphasized that the majority of bereaved pet owners maintain ongoing, meaningful ties with their deceased CA.

Building upon that research, Packman, Carmack, and Ronen (2011–2012) used qualitative methodology to evaluate specific connections that the bereaved maintained with their CA. Findings complimented the quantitative research findings (Packman, et al., 2011). Participants stated that they were often reticent to share their CB experiences with others, as they did not feel as though they would be validated. Drawing from the same pilot study, Packman et al. (2017) examined the relationship among projective drawings and psychosocial adjustment following pet loss. Drawings were developed and combined with a clinical interview and standardized questionnaires of mental health symptoms. The authors found that utilizing projective drawings helped the bereaved create and broaden their stories, especially regarding examples of their memories, dreams, or experiences with their CAs that they might not have expressed because of feelings of disenfranchisement.

More recently, the authors have published several larger empirical studies regarding CB and CA loss (Bussolari et al., 2017; Habarth, et al., 2017; Packman et al., 2014; Packman, Bussolari, Katz, Carmack, & Field, 2016). Packman, et al., (2014) qualitatively investigated grief reactions within a cross-cultural sample (United States and French Canada) of bereaved CA owners. Four major themes emerged from the data: lack of validation and support; intensity of the grief and loss experience; strength of the human–CA attachment bond; and CB to cope with loss. Results supported the adaptiveness of CB as well as both its comforting and distressing aspects, similar to previous research (Packman, et al., 2011). Packman, et al. (2016) later qualitatively investigated post-traumatic growth experienced (PTG) by bereaved CA owners. In regard to CB expressions in relation to PTG, findings suggested that some bereaved CA owners are able to transform the meaning of their loss and use CB as a way of coping. Bussolari, et al. (2017) subsequently conducted a qualitative cross-cultural study assessing PTG responses (United States, French Canada, Japan, and Hong Kong) following the death of a CA. Similar to Packman et al. (2016), participants' responses were coded for CB in the context of PTG. It seemed clear that people utilize CB across cultures. In our view, whether or not a CB is adaptive may depend, in part, on whether it is accompanied by constructive meaning following the loss (Neimeyer, Baldwin, & Gillies, 2006). Consistent with this perspective, positive integration of the loss can bring about post-traumatic growth – transformative positive changes (Calhoun, Tedeschi, Cann, & Hanks, 2010) such as finding new possibilities, increased closeness with others and appreciation of life.

In the largest quantitative CA loss study to-date (N=4,336), Habarth, et al. (2017) investigated how CB related to psychosocial functioning and perceived social constraints. Consistent with our earlier studies on CA loss (Packman, et al., 2011) findings indicated that CB were endorsed by over half of the sample. On average, this study found that owners reported experiencing more comfort than distress across CB efforts. We also found that both higher grief and CA attachment scores were associated with using a greater variety of CB expressions (Habarth et al., 2017). We surmised that if someone were more attached to their CA and engaged in a wide variety of activities with them during their lives that they might find it easier to engage in a greater diversity of behaviors to nurture these connections after their CA died. In addition, higher CA attachment and the experience of PTG ratings together related to higher CB comfort scores. In other words, if a person finds meaning and value in the face of recent loss, it might follow that they would find comfort in their efforts to stay connected to their CA.

Clinical Interventions and Continuing Bonds

Empathic Bridging

In order for bereaved CA owners to disclose their emotions and the depth of their loss, a safe place where empathic bridging occurs must be provided. If unconditional positive regard is the best possible condition for therapy in general, then empathic bridging takes that concept one step further by supporting clients with disenfranchised grief experiences in self-expression. Individuals do indeed engage in CB following the death of their CAs and acknowledging this is one of the initial steps in addressing the death of a CA. This is confirmed by our research as well as previous professional writings, in addition to verification from clinical experience. Assessing a client's experience is an essential first step in determining the degree of value of their CB experiences (Packman et al., 2014). For example, a counselor might say to a client:

> We're finding that often when one loses a loved animal, that person feels or senses his CA's presence or continues to use the CA's belongings or something similar to try to keep and feel an ongoing connection. I wonder if any of that is happening for you.

Or, one could simply ask, "Do you still feel his or her presence?"

We have found that those grieving for their CAs are reluctant to bring these experiences up for fear that the helping person will think they are "crazy." Yet, when a counselor empathically prompts this area of discussion, clients are often relieved to talk about it. If a therapist normalizes and legitimizes an individual's experience, they become more willing to disclose the experiences. Importantly, just as grief continues to evolve, so too is the experience of one's ongoing CB. Clinicians should acknowledge the evolving nature of CB expressions with their potential for comfort and/or distress. For example, we usually say to our clients:

> At times you may be able to look at pictures and feel comfort and at times doing so might feel distressing. Only continue to engage in CB expressions that feel comforting. If something is distressing right now, it may feel comforting in the future.

This is only one example of initiating a conversation to describe the potential comfort one might get from fostering continuing bonds with a CA. It is important for clinicians to help their clients individualize CB expressions based upon each particular person's needs, current intensity of grief, availability of additional supports, and general level of functionality.

Specifically, for some clients, CB may develop immediately after the death, while for others, they may develop over time. At the same time, it is important that clinicians do not burden bereaved CA owners with expectations that they should develop CB. Such bonds are unique to each person and may develop and change over time. Importantly, it is not whether a person experiences CB that is most critical, but rather the degree of comfort or distress that is experienced from a particular kind of connection. Clinicians might consider exploring with their clients their willingness or resistance to engage in CB expressions. For those who fear they may lose the relationship or lose the feelings for their animal, a discussion about how relationships can, in fact, continue through CB might be appropriate. Again, however, it is most essential that the client understand the fluid nature of these expressions and how they ebb and flow over the course of their lives. Thus, they should be encouraged to engage in a variety of CB to determine, at any given time, which feel most helpful.

For many, the concept of a Rainbow Bridge is helpful and comforting. The Rainbow Bridge describes a person being reunited physically with a beloved CA at the time of the person's death. In our studies, several participants have mentioned the Rainbow Bridge when asked about being reunited with their beloved pets and derived considerable comfort from this image. Conversely, for those clients who have been taught, they will never see their animal again, the finality of their loss can be overwhelming because their religious/spiritual teachings do not acknowledge an afterlife. While the CB of Reuniting with a CA may cause distress, clinicians can help clients derive comfort from other CBs.

Finally, those grieving the death of a CA often feel invalidated and unsupported because of their loss. They are reluctant to speak of the intensity of their grief or any experiences of CB either because of previous rejection or fear of their grief being disenfranchised. Statements such as, " It was just a dog" or "What's the big deal, there are lots of cats that need homes" – comments often directed to those in grief – reinforce feelings of disenfranchisement, invalidation, and social constraints (Habarth, et al., 2017). Unfortunately, "Society generally does not acknowledge pet loss as a significant loss, which alienates those who grieve. Clinicians must not fall into the same category" (Podrazik et al., 2000, p. 377). Encouraging clients to seek out supportive situations (e.g., pet loss support groups, online chat rooms) can help them learn what other bereaved individuals do to manage their grief and learn to share their own feelings and coping strategies.

Projective Drawings

Drawings can be a valuable modality for people who have experienced trauma and loss (Reynolds & Prior, 2006). Irwin (1991) suggested that in order for true grief processing to take place, an individual must become fully connected to the emotional challenges of facing loss. Projective drawings are a safe way to access feelings and are useful in allowing the individual to experience cathartic relief, verbally reflect on their drawing to a non-judgmental listener, provide connectors to the deceased, and analyze the drawing's symbolic meanings (Irwin, 1991).

Packman et al. (2017) examined the relationship among projective drawings and mental health symptomatology for 33 adults grieving the loss of a pet. Results showed that those with greater severity of grief displayed poorer psychosocial adjustment scores on the projective drawings. Projective drawings added clinical utility by introducing a nonverbal form of expression helpful in understanding the severity of grief and in opening up shared communication with those experiencing loss. In terms of CB connections, we suggest two directives (Long, 2005) and recommend using a set of colored markers: (1) Draw the current image you "see" when you are thinking about your CA, that is how do you visualize your animal currently? This first drawing can be used as a mental representation of the participant's relationship with the deceased CA, and (2) draw a picture representing how you are now using the time you would have spent with your CA, that is how have you changed the ways in which you use your energy and time since your CA's death? This directive reflects a future orientation, that is, the extent to which the client has integrated the loss (Long, 2005).

Instead of solely keeping to descriptive characteristics of the drawings, the client can create a fuller explanation and story of the drawings with examples of their memories, dreams, or experiences with their pets. This part of the therapy session can open an avenue for the therapist to form an empathic connection, by listening supportively and validating the experiences, which should hopefully decrease experiences of disenfranchised grief. By supporting their clients who are socially constrained and find it difficult to trust that others will validate their loss, therapists are engaging in empathic bridging. These qualitative findings are similar to Irwin's (1991) statements that making art is useful in allowing individuals to verbally reflect on their drawings to a non-judgmental listener, thereby allowing the analysis of the symbolic meanings behind the drawings. "The focus is on the individual's unique understanding and construction of the loss" (Lister, Pushkar, & Connolly, 2008, p. 250).

Self-Compassion

Self-compassion, as described by Neff (2003a, 2003b) is self-directed attention and care. Inspired by a philosophy of Buddhism, self-compassion includes three components. First, *self-kindness* describes when we are caring and considerate towards ourselves without a sense of judgment. Second, is a *sense of a common humanity*, which refers to the idea that all humans make mistakes and have difficulties. The last tenet refers to the *cultivation of mindfulness* which essentially describes being present in the moment with non-judgmental awareness. Overall, self-compassion can be described as a healthy attitude towards ourselves when we are strug-gling. In the psychological literature, self-compassion is related to greater emotional well-being and lower stress (Bluth et al., 2016), plays a role as a predictor for depression and anxiety (Muris, Meesters, Pierik, & de Kock 2016; Ozyesil, & Akbag, 2013), and relates to higher post-traumatic growth (Wong, & Yeung, 2017) as well as higher well-being and less dis-tress (Fong, & Loi, 2016).

At present, there is little research regarding self-compassion and grief (Lenferink, Eisma, de Keijser, & Boelen, 2017). In the only CA loss study, to our knowledge, using the construct of self-compassion, Bussolari, Habarth, Phillips, Katz, and Packman (2018) assessed the use of CB coping strategies in relation to grief and self-compassion. The authors found that the frequency of CB efforts related positively to participants' scores on self-compassion. In essence, we posited that bereaved CA owners with higher self-compassion may be more willing to take risks and engage in more CB expressions to manage grief. This is an important finding, because as clinicians, we want to encourage bereaved CA owners to engage in CB. The more frequently CB expressions are utilized, the better the chance of finding those that are comforting.

For many, being self-compassionate is not easy. This is especially true after CA loss. In our clinical practice, we see bereaved pet owners as some of our most grief challenged. CA owners' feelings of responsibility towards their pet can result in strong feelings of guilt, as well as self-deprecation (Bussolari, et al., 2018). A very important aspect of self-compassion is that it is a skill that can be practiced, learned and assimilated into our daily behaviors. Self-compassion during CA loss can include learning to speak kindly to ourselves, identifying our needs and responding to them, setting boundaries, and/or choosing to only share our grief with those who we know will be supportive. It is important for clinicians to first assess how well a client accepts validation. Often, those who deflect unconditional positive regard from others will have difficulties providing it to themselves. The following interventions are based, in part, upon Germer and Neff's (2013) Mindful Self-Compassion training.

To start, it is important to gain awareness of negative self-talk. A simple way to get clients to pay attention is to have them carry rubber bands. Whenever they notice themselves thinking or saying something negative about themselves, they put a rubber band on their left wrist. When they say or think or do something that is helpful, kind or compassionate (e.g., thinking about euthanasia and feeling like they did the right thing, even though it was still really hard or going out with friends and enjoying them-selves without putting themselves down), they put a band on their right wrist. Each day the slate is cleared and the bands are taken off, in order to start fresh. The goal is not to eliminate the left wrist bands – but that is not realistic. Rather, we want to always have more on the right. Germer and Neff (2013) note:

While self-compassion helps people deal with life struggles, it's important to remember that self-compassion does not push negative emotions away in an aversive manner. With self-compassion, instead of replacing negative feelings with positive ones, positive emotions are generated by *embracing* the negative ones.

(p. 858)

Next, clients can be helped to practice an exercise where the three components of self-compassion are taught. Whenever emotional stress come up, a person repeats phrases such as "This is a moment of suffering" (mindfulness), "Suffering is part of life" (common humanity), and "May I be kind to myself" (self-kindness).

Practicing mindfulness is essential for increasing self-compassion. Mindfulness has to do with experiencing our painful emotions without avoidance in order to cultivate compassion. In addition, while we are seeing our negative emotions, we are also not overly identifying with them. Being mindful of our emotions is a necessary precursor to self-compassion. Thus, the practice of noticing our grief and not pushing away can be helpful. If we were to practice mindfulness after CA loss, we might be better able to tolerate our painful feelings, and have the impetus to explore a variety of CB expressions. Thus, rather than "avoid" distress, we would embrace it as an important aspect of the grief process. Cultivating self-compassion can also involve using a loving-kindness meditation. This can include repeating the phrases such as "May I be safe" or "May I be kind to myself" in a formal meditation or throughout the day. Garmer and Neff (2013) describe this practice as "compassionate exposure therapy" (p. 863). This specific loving-kindness practice can evolve from these rote statements to a more person-specific compassionate voice with supportive language such as, for example, "I care about myself and I am hurting because my CA died. May I forgive myself. May I have courage." Overall, teaching and practicing self-compassionate behaviors can help the bereaved fortify CB expressions by tolerating distressing emotions and nourishing a more self-compassionate foundation.

Conclusion

Research and clinical practice highlight that bereaved CA owners want to maintain continuous and meaningful ties with their CA. Clinical practice suggests that the evolving nature of continuing bonds expressions during the course of grief needs additional exploration. We also need to better understand how CB are experienced in various demographic and cultural groups. Our ongoing international cross-cultural research related to CB expressions and CA loss is significant for clinical practice (e.g., Bussolari et al., 2017).   However, there is still a dearth of information regarding the multicultural and spiritual experiences of bereaved CA owners, and psychology bereavement curricula should always include information about CB and CA loss. Although the grief that bereaved CA owners experience is becoming increasingly acknowledged, there is still a long way to go before pet loss is universally thought of as valid and profound. In fact, many bereaved still do not feel comfortable speaking of their ongoing attachment to their deceased CA. Just as grief related to CA loss has been disenfranchised, so has the experience of CB. Clinicians can affirm and normalize the experiences of CB, especially through the use of a combination of empathic bridging, projective drawings, as well as skills to increase self-compassion. As clients increasingly share their experiences following the death of their CAs with us, our understanding of the CB phenomenon will grow. Our hope is that bereaved CA owners will begin to feel that having a continued relationship with their pet is both a natural and increasingly important part of the healthy grieving process.

Case Scenarios

Case Scenario #1:

Kevin is a young man, aged 26, who has been coming to therapy for the past six months. His reason for the initial visit was:

> Nothing feels good to me anymore. I don't get the same pleasure out of the things I used to do. I love to cook, but haven't in a long time. I actually don't seem to have an appetite and have lost a lot of weight. I try to put on a good face for my friends and co-workers, but it is a lot of effort.

He completed a thorough intake indicating that his brother died when he was a teenager, however, he only recently disclosed that his 15 year-old German Shepherd, Rudy, died seven months ago. He expressed that he has been trying to "get over it" and does not feel comfortable talking with his friends and family members. At the time of Rudy's death, a co-worker said to him, "You can always get another one." Kevin noted that Rudy was given to him as a gift when he was 11 years old by his deceased brother and the dog lived with him his entire life. As you ask more questions about the loss, Kevin notes that he had gotten rid of all of Rudy's belongings the day after he died and actively tries to avoid thinking about him.

Discussion Questions:

1. What are some of the reasons that Kevin might be avoiding talking about Rudy's death?
2. What are the areas where an empathic failure could happen with Kevin? What shouldn't you say or ask? How can you engage in empathic bridging so that Kevin feels comfortable talking about Rudy? What could you say to ensure that Kevin feels seen, heard and valued?

3. What questions would you ask to assess Kevin's level of social constraints? How might you help support him in this area?
4. What are the directives for projective drawings related to CB? What would you look for? What would you reflect?
5. What do you imagine would be the kind of "loving-kindness" statements that would be helpful for Kevin and why?
6. How would a mindfulness practice support Kevin's ability to try out a variety of CB expressions?

Case Scenario #2:

Twenty-two-year-old Sheila has been coming to therapy for two weeks because her 5-year-old cat, Sprinkles, died suddenly. This is the first death she has ever experienced, as both sets of grandparents are still living. She recently moved across the country for a job and hasn't yet cultivated a strong support network. Sheila lives alone in a studio apartment and has developed, what she describes as "panic attacks" whenever she comes home to her empty house. Of her job in the tech industry, she notes, "I have a lot of responsibility and have to work very long hours. I can barely get through an hour without running in the bathroom and crying." Sheila blames herself for Sprinkles death because when she realized she might actually be sick (for the past three days, she seemed lethargic with a decreased appetite), Sheila opted to stay late at work and not take her to the vet until the next morning. While a couple of her co-workers have been supportive, she doesn't want to let anyone know what has happened because, as a woman, she worries that she will be viewed as "weak" or "someone who is not really committed to the mission of the company."

Discussion Questions:

1. How would you start the conversation around CB with Sheila? Are there any CBs that you think would be particularly helpful?
2. What are the areas where an empathic failure could happen as a therapist with Sheila? What shouldn't you say or ask? How can you engage in empathic bridging so that Sheila feels comfortable talking about Sprinkles? What could you say to ensure that Sheila feels seen, heard and valued?
3. What questions would you ask to assess Sheila's level of social constraints? How might you help support her in this area?
4. What are the directives for projective drawings related to CB? What would you look for? What would you reflect?
5. What do you imagine would be the kind of "loving-kindness" statements that would be helpful for Sheila and why?

6.   How would a mindfulness practice support Sheila's ability to try out a variety of CB expressions?

Note

1. We use the term Companion Animal (CA) rather than a pet. We agree with Hewson's (2014) belief that pet "… does not adequately reflect the current scientific understanding of animals' sentience, cognitive complexity and individuality, or the complexity and modern reality of the relationships between animals and their owners" (p. 104).

References

Archer, J. (1997). Why do people love their pets? *Evolution and Human Behavior,* 18, 237–259.

Archer, J., & Winchester, G. (1994). Bereavement following death of a pet. *The British Journal of Psychology,* 85, 259–271.

Bluth, K., Roberson, P., Gaylord, S. A., Faurot, K. R., Grewen, K. M., Arzon, S., & Girdler, S. S. (2016). Does self-compassion protect adolescents from stress? *Journal of Child and Family Studies,* 25, 1098–1109.

Bussolari, C., Habarth, J., Phillips, S., Katz, R., Carmack, B. J., & Packman, W. (2018). The euthanasia decision-making process: A qualitative exploration of bereaved companion animal owners. *Bereavement Care,* 37(3), 101–108.

Bussolari, C., Habarth, J., Kimpara, S., Katz, R., Carlos, F., Chow, A., Osada, H., Osada. Y., Carmack, B., Field, N., & Packman, W. (2017). Post traumatic growth following the loss of a pet: A cross-cultural comparison. *OMEGA: Journal of Death and Dying,* 78(4) 1–21.

Bussolari, C., Habarth, J., Phillips, S., Katz, R., & Packman, W. (2018). Self-compassion, social constraints, and psychosocial outcomes in a pet bereavement sample. *Omega.* doi: 10.1177/0030222818814050

Calhoun, L. G., Tedeschi, R. G., Cann, A., & Hanks, E. A. (2010). Positive outcomes following bereavement: Paths to posttraumatic growth. *Psychologica Belgica,* 50(1–2), 125–143

Carmack, B. J. (2003). Grieving the death of a pet. Minneapolis, MN: Augsburg Books.

Cowles, K. V. (1985). The death of a pet: human responses to the breaking of the bond. *Marriage & Family Review,* 8(3–4), 135–148.

Doka, K. J. (2008). Disenfranchised grief in historical and cultural perspective. In M. S. Stroebe, R. O. Hansson, H. Schut, & W. Stroebe (Eds.), *Handbook of bereavement research and practice: Advances in theory and intervention* (pp. 223–240). Washington, DC: American Psychological Association.

Field, N. P. (2008). Whether to relinquish or maintain a bond with the deceased. In M. S. Stroebe, R. O. Hansson, H. Schut, & W. Stroebe (Eds.), *Handbook of bereavement research and practice: Advances in theory and intervention* (pp. 113–132). Washington, DC: American Psychological Association.

Field, N. P., & Friedrichs, M. (2004). Continuing bonds in coping with the death of a husband. *Death Studies,* 28 (7), 597–620.

Field, N. P., Gao, B., & Paderna, L. (2005). Continuing bonds in bereavement: An attachment theory based perspective. *Death Studies,* 29, 277–299.

Field, N. P., Nichols, C., Holen, A., & Horowitz, M. (1999). The relation of continuing attachment to adjustment in conjugal bereavement. *Journal of Consulting and Clinical Psychology*, 67, 212–218.

Field, N. P., Orsini, L., Gavish, R. & Packman, W. (2009). Role of attachment in response to pet loss. *Death Studies*, 33(4), 332–355.

Fong, M., & Loi, N. (2016). The mediating role of self-compassion in student psychological health. *Australian Psychologist*, 51, 431–441.

Freud, S. (1917/1957). Mourning and melancholia. In J. Strachey (Ed. and Trans.), *The standard edition of the complete psychological works of Sigmund Freud* (Vol 14, pp. 243–258). London: Hogarth Press. (Original work published 1917).

Germer, C. K., & Neff, K. D. (2013). Self-compassion in clinical practice. *Journal of Clinical Psychology*, 69, 856–867.

Gerwolls, M. K., & Labott, S. M. (1994). Adjustments to the death of a companion animal. *Anthrozoös*, VII(3), 172–187.

Habarth, J., Bussolari, C., Gomez, R., Carmack, B. J., Ronen, R., Field, N. P., & Packman, W. (2017). Continuing bonds and psychosocial functioning in a recently bereaved pet loss sample. *Anthrozoös*, 30(4), 651–670.

Hewson, C. (2014). Grief for pets – Part 1: Overview and some false assumptions. *Veterinary Nursing Journal*, 29(9), 302–305.

Irwin, H. J. (1991). The depiction of loss: uses of clients' drawings in bereavement counseling. *Death Studies*, 15, 481–497.

Juth, V., Smyth, J. M., Carey, M. P., & Lepore, S. J. (2015). Social constraints are associated with negative psychological and physical adjustment in bereavement. *Applied Psychology: Health and Well-Being*, 7, 129–148.

Klass, D., Silverman, P., & Nickman, S.L. (Ed.). (1996). *Continuing bonds – New understanding of grief*. Philadelphia, PA: Taylor & Francis.

Lenferink,, L. I. M., Eisma, M. C., de Keijser, J., & Boelen, P. A. (2017). Grief rumination mediates the association between self-compassion and psychopathology in relatives of missing persons. *European Journal of Psychotraumatology*, 8(sup6), doi: 10.1080/20008198.2017.1378052

Lister, S., Pushkar, D., & Connolly, K. (2008). Current bereavement theory: Implications for art therapy practice. *Arts in Psychotherapy*, 35(4), 245–250.

Long, J. K. (2005). The psychosocial adjustment scoring scale. (Unpublished manuscript). Department of Clinical Psychology, Palo Alto University, Palo Alto, CA.

Muris, P., Meesters, C., Pierik, A., & de Kock B. (2016). Good for the self: Self-compassion and other self-related constructs in relation to symptoms of anxiety and depression in non-clinical youths. *Journal of Child and Family Studies*, 25, 607–617.

Nagasawa, M., Mogi, K., & Kikusui, T. (2009). Attachment between humans and dogs. *Japanese Psychological Research*, 51(3), 209–221.

Neff, K. D. (2003a). Development and validation of a scale to measure self-compassion. *Self and Identity*, 2(3), 223–250.

Neff, K. D (2003b). Self-compassion: An alternative conceptualization of a healthy attitude towards oneself. *Self and Identity*, 2(2), 85–101.

Neimeyer, R. A., Baldwin, S. & Gillies, J. (2006). Continuing bonds and reconstructing meaning: Mitigating complications in bereavement. *Death Studies*, 30, 715–738.

Neimeyer, R. N., & Jordan, J. R. (2002). Disenfranchisement as empathic failure: Grief therapy and the co-construction of meaning. In K. Doka (Ed.), *Disenfranchised grief* (pp. 95–117). Champaign, IL: Research Press.

Ozyesil, A., & Akbag, M. (2013). Self-compassion as a protective factor for depression, anxiety and stress: A research on Turkish sample. *The Online Journal of Counseling and Education*, 2(2), 36–43.

Packman, W., Field, N. P., Carmack, B. J., & Ronen, R. (2011). Continuing bonds and psychosocial adjustment in pet loss. *Journal of Loss and Trauma*, 16(4), 341–357. doi: 10.1080/15325024.2011.572046

Packman, W., Carmack, B. J., & Ronen, R. (2012). Therapeutic implications of continuing bonds expressions following the death of a pet. *OMEGA*, 64(4), 335–356.

Packman, W., Carmack, B., Katz, R., Carlos, F., field, N., & Landers, C. (2014). Online survey as empathic bridging for the disenfranchised grief of pet loss. *OMEGA*, 69(4), 333–356.

Packman, W., Bussolari, C., Katz, R., Carmack, B. J., & Field, N. P. (2016). Posttraumatic growth following the loss of a pet. *OMEGA*, 75(4), 337–359.

Packman, W., Kelley, E., Rudolph, B., Long, J., Wallace, J., Hsu, M., Carmack, B. J., & Field, N. (2017). Projective drawings of individuals grieving the loss of a pet. *Art Therapy: Journal of the American Art Therapy Association*, 34(1), 29–37.

Podrazik, D, Shackford, S., Becker, L., & Heckert, T. (2000). The death of a pet: Implications for loss and bereavement across the lifespan. *Journal of Personal and Interpersonal Loss*, 3, 361–395.

Prigerson, H. G., & Jacobs, S. C. (2001). Traumatic grief as a distinct disorder: A rationale, consensus criteria, and a preliminary empirical test. In M. S. Stroebe, R. O. Hansson, W. Stroebe, & H. Schut (Eds.), *Handbook of bereavement research: Consequences, coping and care* (pp. 613–647). Washington, DC: American Psychological Association.

Rando, T. A. (1993). Treatment of complicated mourning. Champaign, IL: Research Press.

Reynolds F., & Prior S. (2006). The role of art-making in identity maintenance: case studies of people living with cancer. *European Journal of Cancer Care*, 15, 333–341.

Stroebe, M., Gergen, M. M., Gergen, K. J., & Stroebe, W. (1992). Broken hearts or broken bonds: Love and death in historical perspective. *American Psychologist*, 47, 1205–1212.

Toray, T. (2004). The human–animal bond and loss: Providing support for grieving clients. *Journal of Mental Health Counseling*, 26, 244–259.

Vevver, J. E. (2008). The social meaning of pets: Alternative roles for companion animals. *Marriage and Family Review*, 8(3–4), 11–30.

Weisman, A. D. (1990/1991). Bereavement and companion animals. *Omega*, 22(4), 241–248.

Wong, C. C. Y., & Yeung, N. C. Y. (2017) Self-compassion and posttraumatic growth: Cognitive processes as mediators *Mindfulness*, 8(4), 1078–1087. doi: 10.1007/s12671-017-0683-4

19 Animal Loss and Interprofessional Practice

A Primer in "Boundary Spanning" for Mental Health Professionals

Jeannine Moga

Introduction

The importance of supporting people through the loss of loved animals cannot be overstated, particularly as the grief experience that results from such losses are often disenfranchised. Veterinary professionals have historically been a foundational source of support for human–animal relationships and animal loss, even when their professional training lacked core instruction in how to understand the facets of these relationships and the impact of their loss. Increasing attention to the non-medical skills required for successful practice, particularly in contemporary veterinary curricula, has provided opportunities for mental health professionals to collaborate with veterinary training programs to help young practitioners develop "soft skills" in communication, teamwork, conflict resolution, and end of life facilitation. However, veterinary curricula are tightly packed and the competition for instructional time is intense; as such, the time devoted to death education – hence, the skills necessary for supporting people through the death and dying of their animals, as well as knowing how and when to refer clients out for additional grief support – is limited. Meanwhile, mental health professionals may avail themselves of instruction and guidance on how to work with the myriad of issues that arise when a client's loved animal dies, but they may not know how to reach out to the larger population of "animal people" who are struggling with loss. The necessity of closing this gap is clear, and the answer to building these bridges can be found in contemporary conversations about interprofessional practice.

Interprofessional Practice in Human – and Veterinary – Healthcare

Recent years have seen growing interest in "interprofessional practice" among healthcare practitioners and social service professionals, particularly with the increased attention on streamlining processes and providing wrap-around service. It follows that most of the research and literature on interprofessional practice is focused on creating interdisciplinary teams with an eye toward improving individual and population health outcomes. As the landscape of healthcare continues to shift toward patient-centered and team-based care, challenges abound in how to create health delivery systems – and healthcare providers – that are collaborative, efficient, and effective.

It is not uncommon for mental health providers to be actively involved in the delivery of human healthcare. Social workers, psychologists, and marriage and family therapists are frequently found on healthcare teams, and their contributions to care are diverse. Whether they are assessing the biopsychosocial impact of illness, providing treatment for primary mental health conditions, facilitating patient discharge, brokering community services, or delivering grief support, they may serve as peripheral actors in primary care or core members of collaborative care teams. It is the latter role that best defines interprofessional practice. Interprofessional practice requires a collaborative process that "facilitates the achievement of goals that cannot be reached when individual professionals act on their own" (Bronstein, 2003, p. 299). Bronstein (2003), described this type of practice as requiring a certain level of interdependence, clearly defined professional activities, flexibility, attention to (and reflection on) process, and a collective ownership of goals. Despite the inclusion of interprofessional ideals in the curricula of many health care students, the wide-scale adoption of them in a rapidly shifting marketplace presents its own challenges, both pragmatic and ethical (Engel & Prentice, 2013). The idiom "*the devil is in the details*" may best describe how multidisciplinary practitioners struggle to define how they will work together.

A recent publication exploring interprofessional practice in veterinary medicine highlights this challenge. Kinnison, Guile, and May (2016) investigated the extent to which interprofessional processes are present in day-to-day veterinary practice. Despite the emergence of the One Health Initiative, which aims to expand "interdisciplinary collaborations and communications in all aspects of health care for humans, animals, and the environment" (2018), Kinnison and colleagues note that veterinary and allied health professionals are still largely trained in isolation, making it difficult to create and sustain collaborative relationships in practice. Multiple weeks of observation in British veterinary practices revealed that veterinary teams are often comprised of veterinarians, veterinary nurses/ technicians, practice managers, and receptionists who must navigate different care perspectives to serve their patients and clients. The absence of mental health professionals (and other allied health professionals) in these clinics was stark, illustrating that while "interprofessional" veterinary teams may include veterinary doctors, veterinary technicians/nurses, kennel staff, and customer service professionals, they rarely include mental health providers who can attend to the needs of the humans in the veterinary service sphere.

However, recent years have seen more intentional interdisciplinary collaboration emerge in American veterinary practices. The challenge of better serving increasingly attached (and demanding) veterinary clients, alongside the need to enhance non-medical/"soft" skills in veterinary practitioners, has opened the door for teaching and specialty hospitals to hire mental health practitioners for client service, teaching, and consulting roles (Hafen, Rush, Reisbig, McDaniel, & White, 2007). These efforts have included psychologists (Siess, Marziliano, Sarma, Sikorski, & Moyer, 2015), marriage and family therapists (Hafen et al., 2007), and, frequently, social workers (Brackenridge & McPherson, 2016; Cohen, 1985; Dunn, Mehler, & Greenberg, 2005; Mertens, 2006) to provide pet loss support, clinical case consultation, euthanasia support, veterinary team debriefing, and skills instruction for veterinary students and staff. While embedding a mental health professional in a veterinary hospital setting is one option for interprofessional work, I argue that having "animal-informed" mental health practitioners (Moga, 2018) available to serve animal people – and animal professionals – in the larger community is critical. It can provide the critical bridge between animal illness/death and the ability to address the impact of animal loss beyond veterinary clinic walls.

Bringing Our Skills to Veterinary (and Allied Animal Health) Practice: Boundary Spanners and Animal Loss

For mental health professionals whose practice interests include the human–animal bond and animal loss, perhaps the greatest challenge is situating oneself among the network of care providers who facilitate animal care and interact with people who are facing the loss of their animals. Whether choosing to serve as a private practitioner with a practice specialty in grief, loss, and human–animal relationships or pursuing a role as an "embedded" veterinary care provider, interprofessional work requires learning how to navigate a somewhat complex web of allied health professionals. The remainder of this chapter will focus on the "how's" of serving in an interprofessional capacity to meet the needs of grievers.

I have developed and led two university-based veterinary hospital programs aimed at addressing the psychosocial impacts of animal illness and death on pet owners, as well as educating and supporting veterinary practitioners. The first program emerged as a trial partnership between the College of Veterinary Medicine and the School of Social Work at a large Midwestern university. A faculty member from the School of Social Work had launched a pet loss support group for clients of the veterinary teaching hospital, and I – still completing graduate training – was searching for an internship related to clinical practice with human–animal relationships. The faculty member agreed to sponsor and supervise a formal field placement at the veterinary hospital, and was able to cultivate an agreement with the hospital director to allow me to provide "support services" to hospital clients 20 hours per week. At the time, there were only a handful of social services providers working in veterinary settings – and there was no precedent for how to set up a more comprehensive human support program at this particular institution. However, I aligned with the hospital director (an RN with abundant experience working with social workers in medical settings), as well as a couple of veterinary faculty who had been trained in veterinary institutions with on-site counselors, to create, and internally market, a client support program modeled on medical social work tenets. This program provided psychoeducation, medical case consultation, crisis intervention, and short-term grief support to the families of veterinary patients, always with an eye toward creating interventions that simultaneously alleviated the time and communication pressures experienced by veterinary teams juggling patient care, client care, and student education. Once faculty and staff began to directly experience the benefits of having a "human handler" on the team, support for a full-time program grew and I was hired to formally launch Veterinary Social Services upon graduation.

It was the success of this program, in part, that led me to launch a similar initiative at a southeastern university's veterinary teaching hospital many years later. In contrast to the first example, this veterinary hospital did not have a formal partnership with a school of social work (or allied field) on which to draw. Additionally, the hospital had enlisted the help of social services students, professionals, and volunteers in a variety of capacities (client counseling, chaplaincy, etc.) in previous years, with varying degrees of success. This College of Veterinary Medicine did have a licensed psychologist on-site to serve students and veterinary trainees, however, so administrators had some foundational familiarity with how human services professionals worked before they decided to hire someone to create and run a veterinary hospital program. As such, I focused on interviewing administrators, faculty, supervisors, and technical staff in order to determine: (1) What "worked" (and didn't) in previous efforts to partner with human services providers, (2) what they thought their teams, students, and clients needed to function successfully, and (3) how they would prioritize the needs they identified. With this information, I was able to collaborate with veterinary hospital – and College of Veterinary Medicine – faculty and staff to launch a program that not only served veterinary clients (via on-site case consultation, crisis intervention, euthanasia support, and grief counseling), but also served veterinary staff (via continuing education related to client care, conflict resolution, and stress management issues) and veterinary students (via presence and involvement in the 4-year veterinary curriculum related to human–animal issues, "human-handling" and communication skills, and professional ethics).

While these programs have been sustained beyond my presence and direction, they were admittedly challenging to create. Upon reflection, it is evident that many of my challenges associated with program development and implementation came from serving as a "guest" within a network of providers that share a uniquely separate knowledge base, language, value system, and skill set. To be successful, guests must assume the role of "boundary spanner," which enables practitioners in nontraditional host settings to bridge these differences in order to accomplish shared goals. The notion of "boundary spanners," or team members that link different groups, bridge communication, and implement collaborative care, is not a new one. Instead, it is an idea that has emerged in the social work literature related to interprofessional practice. Long and Rosen (2017) and Zerden, Lombardi, Fraser, Jones, and Rico (2018) argue that social workers, who comprise the largest group of behavioral health practitioners in the United States, are often trained to operate as boundary spanners in integrated health systems – even when that system may seem an unlikely venue for social work practice. Other mental health practitioners also work as boundary spanners. Examples include when they are working between contexts and systems with multidisciplinary partners who do not share a professional or organizational identity. The key to understanding this role is to focus on critical tasks, not organizational location: boundary spanners must excel at building relationships, taking risks, and navigating differences of opinion in order to facilitate dialog, conduct casework, and serve client/patient needs (Oliver, 2013).

The Competencies Necessary for Boundary Spanning

Few foundational training programs truly prepare mental health professionals for interprofessional work, though opportunities for advanced practice in allied healthcare settings are growing (Brackenridge & McPherson, 2016; Hafen et al., 2007; Long & Rosen, 2017). Ideally, mental health trainees with an interest in human–animal relationships and health should have the opportunity to develop fluency in how veterinary health systems work, as well as basic veterinary terminology and veterinary treatments – and this fluency does not come from being a "pet person." While many mental health professionals with an interest in human–animal relationships come to that interest from a deeply personal place, often having had rich and rewarding relationships with animals themselves, working with animal issues often requires a different – more objective and highly attuned – lens. I often coach young mental health professionals to "not lead with their animal foot," but to step into conversations with veterinary professionals (and veterinary clients) as an "animal-informed" mental health clinician whose skills uniquely situate them to address the psychosocial needs of animal people.

Additionally, those who wish to practice in a more integrated role may need to bolster their training in how to collaborate across settings, contribute to team decision-making, use medical informatics, and provide brief behavioral interventions (Zerden et al., 2018). These competencies align with the *four core competency domains* that have been identified by the Interprofessional Health Collaborative (2016), which include role and responsibilities, interprofessional communication, values and ethics for interprofessional practice, and teams/teamwork. When applied to work with issues of animal loss in interprofessional practice, these competencies can be translated into the following recommendations:

Clearly Define Your Role and Frame Your Skills

A number of studies indicate that interprofessional teamwork may be hampered less by power struggles and more by a lack of clarity and understanding around what the various team members do (see Engel & Prentice, 2013). Likewise, many veterinary practitioners may be largely unaware of the range of behavioral health practitioners' skills. It follows that they may also be unaware of how this work could benefit client and patient care, as well as impact the health/functionality of their team. Regardless of whether you plan to serve as a core member of the veterinary team, to provide on-call or adjunctive service (largely off-site), or to serve as a primary referral partner for a clinic or set of clinics, clearly defining your skills, potential contributions to client care, and what those skills mean for the productivity and functioning of the veterinary team will go a long way toward building a truly collaborative – and integrative – partnership. Brackenridge and McPherson (2016) recommend hosting a veterinary team in-service to explain what mental health professionals do, and how they may assist with veterinary client (or team) needs. I have introduced, and maintained, veterinary-based mental health practices by hosting brief in-services and regular "psychosocial rounds" to discuss practice challenges with veterinary staff. In so doing, both the "guest" and the host team can educate each other on roles, critical issues, and procedural details that often define how people work together.

Hafen et al. (2007) also describe how bringing family therapists into a university-based veterinary hospital can lead to improvements in veterinary team capacity, often related to communication, problem-solving, and conflict resolution skills. This observation illustrates that embedded practitioners may find that their roles will need to flex over time and will rarely be exclusive to provision of direct grief support to clients. Similarly, off-site clinicians who receive grief counseling referrals may find that requests for service may diversify as veterinary staff feel more comfortable with the role of mental health partnership in their practice. Attending to the potential for role conflict and confusion in advance – as the potential for confusion is common in interprofessional settings – will help to clarify the scope of your services and ward off misunderstandings with team members whose needs may exceed your time and capacity (Sweifach, 2015).

Learn the Language of Animal Care to Ensure Clear Communication

It is important to recognize that provision of counseling for grief and loss often entails recounting history of illness/treatment and stories around animal death. I have found the family systems illness model (Rolland, 1994) incredibly helpful as an orienting device to help others understand what family members facing illness may need from their professional caregivers. The family systems illness model describes how family systems make sense of, and respond to, the arc of illness (whether acute, chronic, or terminal) and provides wonderful language to help both clients and veterinary teams normalize and problem-solve the challenges that erupt when a loved animal becomes ill or injured.

Additionally, it is important to recognize that grief experiences may reflect the circumstances around animal death – including the manner in which that death unfolds. As such, practitioners should be fluent in the language around end of life processes and euthanasia in order to fully explore those experiences with clients. Literature reveals conflicting information on whether the act of choosing euthanasia for an animal eases the grief or complicates it. Choosing euthanasia provides both a sense of control and support, as well as a potential source of guilt, for animal owners who are both empowered and troubled by the power to choose death for a loved animal (McCutcheon & Fleming, 2002; Quackenbush & Glickman, 1984). Regardless of whether an animal dies by euthanasia or "natural" death, it is critical that practitioners be able to engage clients in discussions of medical care episodes, including those leading to end of life decisions and processes, in a manner that is well-informed.

Complicating this picture is the knowledge that the majority of Americans have a *below basic* to *intermediate* level of health literacy. "Health literacy" is the degree to which a person can obtain, process, and accurately understand basic health information in order to make appropriate health care decisions on their own or others' behalf. It is startling, then, to learn that 89% of American adults can only understand basic information, locate care, and compare prices (Kutner, Greenberg, Jin, & Paulsen, 2006) – meaning that most are unable to process more complex diagnostic, treatment, and prognostic information. It is not uncommon for grievers to perseverate on the details of an illness or care episode, particularly as they struggle to make sense out of death. Mental health practitioners should therefore be literate in veterinary treatment and end of life care in order to facilitate solutions to whatever questions and concerns make grief resolution difficult. It is sometimes useful to help grievers sort out which unanswered questions necessitate additional conversations with the veterinary team, particularly when there is confusion about how, or why, an animal has died. Practitioners should be alert to the necessity of mediating conversations with the veterinary team (when embedded in a veterinary clinic) or coaching clients on how to reach out to their veterinarian for guidance and resolution.

Be Aware of Practice Standards and Guidelines

While mental health providers are generally encouraged to adhere to best practices in delivering care, there are few standards specific to the provision of grief support for animal loss issues. There are, however, some useful documents emerging from interprofessional veterinary practice that provide guidelines for the mental health/veterinary interface. A working group of animal-informed mental health practitioners worked with the American Animal Hospital Association (2012) to construct guidelines for the provision of human support in veterinary settings. These guidelines describe three levels of social support, ranging from basic social support by trained veterinary staff (minimum) to contracted services with outside human services professionals (medium) to embedded/on-site therapists or social services providers (maximum). While this document was constructed with the veterinary audience in mind, it may also help mental health professionals determine how to frame their work in accordance with how veterinary practices currently assess client needs. Additionally, this document coaches veterinarians to screen mental health providers for "goodness of fit" and training in grief/loss and human–animal bond related issues. As such, it provides useful talking points for counselors who are looking to market their services to veterinary clinics.

The American Veterinary Medical Association (2018) has also published guidelines for the provision of pet loss services. While these guidelines are non-binding for mental health professionals, they do provide important information for practitioners related to the provision of hotline support, pet loss support groups, and short-term telephone counseling. It is important to note that these guidelines do not reflect advancements in the provision of distance counseling, as the current document dissuades veterinary practitioners from supporting internet-based counseling services, despite the growth of telemental health practices providing service for hard to reach consumers.

Finally, the International Association for Animal Hospice and Palliative Care has produced guidelines for the provision of end of life services for veterinary patients. The "Guidelines for recommended practices in animal hospice and palliative care" (2017) include information on mental health considerations during the provision of end of life care. For mental health practitioners who collaborate with animal hospice/palliative care veterinarians, these standards are essential to understanding your role in supporting these end of life specialists and the clients/patients they serve.

Clarify Your Values and Ethics

In their discussion of interprofessional collaboration in human health-care, Engel and Prentice argue that, "Interprofessional care is essentially ethical. Its espoused motivation is that it promotes the well-being of the patient or beneficence, which is to do well by the patient" (2013, p. 427). In human healthcare, where patients' rights are both primary and reflected in both law and ethical codes, the issue of interprofessional ethics may be a bit more straightforward than in veterinary interprofessional care, where the waters are far muddier. In veterinary practice, the patient, who essentially has no personhood and therefore few rights, is the primary focus of attention; meanwhile, the patient's surrogate, to whom rights of ownership provide almost unfettered latitude for decision-making, has his or her own ideas, beliefs, and wants that need to be addressed (Rosoff et al., 2018). Ethical concerns around the provision – or withholding – of veterinary care are not uncommon in practice, and few veterinary facilities have clear processes in place to assist veterinary teams with ethical deliberation and decision-making (Kipperman, Morris, & Rollin, 2018; Rosoff et al., 2018). As such, mental health practitioners working with veterinary teams may well encounter situations that require skillful navigation of competing needs and interests.

Different perspectives on processes and outcomes, say for a suffering dog whose owner wants to pursue treatment in the face of futility, will naturally place mental health providers – whose ethical duty puts the client first – in a position of potential conflict with others on the veterinary team. Attending to, and advocating for, clear communication and problem-solving with the client may also prove difficult when a veterinary team is facing moral distress and frustration in the face of suffering. As such, mental health clinicians working in interprofessional capacities are encouraged to enact the values and ethics of their disciplines while taking collaborative steps to bridge difference and forge solutions, making sure that the needs of both the patient and the client are met.

Relationship Building and Teamwork

Related, many of the challenges inherent to interprofessional work cannot be successfully met without first building a foundation based on relationships. Mental health practitioners working within, or providing adjunct services to, host settings will be most successful when they can establish trust and credibility with the veterinary team. This does not come from being an animal owner, but by showing evidence of clinical experience navigating issues related to animal care, animal loss, and the strains of being an animal care provider (Brackenridge & McPherson, 2016). Trust is further established when boundary spanners show that they understand the unique culture of veterinary medicine. As described by Hafen and colleagues (2007), it is important to demonstrate an understanding of the highly competitive (and demanding) culture of veterinary practice, as well as the myriad challenges of managing these practices, in order to make inroads in interprofessional veterinary settings. Sometimes, this can be most easily accomplished with some degree of immersion at the beginning of a partnership.

Additionally, setting clear expectations about how mental health and veterinary team members will interact, clarifying expectations about confidentiality (particularly related to client disclosures to a mental health provider), and identifying "champions" on the team who can help advocate for, and normalize, collaboration are key. Bronstein (2003) notes that the most successful mental health practitioners in interprofessional settings serve as flexible, adaptable, and reliable resources to the physicians/clinicians with whom they work.

Navigating Sticky Wickets: Problem-Solving the Challenges of Interprofessional Practice

Interprofessional practice in animal care circles is not limited to veterinary clinics, just as animal loss issues are not limited to a narrow population of people or circumstances. Once mental health practitioners establish themselves as having expertise in animal loss, any number of opportunities to expand practice may arise. For example, despite being located in a veterinary hospital as an embedded practitioner, I have received (and fulfilled) numerous requests to assist with animal loss issues outside veterinary hospital walls. These requests range from providing support to a humane organization experiencing a disease outbreak and mass euthanasia, to debriefing the unexpected losses of multiple "charismatic" animals at a local zoo, to consulting with the American Red Cross about animal losses in house fires and other disasters, to working with a local veterinary board when a veterinary provider required remedial education and coaching as part of complaint resolution. If the mental health provider receiving these requests is embedded in a veterinary clinic and does not maintain an outside clinical or consulting practice, the best first step is to clarify the degree to which the request is congruent (or conflicts with) host agency goals and services. Second, and of critical importance, is to assess one's own skills and expertise related to the request at hand. Third, it may be necessary to reach out to allied professionals in animal care, legal, social services, and/or human health care fields to ensure that requests can be fulfilled fully and ethically, whether by you or a team of other professionals.

For example, I received a request from a law firm to assist with a case involving multiple equine fatalities at a horse boarding facility. The request involved forensic evaluation of horse owners' reactions to the loss of their horses, with an eye toward the assessment of loss-related trauma and grief. While I have abundant experience working with human–equine relationships and horse loss, the request to perform forensic evaluation was novel enough to require extensive research into forensic mental health practice, the laws and policies governing such practice, the liabilities associated with forensic work, and the language used to construct forensic service agreements. Additionally, I spent countless hours in consultation with a forensic social work expert before deciding to pursue a business agreement with the requesting attorney. In sum, it was clear that my experience working with horse loss was not sufficient preparation for performing this type of work properly.

Animal loss practitioners must be clear about the scope of their own training and proficiency. Ethical practice requires that we work within the framework of our clinical training and seek consultation, or refer out, when any request – however intriguing – exceeds our capacity as clinicians. While this is certainly true for any of the examples provided above, this is also evident when clients presenting for counseling evolve from "grief" to "grief plus" in their list of clinically relevant problems. I use the term "grief plus" to refer to acute-on-chronic issues that present when an animal belonging to a person with pre-existing health and/or mental health issues dies. Sometimes, animals are the one remaining link to psychosocial functioning and stability for their people; the loss of those animals, then, can endanger sobriety, adherence to treatment, and/or capacity to function in multiple settings.

For instance, I once worked with a gentleman, "M," whose initial request for service revolved around the grief over euthanizing his dog, "Bodie," for severe behavioral issues (anxiety and reactive aggression). "M" was a 20-something gay man who had worked with multiple dog trainers and behaviorists to address Bodie's anxiety. Upon arriving for his first counseling session, M's affect was markedly flat and his appearance was gaunt. He shared that he and Bodie had been together for 6 years, and that Bodie was rescued from M's physically abusive ex-partner. Bodie's anxiety was severe enough to warrant treatment with behavioral modification, strict interpersonal management, and multiple psychotropic medications. M also disclosed his own history with mental health issues, including panic attacks and bulimia for which he had received inconsistent treatment over the past 3–4 years. As our first session came to an end, M commented that he hoped counseling would help him come to terms with Bodie's loss because he was "running out of meds" and wasn't sure he could cope. Upon further discussion, M admitted that he had been self-medicating with Bodie's medications (trazodone and clonidine) since shortly before Bodie's death. Since I was offering short-term grief counseling in a veterinary hospital setting, it was clear that I was not going to be able to fully address the depth and breadth of this client's needs. As such, we worked together twice more to more fully assess M's risks, strengths, and supports, to bolster basic coping skills, and to locate "animal-informed" community providers who were better positioned to assist M with the chronic mental health issues that were being exacerbated by the loss of Bodie. Additionally, I agreed to save a spot for M in a monthly pet loss support group, with the stipulation that M would need to be actively receiving treatment for his anxiety and eating disorder to fully benefit from the group process. When clients such as these present for counseling, treating clinicians should conduct thorough assessments (including risk and safety issues), prioritize carefully, and enlist the help of the client's system and/or additional care providers who can help address the most focal issues.

Concluding Thoughts

Whether a clinician is adding animal loss to a longer list of practice areas or choosing to specialize in human–animal relationships more generally, it will be necessary to engage the veterinary (and larger animal care) community in order to find, and fully serve, "animal people" as a client population. It is increasingly common to find mental health professionals embedded in the veterinary team, enacting some form of interprofessional practice. Serving as an adjunct or referral provider, however, requires similar competencies in understanding veterinary service, speaking the language of animal relationships and care, navigating differences in role and skill, and staying abreast of interprofessional guidelines for practice. Regardless of your practice location, it will be useful to consider yourself a member of an interprofessional care network, the goal of which is to serve the needs of animals and their people.

Ultimately, how a mental health practitioner chooses to work with veterinary and allied service networks, such as animal trainers, animal control officers, animal law specialists, and the like, will depend upon his/her comfort with being a "boundary spanner" and the presence of non-clinical skills like advocacy, outreach, education, and resource brokering. This is particularly true when the demonstrated needs of our clients, whose experiences with animal loss may unveil far more complicated dynamics and risks, go beyond grieving the death of a beloved animal companion. Behaviors congruent with collaboration and partnership will not only engender a higher quality of care to these clients, but will likely support both creative problem-solving and innovation. It is the spirit of innovation that led the very first "animal-informed" mental health professionals to acknowledge, and serve, those struggling with the loss of a pet. It is on their shoulders we now stand as we reach into the future of interprofessional healthcare practice, where human and non-human animal needs will hopefully be met with equal regard, resources, and compassion.

Questions for Reflection

1. Let's revisit the case of "M," the client who presented for grief counseling after the loss of his anxious and aggressive dog, "Bodie." At the
   time of intake, "M" discloses that he has a history of panic attacks and
   bulimia, and is also self-medicating with Bodie's leftover psychotropic
   medications. If you were to serve as the clinician in "M's" case,, consider the following questions:

   a. What issues warrant clinical consideration in this case? How might
      you prioritize them?
   b. What other systems or professionals might you engage to ensure
      that "M" receives the help he needs? How might your approach
      change if you were embedded in a veterinary setting versus
      working as an external referral?

2. Consider a scenario in which a client is referred to you, a therapist in
   private practice, by a veterinarian who is concerned about the client's
   prolonged grief (six months in duration) and "pathological attachment" to her deceased cat, "Socks." The client, "T," is eager to meet
   with you, disclosing that she believes her cat's veterinarian made a
   mistake with Socks' treatment and prematurely advocated for euthanasia in order to cover up that mistake. "T" is considering filing a complaint and asks for your help to formulate a letter to the state
   veterinary board.

   a. What legal, ethical and practical considerations need to be evalu-
      ated with this type of request? How might you respond?
   b. What is the *clinical* relevance of a client's belief that her cat's care
      was compromised (and death was premature)?
   c. How might you help the client find resolution with the reality of
      Socks' death?

References

American Animal Hospital Association. (2012). Human support in veterinary settings. Retrieved from www.aaha.org/public_documents/professional/resources/
   humansupport.pdf

American Veterinary Medical Association. (2018). Guidelines for pet loss support
   services. Retrieved from www.avma.org/KB/Policies/Pages/AVMA-Guidelines-
   for-Pet-Loss-Support-Services.aspx

Brackenridge, S., & McPherson, B. (2016). Developing a successful social work
   practicum in a private veterinary specialty hospital. *Field Educator*, 6(1), 1–6.

Bronstein, L. (2003). A model for interdisciplinary collaboration. *Social Work*,
   48(3), 297–306.

Cohen, S. (1985). The role of social work in a veterinary hospital setting. *Veterinary
   Clinics of North America: Small Animal Practice*, 15(2), 355–363.

Dunn, K., Mehler, S., & Greenberg, H. (2005). Social work with a pet loss support group in a university veterinary hospital. *Social Work in Health Care*, 41(2), 59–70.

Engel, J., & Prentice, D. (2013) The ethics of interprofessional collaboration. *Nursing Ethics*, 20(4), 426–435.

Hafen, M., Rush, B., Reisbig, A., McDaniel, K., & White. M. (2007). The role of family therapists in veterinary medicine: Opportunities for clinical services, education, and research. *Journal of Marital and Family Therapy*, 33(2), 165–176.

International Association for Animal Hospice and Palliative Care. (2017). Guidelines for recommended practices in animal hospice and palliative care. Retrieved from www.iaahpc.org/resources-and-support/practice-guidelines.html

Interprofessional Health Collaborative. (2016). Core competencies for interprofessional collaborative practice: Report of an expert panel. Washington, DC. Retrieved from https://ipecollaborative.org/uploads/IPEC-Core-Competencies.pdf

Kinnison, T., Guile, D., & May, S. (2016). The case of veterinary interprofessional practice: From one health to a world of its own. *Journal of Interprofessional Education & Practice*, 4, 51–57.

Kipperman, B., Morris, P., & Rollin, B. (2018, February14). Ethical dilemmas encountered by small animal veterinarians: characterization, responses, consequences and beliefs regarding euthanasia. *Veterinary Record*, published online first. doi: 10.1136/vr.104619.

Kutner, M., Greenberg, E., Jin, Y., & Paulsen, C. (2006). *The health literacy of America's adults: Results from the 2003 National Assessment of Adult Literacy (NCES 2006–483)*. US Department of Education. Washington, DC: National Center for Education Statistics.

Long, D., & Rosen, I. (2017). Social work and optometry: Interprofessional practice revisited. *Health & Social Work*, 42(2), 117–120.

McCutcheon, K., & Fleming, S. (2002). Grief resulting from euthanasia and natural death of companion animals. *Omega*, 44(2), 169–188.

Mertens, P. (2006). Tapping social workers to help support distressed pet owners. *Veterinary Medicine*, 101(11), 715.

Moga, J. (2018). Integrating clients' animals in clinical practice: Insights from an animal-informed therapist. In L. Kogan, & C. Blazina (Eds.), *Clinician's Guide to Treating Companion Animal Issues: Addressing Human-Animal Interaction* (pp. 253–266). London, UK: Academic Press.

Oliver, C. (2013). Social workers as boundary spanners: Reframing our professional identity for interprofessional practice. *Social Work Education*, 32(6), 773–784.

One Health Initiative. (2018). About the One Health Initiative. Retrieved from www.onehealthinitiative.com/about.php.

Quackenbush, J., & Glickman, L. (1984). Helping people adjust to the death of a pet. *Health and Social Work*, 9: 42–48.

Rolland, J. (1994). Families, illness, & disability: An integrative treatment model. New York, NY: Basic Books.

Rosoff, P., Moga, J., Keene, B., Adin, C., Fogle, C., Ruderman, R., Hopkinson, H., & Weyhrauch, C. (2018). Resolving ethical dilemmas in a tertiary care veterinary specialty hospital: adaptation of the human clinical consultation committee model. *The American Journal of Bioethics*, 18(2), 41–53.

Siess, S., Marziliano, A., Sarma, E., Sikorski, L, & Moyer, A. (2015). Why psychology matters in veterinary medicine. *Topics in Companion Animal Medicine*, 30, 43–47.

Sweifach, J. (2015). Social workers and interprofessional practice: Perceptions from within. *Journal of Interprofessional Education & Practice*, 1, 21–27.

Zerden, L., Lombardi, B., Fraser, M., Jones, A., & Rico, Y. (2018). Social work: Integral to interprofessional education and integrated practice. *Journal of Interprofessional Education & Practice*, 10, 67–75.

Index

Page numbers in **bold** denote tables, those in *italics* denote figures.

For Product Safety Concerns and Information please contact our EU
representative GPSR@taylorandfrancis.com
Taylor & Francis Verlag GmbH, Kaufingerstraße 24, 80331 München, Germany

9 780367 784775